AN AIDE TO CUSTER

AN AIDE TO CUSTER
The Civil War Letters of Lt. Edward G. Granger

Edited by
SANDY BARNARD

Compiled by
THOMAS E. SINGELYN

UNIVERSITY OF OKLAHOMA PRESS ✻ NORMAN

Library of Congress Cataloging-in-Publication Data Names: Granger, Edward G., 1843–1864, author. | Barnard, Sandy, editor. | Singelyn, Thomas, 1929– compiler.
Title: An aide to Custer : the Civil War letters of Lt. Edward G. Granger / edited by Sandy Barnard ; compiled by Thomas E. Singelyn. Description: Norman : University of Oklahoma Press, 2018. | Includes bibliographical references and index.
Identifiers: LCCN 2017055868 | ISBN 978-0-8061-6018-4 (hardcover)
ISBN 978-0-8061-9422-6 (paper) Subjects: LCSH: Granger, Edward G., 1843–1864—Correspondence. | United
States. Army. Michigan Cavalry Brigade (1862–1865) | United States. Army. Michigan Cavalry Regiment, 5th (1862–1865) | United States—History—Civil War, 1861–1865—Personal narratives. | United States—History—Civil War, 1861–1865—Campaigns. | United States—History—Civil War, 1861–1865—Cavalry operations. | Custer, George A. (George Armstrong), 1839–1876—Friends and associates.
Classification: LCC E514.4 .G73 2018 | DDC 973.7092—dc23
LC record available at https://lccn.loc.gov/2017055868

The paper in this book meets the guidelines for permanence and durability of the Committee on Production Guidelines for Book Longevity of the Council on Library Resources, Inc. ∞

Copyright © 2018 by Sandy Barnard and Thomas E. Singelyn. Published by the University of Oklahoma Press, Norman, Publishing Division of the University. Paperback published 2024. Manufactured in the U.S.A.

All rights reserved. No part of this publication may be reproduced, stored in a retrieval system, or transmitted, in any form or by any means, electronic, mechanical, photocopying, recording, or otherwise—except as permitted under Section 107 or 108 of the United States Copyright Act—without the prior written permission of the University of Oklahoma Press. To request permission to reproduce selections from this book, write to Permissions, University of Oklahoma Press, 2800 Venture Drive, Norman, OK 73069, or email rights.oupress@ou.edu.

*To my dear friend,
Bill Lamy,
who was my roommate for four years
at Tennessee Military Institute.*

THOMAS SINGELYN

CONTENTS

List of Illustrations	ix
Preface	xiii
Acknowledgments	xix
Introduction	3
1. A First Letter	31
2. Camp Life and Picket Duty	39
3. A Summer and Fall of Campaigning	97
4. Camp Life, Winter 1863–1864	155
5. Campaigning in the Spring and Summer of 1864	197
Epilogue: Death on a Hot August Day	259
Bibliography	275
Index	283

ILLUSTRATIONS

✹ ✹ ✹

Figures

Lt. Edward G. Granger, circa 1863	2
Brigadier General Custer holding saber	5
Charles Irish Walker	7
Saint's Rest Dormitory, circa 1858	10
Capt. Horace Dodge	25
Capt. Jacob Bristol	25
Capt. Charles H. Safford	29
Lt. Edward G. Granger, late 1862–early 1863	33
Maj. Crawley P. Dake	46
Lt. Walter Stevenson	49
Maj. Noah Ferry	59
Mollie Granger Vernor with children	66
Col. John Mosby	73
Lt. Frederick A. Nims	74
Capt. Robert C. Wallace	81
Lt. William Keith	93
Col. Russell A. Alger	94
Brigadier General Custer and General Pleasonton, 1863	99

Uncle Ferdinand and Aunt Elmira Walker	100
Maj. Gen. J. E. B. Stuart	105
Capt. Robert Judson	109
Custer's brigade at Culpeper, Virginia, 1863	122
Culpeper Main Street, 1862	125
Officers of U.S. Horse Artillery	129
Custer and staff in front of Clover Hill house, circa 1864	154
5th Michigan Cavalry encampment, winter of 1863–64	156–57
Custer and staff on porch at Clover Hill, circa 1864	159
Maj. Smith Hastings	166
Bvt. Maj. Gen. George A. Custer	183
Elizabeth Custer, 1885	183
Lt. Henry W. Granger	204
Gen. Alfred T. A. Torbert, staff, and Capt. Marcus A. Reno	219
Lt. George Hill	234
Capt. William Brevoort	234
Mollie Granger later in life	257
Lt. Edward G. Granger, circa 1863	260
Mollie Granger in her wedding dress	270

Maps

Virginia, Maryland, and Pennsylvania, 1862–63	43
Granger's route during Gettysburg, June 17–July 18, 1863	96
Area of Culpeper, Virginia, fall 1863–winter 1864	127
Granger's hand-drawn map of the action at James City	130
Sheridan's Richmond raid, May 9–14, 1864	200
Union cavalry actions, May 28–June 1, 1864	236
Battle of Trevilian Station, Virginia, June 11, 1864	247
Trevilian Station, early morning opening action	248
Trevilian Station, later action	252
Battle of Crooked Run, August 16, 1864	258

PREFACE

In 1993, my colleague Dr. Thomas Singelyn of Grosse Pointe, Michigan, enthusiastically accepted a friend's offer to let him borrow forty-three historical letters that Lt. Edward G. Granger had written home to his family in Detroit during the Civil War. He quickly realized that the letters had "the makings of a book" in them. The owner of the letters, Lisa Mower Gandelot, is Granger's great-great-grandniece. The letters had come down through the extended Granger family from Granger's sister, Mollie, through Edward Granger's grandniece Virginia Vernor Robinson, to Mrs. Gandelot, who is Virginia Robinson's second cousin.

A history student and a retired dentist, Singelyn immediately set out to transcribe the forty-three letters in the collection. Singelyn and his wife, Denyse, painstakingly transcribed the letters' content. Fortunately, Granger's handwriting was highly readable, but nineteenth-century quirks in word usage, as well as the difficulties Granger himself faced in writing in a wartime setting, often tested their patience. Granger generally had no desk except his knees, his available paper was of poor quality, and he lacked ink or a sharp pencil with which to write. Singelyn eventually submitted the typed letters to the University of Oklahoma Press for possible publication. In early 2015, editor Chuck Rankin asked me to edit the letters, add supporting historical documentation, and create a book-length manuscript.

In October 2016, a forty-fourth letter written by Granger became available to me through Jim Adams of Peterborough, New Hampshire.

It had come down to Adams from his great-great-grandmother Emma Walker, who was Granger's maternal first cousin. In late July or early August 1863, Emma, then an eleven-year-old, had written her soldier cousin, Granger, who was nine years older. On August 22, 1863, Granger replied to Emma. That letter has been inserted chronologically with the others.

A key point of interest in the letters concerns Granger's appointment in late August 1863 to the staff of the Michigan Cavalry Brigade, then commanded by recently promoted Brig. Gen. George Armstrong Custer. In August 1862, Granger had enlisted in Company C, 5th Michigan Volunteer Cavalry Regiment, as a supernumerary second lieutenant. Much of his first year in the regiment was devoted to picket duty along the defensive lines surrounding Washington, D.C. He faced his first significant battle action in the aftermath of the Michigan Brigade's participation in the early July 1863 Battle of Gettysburg. Next, he was active in the following weeks as Gen. Robert E. Lee's Army of Northern Virginia escaped from Pennsylvania, crossed Maryland, and slipped back into the safety of Confederate Virginia.

Thus, Granger's letters can be easily organized, based on his own activities during his two years of service. First, chapter 1 covers the time directly before Granger enlisted. Chapter 2 deals with his early camp life and picket duty as the regiment participated in the Union Army's largely unsuccessful efforts to corral partisan guerrillas commanded by Col. John S. Mosby. Chapter 3 covers the Gettysburg Campaign and the regiment's movements and actions through November 1863. At that point the Michigan Brigade and its subordinate regiments went into winter camp at Stevensburg, Virginia.

In chapter 4, Granger dutifully describes the oft-tedious winter slumber of an army at rest and of a young soldier eagerly awaiting the spring thaw that will bring a renewal of the fighting across Virginia. The letters' final chapter 5 is the most action-packed. Granger writes highly detailed accounts of the regiment's participation in the Union Army's Overland Campaign of May and June 1864. That includes a battle that has often been described as "Custer's First Last Stand," the Battle of Trevilian Station, on June 11 and 12, 1864.

The book concludes with a narrative account of the Battle of Crooked Run, fought August 16, 1864, just north of the town of Front Royal,

Virginia. Late in that day's fighting, sensing victory, Custer directed his aide, just twenty-one years old, to carry orders to the commanders of the 1st and 7th Michigan Cavalry regiments. They were to attack the weakened and reeling Confederate brigades before them. Granger was last seen riding between the two Michigan regiments, urging his comrades on. Tragically, his horse, a replacement mount for his ever-reliable "Bob," who had been captured at Trevilian Station, panicked and carried Granger into the Confederate lines, where he was shot to death.

However, for many months his fate remained uncertain. By July 2, 1865, with the fighting ended, the *Detroit Free Press* published a final tribute to the now-presumed-dead cavalryman. The newspaper quotes from a heartfelt notification letter of August 20, 1864, that Custer wrote to Granger's uncle Charles I. Walker of Detroit: "I sincerely regret even his temporary loss, as no officer of my command has been more faithful and attentive in the discharge of his duties than Lieutenant Granger. In addition to this, the personal relations existing between us from our being members of the same military family, are the most intimate and unreserved."

Granger's letters provide an intimate look into a maturing young man as he meets the ever-challenging experiences of the Civil War. Additionally, during his second term as a student at the Agricultural College of Michigan, Granger had penned a daily journal from November 1858 to February 1859. Even as a teenager, Granger demonstrated superb powers of observation and attention to detail that help modern readers understand the life of a nineteenth-century college student in the years before the Civil War.

My discovery of Granger's journal was fortuitous, coming three months after I began researching his life and military career. One evening, I entered his name into Google and up popped a reference to the journal, housed today in the archives of Michigan State University, the modern descendant of the Agricultural College. Because the journal was more related to campus life, it did not appear in the university's Civil War holdings.

Perhaps of greater historical importance, Granger was an especially astute observer of the world around him, whether describing a soldier's life in camp or rushing orders to subordinate commanders as a staff aide. Not only does Granger offer an insider's view of numerous important engagements of the Civil War, including key battles at Gettysburg, Yellow Tavern, and Trevilian Station, but he also provides unique personal insights into his celebrated leader, General Custer. He frequently comments on Custer's unparalleled abilities as a combat leader on the battlefield, but he also describes the general's personal actions as a still young and single officer who enjoys hanging out with his subordinates in camp and keeping an eye on the young ladies. Later, after Custer marries Elizabeth Bacon of Monroe, Michigan, in February 1864, Granger pens several descriptions of the woman who would prove most influential in Custer's life. More than anyone else, she would assure that her husband would remain an icon in American history after his death in 1876 at the Battle of Little Big Horn in Montana Territory.

Granger also writes frankly, often negatively, about his fellow officers in the Michigan Cavalry Brigade, including the well-known Col. Russell Alger and Capt. Jacob Greene. His criticisms even extend to his mother, Matilda Walker Granger, whom he often chastises, directly or indirectly, for her failure to write frequently to him. His most detailed letters were written to his younger sister, Mollie, with whom he clearly enjoyed a close-knit relationship. Matchmaking in the nineteenth century clearly differed from the modern era, but if the two young Grangers lived in the twenty-first century, undoubtedly the brother would think nothing of dating his sister's many girl friends.

Granger's letters often underscore the serious and sad business that is war. For example, on May 15, 1864, he hastily wrote to his mother to inform her that "Henry Granger is dead. I saw his body." Henry was a much older first cousin who was killed in action May 11, 1864, while commanding the 7th Michigan Cavalry at the Battle of Yellow Tavern, Virginia. The two men were not the only casualties within the large extended family of Lieutenant Granger. Four other members of his family also were either killed in action or by accident during the war.

Granger frequently mentioned the deaths of other comrades in his regiment and his brigade. Surprisingly, he reports their passings in almost matter-of-fact language to his sister or mother. As a staff officer, he remained steadfast and confident on the battlefield. Those were qualities he undoubtedly learned from Custer, who, even in his near disaster at Trevilian Station, provided strong leadership for his brigade. Thus, it is ironic that Granger himself was killed because his horse panicked in the midst of battle. If Granger ever felt fear, he seldom disclosed that to his family members.

On July 2, 1865, the *Detroit Free Press* expressed best the way Lt. Edward Granger should be remembered: "His name belongs to and ranks high in the list of Michigan heroes who have fallen fighting valiantly for the Union and the constitution as our fathers left it to us. His memory will be tenderly cherished by a large circle of attached friends and in the warmer circle of 'home' his place can never more be filled."

For the most part, I have let Edward Granger speak to us in his own words. At times, his paragraphs tended to cover multiple subjects, which I have repaginated for ease of reading today. He often introduced people with an incomplete name if they were otherwise known to the recipients of his letters. To clarify the identity of such individuals, I have surrounded the person's full name in brackets. Similarly, if he misspelled a person's name or a place name, I placed the correct form inside of brackets. If the name occurred subsequently in his letters, I used the correct spelling. Two names in particular were treated that way. Granger frequently left off the closing letter "e" from Capt. Jacob Greene's last name. Likewise, he added an "e" in the middle of Col. John S. Mosby's last name, spelling it as "Moseby." I treated Granger's errors in fact through explanations or clarifications either in the footnotes or in my introductory narratives for each section of the letters. With the exception of people and places, I have preserved Granger's occasional spelling errors without additional clarification.

ACKNOWLEDGMENTS

I F I HAVE LEARNED ONE THING IN ALL MY YEARS AS A researcher-writer studying the Civil War and post–Civil War Indian wars, it is that countless people stand ready to help. Whether they work for a research-related agency or are longtime friends, they inevitably step forward with information and assistance that I need. That has certainly been true with this project, editing the Civil War letters of Lt. Edward G. Granger.

That the project even exists is due to the enthusiasm of Dr. Thomas Singelyn, who quickly realized after reading the letters that they merited publication. Along with his wife, Denyse, he spent considerable time transcribing them and making them available in digital form.

Two friends with years of experience in Civil War research were of immense help. Robert O'Neill made available to me all of his research materials on the Michigan Cavalry Brigade that he had amassed for his superb book, *Chasing Jeb Stuart and John Mosby: The Union Cavalry in Northern Virginia from Second Manassas to Gettysburg*. His willingness to let me review the information saved me travel, expense, and time on this project. Horace Mewborn assisted me at the National Archives one day in Washington, D.C., and reviewed the manuscript for me.

Two other men renowned for their Civil War historical expertise willingly added to my knowledge or clarified events for me. They are John Hennessy, chief historian at Fredericksburg and Spotsylvania National Military Park, and Clark B. Hall, one of the truly significant experts on the Battle of Brandy Station.

Additionally, John Beckendorf, John Ickes, and David Finny provided me with guidance or actual photographs of individuals associated with George Armstrong Custer's Michigan Cavalry Brigade and Granger's own regiment, the 5th Michigan Cavalry. Paul Davis, editor of the book *I Rode with Custer: The Civil War Diary of Charles H. Safford, Brevet Major, 5th Michigan Cavalry*, about one of Granger's comrades, provided photographs of Safford and several other 5th Michigan officers.

One person quite important in my quest to learn about Lieutenant Granger was Jim Adams, the great-great-grandson of Emma Walker, who was Granger's maternal first cousin. Jim has allowed me to use the letter that Granger wrote to then-eleven-year-old Emma on August 22, 1863, as well as two photographs of her cousin that she had kept.

Several of my longtime friends and fellow Indian wars researchers once again stepped forward. They are David Harrington, the Reverend Vincent Heier, David Ingall, Dale Kosman, Bruce Liddic, Jim Mundie, and Pamela Ungar. Additionally, Larry and Cheryl Engle enlisted the aid of their daughter-in-law Katrina Weirauch-Engle. Katrina took matching photographs of the modern Michigan State University campus akin to those of Granger's days when it was known as the Agricultural College of Michigan. At my request, photographer Gail Herschensohn took a series of photographs of the burial site for Charles Irish Walker, the uncle of Edward Granger.

The most important battle for Granger proved to be the Battle of Crooked Run near Front Royal, Virginia, where on August 16, 1864, he was killed in action. Several people from that area proved especially helpful. Joe Whitehorne spent most of a day with my wife and me guiding us on a tour of the area and the Crooked Run battlefield. That was especially important, as modern development has significantly altered the fighting ground itself. Patrick Farris, executive director of the Warren Heritage Society in Front Royal, and Matt Wendling of the Warren County Planning and Zoning Department provided both research assistance and guidance about their area and the battle. Darryl Merchant of Front Royal gave me permission to publish his unique and detailed map on the 1864 Battle of Crooked Run.

We researchers must depend heavily on people who make their living helping others in their communities to find information. As she has done for me on earlier projects, Charmaine Wawrzyniec, curator of the Lawrence Frost Collection, Ellis Library and Reference Center, Monroe, Michigan, eagerly answered my initial and later queries about Edward Granger. Sarah Roberts, acquisitions archivist, Michigan State University Archives, was instrumental in assisting me with a huge step: obtaining a copy of Granger's college journal from 1858 to 1859. She also patiently answered my numerous questions about the university's early days as the Agricultural College of Michigan.

Research personnel at the Detroit Public Library, including Mark Bowden, coordinator of special collections for the Burton Historical Collection, and Joyce Middlebrooks, librarian, as well as the Bentley Historical Library, University of Michigan, were equally helpful.

Over the years my Colorado friend, Gary Raham, has prepared many maps for my previous books. Once again, Gary has used his skills and expertise in my behalf to prepare maps for this book.

I cannot overlook editor Chuck Rankin and his staffers at the University of Oklahoma Press. I deeply appreciate his kind consideration and support in offering me the challenging task of turning the letters of Edward G. Granger into a book. In addition, my two project editors at Oklahoma, initially Emily J. Schuster, before her maternity leave, and Stephanie Evans, revealed their own dedication and professionalism in assuring *An Aide to Custer* made its way through the production process and into print. Copyeditor Kerin Tate, similarly, proved to be an equally superb professional and one of the best editors I have dealt with across my fifty years as a writer. She also produced the index for the book.

Finally, as has been true with all my book projects, my wife, Betty, has been an immense help in completing this project. During our more than fifty years together, she has evolved into my primary research assistant. On this project, one of her greatest skills proved its value once again. She is immensely talented at deciphering handwriting of individuals who lived in the nineteenth century. At least three times she fully compared our copy of the original Granger letters to the transcript prepared by the Singelyns. I am much in her debt.

As with any book project, one statement is always true. While others may assist the author in many ways, in the end he is always responsible for its contents. I accept that responsibility quite readily.

AN AIDE TO CUSTER

Lt. Edward G. Granger,
5th Michigan Cavalry, circa 1863.
Photographer Mathew Brady.
Courtesy of Lisa Mower Gandelot.

INTRODUCTION

> It is a classical maxim that it is sweet and becoming
> to die for one's country; but whoever has seen the horrors of
> a battlefield feels that it is far sweeter to live for it.
>
> COL. JOHN S. MOSBY

IN THE SECOND YEAR OF THE AMERICAN CIVIL WAR, IN August 1862, Edward G. Granger shared with thousands of other young men of his generation an eagerness to serve his country in its time of crisis. However, Americans of the 1860s had little experience with or awareness of the brutality of all-out warfare, except for the relatively short conflict with Mexico between 1846 and 1848. Despite the violence of the Civil War's first sixteen months, youthful Northerners and Southerners largely remained willing to fight for their region's cause.

On August 27, 1862, when Granger mustered into the 5th Michigan Volunteer Cavalry Regiment as a second lieutenant, he was a mere youth, just a few months past his nineteenth birthday. A week short of a year later, on August 20, 1863, he was appointed as an aide on the personal staff of Brig. Gen. George Armstrong Custer, the recently named commander of the Michigan Cavalry Brigade. For the next eleven months, Granger would ride close to Custer, one of the war's most colorful personalities.

In doing so, he would provide an insider's intimate view of the evolution of the Army of the Potomac's cavalry from an amateurish collection of near circus riders who lacked a precise combat role in the early years of the war into an increasingly polished force that seized the momentum from its enemy and became dominant. His commander, Custer, was as responsible as any man for that transformation. Granger's presence by the general's side as an aide-de-camp afforded him a unique opportunity to record the brigade's actions in the field and in camp.

His education, while incomplete as a student at the Agricultural College of Michigan a few years before, had revealed that Granger was both intelligent and an astute observer of the world about him. A schoolboy diary he kept while enrolled at the college further showed he could write not only with precision of thought but also with insight and wit. In his nearly two years of service, crisscrossing Virginia but also reaching as far north as Gettysburg, Pennsylvania, he wrote frequent letters to his sister, Mollie, and to his mother, Matilda, at home in Detroit, Michigan, as well as to his friends and extended family members. Forty-four of those letters survive and have come down to us through his family.

In his letters Granger perceptively detailed his army experiences, ranging from the boredom and hardships of camp life to the dangers of standing in command of a Union picket line on cold, dark evenings or in serving as a general officer's staff aide in the midst of chaos on the battlefield. An avid student of history as a schoolboy, Granger carefully studied the strategy and tactics of cavalry in combat in order to better serve General Custer. Throughout his letters, he wrote frankly about the men he served with, detailing not only their strengths, but also their weaknesses and flaws. He thought Custer, less than four years older than Granger himself, was a "brilliant" general and wrote ever so highly of him to his family. From the so-called Boy General, Granger absorbed the feeling of what some called Custer's Luck in combat, a belief in one's own invincibility in the face of danger. Granger seldom disclosed more than a hint of his own fears about combat to his family; when he felt compelled to address such a topic in a letter, he would defuse it with his customary wit, often bordering on sarcasm. In his letters, his reports about the perils he often faced in combat, especially on such contested ground as the Wilderness and Trevilian Station, revealed his coolness and personal strength of character in the most violent moments a cavalryman might encounter.

INTRODUCTION 5

Brig. Gen. George A. Custer, holding saber. *Courtesy of John Beckendorf.*

Then, in a sudden moment on a nondescript Virginia field of battle, Lieutenant Granger was gone. For one last time, on August 16, 1864, he had faithfully carried orders from his general to the commanders of the 1st and 7th Michigan Cavalry regiments, directing them to attack the reeling enemy on the battlefield of Crooked Run, north of Front Royal, Virginia. In the charge, he rode between the two regiments, but his horse, spooked by the clatter of the battlefield, panicked and carried Granger, just twenty-one years old, into the Confederate lines. For months he was carried as missing in action, while his family and comrades hoped for his safe return. His general, too, remained optimistic that he would rejoin the Michigan Cavalry Brigade. Custer reportedly retained a position on his staff for Granger. But months later word eventually informed his comrades and his family that the enemy had shot him to death that August day.

※ ※ ※

Granger was born on April 10, 1843, in Grand Rapids, Michigan. His parents were a thirty-three-year-old lawyer named Sylvester Granger and his wife, Matilda (Walker), who was the same age as her husband. In the early 1840s, Sylvester wrote partisan articles for the local Democratic newspapers, including the *Grand Rapids Enquirer*, often in collaboration with Matilda's brother Charles Irish Walker. That likely explains how the couple's relationship came about.[1]

Sylvester had been born on October 6, 1810, in Sandisfield, Massachusetts, while his wife's birth had occurred a few weeks earlier on September 18, 1810, in Saratoga, New York. Unfortunately, Sylvester died of unknown causes on July 7, 1845, in Grand Rapids. The loss was made more tragic as Matilda was expecting her second child. On November 25, 1845, she gave birth to Mary Luce Granger in Grand Rapids. Her older brother, Edward, would call her Mollie, especially in his series of forty-four letters during the Civil War.[2]

Sometime in 1846, the widowed Matilda moved to Detroit where she and her children lived with her younger brother Charles, who in the 1850s would become a renowned attorney in that midwestern city.[3]

---

1. *Early History of Grand Rapids City, Kent County, Michigan* (Grand Rapids, Mich.: Dillenback and Leavitt, 1870).
2. In preparation for my research for this book, I used Ancestry.com to create a family tree dedicated to Edward G. Granger, which proved itself as a superb research tool (henceforth, Granger Family Tree, Ancestry.com). I accumulated information on some six hundred members of Granger's immediate and extended families. Much information about Granger and his family members comes from numerous sources available on Ancestry.com. In addition, by July 2, 1865, after Granger had been presumed killed in action, the *Detroit Free Press* published a lengthy account of the young man's life and fate in the war, which provided additional personal information about him.
3. Charles Irish Walker, the son of Stephen and Lydia (Gardner) Walker, was born April 25, 1814, in Butternuts, Otsego County, New York. Educated in district schools, at age sixteen he began teaching in a common school, but soon became interested in mercantile pursuits. In 1836, he moved to Grand Rapids, Michigan. There Charles undoubtedly met Sylvester Granger, whom he introduced to his sister Matilda. In that year Charles was a member of the Second Convention of Assent, and in 1840 he was elected to the state legislature. After completing his law studies, he became partners in 1851 in a Detroit law firm with his brother Edward Carey Walker. One of the original law faculty members at the University of Michigan, he worked for seventeen years, 1859–76, in its law department. He served as chairman twice, in 1879–81

INTRODUCTION

Charles Irish Walker, uncle of Lt. Edward G. Granger. *Courtesy of Bentley Historical Library, University of Michigan.*

A *Detroit Free Press* article about Edward, published on July 2, 1865, noted that "young Granger ever after held towards him [Charles] the relations of an adopted son."

Edward was educated in the city's public schools, including high school. The 1850 census shows that he had attended school within the year.[4] At barely age fifteen, in April 1858, he headed west to Lansing, Michigan, to enroll in the new Agricultural College of the State of Michigan. The newspaper added:

---

and 1886–87. In 1867, he was appointed judge of the Wayne County Circuit Court, but resigned after a few months to resume his law practice. In 1874, the University of Michigan conferred on him the degree of Doctor of Laws. He was twice married: in 1838 to Mary Hinsdale, and in 1865 to Ella Fletcher. He died February 11, 1895. Biographical information courtesy of the Bentley Library, University of Michigan, Ann Arbor, Michigan.

4. 1850 U.S. Federal Census.

He was an excellent scholar and was remarkable for the variety and breadth of his general knowledge especially of history, biography & etc. He was no less remarkable for the perfection of his physical culture. By early systematic and long continued gymnastic training he acquired a very high degree of muscular agility, skill and prowess.[5]

Besides his cache of letters, Granger provided a lengthy account of another important period in his life. During the second of his two terms, 1858–59, as a student in the Agricultural College, Granger kept a daily journal. The two collections of his writings, Granger's forty-four military letters and his 116 pages of college journal entries, provide a fascinating look at a teenager who matured into a highly capable adult and a heroic combat officer.

In the spring of 1858 the institution of higher learning that Edward Granger enrolled in was unique for its time. Prior to then, no schools dedicated to agriculture existed in Michigan, and they were extremely rare elsewhere in the United States. The Agricultural College would evolve into today's Michigan State University. As MSU historian Keith R. Widder has noted:

> America had nearly 200 colleges and universities but none taught agriculture and few offered more than the rudiments of chemistry or biology. Modeled after English universities, their curriculum was dominated by the Greek, Latin, and mathematics that were considered essential to the education of clergyman, lawyers, scholars, and gentlemen. They offered few courses in science. Chemistry was taught by lecture and demonstration, giving the student no experience in laboratory techniques.[6]

The college's birth in mid-May 1857 was heavily overladen with educational controversy and state politics. Its founders persevered and avoided being swallowed up by the larger University of Michigan in Ann Arbor, or the Michigan State Normal School, today's Eastern Michigan University, which had been founded in 1853.[7] When its first students enrolled, they found themselves a significant part of the educational experiment. The school's wilderness location had been dictated by a state law that required locating within ten miles

---

5. *Detroit Free Press*, July 2, 1865.
6. Keith R. Widder, *Michigan Agricultural College: The Evolution of a Land-Grant Philosophy, 1855–1925* (East Lansing: Michigan State University Press, 2005), 1.
7. Widder, *Michigan Agricultural College*, 1.

of Lansing, Michigan. Effectively, in 1857, the school was placed in an undeveloped, inaccessible part of the state. That site was more a political compromise between rival sections than a well-thought-out decision. Fortunately, the Burr farm on which it was sited offered 677 acres of forest land, more than sufficient space for an agricultural institution. It also was convenient to all-weather transportation, including a new plank road connecting Detroit to Lansing.[8]

Besides an academic building called College Hall, a boarding house, dubbed Saint's Rest, was also built out of necessity.[9] The farm was so isolated that few nearby homes existed that could provide students with housing. Granger spent his two semesters at the college living in Saint's Rest. The college opted to accept new students only when others dropped out.[10] That occurred as each new term opened. Kuhn stated, "Some failed to return because of ill health, financial reasons, academic issues, or simply discouragement, but usually an even larger number presented themselves for examination."[11] For example, in the spring of 1858, when Granger initially was admitted, ninety-three applicants applied for only twenty-eight vacancies.

The school's first term in 1857 had run from May 13 to October 28. The winter term opened on December 2 and ended February 22, 1858.[12] Granger's own first term in the school's second year lasted from April 7, 1858, to October 27, 1858. For his second term he was enrolled between November 29, 1858, and February 23, 1859.[13]

---

8. Madison Kuhn, *Michigan State: The First Hundred Years 1855 to 1955* (Lansing: Michigan State University Press, 1955), 12.
9. Both buildings were hastily constructed in 1856 and required frequent repair. College Hall collapsed in 1918, its wooden framework weakened by age, and Saint's Rest burned on December 9, 1876. The latter probably took its name from a popular nineteenth-century devotional guide, *The Saint's Everlasting Rest*, which stressed the need for rest or meditation after a busy day of study and work. Linda O. Stanford and C. Kurt Dewhurst, *MSU Campus, Buildings, Places, Spaces* (East Lansing: Michigan State University Press, 2002), 6–8, 13; Sarah Roberts, acquisitions archivist, Michigan State University Archives, series of emails with editor, May–July 2015.
10. Madison Kuhn, "Spartans in the Civil War," *Michigan State University Magazine*, March 1961, 10–11, 31.
11. Kuhn, *Michigan State*, 11.
12. Ibid., 10.
13. Edward G. Granger Journal, Michigan State University Archives, 1; Sarah Roberts, email to editor, July 29, 2015.

Saint's Rest Dormitory, circa 1858.
Granger has not been identified in this photograph, but he attended the Agricultural College in 1858. *Courtesy of Michigan State University Archives and Historical Collections, A000154.*

But the faculty and the college's supporters also faced a paradox, according to Widder: "If their institution, born of the desire to educate young men from the farm to farm more effectively, was to survive and grow, it also had to educate those young men (and later young women) to find places in a rapidly changing world off the farm as well."[14] As it turned out, many students, including city dweller Edward Granger, had little interest in farming.

The college's original curriculum offered a highly practical education in the study of literature, history, philosophy, and other subjects of the mind, along with chemistry, a science dependent upon research. Each student also spent a portion of his day in manual labor. For their efforts, students received an "equitable remuneration."[15]

---

14. Widder, *Michigan Agricultural College*, 14.
15. Ibid., 34.

Granger's journal reveals him as a serious student who often agonized over the difficulty of his lessons. Yet he persevered and proved successful, or at least he never related any of those moments when his professors found him lacking in readiness for the day's lessons. He enjoyed pranks, he often relied on sarcasm, especially in describing actions of his elders, and he was unafraid of hard labor. He easily formed opinions and stood up for his beliefs. Indeed, his willingness to do so may account for his decision not to return to the college for a third term in early 1859.

While little is known about his first term at the college that began in April 1858, his journal for the second term beginning in November 1858 provides much insight into Granger's time there. The top of his journal's first page states what will become fifteen-year-old Granger's frequent lament, including later in his military letters: his strong dislike of writing. He stated, "The first journal I was ever guilty of attempting to write & I hope it will be the last."[16]

At first, such comments appear surprising, given that Granger was both well-read and an effective, if not colorful, writer. Because he was still in his midteens, he likely remained unsure of his own abilities, including communication. Nonetheless, Granger's journal underscores the relatively mundane academic and social life of the college student of the late 1850s. According to Widder, Granger's "diary gives significant insights into the curiosity and intellectual interests of students, their study habits, and social life at the Agricultural College of the State of Michigan in its infancy. While we must be careful not to draw unwarranted generalizations from the words and experiences of one person, Granger's revelations tell us much about the assumptions and expectations that he had for his own intellectual development and how his studies at the institution could help him grow. References that Granger makes to other students suggest that his outlook was shared by others."[17]

According to his entries, Granger and his friends shared a deep interest in literature and history. They read such literary giants as John Milton, Sir Walter Scott, William Shakespeare, Oliver Wendell Holmes, and Harriet Beecher Stowe. Granger added to his knowledge

---

16. Granger, Journal, 1.
17. Widder, *Michigan Agricultural College*, 35.

of history by reading Jacob Abbott's *History of Hannibal*, Mrs. E. M. Sheldon's *History of Michigan,* and *Life of the Duke of Wellington by an Old Soldier.* He was pleased when a roommate, Harvey Bush, subscribed to the *Atlantic Monthly,* but Granger was equally upset when Bush, in a huff, locked away the latter's copy of Milton's *Paradise Lost.*

Granger and his peers also revealed an interest in politics. On January 8, 1859, he accompanied his friends Elbert J. Clark and William A. Thomas into Lansing to observe the Michigan State Legislature in session. Granger's broad intellectual and political interests prepared the youth well for the instruction he received from his professors.

At the same time Granger showed how advanced he was, despite his youth, at forming his own opinions. Granger and his classmates did not tolerate what they deemed to be violations of their own rights as American citizens. In his diary entry for December 17, 1858, he strongly demanded that the college not interfere with the students' exercise of democracy.[18]

According to Widder, Granger frequently bounced between excitement and frustration over his studies. When a professor asked Granger to write a composition, he chose the topic "Sir Walter Raleigh and His Times." As Granger developed his composition, he knew that his professor would demand that his work be of high quality. At the same time, he proved the truth of his early prognosis that "literature is the hardest thing I ever studied, but I guess it will be interesting after a while."[19]

Granger not only recorded his thoughts and opinions about his schooling and related activities, but he meticulously listed his near-daily efforts at manual labor. For about three hours almost every afternoon, Granger and his fellow students hacked a working farm out of the wooded, swampy terrain that comprised the college lands. Among his tasks, Granger planted trees and gardens, laid brick, weeded, sowed turnips, planted potatoes, cleaned the barn, spread manure, logged, picked brush, split wood, and ground corn. More than anything, he chopped and split wood.[20]

In some ways, students at the agricultural college mirrored their peers at the classical colleges. Granger and his friends enjoyed the

---

18. Ibid., 36.
19. Ibid.
20. Ibid., 37.

INTRODUCTION 13

intellectual exercises offered by the Lyceum and many mornings participated in religious services conducted by faculty members in the lecture hall. Religious belief was clearly important to Granger, who in 1858 took pride in reading through the entire Bible.[21]

Early in his winter term, Granger seemed devoted to his studies, but as the weeks passed, he resembled more a typical college student of today. Dedicated to his studies when circumstances demanded, he often found opportunities to slack off. He noted when he was ill-prepared for a class and optimistically hoped the professor would not call on him to recite that day.

In his journal Granger did not stand out as a strong, out-in-front leader, but rather as someone who supported his peers who were. His classmates clearly liked him. They sought out his companionship and enjoyed interacting with him in discussions and games. Granger also revealed an introspective side. On one occasion, he noted that studying was difficult for him, despite spending three or four hours some nights on his academic tasks. He proved to be an inveterate reader.

However, Friday night, December 17 also revealed Granger's strong thoughts about politics. His friend Charles A. Foote[22] and he attended the Lyceum, where President Joseph R. Williams introduced a proposal

---

21. Ibid., 38.
22. Charles Augustus Foote, Granger's roommate and best friend, was the eldest son of the Reverend and Mrs. Charles C. Foote. Although he was born September 10, 1841, at Maumee, Ohio, where his father was pastor of a Presbyterian church, his family eventually settled in Detroit. Just as Granger, Foote did not remain enrolled long in the college. After a term or two, Foote spent a winter in Canada as teacher in a School For Freemen, a school for former slaves who had sought refuge there. On June 24, 1861, he enlisted in the 7th Michigan Infantry. Before the end of the year, Foote was seriously wounded by a bullet in his right arm near his shoulder in the Battle of Fair Oaks, Virginia. Badly disabled, he received an honorable discharge on March 1, 1863. After working in the grocery business while recovering from his wounds in Quincy, Iowa, he reenlisted on March 30, 1864, in the 146th New York Volunteer Infantry Regiment. After his final discharge on July 16, 1865, Foote returned to Adams County, Iowa, where he worked a farm for seventy years. Foote died on March 19, 1936. Charles Augustus Foote obituary, *Adams County Free Press*, March 26, 1936, posted by Marlene Skalberg, September 22, 2012, http://iagenweb.org/boards/adams/obituaries/index.cgi?read=408303. See also U.S., Civil War Soldier Records and Profiles, 1861–1865, database at Ancestry.com, original data from Historical Data Systems (hereafter cited as Soldier Records and Profiles), and New York, Civil War Muster Roll Abstracts, 1861–1900, database at Ancestry.com, original data from New York State Archives, Albany, New York.

that Granger personally rejected. Williams asked the boys to amend the Lyceum's constitution to assure nothing would be said "in the Lyceum or in the paper disrespectful to the faculty or ridiculing any of their sayings or doings."

In response, Granger wrote in his journal, with underlining for emphasis, "<u>Free</u> <u>country</u>." The students voted the measure down, Granger stated. He added, "President Williams requested us to pass the amendment but fortunately [there] was more of the spirit of liberty in the society than to pass such an abomination."

Perhaps of greater significance, his attitudes were clearly changing. His January 3, 1859, entry included the information that he "did not go to chapel this morning. This makes the third time this term. Last term I was not quite so apt to be absent. Am afraid I am becoming more lax in my morals or something else. Went over to my classes this morning without having looked at any of my lessons for the first time this term."

On January 11, Granger ran afoul of President Williams, who had lectured the students for too long a time to suit the youth. Granger felt compelled to tell the president, perhaps foolishly, that his talk went "so long without saying anything that I cared about hearing, that I reminded him that we had to get our lessons. This made him mad, and he told me that I might go, and afterwards gave me what Foote calls a 'one horse blessing,' for which I was much obliged to him. He said that this was the first act of impropriety which he knew of my committing since I had been in the institution."

As the term progressed, Granger's journal provided more indications that he was standing up for himself, even rebelling, and was no longer guided by what he considered petty rules. On Thursday, January 20, when the night bell sounded for retiring, he chose to ignore it. "I shall so far disobey the rules of the institution, as to stay up till I get ready to go to bed."

On January 24, 1859, he realized only a month remained in the term. "Hurrah!" His strong desire for the end of the term surfaced again on January 31. "Only three weeks more before examinations. Wish it was vacation, but dread examination."

His overall attitude continued to be surly. He frequently slept in later and intentionally missed the required morning chapel. His annoying problems with his roommate Harvey Bush continued unabated. He paid little heed to the nighttime bell most evenings. Granger provided little insight into the reasons for his behavioral changes. Likely, he was bored with the pettiness of the rules promulgated by the faculty. Or, to look at it another way, Granger was acting out as what he was—a teenager! By comparison, his military letters, written between four and six years later, reveal no similar signs of immaturity.

In February, as the term was winding down, Granger found himself involved in some controversy that involved the faculty and the college. On February 15, he wrote, "Have been before the faculty for the first time since I have been in the institution." Unfortunately, he failed to provide any further background about the matter or the extent of his involvement.

Instead, he offered a rambling statement:

> Bush saved me the trouble of telling ever so many lies by telling everything he was requested to and some things which he was not. This morning just after literature class we all had to go into the lecture room for some reason which was then unknown to me. Prex. [President] began by calling the roll so as to be sure that were all present.
>
> Prex. then told us that there was an offense committed last night which was equivalent to a suspension. Old Blucher's [a college horse] harness was cut up in such a manner as to have endangered the life of any person who attempted to drive him with it on. Fortunately this was discovered before he was fastened into the cart. He said that it was time for the institution to discontinue operations, if the faculty could not discover the perpetrators of the crimes which had been committed in the institution.

On Wednesday, February 16, Granger again found himself in trouble with the faculty, who "laid into me rather strong generally." Granger further claimed one of the faculty members accused him of lying to them. While the details of the accusations remain muddled, the episode evidently impacted Granger's future in a major way, especially coming so close to the end of the term as it did. Later in that day's journal entry, he noted that two classmates had been "sent off, some say they were expelled and others say they were not."

He added, "If they don't suspend me this term I will try not to give them another chance by coming back here."

After completing that academic term, Granger never did return to the college. Sketchy early records of MSU provide no further insight into the turmoil of February 1859 or how Granger, still only fifteen, was involved.[23] Except for mundane references to his academic work, Granger ended the school-based portion of his journal. A little more than ten months later, on January 1, 1860, Granger did briefly resume recording his thoughts. This time he wrote from his Detroit home. Fortunately, at the beginning, he offered a few tidbits about the close of his last college term, including that he had again been ill. For about a week after his return home, he remained ill. He claimed that for much of the summer he had the ague, "though I hope I am now rid of it."

According to Granger, in March 1859, another of his mother's brothers, Ferdinand Walker, arrived from New York with his family and soon launched a department store in Detroit. In April, Granger went to work as an errand boy in the store. Shortly after, the store's cashier left and Granger was promoted. However, he closed his first day's entry with a typically obscure remark: "As it is time for me to study my school lesson I must leave this until some other time when I feel disposed to take it up." He obviously was not back in Lansing at the college so what did his school reference pertain to? He never explained.

On New Year's Day, Sunday, January 1, 1860, an excited Granger also talked about his holiday visits, made along with his cousin Hobart M. Walker.[24] "The young ladies whom I honored by my visits were Miss

---

23. Later that year, President Williams resigned, as members of the State Board of Education complained that the college was too elitist and extravagant. Farmers, too, were unhappy that the school's curriculum seemed less focused on farming itself. For a time, the curriculum was reduced to a two-year, vocation-oriented farming program, which may better explain why Granger did not return. In the early 1860s, the state's Reorganization Act of 1861 and the federal Morrill Land-Grant Colleges Act of 1862 restored the school's four-year curriculum and assured its growth.

24. Hobart M. Walker's information was gleaned from various entries and family trees on Ancestry.com as well as the editor's own Granger Family Tree. Historical sources confirm that Granger's cousin was actually an army lieutenant who died in the sinking of the SS *General Lyon* on March 31, 1865, off Cape Hatteras, North Carolina. Findagrave.com shows Hobart's name listed on a gravestone over a family plot in Greenwood Cemetery in Brooklyn, New York, with a death date of 1865, but that is a cenotaph, or monument, in his honor. Nothing in the historical record suggests his body was recovered from the Atlantic Ocean. Compiled military service records in the National Archives and on Ancestry.com indicate Hobart served several times for short periods in different units during the Civil War. He first joined the 44th New York Infantry on August 30, 1861, and was wounded and captured at the Battle of Malvern Hill on July 1, 1862. His brother Jerome, later a doctor, was a short distance away. Hobart was discharged for disability later that year. In December 1862, he was

INTRODUCTION   17

Strong, Georgie Harris, and Carrie Thompson." Apparently, the young people wanted to go ice skating, but they could not locate a suitable, presumably safe place.

Granger also mentioned having studied French in the spring with Hobart's sister Adaline Walker, whom he calls Ada.[25] He refers to another friend, Theodore McGraw, who was studying languages in Europe. McGraw surfaces later in Granger's military letters home.[26]

    mustered into Company D, 12th New York Cavalry, as a private, but was discharged in June 1863 without being commissioned. Then from May 2 to August 23, 1864, Walker served in the 150th Ohio, which garrisoned Washington, D.C., forts during Confederate major general Jubal Early's raid toward Washington. Finally, on September 27, 1864, perhaps out of respect for his cousin Edward Granger, who had been killed the previous month, Walker enlisted as a lieutenant in the 106th New York Infantry. The unit was stationed as part of the permanent party at the draft rendezvous on Hart Island in New York Harbor. An obituary for him, published April 8, 1865, in the *New York Times,* confirms the manner of his death: "Lost on the steamer *Gen. Lyon,* on Friday, March 31, near Cape Hatteras, HOBART M. WALKER, aged 22 years, son of Ferdinand and Elmira Walker, of Brooklyn, N.Y." Those are the names of Hobart's parents and Edward Granger's aunt and uncle. In March 1865, Walker was part of a twenty-two-man detail that escorted recruits to Wilmington, North Carolina. For the return trip, the detachment's members were detailed as "ship guard" when they boarded the steamship SS *General Lyon* at Wilmington, en route to Fortress Monroe, Virginia. On March 31, the *Lyon* ran into heavy weather off Cape Hatteras. Barrels of kerosene, illegally stored in the engine room, tipped over and ignited. The blaze engulfed the entire ship, which sank, taking with it the vast majority of those onboard, including Walker. Granger and Walker were two of at least a half dozen members of their extended family who died in the war. "Hobart Walker," memorial and cenotaph at Findagrave.com, 98502007.

25. Adaline Walker, the daughter of Granger's uncle Ferdinand Walker and his wife, Elmira, was born on November 8, 1839, and would have been about three years older than Edward.

26. Dr. Theodore A. McGraw was born either November 11 or 18, 1839, and died September 6, 1921, in Detroit. His obituary and gravestone provide conflicting birth dates. In 1863, he received his medical degree from the College of Physicians and Surgeons, New York, and on March 30, 1864, he was commissioned as an assistant surgeon in the Union Army. He was mustered out on June 12, 1865, as a brevet captain. After the war, he returned to Detroit to begin a highly successful surgical practice. He later served as a vice president of the American Medical Association and the American Surgical Association. John H. Jopson, ed., "Report of the Committee on Necrology," *Transactions of the American Surgical Association* 40 (1922): xiv; Soldier Records and Profiles; "Dr. Theodore Andrews McGraw," memorial and gravestone at Findagrave.com, 76461516.

After citing books he has read, he noted he had corresponded with two or three unnamed former classmates at the Agricultural College, who also had dropped out.

"The Agr'l college has been remodeled lately but I have not yet seen the plan of operations. The *Tribune* said that it was to be more entirely agricultural." After Granger's departure, the school's curriculum did undergo another revision to emphasize its agricultural roots. Clearly, the Detroit youth did not see himself as a farmer and was certainly more intellectual than the school apparently considered its student body.

His tasks at his uncle's store afforded him plenty of leeway in his work schedule. On January 6, 1860, for example, Granger observed that "the dry goods business is now in its doldrums from 1 January to 1 March. Dullest time of the year. Shall have to take a book down to the store to read as there is nothing so dull for me as to sit in the house all day with nothing to do. I have a better chance to read in the store than the other boys as I am behind the desk all the time."

By late January, Charles Walker employed his nephew in some law-related writing. In a few sentences Granger summed up his current life: "Commenced copying for Uncle Charles tonight. Got along tolerably though his writing is none of the plainest and I can't make out the law terms very well. Terribly dull in the store and the boss feeling rather cross of course I took the benefit."

As the calendar advanced into February 1860, Granger wrote less and less often. Many of his remarks related to books he had been reading, with an occasional reference to the store's workload. His last entry appeared on February 29, 1860. From that point until he joined the army in August 1862, we know little about Granger's activities. Detroit city directories for 1861 and 1862 list him as a clerk in Charles Walker's law office, Walker and Kent, 4 Larned East Street. By 1862, about age nineteen at that time, he also was no longer living at home. The directory shows him boarding at 99 Fort Street West. His mother, Matilda, was listed at 40 Montcalm West. Presumably, his younger sister, Mollie, was living with her. Charles Walker's house in 1862 was at 19 Fort Street West, not far from where his nephew was boarding. Of significance, Edward Granger and his uncle Edward Walker boarded at the same address.[27]

---

27. Charles F. Clark, *Annual Directory of the Inhabitants, Incorporated Companies, Business Firms, etc., in the City of Detroit for 1862–'63* (Detroit: Charles F. Clark, 1862), hereafter cited as *Detroit City Directory 1862*, 28; *Detroit Free Press*, July 2, 1865.

INTRODUCTION

In its tribute article to Granger on July 2, 1865, the *Detroit Free Press* stated that Granger, who was a law student in 1862, "determined to enlist in the army as a private. Earnest efforts were made to dissuade him from his purpose, as he was the only son of his mother, and she a widow, but that purpose was inflexible, as it was founded in a deep sense of patriotic duty."[28]

Undoubtedly, his politically connected uncles, Charles and Edward Walker, influenced the young man to join. Edward Walker, as the head of the state's Republican Party, secured a commission for Edward Granger as a second lieutenant in the 5th Michigan Volunteer Cavalry Regiment at the time of its formation in August 1862.[29]

In a letter, Granger indicated he reported to the regiment two weeks ahead of its formal mustering in on August 27, 1862.[30] His early letters

---

28. *Detroit Free Press*, July 2, 1865.
29. Edward Carey Walker, Granger's maternal uncle, was born on July 4, 1820, in Butternuts, Otsego County, New York. He was a younger brother of Granger's mother, Matilda Walker Granger, and Granger's uncle Charles I. Walker. Edward Walker was also a lawyer and for a time had been in practice with Charles. However, Charles was a Democrat, and Edward was a Whig and later a Republican. During the Civil War years, he was chairman of Republican State Central Committee and had close political ties to Governor Austin Blair. In 1863, Walker was one of the organizers and chairman of the Michigan Branch of the U.S. Christian Commission, which sent representatives to the hospitals and spent more than $30,000 ministering to the welfare and comfort of Union soldiers. He himself spent six weeks in the field caring for the wounded after the May 1864 Battle of the Wilderness, an engagement in which his nephew Edward Granger participated with the Michigan Cavalry Brigade. He was married on June 16, 1852, to Lucy Bryant, and the couple had two children, Bryant Walker (1856–1936) and Jessie Rawson Walker (1859–1934). Edward Walker died on December 28, 1894, in Detroit. Granger Family Tree, Ancestry.com; *Detroit City Directory 1862*; Silas Farmer, *History of Detroit and Wayne County and Early Michigan*, vol. 2 (Ann Arbor: University of Michigan Library, 1890), 1129–30; S.D. Bingham, *Early History of Michigan, with Biographies of State Officers, Members of Congress, Judges and Legislators* (Lansing, Mich.: Thorp & Godfrey, 1888), 664–65.
30. President Abraham Lincoln's call for three hundred thousand additional troops in July 1862 set in motion a flurry of events in Michigan. Politicians and potential commanders jockeyed for positions and rank in the new regiments that Michigan would create, including three cavalry regiments to be designated the 5th Michigan, 6th Michigan, and 7th Michigan. Historian Edward Longacre designated Capt. William D. Mann as the "prime mover" in the creation of the 5th Michigan. See Edward G. Longacre, *Custer and His Wolverines: The Michigan Cavalry Brigade 1861–1865* (Conshohocken, Pa.: Combined Publishing, 1997). Mann enlisted his fellow member of the 1st Michigan, Lt. Col. Joseph T. Copeland, as his assistant *(continued)*

home during his first six months document that he was carried as a supernumerary second lieutenant, waiting for an actual roster space to open.[31] Among his fellow recruits were his friends Edwin B. Bigelow,[32] a former Agricultural College classmate who was appointed a sergeant in Company B, and Myron Hickey,[33] a son of a storekeeper

---

by offering the regiment's colonelcy to him. Within six weeks, the 5th Michigan had enrolled its full complement of men, forcing the two men to cease their recruiting.

31. Edward G. Granger, Compiled Military Service Records, Record Group 94, Entry 519, National Archives and Records Administration, Washington, D.C.; Granger letters. Various definitions for supernumeraries exist. Generally, such men were authorized to act as officers but were considered "extra" to the unit. Often they were placed in the rear waiting to replace those who fall in action, or for preserving order and regularity in the rear ranks while the front rank was engaged or was advancing. According to his letters, Granger seems to have had only secondary assignments given to him, primarily as an officer overseeing men on the picket lines in the defenses around Washington, D.C. Charles H. Safford, then a lieutenant in Company I, listed in his diary all the officers of the regiment at the time of their mustering in August 1862. According to his list, each of the regiment's companies had an additional second lieutenant, including Granger for Company C. See Paul Davis, ed., *I Rode with Custer: The Civil War Diary of Charles H. Safford, Brevet Major, 5th Michigan Cavalry* (Michigan: Ashton Z. Publishing, 2014).

32. *Detroit Daily Advertiser*, July 10, 1858; *History of Oakland County, Michigan* (Philadelphia: L. H. Everts, 1877), 280. Edwin Bigelow enlisted at age twenty-three as a sergeant on August 20, 1862. As he was born December 9, 1838, he was considerably older than his schoolmate Granger. He was later promoted to first sergeant. On October 19, 1863, he was taken prisoner during the Battle of Buckland Mills, Virginia, and was held until June 15, 1864. On August 9, 1864, he was discharged to accept promotion in the U.S. Colored Heavy Artillery. On October 20, 1864, he was promoted to captain in the 1st Colored Heavy Artillery. He was honorably discharged at Chattanooga, Tennessee, on March 31, 1866, and returned to live in Jackson, Michigan. He died on September 22, 1916, in Jackson, and is buried in Woodland Cemetery. "Edwin B. Bigelow," memorial and gravestone at Findagrave.com, 25163308; Soldier Records and Profiles; U.S. Civil War Soldiers, 1861–1865, database at Ancestry.com, original data from National Park Service, Civil War Soldiers and Sailors Database (hereafter cited as U.S. Civil War Soldiers).

33. Myron Hickey, born in 1833, enlisted on August 14, 1862, as a second lieutenant in Company B, 5th Michigan Cavalry. He was promoted to captain on June 6, 1864 and major on April 13, 1865. At least one author credits Hickey with being a staff officer for Gen. Philip Sheridan from 1864 through the end of the war in April 1865. At first, he was chief ambulance officer and later ordnance officer. Hickey was mustered out on June 13, 1865, but may have joined the 1st Michigan Cavalry for three months' service at Fort Leavenworth, Kansas, from June to September 1865, when he received his final discharge on September 5, 1865. Research indicates Hickey returned to Davisburg,

in the small village of Davisburg, Michigan, who was named a second lieutenant in Company B.

An article about the Civil War sesquicentennial published in April 2011 on the Michigan State University website indicates "the Civil War influenced Michigan Agricultural College as well as many other schools at this time."[34] The document indicates that a few students did enlist in the war's first summer of 1861, but "a mass exodus" did not threaten the university's enrollment until that fall. Seven seniors and two underclassmen were excused in order to serve. The seven seniors received their degrees in absentia that December.

A casualty list in the university archives suggests at least sixteen graduates or men who withdrew for service were killed or wounded during the war.[35] Because Granger had withdrawn from the school well before the war, he was not included on the list, but at least thirteen of the men were likely known by him during his year as a student. At least three of the casualties were men who served with him in the Michigan Cavalry Brigade.

—Capt. James G. Birney, Company C, 7th Michigan Cavalry, who apparently entered the school with Granger, but withdrew at some point. He was wounded July 3, 1863, at Gettysburg, Pennsylvania, and died in 1870 while serving as an officer in the postwar army.[36]

---

where he had earlier married Hepsebeth Losee prior to 1860. He likely resumed his occupation as a merchant, but he died at age thirty-five on August 24, 1868, in Springfield, Michigan, apparently the result of "a chronic illness" contracted while in the army. He is buried in Davisburg Cemetery. Soldier Records and Profiles; U.S. Civil War Soldiers; "Maj. Myron Hickey," memorial, photograph, and gravestone at Findagrave.com, 15927793; Abbott M. Gibney, "Major Myron Hickey, Civil War Veteran is Mystery," *Lake Orion (Mich.) Review*, December 12, 1963.

34. "Exhibits: Civil War Sesquicentennial," Michigan State University, April 2011, http://onthebanks.msu.edu/Exhibit/1-6-7/civil-war-sesquicentennial/.

35. Casualty List provided by Sarah Roberts, Michigan State University Archives.

36. James G. Birney IV was born April 12, 1844, in New Haven, Connecticut, and died June 16, 1870, while stationed with the 9th U.S. Cavalry at Fort Davis, Texas. On September 14, 1862, he enlisted as first sergeant in Company C, 7th Michigan Infantry, but on October 15, 1862, he was reassigned as a second lieutenant to Company A, 7th Michigan Cavalry. At Gettysburg, he was wounded and captured, but soon escaped. According to an account on a Bay County, Michigan, web page, he had been wounded by a slash to the head. When his color bearer was killed, he dismounted, took the colors, rallied his men and continued the charge, before he was captured for a time. On March 18, 1864, he was promoted to captain. *(continued)*

—Sgt. Otis W. Carpenter, Company M, 7th Michigan Cavalry, who attended in 1861–62, but withdrew. He went missing on June 11, 1864, during the Battle of Trevilian Station, Virginia, and became a prisoner of war. Later released, he died December 6, 1864, in General Hospital Division 1 in Annapolis, Maryland.[37]

—Capt. Alphonso (or Alpheus) W. Carr, Company I, 1st Michigan Cavalry, who attended in 1858–59 with Granger. He was killed in action June 12, 1864, at Trevilian Station, Virginia.[38]

On April 1, 1863, Granger was rescued from his temporary status when he was officially promoted to second lieutenant.[39] One of the

---

Marvin Kusmierz, "James G. Birney IV," Bay-Journal, October 2007, http://bay-journal.com/bay/1he/people/fp-birney-james-gson.html. Brief accounts of Birney's exploits at Gettysburg can be found in Asa B. Isham, *Seventh Michigan Cavalry of Custer's Wolverine Brigade* (Huntington, W.Va.: Blue Acorn Press, 2000), 27; and William O. Lee, comp., *Personal and Historical Sketches and Facial History of and by Members of the Seventh Regiment Michigan Volunteer Cavalry 1862–1865* (Detroit: 7th Michigan Cavalry Association, 1902), reprint by Forgotten Books, November 26, 2015, 157–59. On September 17, 1865, he was mustered out of the 7th Michigan and mustered into the 1st Michigan, serving until June 6, 1866, and mustering out at Salt Lake City, Utah. About a month later, on July 28, 1866, he was appointed as a lieutenant in the 9th U.S. Cavalry, but died of illness on June 16, 1870. He was buried in Greenwood Cemetery, Brooklyn, New York. "Capt. James Gillespie Birney, IV," memorial and photograph at Findagrave.com, 66530190. Also, see Tim Younkman, "Bay City Profile: Capt. James G. Birney IV Served under Gen. Custer in 7th Michigan Cavalry, Received Sword on Display at Bay County Historical Museum," *Bay City Times*, April 9, 2011; U.S. Civil War Soldiers; Soldier Records and Profiles.

37. Otis W. Carpenter of Delta, Michigan, enlisted at age twenty-two in September 1862 as a sergeant in Company D, 7th Michigan Cavalry. He reportedly died in the hospital of chronic diarrhea and was buried in the Annapolis National Cemetery. Soldier Records and Profiles; U.S., Registers of Deaths of Volunteers, 1861–1865, database at Ancestry.com; U.S. National Cemetery Interment Control Forms, 1928–1962, database at Ancestry.com.

38. Alpheus W. Carr was born in 1834 in New York. He enlisted as a captain on November 1, 1863, in Company I, 1st Michigan Cavalry and was killed in action on June 12, 1864, at the Battle of Trevilian Station, Virginia. He was buried in Evergreen Cemetery in Union City, Pennsylvania. Soldier Records and Profiles; "Alpheus W. Carr," memorial and gravestone at Findagrave.com, 49983173.

39. Granger's uncle Edward Walker was busy behind the scenes working in his nephew's behalf. On March 28, 1863, he wrote to Governor Austin Blair expressing his concern that Granger might be axed from the regiment. In a second letter to the governor, April 7, 1863, Walker advised Blair that Granger had told him that

company muster roll cards in his NARA military file actually gave his rank as private as of March 31, 1863, as he was discharged to accept his commission effective April 1, 1863. However, even earlier cards recording his whereabouts list him as a lieutenant, including from August 27 to October 31, 1862. Almost certainly within the 5th Michigan Cavalry he always functioned as and was recognized as an officer.

At age nineteen, Granger was by far the youngest of his company's four original officers, all of whom were from Detroit and Wayne County. At age twenty-nine, Capt. George Wellington Hunt[40] was the oldest. First Lt. Horace W. Dodge[41] was twenty-six and Second Lt. Jacob Bristol[42] was twenty-eight.

---

a vacancy had occurred in the regiment. Governor Austin Blair Papers, Burton Historical Collection, Detroit Public Library.

40. George Wellington Hunt enlisted at age twenty-nine on October 1, 1861, as a first lieutenant in Company A, 1st Michigan Cavalry, and was mustered in on November 1. He was mustered out on March 20, 1862, according to Soldier Records and Profiles. According to U.S. Civil War Soldiers, he was mustered in as a captain in Company C, 5th Michigan Cavalry, on August 27, 1862. He was mustered out on March 23, 1863. Born in either 1832 or 1833, he died on May 21, 1881, and was buried in Elmwood Cemetery in Detroit. According to Edward Walker's letters (see note 39) to Governor Blair, Captain Hunt's early resignation in March 1862 assured that Granger would retain his officer's position within the regiment.

41. Horace W. Dodge, age twenty-six, enlisted on August 27, 1862, as a first lieutenant in Company C, 5th Michigan Cavalry. He had been born on February 18, 1836, in Newburyport, Massachusetts. On April 1, 1863, he was promoted to captain, which allowed both Lieutenants Bristol and Granger to move up in rank within the company. Wounded in action on June 12, 1864, at Trevilian Station, Virginia, Dodge was honorably discharged for disability on October 21, 1864, and promoted to brevet major on March 13, 1865, for "gallant and meritorious service." His death proved to be unique. He was killed in a western gunfight of some sort on March 22, 1868, at Cheyenne Crossing, South Dakota, then part of Dakota Territory. He was buried in his hometown of Newburyport. Soldier Records and Profiles; U.S. Civil War Soldiers; "Horace W. Dodge," memorial and gravestone at Findagrave.com, 101131463.

42. Jacob Bristol, twenty-eight, of Detroit, Michigan, was the original second lieutenant of Granger's Company C. Born on October 11, 1833, in New York state, he was commissioned as a second lieutenant on August 14, 1862. He was promoted to first lieutenant on April 1, 1863, which enabled Granger himself to move up from supernumerary status to second lieutenant. The two men evidently became close friends. Bristol died on December 21, 1915, and was buried in Woodmere Cemetery in Detroit. He was discharged for disability on July 5, 1864. However, Gen. Judson Kilpatrick's General Order No. 7, August 16, 1864, lists Bristol as "Assistant Commissary of Musters." He received a brevet for captain on March 13, *(continued)*

A card in Granger's National Archives military file shows he actually reported for duty on August 15, 1862, at the 5th Michigan's camp twelve days before he was mustered in. The regiment's training area was located at Camp Banks (sometimes called Banks Barracks) in Detroit, not far from Granger's uncle's house.[43] For his first year in the army, Granger was always listed as present for duty. Beginning with the muster card covering July and August 1863, Granger was listed as either present or "absent on duty" on General Custer's staff. The difference describing his status appears to be simply an administrative choice of words. He was appointed to Custer's personal staff on August 20, 1863.[44]

On July 17, 1864, he was discharged to accept promotion to first lieutenant. After his death on August 16, 1864, during the Battle of Crooked Run north of Front Royal, Virginia, the company muster roll card for July and August 1864 listed Granger as missing in action. The combined card for November and December 1864 stated that he died of wounds received on or about August 16 at Front Royal. On June 19, 1865, when survivors in his regiment were mustered out of service, Granger was listed as killed in action on August 16, 1864.[45]

When the Civil War began in April 1861, most Americans expected it would last no more than a few short months. By the summer of 1862, President Abraham Lincoln and his Union Army generals realized that the war would last much longer. Fighting would continue

---

1865, for gallant and meritorious service. Soldier Records and Profiles; "Kilpatrick Staff," Civil War Talk, http://civilwartalk.com/threads/kilpatrick-staff.115131/; "Cpt. Jacob Bristol," memorial and gravestone at Findagrave.com, 10305702.

43. Camp Banks, also known as Banks Barracks, was a Civil War mustering and training facility for new regiments to prepare for the fighting that lay ahead of them. Located in Detroit, it was maintained by the state of Michigan. The 5th Michigan Cavalry Regiment initially was trained there. See Eric J. Wittenberg, ed., *Under Custer's Command: The Civil War Journal of James Henry Avery* (Washington, D.C.: Brassey's, 2000), 9n8, 9–16, 161. Also, see Paul Taylor, *"Old Slow Town": Detroit during the Civil War* (Detroit: Wayne State University Press, 2000), 59–60. In his memoirs Captain Safford located the camp on the north side of Clinton Street near Elmwood Cemetery in Detroit. He noted that the open fields between Clinton Street and Jefferson Avenue were used for drill grounds. Davis, *I Rode with Custer*, 8.

44. Edward G. Granger to Emma Walker, letter, August 22, 1863.

45. Edward G. Granger, Compiled Military Service Records; Soldier Records and Profiles.

INTRODUCTION 25

(left) Capt. Horace Dodge. *(right)* Capt. Jacob Bristol.
Courtesy of John Beckendorf.

indefinitely, and more soldiers were needed. In July 1862, Lincoln called for an additional 300,000 volunteers to serve three years in the Union Army to combat the Confederate states. By July 1862, the state had already contributed three cavalry regiments, sixteen infantry regiments and eight batteries of light artillery. By the war's end, nearly 90,000 Michigan men would serve the Union cause. When the president's 1862 order reached the state, a fourth cavalry regiment and another infantry regiment were already being formed. However, Michigan was expected to provide another 12,000 men, assigned to six new infantry and three cavalry regiments for the Northern army. The added horse soldier regiments were designated as the 5th, 6th, and

7th Michigan Cavalry regiments.[46] The year before, the 1st Michigan Cavalry had been formed, and since then had earned a reputation as a hard-fighting unit.[47]

By the next month, August 1862, recruitment for the 5th Michigan Cavalry was in high gear. Joseph T. Copeland, a well-known judge from Pontiac, Michigan, and then lieutenant colonel of the 1st Michigan Cavalry, was given responsibility for raising and equipping the 5th Michigan, but he was ambitious for more than a regimental command.[48] Still, he went about his duties forming the 5th, which, like

---

46. For further background on the 5th Michigan and its sister regiments in the Michigan Cavalry Brigade, see the following several works: Longacre, *Custer*; Wittenberg, *Under Custer's Command*; Robert F. O'Neill, *Chasing Jeb Stuart and John Mosby: The Union Cavalry in Northern Virginia from Second Manassas to Gettysburg* (Jefferson, N.C.: McFarland, 2012); and Davis, *I Rode with Custer*. The creation of the three cavalry regiments proved contentious and involved such political figures as then–lieutenant colonel Joseph T. Copeland, then-captain William Mann, and congressman Francis Kellogg. See O'Neill, *Chasing Jeb Stuart*, 21–23, for further information on the political bickering that overlay the creation of the three regiments and the choices of the men who would serve as their higher-ranking officers.
47. The 1st Michigan Volunteer Cavalry Regiment was organized by the state of Michigan between August 21 and September 6, 1861, in Detroit under command of Col. Thornton Brodhead. It left for Washington, D.C., in late September. Initially, its companies were divided into three battalions that served apart from each other. Two saw action in the Shenandoah Valley while the third campaigned through Loudoun and Fauquier counties in Virginia. The regiment was re-formed in July 1862 as part of the Army of Virginia under Maj. Gen. John Pope. On August 30, 1862, the regiment suffered terribly when it clashed with Confederate Cavalry under Maj. Gen. James Ewell Brown (J. E. B. or "Jeb") Stuart at Lewis Ford near the close of the Battle of Second Manassas. Among its casualties was Colonel Brodhead, who was mortally wounded. Its total loss in killed, wounded, captured, and missing numbered about 130 officers and men. For the next ten months, the regiment would remain on duty within the defenses of Washington, D.C. See O'Neill, *Chasing Jeb Stuart*, 8–9, 18–26.
48. Before the war, Joseph Tarr Copeland (May 6, 1813–May 6, 1893) was a highly placed figure in Michigan politics and served as a justice on the Michigan Supreme Court from 1852 to 1857. Initially, Copeland served as the lieutenant colonel and commander of the 1st Michigan Cavalry Regiment and then, briefly, as commander of the 5th Michigan Cavalry. Promoted to brigadier general, he commanded the Michigan Cavalry Brigade for about the first six months of 1863. Days before the Battle of Gettysburg, he was abruptly replaced by newly promoted Brig. Gen. George Armstrong Custer, who would eclipse him in history as the brigade's

INTRODUCTION 27

the 6th and 7th, would draw upon experienced officers who had served with the 1st, 2nd, or 3rd Michigan Cavalry regiments. However, the 5th would be unique compared to its predecessors in how it was armed. Its soldiers would carry the popular seven-shot Spencer repeating rifle. A new mass-production weapon, it offered tremendous firepower that could significantly influence the outcome on the battlefield. Soldiers armed with the Spencer could fire seven rounds in about a minute, more than twice what a well-trained infantryman could do with the more common muzzleloaders.[49] Some may have been capable of firing as many as ten rounds in a minute.

Young Edward Granger's decision that summer of 1862 to join the army must have caused consternation within his family. From the *Detroit Free Press* article of July 2, 1865, we know his mother was opposed to her only son serving in the army. But his uncles Charles and Edward Walker significantly supported the Union's cause, and Edward Walker, the state Republican leader, enjoyed close political ties with Michigan's governor, Austin Blair, a staunch abolitionist and supporter of President Lincoln. Undoubtedly, the two men placated their sister and relied on their political pull to gain an officer's commission for their nephew.

Recruitment for the 5th Michigan had begun only in July in Detroit, led by Capt. William D. Mann, an overly ambitious member of the 1st Michigan Cavalry.[50] Six weeks later, as the end of August neared,

---

commander. For the rest of the war, Copeland handled mostly administrative assignments, including commanding a depot for drafted men at Annapolis, Maryland, and later Pittsburgh, Pennsylvania. He also commanded a military prison at Alton, Illinois, until his resignation on November 8, 1865. He spent his final years in Florida.

49. In their books, both Wittenberg and O'Neill note that actually manufacturing and putting Spencers into the hands of the 5th Michigan proved to be a challenging task. The first shipment of the repeaters did not arrive until December 2, 1862, about the time the 5th departed Detroit for Washington, D.C.

50. William D. Mann was born on September 27, 1839, in Sandusky, Ohio, and at age twenty-one accepted a commission as a captain in the 1st Michigan Cavalry on August 12, 1861. Ambitious for greater command, he resigned on July 5, 1862, and proposed that he raise a new regiment of mounted riflemen to combat the ever-increasing threats from Confederate guerrillas. In the summer of 1862, he enjoyed great success in recruiting men and training them for his new regiment. Michigan governor Austin Blair opted to count Mann's personnel against the state's *(continued)*

so many men had rushed to join that the 5th was essentially full. Additional recruits were funneled to the respective camps of the 6th Michigan in Grand Rapids, and to the 7th Michigan from that point, until both of those regiments were ready to take the field early in 1863.[51]

Author Eric Wittenberg has noted that the 5th Michigan served with distinction for the balance of the Civil War. While 272 cavalry regiments served the Union cause, the 5th Michigan suffered the third highest number of men to die on the battlefield.[52] Among that number were ten commissioned officers, including Lieutenant Granger.

According to Wittenberg's figures, 1,866 men served in the regiment, and 101 were killed in action. Another 24 died of combat wounds, and 69 more died as prisoners of war in Southern camps. Disease claimed another 109 men, and 196 men were lost on disabilities resulting from either combat wounds or illness. All told, 303 of the regiment's 1,866 men, or 16 percent of its numbers, never came home. That casualty rate rises to 27 percent when the men who were disabled are added to the total.[53]

Unfortunately, Granger either wrote no letters from Camp Banks or they have not survived. More likely, as an officer, he lived at home during much of this time.[54] Thus, we have little idea what the camp

---

new manpower quota. Mann's First Mounted Rifles, instead, became the base for building the 5th Michigan Cavalry. After the governor offered Mann the colonelcy of the 6th Michigan, state politics intervened. Instead, Mann gained command of the 7th Michigan Cavalry. He served at length in that role, especially at Gettysburg on July 3, 1863, but his tenure was controversial. He endured numerous problems with his officers. On March 1, 1864, Mann resigned his commission. After the war, Mann became a businessman, and newspaper and magazine publisher. He died on May 17, 1920, in Morristown, New Jersey. See O'Neill, *Chasing Jeb Stuart*, 18–23; Eric Wittenberg, "Col. William d'Alton Mann," *Rantings of a Civil War Historian* (historical blog), April 15, 2011, http://civilwarcavalry.com/?p=2492; Robert O'Neill, "Col. William Mann and the 7th Michigan Cavalry," *Gettysburg Magazine*, January 2013; also, Soldier Records and Profiles; U.S. Civil War Soldiers.

51. Longacre, *Custer*, 83–94. The 7th Michigan's first recruits were mustered in on October 13, 1862. Many of them were excess to the personnel needs of the 6th Michigan.
52. Wittenberg, *Under Custer's Command*, 3–4n.
53. Wittenberg, *Under Custer's Command*, 4.
54. Granger's first letter, August 12, 1862, written to his cousin Alexander Caskey, is datelined Detroit, but he gives no indication that he was writing from the camp. Because the camp was located near his residence, it seems likely that he wrote to Caskey from his boarding house.

INTRODUCTION

Capt. Charles H. Safford.
Courtesy of John Beckendorf.

and training were like from his officer's perspective. However, Wittenberg's book, *Under Custer's Command*, containing the Civil War journal of James Henry Avery, provides insightful details about camp life. Captain Safford's memoir also provides details of the Detroit camp.

Many historical accounts indicate that the men of 5th Michigan began their lengthy trek to the east on December 4, 1862, going by train from Detroit to Washington, D.C., where they went into camp on East Capitol Hill in sight of the Capitol Building itself. Safford's memoirs state that the regiment's departure actually took place over three days, December 3–5. He also says the new Washington camp was located on East Capitol Hill, about one mile from the Capitol Building, and adjoined Lincoln Hospital.[55] The site was named Camp

---

55. Davis, *I Rode with Custer*, 8, 11–12. Charles H. Safford, twenty-four, of Detroit was commissioned as a second lieutenant on August 14, 1862, in the 5th Michigan Cavalry, the same day as Edward Granger, but he would serve until January 23, 1865. During his service he kept a diary and collected notes and newspaper clippings about the experiences of the 5th Michigan and the Michigan Cavalry Brigade. That material forms the basis for the Davis book. Safford was born on March 10, 1838, in Lockport, New York. He was promoted to first lieutenant on June 13, 1863, and to *(continued)*

Copeland after the regiment's original commander, himself a newly named brigadier general.

Much of their early activity was taken up in drill and review. Safford's files for his book included a number of mostly undated newspaper clippings that also provide insights into Camp Copeland's activities and the soldiers' training. The regiment would not be fully trained and equipped, ready for field duty, until early February 1863. More important, Copeland himself had been instrumental in having the 5th brigaded with the 6th and 7th as an all-Michigan cavalry force.[56] Another organization, the 1st Michigan Cavalry, had been formed a year earlier and had already been bloodied in action in Northern Virginia against the enemy. In time, it, too, would become part of the Michigan Cavalry Brigade.

> captain on July 15, 1864, two days before Granger himself was promoted to first lieutenant. Sgt. James Avery of Company I described Safford as "a small man, with sandy beard, and very light complexion, generally quiet, always neat and military in camp, but a very lion in battle." In January 1865, Safford's father took ill back in Detroit and he went home on leave. His father died and Safford subsequently resigned his commission on January 23, 1865. On March 13, 1865, he received a brevet promotion to major for gallant and meritorious service. After the war, he became a merchant in Black River, Michigan. His former commander, Col. Russell Alger hired him to work for him in Detroit and later in Duluth, Minnesota. In 1920, he suffered a stroke and died on December 10, 1924, in the Minnesota Soldiers' Home in Minneapolis. He is buried in Elmwood Cemetery in Detroit.
>
> 56. Although the 5th and 6th Cavalry regiments were mustered into federal service weeks apart from each other, both headed for the war in December. A lack of arms and equipment had delayed the 5th Michigan's departure. Most of the troopers still had no Spencer rifles and other equipment. The 5th also traveled without its highest-ranking field officers. Colonel Copeland had been named a brigadier general and Lieutenant Colonel Mann had moved to command the 7th Michigan. Maj. Freeman Norvell was left with the regiment's colonelcy. By late December, he had been promoted to colonel. By January 27, 1863, the 7th Michigan was sworn into federal service. Between February 20 and 22, 1863, the regiment began its travel by train to Washington, D.C. The now-veteran 1st Michigan Cavalry remained within the Washington defenses at Fort Scott between Washington and Alexandria. It would not join the other three regiments as the Michigan Cavalry Brigade until June 28, 1863.

CHAPTER I

A FIRST LETTER

IN HIS FIRST SURVIVING LETTER, PROBABLY WRITTEN FROM his boarding house at 99 Fort Street West in Detroit, Edward G. Granger offered a recruitment pitch to one of his many first cousins, Alexander Carey Caskey.[1] Granger indicated he would be going away soon. According to his military records at the National Archives and Records Administration, Edward Granger signed up two days later as a supernumerary second lieutenant in Company C, 5th Michigan Volunteer Cavalry Regiment, or what he referred to as a third lieutenant in this letter.[2] Fifteen days later, on August 27, 1862, he and many of his regiment's original complement of troops were formally mustered into U.S. service. For nearly seven months he served as an "extra officer" available for whatever mundane tasks might be assigned

---

1. Alexander Carey Caskey (July 20, 1844–December 1, 1904) was a paternal first cousin of Edward G. Granger. Edward's mother, Matilda, was a sister to Alexander's mother, Caroline Walker, according to the Granger Family Tree compiled by the editor from Ancestry.com records (henceforth, Granger Family Tree, Ancestry .com). Two days after Granger wrote to him, Alex, fifteen months younger than Edward, enlisted as a corporal in the 124th Ohio Infantry Regiment. It would serve in the war's western theater, first in Kentucky and Tennessee, and in 1863 and 1864 in the Chickamauga and Atlanta Campaigns. For the balance of the war, it fought in Alabama and Tennessee, including at the Battle of Nashville, December 15–16, 1864. On March 16, 1863, Caskey was promoted to sergeant and on May 1, 1864, to sergeant major. On October 13, 1864, or almost two months after Edward's death in Virginia, Caskey was promoted to first lieutenant. He mustered out on June 9, 1865. After the war, he lived in Ohio until his death in 1904.
2. Edward G. Granger, Compiled Military Service Records.

to him. He was finally mustered in as the second lieutenant of Company C on April 1, 1863.

Although they would not serve together in the Union Army, the two cousins were close. In his will probated after his own death in 1904, Caskey left a photograph of Granger to his own son Edward G. Caskey, "for whom he was named."[3] Just prior to writing this letter, according to the Detroit city directory for 1862, Granger had been working as a law student in the firm of Walker and Kent, one of whose partners was the boys' uncle Edward Carey Walker.[4] Caskey was a clerk at A. C. McGraw and Company, whose partners included his much older brother Samuel G. Caskey. It is unclear how a letter to a cousin ended up in the Granger family's collection after Edward's death in 1864. However, given the apparent close bond between Edward and Alex, the latter may have given this letter and another from March 1863 to the Granger family after Edward's death in 1864.

The second item in this section is not an actual letter written by him, but is included here because of its relevance. After Granger's mustering into his regiment, his many friends gathered to send him off on his military career with the presentation of a new revolver. Several of these young men will be mentioned later in Granger's letters to his family members.

At the same time we can learn a great deal about Edward himself by analyzing his friends' own backgrounds. Except for his uncle Edward Walker, almost all were youths, like Granger himself, in the beginning stages of their own careers. Documents gleaned through Ancestry.com clearly indicate they were men of the middle class. They also confirm that in the years after his return from the Agricultural College, Granger built up a wide circle of friends. As customary for that era, the men were usually referred to by their first initials and last names. The *Detroit City Directory 1862* fleshes out names and other details about almost all of them.

---

3. Alexander C. Caskey, Ohio, Wills and Probate Records, 1786–1998, doc. 72, no. 35531, Ancestry.com.

4. *Detroit City Directory 1862*. Other sources say Granger worked for his other uncle, Charles Walker, but it is unclear whether the two Walker men worked together in 1862.

Lt. Edward G. Granger,
5th Michigan Cavalry, circa late 1862–early 1863.
Courtesy of Jim Adams.

[LETTER 1]

Detroit, August 12th 1862

Alex.

I expected to answer your letter verbally but, as you have given up coming here I suppose, I must write which you know is much harder for me to do.

We have not heard, as yet, your reasons for changing your mind, but suppose they were sufficiently weighty.

Theodore McGraw[5] is coming home as soon as his father sends him the money: probably he intends to get a place as assistant Surgeon in the army. He will make a good one.

Gus Buhl[6] is 2nd Lieut. in I. W. Ingersoll's Company in the 24 Regt. and Price Quincy's Clerk is first sergeant of the same Company.

---

5. According to his gravestone, Doctor Theodore A. McGraw was born November 11, 1839, but his obituary provides a November 18 birth date. He died in Detroit on September 6, 1921, and was buried in Detroit's Elmwood Cemetery. In 1863, he graduated in medicine from the College of Physicians and Surgeons, New York, and on March 30, 1864, he was commissioned as an assistant surgeon in the Union Army during the Civil War. He was mustered out on June 12, 1865, as a brevet captain. After the war, he returned to Detroit to begin a highly successful surgical practice. He later served as a vice president of the American Medical Association and the American Surgical Association. Jopson, "Committee on Necrology," xiv; Soldier Records and Profiles; "Dr. Theodore Andrews McGraw," memorial and gravestone at Findagrave.com, 76461516.

6. At age nineteen, F. Augustus Buhl enlisted as a private on July 26, 1862, in the 24th Michigan Infantry Regiment. On August 13, 1862, he was commissioned as a second lieutenant in that regiment. On Dec. 13, 1862, he was promoted to first lieutenant. When his company commander was wounded early in the fighting at Gettysburg, Buhl assumed command. He was badly wounded in the leg. After his recovery, he returned to duty that September, but on November 10, 1863, he accepted a commission as a captain in the 1st Michigan Cavalry. For a time Buhl served as an aide on the staff of Brig. Gen. George A. Custer along with Edward Granger. During Confederate Gen. Jubal Early's invasion of Maryland, Buhl was badly wounded on August 25, 1864, in a fight at Shepherdstown, Virginia. This was nine days after Granger himself had been killed in action at Front Royal, Virginia. After reaching the hospital, Buhl wrote a brief letter to his younger brother Walter Buhl, in which he described his wounding by a ball that lodged in his right hip. Although he expected to recover, he died suddenly on September 1, 1864, at a military hospital at Sandy Hook, Maryland. Also, see J. H. Kidd, *Personal Recollections of a Cavalryman* (Grand Rapids, Mich.: Black Letter Press, 1969), 383–84. Kidd

Sam Warren[7] says he is going in the 17th but whether he has enlisted yet, I don't know.

Hunter[8] is going if he can get his Father's consent, and Stanton[9] says he is going.

Judge Copeland of Pontiac, late Lieut. Col. of the 1st Cavalry, has received authority from the Governor to raise a Regiment of Mounted Riflemen. Wellington Hunt of Detroit is to be Captain in said Regiment; and if he can raise men enough, E. G. Granger (also of Detroit) may get the place of 3d Lieut. in Hunt's Company. I have not seen Hunt yet and so don't know how many men he will want me to raise but C. I.[10] was talking to him yesterday. Uncle thinks that by going out to Fowlersville and getting Ben to help me, I could raise some men in Livingston Co. so I shall probably go and try my luck. You know you promised to go when I went; if you will come up now you can get the chance as I shall go some way, even if I don't get the Lieutenancy. Don[11] seems to have some inclination to go, though I have not yet said anything to him about my intentions.

If you know of anyone who wishes to enlist in such a Regiment just send him to me. Wonder if "Old Scott" wouldn't like to go.

By the way, I met George Davis[12] yesterday and he wanted me to

---

wrote: "He was a Detroit boy, and a classmate of mine in Ann Arbor when the war broke out. I was deeply grieved at his death as I had learned to love him like a brother." Soldier Records and Profiles; "Capt. Frederick Augustus 'Gus' Buhl," memorial and photograph at Findagrave.com, 10323572.

7. This may have been Samuel E. Warren, who was born in 1843 and died on April 19, 1900. He enlisted on August 24, 1861, as a private in the 11th Michigan Infantry and was mustered out on June 24, 1862. Despite Granger's statement, Warren does not appear to have reenlisted in any other regiment. Soldier Records and Profiles.
8. This is probably Hammond Hunter, who is listed among Granger's friends who gave him a revolver as a going-away present. See letter 2 in this chapter.
9. This is either S. K. or William Stanton, both of whom are listed as friends of Granger.
10. Granger is referring to his uncle Charles Irish Walker.
11. This is likely Donald MacDonald (sometimes McDonald), who is mentioned frequently by Edward Granger. Initially, it appeared that Don may have been a suitor for Granger's sister, Mollie. According to the 1860 Detroit census, Donald MacDonald lived with the family of the Grangers' mutual friend George A. Sheley. Both Sheley and MacDonald were born in 1845. The *Detroit City Directory 1862* lists MacDonald as a clerk at Farrand, Sheley & Co., a firm of druggists and grocers owned by Sheley's father, Alanson. MacDonald was also boarding with the Sheley family. 1860 U.S. Federal Census, Detroit.
12. This individual is unidentified.

tell you to hurry up and answer his letter. He says he wrote to you six weeks ago and has not heard from you yet. I am surprised at your treatment of the poor boy.

Don had a first rate time up the lakes but poor Wenus[13] got decidedly cut out by a handsome young Lady, who was away at a boarding school when Don was up there last, who proved so attractive that Don's stay was prolonged from two to four weeks and the hunting was entirely neglected.

Mollie and I went to one of Philbrick's concerts[14] last night and one of the principal performers was your bashful friend Dell Beardsley.[15] Uncle Edward just got home from down East and brought Mother a photograph of Ada for Mother.[16] Mother says "tell Mr. Adams I want his to put with it," for a contrast I suppose. You may tell Ada for me that I should like one like the one Mother has of her, as I am going away.

Mollie sends love to Maria & Alex and Carrie sends hers to one or the other, I forgot which, & I guess she is not very particular.[17]

Write soon to
Your Cousin
Ed.

[LETTER 2]

Lieut. Ed. G. Granger

Detroit, September 3rd 1862

Your undersigned friends and fellow gymnasts beg your acceptance of the accompanying revolver, presented as a slight mark of their esteem

---

13. This may be a reference to Venus, the Roman goddess of love.
14. Philbrick may possibly have been Henry Philbrick, a native of New York state and successful voice teacher in Michigan in this period. However, this is not certain.
15. This individual is unidentified.
16. Edward was Granger's uncle Edward Carey Walker. Ada was Adaline Walker, daughter of Granger's uncle Ferdinand Walker and his wife, Elmira. Ada married Jarvis Martin Adams in 1861. See introduction, notes 25 and 29.
17. Alex was undoubtedly Alex Caskey himself. Maria was likely Caskey's younger sister Maria Louisa, born in 1846. Carrie was likely Carrie B. Hawley, who was friends with both Grangers.

for you, at the same time expressing the hope that you may be as active and energetic in the cause of Union as you have been in the Gymnasium:

    S. K. Stanton[18]
    L. H. Baldwin[19]
    William Stanton[20]
    F. R. Hallock[21]
    Hammond Hunter[22]
    E. W. Hudson[23]
    John Stevenson[24]
    James Craig[25]
    W. C. Williams[26]
    E. C. Hinsdale[27]
    Robt. Beveridge[28]
    W. G. Pungs[29]

---

18. Stephen K. Stanton was a partner in the insurance agency of Biddle & Stanton. He boarded at 103 Fort Street, near Granger who lived at 99 Fort Street at that time. *Detroit City Directory 1862.*
19. Lyman H. Baldwin was a bookkeeper for his brother's firm, Hayden & Baldwin, a carriage hardware company. *Detroit City Directory 1862.*
20. William Stanton was probably Stephen Stanton's brother or father, but he did not appear in the *Detroit City Directory 1862.*
21. Francis R. Hallock was a bookkeeper for the Horace Hallock clothing store, another family store. *Detroit City Directory 1862.*
22. Similar to Edward Granger, Hammond Hunter was a law student in the firm of Douglas & Andrews. *Detroit City Directory 1862.*
23. Edon W. Hudson was listed as a "vessel owner." *Detroit City Directory 1862.*
24. John Stevenson was a merchant tailor in Detroit. His son Walter Stevenson is one of Granger's fellow lieutenants in the 5th Michigan Cavalry, whom he mentions in a later letter. *Detroit City Directory 1862.*
25. James Craig is a commission merchant in the city. *Detroit City Directory 1862.*
26. William C. Williams worked for Farrand, Sheley & Co., a firm of druggists and grocers. *Detroit City Directory 1862.*
27. Edwin C. Hinsdale was a Detroit lawyer. He may have been related to Mary Ann Walker, Charles Walker's wife, whose maiden name was Hinsdale. *Detroit City Directory 1862.*
28. Robert Beveridge was a clerk with the Genesee & Wyoming Railroad. *Detroit City Directory 1862.*
29. No William G. Pungs was listed in the *Detroit City Directory 1862.* A William Pungs was listed as a blacksmith, while William L. Pungs is cited as a clerk at the Russell House. The 1870 census lists blacksmith Pungs as sixty-two years old, and his son as a bookkeeper at age twenty-eight. That would suggest an 1842 birth date for the latter and would put him in the age bracket of Granger and his other friends. Both father and son were born in Prussia. A William G. Pungs *(continued)*

J. Dean[30]
A. Ives, Jr.[31]
W. H. Allen[32]
E. C. Walker[33]
Frank Folsom[34]
J. M. Arnold[35]
D. B. Whitwood[36]
L. E. Clark[37]
Geo. A. Sheley[38]
Wm E. Quinby[39]

---

was listed in the U.S., Civil War Draft Registrations Records, 1863–1865, but for Toledo, Ohio. His birth date was given as 1842 in Prussia and his occupation as a bookkeeper. Thus, he seems to be the same individual. He also appeared to have had prior military service in a Michigan regiment. 1870 U.S. Federal Census.

30. This was most likely Joseph Dean, a salesman with F. Buhl & Co. The 1862 directory listed five possibilities, but from an occupational standpoint as well as the Buhl name, Joseph Dean seems the most probable individual. *Detroit City Directory 1862*.
31. Albert Ives Jr. was a teller at the C. & A. Ives Bank, suggesting another family business. *Detroit City Directory 1862*.
32. William H. Allen was a clerk at Moses Sutton Photography. *Detroit City Directory 1862*.
33. This is Granger's previously mentioned uncle, Edward Carey Walker.
34. Frank Folsom was the son of Simeon Folsom, a dealer in wool, and worked in the family concern. He also was listed as the treasurer for the Detroit baseball club. Albert Ives was listed as its treasurer and James Craig was a member of its board of directors.
35. John M. Arnold was a minister. *Detroit City Directory 1862*.
36. Deodatus B. Whitwood was a teller at Merchants Bank. *Detroit City Directory 1862*.
37. Lorenzo E. Clark was a vice president of the State Bank of Michigan. *Detroit City Directory 1862*.
38. George Alanson Sheley, born September 8, 1844, in Detroit, enlisted on March 15, 1863, as a private in Battery M, 1st Michigan Light Artillery Regiment. He was promoted to second lieutenant on August 24, 1863, and was discharged for wounds on October 15, 1864. His father, Alanson, was a partner in Farrand, Sheley & Co. *Detroit City Directory 1862*; Soldier Records and Profiles.
39. William E. Quinby was the locals editor for the *Detroit Free Press*. *Detroit City Directory 1862*.

CHAPTER 2

CAMP LIFE AND PICKET DUTY

✻ ✻ ✻

Nine of Granger's surviving letters were written between February 4 and June 12, 1863. In that period, the 5th Michigan Cavalry spent most of its time in Camp Copeland finalizing training for combat and gaining field experience. Later in the spring, they manned the picket lines in the area of today's modern northern Virginia suburbs of Washington, D.C. Given the rotating schedules of field duty that the various regiments and companies followed, Granger often had time to write home in this period. Several of his letters are quite lengthy. While he reveals his eye for detail, the subjects that he broaches generally are chosen for their value and interest to his family back home. He frequently comments about people, including relatives, with whom the Grangers and Walkers would be familiar. In the multiple letters to his sister, Mollie, he more often focuses on the simple chitchat between a brother and a sister about such mundane topics as the sad state of his clothing, his attempts to secure his back pay, a night at the theater, and his visit to a government greenhouse to look at plants and flowers.

However, his letter of February 4, 1863, to his uncle Edward Carey Walker differs significantly in its emphasis on harder matters, presumably more of interest to an older uncle than a teenage sister. It is full of politics and personalities, especially about individuals in the regiment competing for line or field officer command positions. Volunteer regiments were raised by politicians in their respective states under the authority of their governors until the units were accepted by the federal government for service. As Granger outlines his experiences, the 5th Michigan Cavalry Regiment was rife with the bickerings and backstabbings of citizen soldiers suddenly introduced to the highly competitive military life. In this period the 5th Michigan Cavalry and its sister cavalry regiments, the 6th and 7th Michigan, were classic examples of regiments beset with such problems.

Whether his February 4 letter was his first letter home from his wartime camps or merely the first one that survived is unclear. Inasmuch as his regiment had departed from Detroit two months earlier, he presumably would have written home before this date. As a counter to such an expectation, Granger instead reported on the 5th Michigan Cavalry Regiment's Camp Copeland in Washington, D.C., set up on East Capitol Hill near the Capitol Building. The 5th Michigan served with a provisional cavalry brigade among the troops guarding the defenses of the nation's capital.

In a letter of March 6, 1863, to his mother, Matilda, Granger commented on the poor state of his uniform, and reflected on his feelings of sadness in passing over the grounds of past battlefields, including First and Second Manassas and Fredericksburg, Virginia. While Granger often commented about the effects of rain and mud on the troops, such hardships seldom seemed to bother him. He also introduced his mother to his orderly, Augustus F. Corser.[1]

---

1. This was Pvt. Augustus Friend Corser from Sandstone, Michigan, of Granger's Company C, who enlisted on August 25, 1862. Born in 1838 in Ogden Center, New York, Corser had married Sarah Pratt in Jackson, Michigan. Their son Marion Augustus Corser was born on October 2, 1862, in Jackson, and lived until July 23, 1922. In a later letter, Granger mentions the circumstances of Corser's death, when he was killed in action by Confederate guerrillas near the regiment's camp at Stevensburg, Virginia, on October 29, 1863. Some online listings indicate that Corser himself was buried in Aumsville Cemetery, Aumsville, Oregon, but that seems unlikely in 1863. Mrs. Corser later remarried and died on Feb. 20, 1918, in Marion County, Oregon, where she was buried in Aumsville Cemetery. Their son Marion is also buried in Aumsville Cemetery. William F. Corser, a descendant, does not believe Corser's body was moved later by his widow or son, although that might have been a possibility. Patricia Carson, who posted the information about Corser on Findagrave.com, said that her group photographs gravestones before they are lost to age or vandalism, but found no marker for Corser himself. Ancestry.com;

CAMP LIFE AND PICKET DUTY

Of note, this is Granger's first letter, among those that have survived, to his mother. Frequently in his correspondence, he would be testy either directly in writing to her or in telling his sister about Matilda's own infrequent letters to him. Unfortunately, without her own responses to him, we cannot know the other side of the story. Thus, we can only speculate about how close the bonds may have been between mother and son.

His seventh letter, begun on April 3, 1863, and completed on April 6, to Matilda was initially misdated. In it, Edward wrote about the 5th Michigan Cavalry's camp life in the field and its permanent move from Camp Copeland, Washington, D.C., to Fairfax Court House, Virginia. The regiment would spend most of its next three months serving on picket duty on the massive network of Union lines that protected the nation's capital. Because of his busy service in the field, Granger apparently became confused about the months and dates of writing. He began this letter on April 3, but dated it originally as March 3, and concluded it on April 6, 1863.

As noted earlier, on April 1, 1863, Granger's appointment as a full-fledged second lieutenant was confirmed, ending his status as a supernumerary officer. While his uncles clearly had a hand in his success at retaining his commissioned status, one of his fellow officers also sought to claim credit for Granger's appointment. One of the candidates for the then-open colonelcy of the 5th Michigan Cavalry, Lt. Col. Ebenezer Gould, played politics behind the scenes with Granger's uncle Charles Walker. In an April 1, 1863, letter to his brother, Gould revealed, "I had a letter today from C I Walker. He said his brother had written to the Gov. for me. He had also seen Howard who had also written and would see Chandler and get him to work for me. C I has a nephew in the regiment whom I have been able to help."[2]

Throughout the spring of 1863 the 5th Michigan Cavalry had remained on picket duty in defense of Washington, D.C. All the while, they endured raids from guerrillas under John Mosby, then a

---

U.S. Civil War Soldiers; "Augustus Friend Corser," "Sarah Corser Huston," and "Marion Augustus Corser," memorials at Findagrave.com, 6345547, 47183735, and 47183669; William F. Corser, phone interview with editor, April 14, 2016; Patricia Carson, email to editor, March 20, 2016.

2. Ebenezer Gould to Amos Gould, letter, April 1, 1863, Amos Gould Papers, Clarke Historical Library, Central Michigan University.

major.³ With the change of seasons from spring to summer, Granger and his comrades would begin to experience their most serious combat to date, beginning with the Gettysburg Campaign between June 13 and July 14, 1863.

❋ ❋ ❋

[LETTER 3]

Camp Copeland
Washington D.C. Feb. 4th 1863 [Wednesday]

E. C. Walker Esq. Detroit
Dear Uncle

Yours of the 21st ult., duely received enclosure of Postage Stamps for which I am obligated.

The package of books has not yet arrived and we don't know as it is likely ever to get here, but still, it may, as some packages have been delivered here after a journey of nearly a month. Our mails were equally irregular at first but have improved very much. I don't know whether Ed. Walter⁴ is to be considered fortunate or unfortunate—fortunate

---

3. John Singleton Mosby (December 6, 1833–May 30, 1916) commanded a Confederate cavalry battalion, the 43rd Battalion, 1st Virginia Cavalry, also referred to as Mosby's Rangers or Mosby's Raiders. It was a partisan ranger unit noted for its lightning-quick raids and its ability to elude Union Army pursuers and disappear into the surrounding countryside by blending in with area farmers and townspeople. His area of operation became known during the war and ever since as Mosby's Confederacy. Major books written about Mosby include *Ranger Mosby* by Virgil Carrington Jones (1944) and *Mosby's Rangers* by Jeffry D. Wert (1990). Granger misspelled Mosby's name every time with an extra "e." Henceforth, the spelling has been corrected.

4. This was likely Granger's first cousin Edward L. Walter, the son of his mother's sister Sarah Walker and her husband, Edwin Walter. Edward Walter was born February 2, 1845, in Litchfield, Michigan, and died July 4, 1898, in the sinking of the *La Bourgogne* off the coast of Nova Scotia. Walter enlisted in Company H, 4th Michigan Infantry, on August 22, 1862, five days before Granger mustered into the 5th Michigan. Edward Walter was mustered out for disability on February 20, 1863. In 1864 he entered the University of Michigan and was graduated in 1868 with a bachelor of philosophy degree. He was immediately appointed as an assistant professor of Greek and Latin for a year. The next year he was appointed an assistant professor of Latin, a job he held until 1879. "Edward Lorraine Walter," memorial and cenotaph at Findagrave.com, 30523007; Burke A. Hinsdale *(continued)*

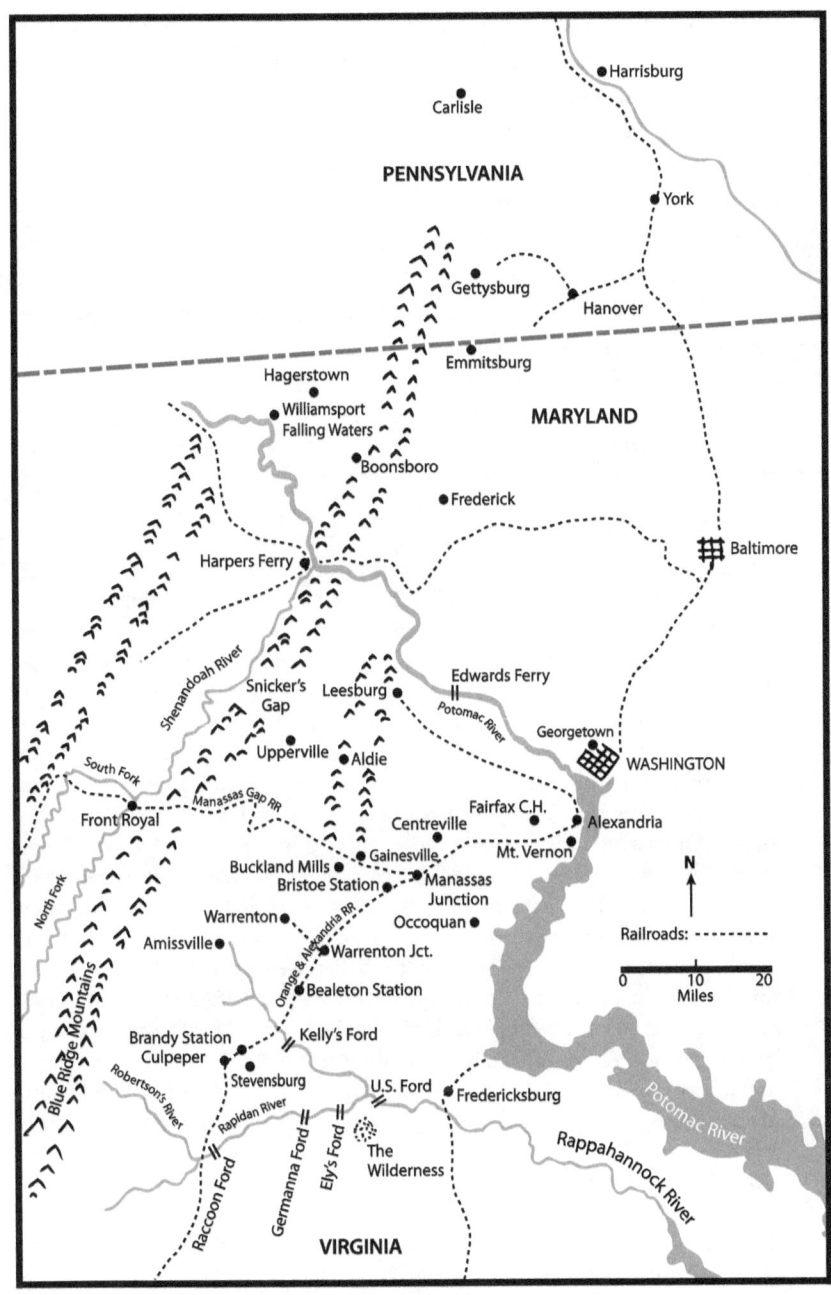

Virginia, Maryland, and Pennsylvania, including Gettysburg and Fredericksburg, 1862–63. *Map by Gary Raham.*

he certainly was in seeing one battle, and most people who have seen one, say that they never want to see another; if he feels so his discharge will not be very unwelcome to him. I never thought there was anything in him which would enable him to endure the fatigue and exposure to which a private in the Infantry is subject.

Last Saturday [January 31, 1863] our Regt. was ordered to report for duty.[5] Accordingly, we got all packed up and ready to start, but our former experience made Bristol and me sufficiently cautious not to pack up our bed clothes or take down our stove. It was fortunate for us that we did not, for only two Companies marched. Company H (Capt. Purdy's)[6] and Company D (Capt. Simonds)[7] and they did not

---

and Isaac N. Demmon, *History of the University of Michigan* (Ann Arbor: University of Michigan Press, 1906), 258; Soldier Records and Profiles; *History of Washtenaw County, Michigan*, vol. 2 (Chicago: Chas. C. Chapman, 1881), 1052.

5. In his diary entry for January 31, 1863, Capt. Charles H. Safford included a newspaper clipping indicating that many officers of the 1st, 5th, and 6th Michigan Cavalry regiments attended a dinner at the Capitol, given by a P. Parsons, identified as "a prominent business man of Detroit." Some one hundred "gentlemen" were present at the event that was held in the vestibule of the lower story of the north wing of the Capitol. The audience heard numerous "able and patriotic speeches." Safford's statement suggests that all the officers were invited, but Granger fails to mention whether he attended. Safford was born on March 10, 1838, in Lockport, New York. At the time of his mustering on August 14, 1862, as a second lieutenant in Company I, 5th Michigan Cavalry, he lived in Detroit with his father, a brother, and a sister. Otherwise, little is known about him. On June 13, 1863, he was promoted to first lieutenant and on July 15, 1864, to captain. According to Sgt. James Avery, "1st Lieutenant Safford, a small man, with sandy beard, and very light complexion, generally quiet, always neat and military in camp, but a very lion in battle. I have seen him in front of his company, where the bullets were flying thickest, waving his sword and leading on his men to victory." In January 1865 Safford's father fell gravely ill and he went home on leave. After his father died, Safford filed his resignation on January 23, 1865. After the war, he became a merchant in Black River, Michigan. Later, he worked for his former colonel, Russell Alger, in Detroit and Duluth, Minnesota. After suffering a stroke in 1920, he died on December 10, 1924, in the Minnesota Soldiers' Home in Minneapolis and was buried in Detroit's Elmwood Cemetery. Davis, *I Rode with Custer*, 1–2, 24.

6. Capt. Stephen P. Purdy, thirty-six, of Detroit, Michigan, was born about 1826. He signed up with the 5th Michigan Cavalry Regiment on August 14, 1862, and was commissioned as a captain in Company H on August 30, 1862. He was promoted to major on October 24, 1863. At the time he was commanding the 5th Michigan during the Mine Run Campaign. He was mustered out of the regiment and discharged for disability on May 15, 1865. Soldier Records and Profiles.

7. After signing up on August 14, 1862, Eli K. Simonds of Northville, Michigan, was

CAMP LIFE AND PICKET DUTY

leave till Sunday morning [February 1]. They went to garrison Poolsville [Poolesville], Maryland.[8] Capt. Clark's[9] Company had left a week before, as we all supposed, to act as body-guard to Gen. Casey[10] in an inspection of his division; but some of the men have been back since they went and it appears that the Company is at Fairfax Court House and the men are employed as bearers of dispatches.

To day the Major has ordered us to be in readiness to move to night if the Colonel, who is now down town, should bring up orders to that effect. But we give ourselves no trouble. I don't think there is any particular danger of our leaving immediately.

Lieut. Dodge has just told me that Capt. Hunt has received a letter from you, I suppose, in relation to the vacant Majority.[11] Do you know any-thing how that is going to be decided? It is the great question of the Regiment.

Thursday February 5th—Just at this point I was interrupted by the

---

mustered into the 5th Michigan as a captain commanding Company D on August 27, 1862. He was thirty-three years old, having been born on November 16, 1828, in Walpole, New Hampshire. He was mustered out for disability on July 27, 1863, after serving heroically at Gettysburg. An insurance agent later in life, Simonds died on April 20, 1912, and is buried in Oakwood Cemetery in Northville, Michigan, where he lived after the war. Soldier Records and Profiles; "Eli K. Simonds," memorial and gravestone at Findagrave.com, 41601437.

8. The two companies, or a squadron, were assigned to patrol along the Potomac River. A few days later, Companies I and M, under Capt. Charles W. Deane, joined them in the same vicinity, but were assigned to disrupt civilian groups involved in smuggling medical supplies and other goods to the enemy. Longacre, *Custer*, 107–8.
9. Signing up on August 14, 1862, John E. Clark, thirty, of Ann Arbor, Michigan, was commissioned as a captain in Company K, 5th Michigan Cavalry Regiment, on September 2, 1862. He was promoted to major on July 3, 1863, and to brevet lieutenant colonel on March 13, 1865. He was mustered out on February 25, 1865. Soldier Records and Profiles.
10. This was Maj. Gen. Silas Casey, an 1826 graduate of West Point and a veteran of both the Second Seminole War (1837–42) and the Mexican-American War (1847). During the early Civil War, he served as a division commander under Maj. Gen. George B. McClellan, but lost his post after his division suffered heavy losses at the Battle of Seven Pines on May 31, 1862. After this, he never held another combat command during the war. John Eicher and David J. Eicher, *Civil War High Commands* (Stanford, Calif.: Stanford University Press, 2001); Ezra J. Warner, *Generals in Blue: Lives of the Union Commanders* (Baton Rouge: Louisiana State University Press, 1989), 74–75.
11. One of the positions for a major was vacant at the time. A number of officers were competing to gain the appointment from Governor Blair.

Maj. Crawley P. Dake.
Courtesy of John Beckendorf.

announcement of supper and in the evening I heard that the great question was settled. Capt. Dake[12] had been appointed Major. The long agony was over, or rather had just culminated as far as Capt Hunt

---

12. Crawley P. Dake (1836–1890) was one of the more interesting individuals to serve in the 5th Michigan Cavalry, especially because of his law enforcement career in his postwar years. Appointed as U.S. marshal for Arizona Territory from 1878 to 1882, he was known for his innovative techniques in enforcing the law in the far-flung territory. After the Posse Comitatus Act, which restricted the use of U.S. troops to pursue outlaws, was passed in 1878, Dake creatively deputized civilian posses to control the lawlessness along the United States and Mexican border. Among his controversial acts, he appointed Wyatt and Virgil Earp as deputy marshals, but that led to the Gunfight of the O.K. Corral on October 22, 1881. Dake was heavily criticized and a few months later he was replaced. He died on April 9, 1890, in Prescott, Arizona Territory. He had been born on September 15, 1836, in Kemptville, Ontario, Canada, but his family moved to New York and then Michigan. When the Civil War broke out, he raised a company of soldiers and was commissioned as a captain in the 5th Michigan Cavalry. He was promoted to major on December 31, 1862. He took part in all of the regiment's major engagements beginning with Gettysburg in July 1863 through the rest of the year. Wounded in the leg, he was discharged as a major in August 1864. He served briefly as chief deputy marshal in Detroit and later for the U.S. Internal Revenue Service. See Larry D. Ball, "Pioneer Lawman: Crawley P. Dake and Law Enforcement on the Southwestern Frontier," *Journal of Arizona History* 14, no. 3 (Autumn 1973): 243–56. Soldier Records and Profiles; U.S. Civil War Soldiers.

CAMP LIFE AND PICKET DUTY   47

was concerned. Capt Hunt was raving mad. He cursed the "political influence" which had obtained for Dake the Majority, he was going to resign and charges would be preferred against Dake, etc. Now I believe the game is to have Dake brought up before a Board of Examiners.[13] If this is done, he will certainly be thrown out as, like some of his brother officers, he has been so busy figuring for promotion that he knows nothing about the tactics. You would be perfectly surprised if you could see the ignorance displayed by some Commissioned Officers of this Regiment, though owing to Colonel Mann's instruction, we are said to be better posted than the Officers of some old Regiments.

Of course you remember [Henry] Starkey[14] of Capt. Purdy's Company.

---

13. With the great expansion of the army to fight the Civil War, huge numbers of civilians found themselves assigned to military tasks for which they were ill-prepared. Examining boards were established as early as July 1861 which required would-be officers to demonstrate their proficiency and knowledge in military science. These boards were designed to weed out individuals who might be ill-suited to lead men in combat. Edward G. Longacre, *From Antietam to Fort Fisher: The Civil War Letters of Edward King Wightman, 1862–1865* (Cranbury, N.J.: Associated University Presses, 1985), 252n2.

14. Granger is exhibiting his humor here, as First Lt. Henry Starkey, Company H, was a highly efficient officer. A veteran of the Mexican War, he was born on May 11, 1828, in Binghamton, New York. By 1833, his family had moved to Kalamazoo, Michigan. Before and after the Mexican War, he worked as a printer, including in the 1850s on the *Detroit Free Press*. Subsequently, he organized the Detroit Typographical Union, although he later was appointed clerk of the Recorder's Court. Signing up for the 5th Michigan Cavalry on August 14, 1862, he was wounded at Gettysburg, which disabled him. He was mustered out November 2, 1863. Returning to Detroit, he was elected city clerk and later appointed secretary of the Board of Water Commissioners, a position he retained until his death on October 28, 1888. According to one local history, "Henry Starkey was considered the encyclopedia for all information relating to the proper methods by which the city and its inhabitants are supplied with water; the appliances, cost and dispensing were as familiar to him as the letters of the alphabet. Mr. Starkey devised the present system of house numbering in Detroit, giving each twenty feet a number, whether occupied or not, and was recognized as authority on all matters relating to the municipal government, many knotty questions being submitted to him to solve." Starkey also was an early baseball enthusiast, known for his umpiring of games. Fred Carlisle, *Wayne County Historical and Pioneer Society: Chronograph of Notable Events in the History of the Northwest Territory and Wayne County* (Detroit: O. S. Gulley, Bornman, 1890), 385–86; Peter Morris et al., eds., *Base Ball Pioneers, 1850–1870* (Jefferson, N.C.: McFarland, 2012), 174–75; Davis, *I Rode with Custer*, 62; U.S. Civil War Soldiers.

He and our First Lieut., Dodge, are considered (especially by themselves) the two best posted men in the Regt. When Starkey was here, they used to go around trying to catch every-body on some little technical point in the Tactics. They used to come in here at first, but they soon got sick of that, as they always got as good as they gave. In the course of their travels they picked up young [Walter] Stevenson,[15] brother of the Merchant Tailor in Detroit, and finding that he knew nothing brought him over to our tent to exhibit him. There they kept him all the evening showing off his ignorance for the benefit of a whole tent full of Officers, who were laughing at him all the time and he did not know that they were laughing at him at all. Stevenson had heard Starkey explain to Lieut. Lee[16] the manner of encamping, and when Starkey asked Stevenson what he would do if ordered to take a grand guard and relieve another officer across the river, he said he would have the men pitch their tents etc. going on to give as well as possible the process of encampment. Starkey asked him how long it

---

15. Walter Stevenson enlisted in Company D, 5th Michigan Cavalry, as a quartermaster sergeant on August 18, 1862, and was mustered in nine days later. On December 1, 1862, he was commissioned as a second lieutenant and promoted to first lieutenant on March 3, 1864, and captain on October 28, 1864. Wounded at Winchester, Virginia, on September 19, 1864, he was mustered out with many others in the regiment on June 22, 1865, at Fort Leavenworth, Kansas. Tragically, especially for a cavalry officer who had just survived three years of combat, he was injured severely when his horse fell on him on July 7, 1865, in Detroit. He died two days later and was buried in Elmwood Cemetery after services attended by a number of his now-former comrades. See John Peter Beckendorf, "Finding Major Wallace of the 5th Michigan Cavalry," *Military Images* (Export, Pa.) 26, no. 5 (March–April 2005): 20–22; U.S. Civil War Soldiers.
16. Edward M. Lee, born in Connecticut in 1835, was commissioned as a first lieutenant in Company E, 5th Michigan Cavalry on August 14, 1862, and promoted to captain on January 1, 1863, and lieutenant colonel April 13, 1865. That same day, he received brevet promotions to colonel and brigadier general. Lee was taken prisoner at Buckland Mills, Virginia, on October 19, 1863. After the war, on April 7, 1869, President Ulysses S. Grant appointed Lee as secretary, the highest-ranking officer after the governor, of Wyoming Territory. During his tenure, Lee introduced on December 10, 1869, a bill, later signed by Governor John A. Campbell, which for the first time gave women in the United States the right to vote. He died on January 2, 1913, in New York City and was buried in Guilford, Connecticut. American Civil War General Officers, Ancestry.com; U.S. Civil War Soldiers; Edward M. Lee obituary, *New York Times*, January 3, 1913.

Lt. Walter Stevenson.
Courtesy of John Beckendorf.

would take him to get across the River. He had heard Capt. Purdy give the definition of Abbattis[17] and he tried to give the same as the definition of Cantonment.

This morning Company E, the Company from which Capt. Dake was promoted, started for the front, it is said, to relieve Company K. I pity them, for it is freezing cold this morning.

We have had the most peculiar winter here. Last December was

---

17. Variously spelled as abatis, abattis, or abbattis, this military term refers to field fortifications commonly created as defensive obstacles by Civil War military units, using tree branches laid in a row, with the sharpened tops directed outwards and facing the enemy. The trees were usually interlaced or tied with wire. Abatis were either used alone or combined with wire entanglements and other obstacles. However, they could be destroyed by fire.

very mild indeed, more like May than any other month. January was equally mild but somewhat more rainy and the first five days of February have been as cold as any weather we ever saw in Michigan. It is so cold here that we can not drill or do any thing else except stay in doors and talk, study or write, and wait patiently for meal times and bed-time. We only have to go out doors to attend to the water & feed calls, and unfortunately it is my week to go to water.

Lieut. Dodge is here and consequently my letter gets along but slowly, for he is a very interesting talker indeed, and besides that, my material is about used up. Dodge says that Capt. Hunt intends to resign. I don't know whether he will or not, but if they can't throw out Dake, I shouldn't wonder if he did: for a more homesick man is seldom seen, I should say. He has been as blue as he could be ever since he came here.

Tell Kent[18] that he ought to be down here, there is need for men of common sense and honesty here among Commissioned Officers, and no man possessing those two qualities should stay at home if he could have a Commission by applying for it, but if he is going to come he don't want to be a private.

Write again and more at length if you have time.

Remember me to Aunt Lucy[19] and the children. Tell Jessie I will give her a non-commissioned office if she will come down here as she has better power of command than most of our officers.

Yours
E. G. Granger

---

18. This individual is unidentified.
19. Granger's mother, Matilda Walker Granger, was one of nine siblings, six of whom were women. Her brother Edward Carey Walker was married to Lucy Bryant (1827–1883). The couple had two children, Bryant Walker (1856–1936) and Jessie Rawson Walker (1859–1934). Granger jokingly refers to three-year-old Jessie and her "power of command." See introduction, note 29, for more about Edward Carey Walker.

[LETTER 4]

Camp Copeland
Washington D.C. Mar 6, 1863 [Friday]

Dear Mother

Till I received your last letter I did not remember which of us owed the other a letter, but Mary said that you said you would "answer my letter soon," so I supposed that you considered yourself the debtor and that was sufficient for me. I didn't care to investigate that matter any further. Colonel [Freeman] Norvell's resignation[20] has just been

---

20. One of Captain Safford's newspaper clippings, likely from December 1862, highly praises Major Norvell. The regiment's officers had petitioned for his appointment as the commander, but within weeks, Norvell's alcohol problems led to his ouster. For example, an expedition he ostensibly led February 8–11, 1863, from Aldie to Manassas Gap only reached Ashby's Gap in the mountains to the west and had to be canceled when Norvell was "so drunk as to require five or six men to take care of him." By February 23, the colonel had apologized for his behavior and had pledged to remain sober, but his ability to command had been undermined. Despite a revolt among the regiment's officers, more senior officers, including Col. Joseph T. Copeland, sought to keep Norvell in command. By early March, Norvell's situation had not improved. On February 26, Lt. Col. Ebenezer Gould wrote to his brother that "if it should be our drunken colonel I am afraid there will be some unpleasant scenes as some of the officers have said they would never go under him." About that time Norvell submitted his resignation, which was accepted, as Granger said in his March 6 letter. Gould served for a couple of months as the regiment's colonel, but he never gained the final appointment. That led to months of scheming and politicking both within the regiment and at home in Michigan. One of the purported candidates in April 1863 was a young Regular Army lieutenant named George Armstrong Custer, formerly a captain on General McClellan's staff. Custer was unable to secure the appointment from Governor Austin Blair. Eventually, the appointment went to Lt. Col. Russell Alger, 6th Michigan Cavalry. For Norvell, who had been born on January 15, 1827, the loss of his command was a personal tragedy. As a second lieutenant with the U.S. Marine Corps in the Mexican-American War, he had served heroically, including in the storming of Chapultepec and the capture of Mexico City. After the Civil War, he became part owner of the *Detroit Free Press* newspaper until 1872. Norvell died at age fifty-four on May 13, 1881, in Detroit. See O'Neill, *Chasing Jeb Stuart*, 58–59, 85–89, 97–98, 180–81; also, Soldier Records and Profiles; John E. Norvell, "Freeman Norvell and the Detroit Free Press," *An American Family* (historical blog), July 22, 2015, https://jenorv66.wordpress.com/2015/07/22/freeman-norvell-and-the-detroit-free-press/; Davis, *I Rode with Custer*, 8–9; "Col. Freeman Norvell," memorial, photograph, and gravestone at Findagrave.com, 25422142.

accepted and Lt. Col. Ebenezer Gould[21] is in Command today. It is the unanimous wish of the Officers of the Regt. that Major [Luther S.] Trowbridge[22] may be made Colonel, and, if they get any chance to do so they will express their opinions pretty decidedly. The only trouble is that the Major will not work for the place, at all, or get his friends to use their influence.

You were a poor prophet in the matter of Capt. Hunt. He has sent in his resignation, though I think it very doubtful whether it will be accepted. There is a rumor around Camp that we are to be payed again very soon; if we are, I shall probably get enough to pay my indebtedness to Uncle Charles all but $100 which he offers to pay himself.

If you think my wardrobe is <u>giving</u> out, you are mistaken, it has given out long ago, that is that portion of it which I brought with me except my coat which is so small I can't wear it with any degree of comfort. My jacket is minus half the regulation number of buttons, there is a hole under the arm through which I get my fist, once in a while, by mistake, and now one of my shoulder straps is torn off. My pantaloons are some that I drew—regulation—and pretty shabby at that. My cap looks as if it had been in the service six years, instead of six months. My boots are a pair which constituted part of the cargo

---

21. A lawyer from Owosso, Michigan, who had been born on April 10, 1818, in New York, Ebenezer Gould, forty-four, was among the oldest officers when he mustered into the 5th Michigan Cavalry on September 2, 1862. By December 31, 1862, he was a lieutenant colonel and was promoted to colonel on September 21, 1864. On July 13, 1863, he was wounded in the foot at Hagerstown, Maryland. Poor health led to his mustering out on November 10, 1864. He continued to work as a lawyer until his death on September 7, 1877, in Owosso. Soldier Records and Profiles.
22. Despite Granger's wish, Luther S. Trowbridge, a lawyer before the war, would earn his colonelcy much later in the Civil War and in a different regiment, the 10th Michigan Cavalry. Born July 28, 1836 in Troy, Michigan, Trowbridge attended Yale University, but dropped out before graduation to focus on a legal career. He joined the 5th Michigan in 1862 as a major. After seeing combat at Gettysburg in early July 1863, Trowbridge was promoted to lieutenant colonel in the 10th Michigan and a year later to colonel. With the 10th, he served in the western theater. The end of the war found him stationed in Tennessee. Remaining in Tennessee after the war, he returned to Detroit in 1868. On September 1, 1865, he was brevetted major general in recognition of his service. He died February 12, 1912, after a career as a civil servant and banker in Detroit, and was buried in the city's Elmwood Cemetery. "Luther Stephen Trowbridge," memorial, photograph, and gravestone at Findagrave.com, 8150811; U.S. Civil War Soldiers.

CAMP LIFE AND PICKET DUTY 53

of a British steamer caught running the blockade. They are made, for use, not ornament, of leather which has never been colored, and the counters are outside—the legs come up to my knees, and the first pair of the kind I had were so large that I could take hold of the tops of the legs and <u>push</u> them off. I like a boot loose—but I thought that was too much of a good thing so I traded them off for a smaller pair.

Tell Mollie that when I get my hair cut fighting fashion, and a Regulation Plug hat on, I will get my photograph taken for her particular benefit.

I haven't had my hair cut since I left Detroit and it is pretty long now, and on our last raid I forgot to take a comb along with me, consequently my hair remained uncombed from one Wednesday to the next. You may imagine the time I had with it when I got back and I resolved that I would have it cut the first time I got down town. By the way, I haven't given you any description of our last Raid.[23] It was so nearly like the other, especially in its results, that it may not be very interesting but if you don't like it it will be a proper punishment for your demand for particulars. A week ago last Wednesday night [February 25], about 11 o'clock we waked up by the Officer's Call. I chose to consider it a call for Commanders of Companies as it proved

---

23. Granger is referring to the regiment's second expedition. Its first was a three-day scout February 8–11, 1863, under the command of Sir Percy Wyndham, who led two columns of cavalry, about one thousand men, one of which went to Aldie and Middleburg, Virginia, and reached Ashby's Gap on February 10. But Majors Gould and Ferry had to relieve Colonel Norvell, who was drunk. The regiment and its fellow units returned to camp on February 11. Norvell was arrested upon his return and resigned February 27. The second expedition began on February 26, when the 5th Cavalry joined with the 6th Michigan Cavalry to travel from Washington, D.C., through Centreville, Virginia, to Falmouth, Virginia. Lieutenant Colonel Gould commanded. Their brigade's mission, under Col. Percy Wyndham, seemed obscure to many of them, including Granger. Most thought they were chasing Mosby. However, Wyndham may have been ordered to prevent Confederate cavalry leader, Brig. Gen. Fitzhugh Lee, from reaching the Rappahannock River. They reached Centreville at noon, where they remained until the morning of the next day. By noon February 27, they had reached the Bull Run battlefield and traveled about 10–15 miles past Warrenton, Virginia, where they camped that night. On February 28, they marched to Falmouth, Virginia, across the Rappahannock River from the site of the Fredericksburg battle the previous December. The Army of Northern Virginia under Gen. Robert E. Lee remained camped on the city side of the river. The Union cavalrymen remained in the Falmouth area until March 2.

to be, and did not get up till Capt. Hunt came and told us that we were ordered to be ready to march by day-light. We then put a piece of ham on the stove to boil, for rations on the way, and I stayed up to watch it while Bristol lay down till 4 o'clock. By the time we were ready to start it was raining beautifully, a steady drizzling rain which gave promise of "more of the same" and as the snow was several inches deep p there seemed to be a fair prophecy of mud, to be waded through before we got back.

At Gen. Price's[24] [Col. Richard Butler Price's] Head Quarters, across the River, we were joined by the Sixth, and then wandered around in the mud and rain for several hours without making any essential progress till we struck the Little River Pike, the one on which we came in from the first Raid. At Fairfax we were put under command of the same Sir Percy Wyndham[25] who came out to Detroit, once, to take command of the Lancers. About dark that night we stopped at Centerville [Centreville], at the Head Quarters of the Commander of the Post. As it was still raining slightly, most of the officers immediately looked out for themselves, among others, Capt. Hunt & Lieut. Dodge but Capt. [Hunt] made Bristol & I stay with the men "to see that they were all straight" long after there was no need of our presence so that when we went to find lodgings we could not succeed, partly because of the stupidity of the sentinels who were guarding the house where most of the officers slept. The aforesaid sentinels belonged to the 17th [18th] Penn. Cav.[26] were all Dutch and could not speak English at all, and they understood it less than they spoke it.

The boys built a fire with what little green wood and brush they could scrape together and I took off my boots and stockings and dried

---

24. Col. Richard Butler Price was born December 15, 1807, in Philadelphia and died there on June 25, 1876. He was commissioned on January 23, 1862, as the colonel of the 2nd Pennsylvania Cavalry and was brevetted brigadier general on March 13, 1865. "Richard Butler Price," memorial, photograph, and gravestone at Findagrave .com, 10877564; Soldier Records and Profiles; U.S. Civil War Soldiers.
25. Civil War historian Eric Wittenberg has labeled Sir Percy Wyndham as "an English lord and notorious fop." Indeed, he was a controversial figure, who enjoyed little success as a Civil War commander. The February 26–28 expedition, no matter what its true goal may have been, was a notable flop. Wittenberg, *Under Custer's Command*, 24n.
26. Granger erred. The Pennsylvania regiment was the 18th, not the 17th. O'Neill, *Chasing Jeb Stuart*, 98.

my feet which had been soaking wet all day. Then I tried to dry my boots & stockings but had to give it up, the fire was so poor. After a long while I spread my rubber blanket in the mud, took a saddle for a pillow, stuck my feet into the fire, they were so wet that they couldn't burn, and tried to go to sleep. Meanwhile Bristol had curled himself up onto a saddle, with his head on the Cantle and his feet on the pommel, some distance from the fire. This was a splendid way to rest, to be sure, still I could not go to sleep, and when I thought it must be most morning it was only ten o'clock. Once in a while Bristol would get up and come over to the fire to warm himself and as the water began to soak through my rubber blanket soon after I lay down, I had to get up occasionally and get out of the water as much as possible. It was the longest, most dismal night I ever spent. About 12 o'clock Bristol & I got up and went into the house and lay down on the floor of the Hall floor. Both doors being open, it was colder than our former position, but it was dry. Here I fell asleep after another long time of freezing. About 3 A.M. we were awakened by the noise of a violent rain storm and from that time we didn't sleep any more that morning.

When we got up the boys were nearly drowned. The water was so deep where Bristol's bed was that one of the Rifles was lost in it and they only found it by good luck. When we left we were lef accompanied by part of the N.Y. Fifth, Penn. Seventeenth [18th] (the aforesaid wooden heads) and the First [West] Virginia.[27] Near Centreville a picket had been captured the night before we were there. Several of the privates and the Lieut. commanding the pickets were severely wounded. The second day of our journey was much pleasanter than the first had been. Just after leaving Centreville we crossed Bull Run and passed the field of the first battle.[28] A little further on, we halted

---

27. This regiment was actually from West Virginia. Again, the Pennsylvania regiment was the 18th, not the 17th. O'Neill, *Chasing Jeb Stuart*, 98.
28. The First Battle of Bull Run, or First Manassas, was the first major battle of the American Civil War when it was fought on July 21, 1861, in Prince William County, Virginia, near the city of Manassas, not far from Washington, D.C. For a time, Union forces held the edge, but slow in positioning themselves, they allowed Confederate reinforcements time to arrive by rail. Each side had about eighteen thousand poorly trained and poorly led troops in their first battle. In the end, the battle was a Confederate victory and a near-disastrous loss for the Union, whose army virtually fled in a disorganized retreat back to the safety of the defenses of Washington, D.C.

on the Second Bull Run Battle Field.[29] Scattered around the field were musket balls, grape, and round shot, and shells. The projectile most used, appeared to have been the 3 inch conical shells, a great many of which were scattered all over the field and also along the road for two or three miles. All the bodies had been buried, but so ineffectually, that hands and feet protruded from every grave that we saw. I don't want to gove over another Battle Field so long after the Battle.

When we started this morning we were only one day's march behind the body of Rebel Cavalry of which we were in pursuit. We always have the luck to be that distance at least. We passed through Warrenton this afternoon and made for the valley of the Rappahannock. Halted for the night 10 miles beyond Warrenton. Here there were plenty of rail fences with which to make fires, and soon after we stopped Company "C" had three roaring fires, and as we had run out of provision the first day we detailed one of our men to go and look at the flock of sheep which we had seen on the other side of the Road. He soon returned with a fine specimen of the genus mutton and he (the sheep not the man) was soon cut up and distributed among the boys. Bristol & I got part of a forequarter and stuck it in the fire and kept it there till it was supposed to be done. You know how fond I am of mutton anyway—well this piece was burnt on the outside and raw on the inside and so tough that it was hard work, even for a gymnast like myself, to get a mouthful off the bone. To cap the climax, we had neither salt nor pepper to eat with it. The ration I ate that night was a small one, though I was nearly starved.

But what more than made up for the lack of supper, was the splendid bed we had. Near us was a pine forest, (Virginia is all pine woods of about 20 years growth) and we brought a heap of pine boughs and laid them down on rails for our bed, then put our feet to the fire covered ourselves with our blankets and slept as only men can sleep who are as tired out as we were. In the night I waked up and found that the fire was so hot that it had warped the souls of my boots so as to make them feel rather uncomfortable for the rest of the trip. The mud at this place was

---

29. The Second Battle of Bull Run, or Second Manassas, was fought August 28–30, 1862, in Prince William County, Virginia. It marked the culmination of an offensive campaign by Confederate general Robert E. Lee's Army of Northern Virginia against Union major general John Pope's Army of Virginia. The battle was of a much larger scale and involved more troops than the 1861 Battle of Bull Run that was fought on much of the same ground.

the worst I ever saw. I could pull my boots off any time by stepping into the mud and then just taking the foot out of the boot. It was as much more sticky than Detroit's clay as that is, than Pontiac sand. As one of the men was marching on foot through this mud (his horse having given out) he said "This is what we call crushing this unholy Rebellion."

Some of the remarks the men make, on a march, when they are all in the best of spirits, are pretty good. One of our boys gave the most flattering opinion I ever heard of one of the Sergeants of the Regt. 'That's the meanest looking man I ever saw & I believe his looks are deceiving, for I think he is a darn sight meaner than he looks.' I don't know whether it was original or not, I never heard it before.

As we had nothing to eat the next morning, before leaving, we were pretty hungry and the boys stopped at the houses along the road and confiscated what fowls they could get. About ten or eleven o'clock I stopped, tied my horse to the fence and went to see what I could raise to eat. The darky girl was just baking a couple of loaves of corn-bread by the kitchen fire place, and I concluded to wait till they were done. But after awhile I looked out and saw Major Ferry[30] leading my horse off, so I had to leave my bread, hungry as I was, and run after my horse. When I overtook him, the Major said I had had orders not to leave the ranks. I had not had any such orders & I told him so & it afterwards turned out that no such orders had been given. But I was cheated out

---

30. Maj. Noah Ferry was born on April 30, 1831, on Michigan's Mackinac Island, but when he was age three, his family moved to Grand Haven, Michigan, south of Muskegon. After working in the lumber business before the war, Ferry was appointed captain of Company F, 5th Michigan Cavalry, on August 14, 1862. Within a few months, he was promoted to major, the rank he held when he chastised Lieutenant Granger in March 1863. He died heroically on the field of battle on July 3, 1863, while rallying his company during the Gettysburg fighting. In a letter to Ferry's father, the commanding officer of the 5th Michigan Calvary, Lt. Col. Allyne C. Litchfield wrote, "He died as a soldier should die, doing his whole duty fearlessly." A few days later, his father, the Reverend William Ferry, recovered his remains and had them interred in Lake Forest Cemetery, Grand Haven, Michigan. "Maj. Noah Ferry," memorial, photograph, and gravestone at Findagrave.com, 23442630; Dave LeMieux, "150 Years Ago, Muskegon Residents Filled Regimental Ranks after Attack on Fort Sumter," *Muskegon (Mich.) Chronicle* (online edition), April 12, 2011; U.S. Civil War Soldiers; Rev. David M. Cooper, *Obituary Discourse on Occasion of the Death of Noah Henry Ferry, Major of the 5th Michigan Cavalry, Killed at Gettysburg, July 3, 1863* (New York: John F. Trow, Printer, 1863).

of my breakfast & dinner and a madder individual is seldom seen than I was that morning. It was a most ungentlemanly trick any-way, even if I had had orders to stay in the Ranks as Major Ferry thought I had.

I hope I may get a chance to starve him sometime and see how he will like it. This day was rainy to add to the pleasure of a long tramp through the mud without food for either horses or men. About dark we arrived at Falmouth on the Rappahannock, opposite Fredericksburg [February 28]. Here we went into camp and having obtained some cookies from the sutler at the rate of two cents apiece and a piece of cheese for which we paid 40 cts pr. We made a fire, cooked cup of coffee, we had a good supper & went to bed. Being very tired I went to sleep immediately, but was soon waked up by a terrible noise—men shouting—horses running, etc. etc. I was half asleep still so that I didn't know what was the matter, but the first man I saw had a broken head and the horses were apparently scattered in every direction and I made up my mind that we were attacked and I was just about as badly scared as I could well be. The trouble turned out to be nothing but a runaway horse, which had galloped right over us striking square on the head of the man next to me. Luckily [Pvt. George] Geigrich[31] had his head all wrapped up in his blankets & overcoat, as it had by this time commenced to rain again, so he was not severely hurt though his head was pretty well bruised & slightly cut.

As it was raining our boys now put up our shelter tent over Bristol & I and we slept very well for the rest of the night considering the fact that we were pretty near the foot of the hill from which all the water ran under our beds so that in the morning we were pretty well soaked. About eight o'clock the boys drew rations for three days for themselves and their horses. I tell you the bread and pork disappeared with wonderful rapidity in that camp that Sunday morning.

About ten or eleven A.M. Bristol called me and I found that Lycurgus [Granger][32] had come over to see me. You may believe I was surprised

---

31. Pvt. George Geigrich of Saginaw, Michigan, enlisted at age eighteen in Granger's Company C on August 20, 1862. He was taken prisoner at Kelly's Ford, Virginia, on October 14, 1863, and was released February 6, 1865. For a time he was hospitalized in Milwaukee, Wisconsin. U.S. Civil War Soldiers.

32. Lycurgus Granger was the son of Thomas A. Granger (1808–1901), who was a brother of Granger's own father, Sylvester. Thomas and Sylvester's brother Austin Granger (1791–1863) had died on March 5, 1863, at his home in Rochester, New York. Thus,

Maj. Noah Ferry,
5th Michigan Cavalry.
Ferry was killed in action at
Gettysburg, Pennsylvania,
July 3, 1863. *Courtesy of Paul Davis.*

for we had been told that the 3rd [Michigan Infantry] was a good many miles from our Camp, but down in Virginia not one man in a hundred knows the difference between one mile & five. Lycurgus staid over with me till afternoon & then asked me to go to his Camp. I got permission of the Col. to be absent till sunset, mounted Bob & we started off. First we went over to the Camp of the Fourth [Michigan

---

Lycurgus was a first cousin to Edward Granger. He was born on November 19, 1839, in Grand Rapids, Michigan. Lycurgus had enlisted on May 13, 1861, in Company F, 3rd Michigan Infantry. He reportedly drove an ambulance from July 1862 through March 1863, which fits with Granger's account. By June, he was with the ammunition train, probably as a guard. In August 1863, he was reported as absent without leave. At some point, he apparently lost his right eye and was transferred to the Veteran Reserve Corps on September 14, 1863. He reportedly deserted from the VRC on December 4, 1863, in New York City. He later may have married Eliza Ann Kidd, but the marriage seems to have ended in divorce. Lycurgus died on May 5, 1915, and was buried in the Grand Rapids Veterans Cemetery. U.S. Civil War Soldiers; Steve Soper, "Lycurgus E. Granger," *Men of the 3rd Michigan Infantry* (historical blog), updated January 3, 2009, http://thirdmichigan.blogspot.com/2008/11/lycurgus-e-granger.html.

Infantry] which is about a mile beyond that of the Third. Found Sam Walker[33] all well. He had grown a great deal since I had seen him before, and a slight gotee [goatee] served to alter his appearance some what but I should have known him any where. He didn't know it me though at all. Ed. Walter had gone home six weeks before. Had a pleasant visit with Sam, saw the dress parade of the Regt. and went back to the Camp of the Third or rather of the Ambulance Corps of the 3d. Lycurgus has not been with the Company much for a long time. His place in the Ambulance Corps is a very good one, but with little or no chance of promotion. He has a nice log hut with a roof made of shelter tents, a fire-place and two good bunks. They have all conveniences for cooking and I had as good a supper there as I have had since I left Detroit. Lycurgus has improved very much since I saw him before, in appearance & other ways.

The field of the Battle of Fredericksburg could not have been better—for the Rebs. The River is not much, if any, wider than Jefferson Ave. the bank gradually sloping up to the plain on which the Battle commenced, and just beyond the plain, rise the hills on which can be seen the Rebel Rifle Pits & Fortifications. These hills are neither high nor steep but just the kind of hills from off which artillery could sweep an army, without any possibility of the army ever getting near enough to do their Artillery any harm. The Pickets can walk across the River, though I believe it is against orders to do so, now. It was here that the Conversation just after the Battle took place of which the Rebels tell the story.

Rebel Picket—Stonewall Jackson is going to resign

Yankee—Why?

---

33. Samuel G. Walker, a maternal first cousin to Edward Granger, had been born in Tecumseh, Michigan, in 1841. He was living in Adrian, Michigan, when on June 20, 1861, he enlisted as a corporal in Company H, 4th Michigan Infantry. He was promoted to sergeant on January 1, 1862, and to second lieutenant on July 18, 1862. He was wounded in action, shot through the arm and back, on July 2, 1863, during the fighting in the Wheatfield at Gettysburg, Pennsylvania. He was taken prisoner, but escaped. In September 1863, he was transferred to the Invalid Corps, serving until he was mustered out on June 30, 1864, at Detroit. He died on November 5, 1914, in Buffalo, New York, and was buried in Forest Lawn Cemetery. Soldier Records and Profiles; "Samuel G. Walker," memorial and gravestone at Findagrave.com, 50569904.

Reb—Because they have taken away his Quartermaster & Commissary.

Yankee—Who was his Quartermaster & Commissary?

Reb—Banks—They say that Stonewall took 8 miles of waggon trains from Banks' his (Bank's) celebrated retreat.

We left Falmouth Monday morning (March 2] and travelled over, or rather ~~passed~~ past, some of the worst roads I ever saw. We had to go through the woods on each side of the road most of the time but not withstanding the state of the roads we must have marched fifty miles that day, for Wyndham is a great hand to keep a Column closed up so that I had to go a good deal further than the others, and whenever the road was half way decent I would ~~now~~ let Bob gallop as he was always anxious to do so. I thought I would have him tired out, once, at any rate. But the next day he was as fast as ever. Monday night we bivouacked in the woods, & it was so pleasant that we didn't put up our tent, and of course it rained before morning.

Tuesday I was again on the "Staff" and again I kept Bob on the gallop all day, but I got the worst of that, for when it got dark, and I wanted to go slower he was most unreasonably opposed to any gait short of a dead run, and would not stop for anything. He would pay no attention to a horse in front of him, but run onto him sometimes in spite of my best endeavors to hold back. Finally we got here safe [Tuesday, March 3] & I was sure that Bob must be used up the next day—but Corser had to get extra strict and grab his jaw (But not Corser's) to hold him when he took him to water.

The last two or three days I had got used to the style of our trip that I was as well as ever, though the final day or two did go rather hard.

When I got here I found four letters waiting for me one of which was from Mollie—Tell her I will answer hers in due time.

I have not seen Mrs. Sheldon[34] yet I don't find the lack of female society any particular deprivation yet, as you seem to think I must.

Your Son
Ed. G. Granger

---

34. Mrs. Sheldon is unidentified.

[LETTER 5]

Camp Copeland
Washington D.C. Mar. 8, 1863

Alex[35]

I hope you will make all sorts of allowances for my tardiness in writing, as you know, as well as I do, why I don't write oftener; that is, because I am too lazy, and hate to write as I hate nothing else in the world. Then too there is nothing of any importance or which would be interesting to you, going on here.

Of course you know the routine of Camp life, and that is probably the same with you as it is here. Probably you have seen more of field service than we have, for they have a way of fighting out West which has not been very extensively introduced around here, and has not found favor when tried; Nevertheless, we "The Fifth," being Michigan men, are supposed to be fighting men, so we have been sent on two grand "Raids" into Virginia.[36] The first time we went about one hundred and twenty miles in four days and as it was the first riding we ever did except on drill &c, we thought that was doing pretty well.

We had a first rate time, as the weather was beautiful, the roads, were the best I ever saw and there were plenty of rich old Secessionists on whom we lived.

They talk about Virginia being all desolated by the war! It's all humbug. There were several planters, at whose houses we stopped, who had thousands of bushels of grain in their barns, and hundreds of tons of hay in their yards and fields. All this will, of course go to the Rebs except the little we used. One of these Planters had five sons in the Rebel Army and still, as his negroes were left him, he could raise grain to keep himself and sell to the C.S.A. Thanks to the EMANCIPATION-PROCLAMATION, that game will soon be "played out." Isn't it glorious

---

35. This is again Alexander Caskey, Granger's first cousin.
36. As documented in chapter 2, notes 20 and 23, the first "raid" began February 8 when the regiment was part of a force seeking to find the partisan rangers of then-captain John Singleton Mosby and his 43rd Battalion of Virginia Cavalry. It proved highly unsuccessful, in part because of the Union leadership, but also because Colonel Norvell's problems with alcohol required Lieutenant Colonel Gould and Major Ferry to remove Norvell from command and end the expedition. The 5th Michigan returned to Camp Copeland on February 11.

that Old Abe has at last got around to Fremont's Position.[37] We exercised the right of confiscation pretty freely, taking all the horses and mules we came across that were worthwhile. We went as far as Ashby's Gap in the Blue Ridge and then our Colonel was so drunk that we returned, without having accomplished anything—Our Colonel (as Bristol says) in Command of the Ambulance Corps. Our next "Raid" was under the command of the <u>celebrated</u> Sir Percy Wyndham of Lancer memory. This time we got more real "Soldiering." It rained most every night. The mud was about eighteen inches deep and we passed through the most God forsaken Country ever seen. Half starved—wet and cold it was not so funny as the first trip. We passed through the field of the first Bull Run Battle and halted, a little while, on the scene of the second Battle. A pleasant place to contemplate, certainly; just when expecting to get into a fight. The bodies were, of course, all buried; but dead horses by the dozen were "wasting their fragrance on the Desert air." From here we went to Warrenton Junction and then to Falmouth on the Rappahannock, opposite Fredericksburg. Here we stayed over Sunday and I saw my Brother,[38] and Sam. Walker. Ed Walter had gone home six weeks before having been discharged on account of disability. They were very comfortably situated down there as they are in the middle of pine woods so that they can build very good huts of small Pines and use their shelter tents

---

37. John C. Frémont (1813–1890), a controversial figure in American history, was an army officer, explorer and politician, who ran unsuccessfully in 1856 for president as the first candidate of the antislavery Republican Party in 1856. During the Civil War, President Abraham Lincoln appointed him as commander of the Department of the West, but his independence and hasty decisions ran afoul of the administration. After Frémont issued an emancipation edict that freed slaves in his district, the president removed him from command for insubordination. From 1878 to 1881, he served as governor of Arizona Territory. He died in 1890 in New York City, long retired from politics and financially destitute. While Radical Republicans were pleased when Frémont sought to free the slaves, it is highly unlikely that Granger's praise here indicates that he, too, was a Radical Republican. At the time Granger wrote this letter in March 1863, he was still a month shy of his twentieth birthday. Heretofore, he had shown modest interest in politics. Finally, his uncles Charles and Edward Walker loomed large in his life. Charles was a Democrat and Edward was a Republican. Warner, *Generals in Blue*, 160–61.

38. With his use of the word "brother," Granger may be referring to his cousin Lycurgus Granger, as he met both Lycurgus and Samuel Walker that day. He, of course, had no male siblings.

for roofs. Fredericksburg is fortified, so as to make another attempt to cross there w very unlikely.³⁹ The Battle Field could not have been better—for the Rebels. A long sloping hill on top of which were their rifle pits and batteries, from which it was impossible to drive them.

We left Falmouth Monday morning and arrived at Washington Tuesday night, glad enough to get home, though we had again, done nothing but use up our horses, many of which we had to leave on the way. My horse is the toughest & wickedest brute in the Company.

Soon after our return the resignation of Col. Norvell was accepted. We are consequently temporarily without a Colonel. Lieut. Col. Gould will probably get the Colonelcy though it is the unanimous wish by the Regt. that Major Trowbridge may be made Col.

I suppose your numerous lady friends in Detroit keep you posted on all home matters. Don you know is Sutler's Clerk in the 27th Infty., his Brother, Dick, being Sutler thereof.⁴⁰ He sent me lately the <u>Carte de visite</u> (Auglice "Photg") of Miss Celia Goodell,⁴¹ perhaps you may remember hearing something of her when Don went to the D. H. School. I haven't got any of my Photographs or I would send you one. You don't suppose I could keep any in Detroit do you? With my many near & dear friends all wanting one. You know how affectionate it makes all one's friends, but it would have done your soul good to have seen the loving interest taken in your humble servant by his aunt Mary Ann Walker—<u>nee</u> Hinsdale.⁴² Ada says she asked you to write to her but you have not done so. Alex, I am surprised at you! Why don't you behave yourself like a good boy and write to your friends as you ought? Or do you think your letters would have to be read by him as well as her. I am going to ask Ada whether she shows him all her letters or else put something in one of mine for his special benefit. Write

---

39. Granger is referring to the Battle of Fredericksburg, Virginia, fought on December 13, 1862, which ended in a Union disaster.
40. Neither man has been identified. Don is not likely to be Donald MacDonald, whom Granger frequently mentions.
41. Celia Goodell was born September 18, 1847, in Canada, and died February 27, 1927. At the time of her death from diabetes she was the widow of William Rouse.
42. Mary Ann Walker, a Hinsdale before her marriage, was the first wife of Granger's uncle Charles Irish Walker. Born July 14, 1811, she married Walker on April 12, 1938, and gave birth to three children during their marriage. She died at age fifty-two on February 16, 1864, in Detroit. Charles Walker fathered two additional children after he married Ella Fletcher on May 18, 1865.

soon and I faithfully promise to turn over a new leaf in the matter of writing (whether that will better the thing or not time only can tell) Anyway <u>write soon</u>.

Yours
E. G. Granger

※ ※ ※

[LETTER 6]

Camp Copeland Washington
Mar. 14, 1863 [Saturday]

Dear Mollie

You see my stock of Government paper is used up, to my great relief—for it is so much easier to fill a sheet of note paper like this, that the task of writing a letter is deprived of half its terrors.

On my return from the second Raid I found four letters waiting for me, making in all, seven that I had received since I have written and I did not know till then what an enormous correspondence I was carrying on [illegible] realized I had seven letters to write so overcome me that I had not recovered from the shock when we were ordered off again, this time we went to Fairfax Court House Wednesday morning [illegible] [March 11] there till Saturday (this) morning [illegible] [March 14] then returned in peace safely to Camp Copeland. The object of our expedition was to surprise a large force of Rebel Cavalry which was at Culpeper Court House.[43] We didn't do it though. It was the intention that we, (the Fifth & Sixth with other Regts. of Cavalry) should go through Ashby's Gap and attack them in front, while a force under Gen. Pleasonton should march from Falmouth to get in their rear. The cause of the failure of the expedition was the inability of Gen. Pleasonton to come in time, on account of the bad state of the roads.

---

43. Union leaders were concerned about possible Confederate forces massing near Winchester coming out of the Shenandoah Valley. This led to the movement of Union troops, more on a scouting mission, to fend off the feared attacks. Copeland's Michigan Cavalry Brigade left Washington, D.C., on the morning of March 11, as Granger notes, marching to Fairfax Court House. After three days camping in the vicinity, the brigade returned to Camp Copeland. O'Neill, *Chasing Jeb Stuart*, 115–16; Longacre, *Custer*, 112.

Mollie Granger Vernor with three of her six children.
Given the number of children in the photo and their size, the girl on the left is likely Edna, born in 1869, and the boy is her brother, Benjamin, born in 1871. A third child, Charles Vernor, was born in 1875 but died in 1879, while a fourth, Ellen, was born in 1876 and died in 1878. A fifth, another daughter, Winifred (1877–1963), proved long-lived. Sadly, a sixth child, Frederick, was born in 1883 but died that year. Thus, given the tragedies of the several children's early deaths, it seems likely that the baby Mollie is holding is Winifred. After the death of Charles in 1879, Mollie may have had a family portrait taken with her surviving children. The two older children that year would have been ten and eight, about the age of the youngsters in the photo. *Courtesy of Lisa Mower Gandelot.*

CAMP LIFE AND PICKET DUTY

I believe we would have had a first rate time at Fairfax. Our Camp was in the woods and we had nothing to do but cut wood to keep up our own fires, eat and sleep which is just about a soldier's idea of Paradise. It is wonderful what an appetite living in the open air gives a man. You would think so if you could see me eat a piece of salt pork, pure fat, which I had just roasted by holding it over the coals on the end of a long stick. This is an excellent mode of cooking that luxury, pork, the worst inconvenience being a liability to ~~fall~~ drop the pork into the fire two or three times before you get it cooked, but that don't hurt it much, for me, you know I like meat well done.

Some of our boys went off foraging and got some ham and eggs, some salt herring (not smoked) and a little honey which last was very good, as I can [illegible]. The boys took their articles from families of Secesh proclivities paying them in River Raisin and [illegible] money.

Tell Miss Polly[44] that I saw near in Fairfax, a blossom of the <u>Symplo-Carpus-Foetidus</u>[45] but being on horseback could not conveniently get it. I send you a sprig of Holly which was given me by a female "American citizen of African descent" from a bush which I saw in one of our former Raids, in a yard near Fairfax. I don't know as I shall be able to put the beans in the letter at all & if I can, I presume they will all be <u>smashed</u> before they reach you, but you will at least see what kind of leaf the Holly has.

Now for your letter.

In the first place, if you ever get Annie[46] to direct your letter again I want her to write more indeed than she did in that.

I saw the direction of the letter and supposed I had an epistle from some beautiful Young Lady but did not try to make out who it was, from the writing. I left it till the last of the four I had, so as to have the full benefit of the anticipation which in this case was so much more brilliant than the reality. Imagine my "pheelinks" when the first signature that I saw was that of C. W. Welmore[47] and the next Sister

---

44. Polly Walker (1797–1886) was a sister of Granger's mother, Matilda. She was married to George Andrews (1793–1873).
45. This is a deciduous perennial low-growing fetid swamp plant of eastern North America having minute flowers enclosed in a mottled greenish or purple cowl-shaped spathe.
46. Annie is unidentified.
47. C. W. Welmore is unidentified.

Mollie: both well enough in their place but under such circumstances!! In conclusion let me advise you to direct your own letters if you want to have them answered.

Secondly, if you are so foolish as to believe any such story as the one you tell about D. M. D. I am glad Don[48] has cut you though he says that the cause of the trouble came from Mother. You ought to have known Don well enough to know that he would never say any such thing. I should have been perfectly sure of that even if he had not in his letter to me denied ever having made any such remark. For he said there was such a story afloat though he did not get it just as you did.

3d Subject—Photographs—I don't have any more, only I was thinking there must be two or three more than I had lying around loose somewhere; but come to look up the matter I guess that I have given them all away.

I am glad Lucy[49] passed so well. Is she going to teaching? I should like to see Miss Maggie Buchanan's[50] performance as "School-marm."

Capt. Hunt has the will to get out of the service, and you know the old saying "Where there's a will there's a way," but I rather doubt whether he can get out. He has sent in his resignation but I don't know whether it is accepted yet as I haven't seen Capt. since our return, he having been down town, all day. But I hardly believe he will get it accepted. He is terribly Home sick, but, he has not, a tithe of the reason to go home that one of our Privates has, poor fellow!! His wife lost a young babe a few weeks ago, and now his daughter writes that "Mother is deranged by spells and you must come home." I am afraid his chances of going home are small, it is such hard work for anyone to get a furlough now.

I tell you it need young men for soldiers, a married man is always home sick, and their wives are always wanting for them to come home. The women of the North are shamefully selfish and unpatriotic in that matter of writing to their husbands in the Army. They ought to know that it only makes the poor men unhappy without doing any possible good. What fools men are to get married anyway!! I sometimes think they don't deserve any pity.

---

48. This is likely the previously described Donald MacDonald.
49. Lucy is unidentified.
50. Maggie Buchanan is unidentified.

CAMP LIFE AND PICKET DUTY

Alex & I corresponded: I know as I have just written to him after owing him a letter for some months.

E. G. Granger

❈ ❈ ❈

[LETTER 7]

Camp Copeland Washington, D.C.
Mar. 3, 1863 April 3d, 1863 [Friday]
Camp near Fairfax C. H. Virginia

Dear Mother

You see I am as absent minded as ever. That first date as I wrote before I thought of the fact that I had not seen Washington for more than a week and that it was now April instead of March.

From this time forward, you must not expect to hear from me with any regularity as there is no certainty of my being in camp any great length of time at once.

It is so long since I have written home that I hardly know where to commence my history of our proceedings and may perhaps repeat some things that I have written before.

About 3 weeks ago Bristol & I drew an "A" tent[51] & pitched it up behind our own for Corser, my hired man who went into it and commenced to cook for us. As we were, at that time, "strapped," the cooking for our mess was rather slim but it suited me exactly as our only dependence was on cakes & Bread & butter. The cakes were not such as I have had at home, but they were very good.

On the 19th of March [Thursday], I was surprised by a visit from Lycurgus [Granger]. His team had run away with him & he had been hurt enough to prevent his doing duty for a few days so he got a furlough for seven days & came to Washington. He stayed from Friday to Tuesday [March 20–24], part of the time with us & part, down town. We had a very good time, went to see the Sixth & Seventh Regiments & the Smithsonian Institute. At the camp of the Sixth I saw George

---

51. The A-frame, or wedge tent, was used during the Revolutionary War through Civil War times. Modern replicas can be easily found for sale on the internet and are common purchases by Civil War reenactors today.

Granger[52] who had just received a notice of Uncle Austin's death. George came out as Regimental Wagon Master, but that office was abolished at the same time that the rank of Supernumerary Sec. Lieut was, and Geo. had not yet got any pay at all & I didn't know whether he should get any. I also saw Sheldon[53] & his wife who was with him at Camp. They had an old tent fitted up as comfortably that it looked more like home than any thing I have seen since I left Camp Banks. They did not know me at first & I should not have known either of them but when I told them who I was, they appeared to be very glad to see me. They inquired particularly about Mr. Taylor's health & Mrs. Sheldon said she wished Jule would write to her.[54] She took me into the kitchen & gave me a piece of mince pie to show me how well they lived there.

Lycurgus went to get some photographs taken before he left, but the negatives got broken when they had taken but two impressions. Those two he gave me, one for you which I enclose, & one for myself.

The same day that Lycurgus left we were told about 10 A.M. to be in readiness to receive marching orders if they should come.

At 4 A.M. the next morning [Wednesday, March 25] we were ordered to be ready to move everything in an hour.[55] We got ready all but

---

52. Another Granger first cousin, George Warner Granger (1825–1894) was the son of Austin Granger (1791–1863), who had died March 3, 1863, and his late wife, Rhoda Bostwick (1795–1849). He was about eighteen years older than Edward Granger. He must have been a civilian employee of the 6th Michigan Cavalry, as Civil War records do not disclose any service time for him. Granger Family Tree, Ancestry.com.
53. The identities of Sheldon and his wife are unconfirmed. In Granger's extended family appear George Sheldon Walter (1833–1907) and his wife, Hannah (1837–1922). However, by this date in 1863, the couple had two children, one a toddler and the other an infant, making it highly unlikely that the people Granger is referring to are them. No Civil War records indicate that this Walter served in the Union Army during the Civil War. Too, their last name is different from the one that Granger cites.
54. The identities of both Mr. Taylor and Jule are unknown. A first cousin in the Granger line, Julia C. Granger (1846–1920), could be a possibility as Jule is often seen as a shortened version of Julia, but that would be speculative.
55. These orders were significant for Granger's regiment, as it would virtually end their stay at Camp Copeland and duty in Washington, D.C. The three Michigan cavalry regiments had been formed into an independent cavalry brigade that remained assigned to the defense of Washington, D.C. While they would still endure their share of picket duty for two more months, more action would soon loom ahead for the men of what was now the Michigan Cavalry Brigade. O'Neill, *Chasing Jeb Stuart*, 131; Longacre, *Custer*, 114.

CAMP LIFE AND PICKET DUTY

striking our tent and taking down our stoves, and then had to wait till about noon when we started off with only our blankets & shelter tents. We camped that night about ten miles from Washington in the woods.[56] We pitched our tents and went to bed but I was soon waked up by the rain dropping into my eyes. We had got our tent so slanting that it did not shed rain very well & consequently were soon soaked through. Soon after Bristol waked up & found himself lying in quite a pool of water. This was rather rough but we were so sleepy that we slept there till morning only waking up occasionally when we got pretty well soaked up.

The next day [Thursday, March 26] we waited till two o'clock for orders & then started for Fairfax C. H. [Court House] where we arrived a little after dark, or, rather, we arrived at our present camping grounds which is about a mile from the Court House, on the road to Washington. It had been raining just enough to make the leaves so wet that it was almost impossible to get a fire started and it was 10 or 11 P.M. before we got to bed & then the ground was so damp & the wind had such a good sweep through our shelter tent that we slept but little that night. The next day we cut some cedar boughs and made a splendid bed and that (Friday) night we slept as tired men could.[57] Saturday I was on guard & as I had not got the run of things yet I slept but about an hour till about 5 A.M. Sunday when I retired & slept till 8 A.M. Sunday [March 29] our tents and other traps were brought to us from Washington.

We put up our tent Sunday afternoon and had a supper of buckwheat cakes which went well, you may imagine, after living on hard tack & coffee, the latter of the poorest quality.

---

56. During this period Confederate cavalry leader major general J. E. B. Stuart was reportedly in the area and Union leaders greatly feared he might attack along their lines. Union forces were constantly shuffled about, going forward or backward as circumstances seemed to dictate. This is probably why Granger's company moved the ten miles from Washington, D.C. They crossed the Potomac River on the Long Bridge from Washington and camped near Bailey's Cross Roads. O'Neill indicates this move occurred on March 23–24, while Granger suggests it was March 25–26. Captain Safford's diary has a brief entry for March 25 indicating "Broke camp at 4 P.M. marched to Fairfax C. H." O'Neill, *Chasing Jeb Stuart*, 131; Wittenberg, *Under Custer's Command*, 24; Davis, *I Rode with Custer*, 27.

57. According to Longacre, by March 27 the three Michigan regiments were encamped within five miles of each other between the Loudoun & Hampshire and Orange & Alexandria Railroads. Longacre, *Custer*, 114.

Monday morning [March 30] Co. C. with four other Companies of the 5th were ordered out on Picket. Dodge being on the Staff, Bristol was in command of the Company.

O! I forgot to say that when we left Washington, Capt. Hunt begged to be left behind. He was left, but when the baggage was sent for, he was ordered on.

Easter Sunday ~~Mar.~~ April 5th 1863

Just here my letter was interrupted by an order to be ready to move within an hour with three days rations & we did move, but of that I will speak again.

We received the order to leave for picket duty at 9 A.M. Monday [March 30]. We were to take one day's rations and one feed for our horses and no blankets. We were posted at a fork in the road where the picket of the 18th Pennsylvania was captured by Moseby [John S. Mosby] at the time of the Falmouth Raid. It is about five miles from Fairfax and a mile and a half from the Pike.[58]

The day was pleasant but rather cold and as the post was an outside one, Lieut. Bristol thought it best not to build any fire. There were only 42 men of our Company out and the number of posts we had to keep on was so great that all the Corporals & Sergeants except the orderly had to act as privates. Fred Nims[59] & I went around as a Patrol to visit the posts every hour or two. This was all very nice, but we

---

58. Granger is referring to the Little River Turnpike, which was built in the early nineteenth century by private interests and which operated as a toll road. It ran from Alexandria, Virginia, to Aldie, Virginia, in Loudoun County. Numerous relocations and other changes have occurred to the highway since the nineteenth century. Today, the portion of the historical turnpike between Aldie and Fairfax is part of U.S. 50. Only the State Road 236 section continues to carry the Little River Turnpike name. Captain Safford's entry for April 1, 1863, places the 5th Michigan's pickets on the Ox Road, seven miles from Fairfax.

59. First Sgt. Frederick A. Nims was born on May 16, 1841, at Monroe, Michigan, and enlisted on August 22, 1862, in Granger's Company C, 5th Michigan Cavalry. He was promoted to second lieutenant, Company F, on January 12, 1864, and to first lieutenant on March 7, 1865. As a second lieutenant, Nims also served as an aide on General Custer's staff from July 1864 to September 30, 1864. Nims was mustered out on August 22, 1865, in Detroit. A farmer after the war, he died October 2, 1921, in Monroe. Nims was buried in his family plot, next to the Custer's family lot in Monroe's historic Woodland Cemetery. David Ingall, "Lieutenant Frederick Nims," *River Raisin News & Dispatch* 3, no. 3 (July/August/September 2008): 3; Soldier Records and Profiles.

CAMP LIFE AND PICKET DUTY

Col. John Mosby.
Courtesy of Library of Congress, 03240u.

had to "Dismount and advance & give counter signs" every time we approached a Picket: and the boys thought it was such a good joke that they would halt us about as far as they could see us & make us walk up to them through the mud. Fred & I thought we would like to try a little "active service" so we agreed to stand one "trick:" as the boys call it, that is stand on post for two hours. About one A.M. Tuesday [March 31] it commenced snowing and as Fred was asleep, I thought he was enjoying himself more than became a soldier on Picket duty; so I waked him up and told him it was time for us to go on. He got up grumbling, and we went out to our post, which was the most advanced on the road on which Mosby usually comes.

Fred is a dangerous companion on a Picket post as he keeps one laughing a good part of the time. He is a well informed fellow & has been pretty much all through the U.S. and a more sensible and pleasant companion than most of the Commissioned Officers. The

Lt. Frederick A. Nims.
Courtesy of John Beckendorf.

only trouble with him is that he will drink occasionally and that he is with the boys in all their deviltry.

That two hours from one to three O'clock was about as long as any two hours I ever spent. It snowed steady all the time and I wished I had one of the plug hats that the boys had just drawn. The snow got down my neck altogether too much for comfort while the others were protected by the brims of their hats. The place where we were posted was at a crossing of an old road through the woods and along both roads were large chestnut trees. The snow was just damp enough to cling to the branches of the trees making a most beautiful picture. We had been dismounted & made to walk so much that night we were determined to have revenge on some one, so when it was about time for the relief to come around I kept a sharp lookout for it and halted it as soon as it came in sight. The poor Corporal had to walk about half a mile in the snow and mud. The next day we should have been relieved at ten A.M. but no relief came and a more dismal day was never seen, I believe. The snow was several inches deep and it kept coming till after noon, when the fire we had finally built about midnight, was but a poor affair, as there were no rails anywhere within half a mile that we wanted to confiscate and the green pine, which was the only wood at hand, was miserable stuff to burn. But the principal sources of our comfort were the fact that our provisions had nearly all given out the night before, while our horses had been half rations for about a week & had had but one feed since 9 A.M. Monday: and the prospect fast growing more delightfully certain that we should have to stay again that night on Picket.

However, at 4 P.M. the welcome news came that relief was at hand, and soon Company M made its appearance, having come to take our place. They brought news of the acceptance of Capt. Hunt's resignation which was received by his bereaved Company with three cheers. They also told us that Dodge had left his position on the Staff and was made Capt. of Co. C. This was also welcome news, to me, for though I had rather have had Bristol Capt. I knew that they did not intend to appoint him, and Dodge is a great deal better than any other 1st Lieut. in the Regt.

On our return we found Capt. or rather G. W. Hunt fast getting ready to leave and though he only heard of the acceptance of his resignation on Tuesday he left so early Thursday morning [April 2] that I did not see him to bid him good-by whereupon I wept bitterly—perhaps.

The reason Hunt got his discharge was his "inability to ride" but he went into Washington on the hardest riding horse in the Company, just because he was fast.

Wednesday [April 1] I spent sleeping and that evening the Col. sent for Lieut. Granger. I went over to Head Quarters and Col. wanted to know if I was fit for duty, of course I was, and he accordingly ordered me to report to Capt. Grey [Wellington W. Gray][60] (of Co. A.) mounted & with an orderly. Capt. Gray had one orderly & one of his Sergeants who wanted to go with him. Our mission was to visit all the Pickets from our Regt. We went to General Copeland's Head Quarters for instruction and he showed us the line of our Pickets on a map which he had on his table.

We had a good deal of fun trying the men to see if they knew their business. I learnt a great deal as Capt. Gray is an old officer (Comparatively having been 18 mos. in the service) and is well posted. On

---

60. At age thirty-four, Wellington W. Gray of Romeo, Michigan, was commissioned as a first lieutenant in Company A, 1st Michigan Cavalry, on August 22, 1861, at Detroit. On June 10, 1862, he was mustered out of the 1st Michigan at the rank of captain. Two months later, on August 14, he was commissioned as an officer in Company A, 5th Michigan Cavalry, and was mustered out on account of disability on February 4, 1864. Soldier Records and Profiles.

approaching one Picket & in answer to the usual challenge "Who goes there," Capt. said, "Soldiers."

This appeared to puzzle the Dutchman a little but he finally answered. "Well, give me the countersign."

Capt—"Come and get it."

Dutchman—after some deliberation "No you come and give it to me."

Capt. "Well come on boys"—and we all went up together till we got within a few paces when the Dutchman sings out "Halt" & then "give me the countersign."

Capt.: "That's just what we were going to do! What did you halt us for? Come on" and again we advanced in a body & the Capt. rode up to him to give the Countersign.

—Capt. "Newtown"

—Dutchman—"No its Newburn"

Capt.—presenting a pistol at the head of the other—That's just what I want—the Countersign. Do you know me?

D— [illegible]

Capt. "I'm Mosby. You've heard of Mosby?"

D—still more frightened—"yes."

Then the Capt. proceeded to extract from him all the information he could give. He answered correctly to the best of his knowledge every question asked him; gave the name of his Regt., told where it was stationed & how many more Regts. there were here, the letter of his Company where the Lieut. commanding it, was and expressed his belief that we could take him.

Capt.—"Are you willing to take the oath not to fight against the Southern Confederacy?"

Du "Yes"

Capt. "and to go to Richmond?"

Du—"Yes,"

Capt. "Won't you join my band"

Du "No. I'm sick of fighting, I didn't want to fight anyway but they made us come, if we hadn't enlisted. They would have drafted us."

Capt.—to me [Granger] "Well I guess we'll take his horse, overcoat and arms, and go on to take the rest of the Pickets."

The man then began to take off his Rifle to give it to me, but Capt. Gray stopped him, told him who he was & gave the poor Dutchman the hardest lecture I ever heard a man get. It was a good lesson for him & a while after, when he had been relieved he swore that they would never catch him again.

As I have said before, we were ordered to move last Friday [April 3] with three day's rations.[61] We started just afternoon and stopped at Chantilly which is of about around 8 miles from the Court House till nearly dark when having been joined by parts of the First & Sixth Mich.; & the 2nd Regt. Penn. and the 1st [West] Virginia we proceeded to a spot where the Pike crosses the is crossed by a small road called the gum spring road.[62] Here Co. C. was left to Picket the two Roads while the Regt. went on a few miles further.[63] On the next day morning we moved on nearly to Aldie where we stayed nearly all day, sending out scouting parties which brought in large quantities

---

61. According to O'Neill, on the morning of April 3, the 5th and 6th Michigan Cavalry regiments were ordered to take the field with three days of rations. General Copeland led the expedition which departed about 3:00 P.M. The men rode to Aldie, Virginia, where they camped for the night. However, they got little rest, as they were ordered to stand to horse "nearly all of the time." The area was considered "Mosby's Confederacy." Some signs of his presence were found, but no troops were encountered. Some individuals suspected of being close to him were arrested. O'Neill, *Chasing Jeb Stuart*, 147; Longacre, *Custer*, 115.
62. Granger is likely referring to the intersection of modern State Route 659, otherwise known as Belmont Ridge Road north of Arcola, and south as Gum Spring Road, and U.S. 50. The intersection today is about 6.5 miles from Chantilly and not far from Dulles International Airport. The road is heavily traveled by commuters in the suburbs and bedroom communities of Loudoun County, Virginia. In his letter Granger inaccurately identifies the 18th Pennsylvania Cavalry as the 2nd Pennsylvania, and he omits the 5th New York Cavalry. O'Neill, *Chasing Jeb Stuart*, 147.
63. According to O'Neill, Copeland left Companies A and E to search the countryside around Aldie, while he took the rest of his command, which include elements of the 1st West Virginia, 5th New York, and the 18th Pennsylvania, on to Middleburg, Virginia, in a search for guerrillas. Granger's Company C apparently remained on picket duty until the next morning, when they, too, moved to join the regiment at Aldie. O'Neill, *Chasing Jeb Stuart*, 147.

of forage so that we lived on the best the country afforded and it was literally a land "flowing with milk & honey!"[64]

The house of Major Fairfax, whose wife said he was Inspector General in Longstreet's army, was pretty well ransacked. The house was formerly occupied by President Monroe.[65] Sunday [April 5] we returned to Camp bringing some fifty or sixty prisoners, some of whom must have been of some importance as they were the ones whom we had been specially ordered to take.[66]

This morning [April 6] there was an Undress Parade at which were announced the promotion of Lieuts H. W. Dodge, Jacob Bristol and Edward G. Granger. So I am all safe. Please let Uncle C. I. know this as soon as you can, though I shall probably write to Uncle Edward, so that the letter will go out only when this does, unless I am too tired to write tomorrow and am to go as Officer of the Guard to night.

I had my hair cut "Fighting fashion" to day & enclose a lock to show you the length before the operation.

Your son
Ed. G. Granger

I would send a lock as it is now but it is so short—I can't get hold of it with the scissors.

E. G. G.

---

64. O'Neill identifies the scouting parties as Companies A and E, 5th Michigan Cavalry. Copeland reportedly headed west to Middleburg, Virginia, where his troops helped themselves to what they could carry.
65. Aldie is an unincorporated community located between Chantilly and Middleburg in Loudoun County, Virginia. During the Civil War, the village was the scene of numerous small engagements, especially with Mosby's partisan rangers, as well as the Battle of Aldie during the Gettysburg Campaign of 1863. It is nearly thirteen miles from Chantilly along modern U.S. 50. As Granger suggests, President James Monroe once owned the house that in 1863 belonged to Confederate major John W. Fairfax. Monroe constructed his private residence at Oak Hill about 1820 and owned the property until his death in 1831. The house still exists today as a private residence. Oak Hill, National Register of Historic Places Nomination Form, no. 053-0090, Virginia Department of Historic Resources, http://www.dhr.virginia.gov/registers/Counties/Loudoun/053-0090_Oak_Hill_1960_Final_Nomination_NHL.pdf.
66. This camp was at Fairfax Court House. The command brought in sixty-one prisoners while enduring a violent snowstorm. Some of the prisoners were believed to have been connected with Mosby's command. O'Neill, *Chasing Jeb Stuart*, 148–49.

[LETTER 8]

Camp Near Fairfax Court House
May 5, 1863 [Tuesday]

Dear Mollie

I should have answered your letter long ago but we have been on Picket since the 1st of last month and I have had absolutely no time to write.

Since the 10th Ult., the whole Brigade has been out at a reserve Camp some five miles from Fairfax under command of Col. Gray of the 6th, and when we are relieved we only come back to the Camp & stay one night and then start off the next day for some other post.

This makes it very hard for the men and still harder for the horses: but we hope to be relieved Friday [May 8] by the second Brigade, and then the horses will have a chance to rest, though the men will probably have to drill.

The weather is still delightfully moist down here and Company C never leaves Camp without getting caught in a storm. One time, when we were out at Hawkhurst's Mills where one part of the Company had to relieve the other part every six hours; a small stream, which we had to cross to relieve each other, became so swollen that we had to let Bristol and his relief stay on all night, as we could not get across the Run. Of course Bristol had a nice time as it rained copiously all day night.

This place, Hawkhurst's Mills, is where Bob. Wallace[67] was taken. Of course you have read of his capture in the Detroit papers. Poor

---

67. Robert C. Wallace was born in Scotland on February 26, 1837, and his family and he immigrated to the United States in 1844, when he was age seven. He enlisted in Company A, 1st Michigan Infantry on April 18, 1861, for ninety days service. On August 14, 1862, he joined the 5th Michigan Cavalry as a second lieutenant in Company L. As Granger mentions, Wallace was seized by Mosby's men near Hawkhurst's Mills, Virginia, on April 19, 1863, when he rode outside the Union lines with Pvt. Samuel Earle on a scouting mission checking out area roads. Union newspapers first reported they had disobeyed orders by going beyond the lines, as Granger stated. Wallace was imprisoned for a few months in Libby Prison in Richmond, Virginia, but was soon exchanged and returned to the 5th Cavalry. After the war, Wallace went west in 1869 and eventually settled in Helena, Montana, where he became a leading citizen. Davis, *I Rode with Custer*, 26; O'Neill, *Chasing Jeb Stuart*, 152–53; Robert C. Wallace, *A Few Memories of a Long Life*, ed. John M. Carroll (Fairfield, Wash.: Ye Galleon Press, 1988), 21–27.

fellow! he was caught outside of the lines in disobedience of recent stringent orders, and if he is returned to the Government he will be dismissed, I suppose. Luckily I have no inclination to get myself into any such scrape <u>in the same way</u>, that is, by going to see any good looking Rebel of the female persuasion. I have hardly been into a house since I have been out here, and then only for the laudable purpose of getting something to eat. But now, even that, is stopped and it is ~~going~~ against the rules to go into any house.

But while we were out at Hawkhurst's, [Elliott] Stedman[68] (who is now a Sergeant) took several men & went outside of the lines, <u>without our knowledge</u>, for the purpose of foraging. On his return he handed over to Brown,[69] the cook, 9 Chickens, 3 Geese and a Turkey. Of course we (Bristol and I) were terribly shocked to find out that the boys had been outside of the lines, but we had a <u>first rate</u> dinner.

One of the boys brought in about ten pounds of a mixture, new to me, of butter & honey, and of this I had what I wanted for breakfast and dinner. The day before this we had so short of rations that we thought ourselves nearly starved & one of our boys offered a quarter of a Dollar for a hard tack, but could not get it. So we live, one day a piece of hard tack is "first rate" eating, and a small bit of fat pork a luxury only to be enjoyed by a few, more lucky, or more provident than the rest. The next day we live on the fat of the land. Turkeys, Geese, Chickens, honey & milk in abundance "without money & without price."

The next time we started out on Picket it rained harder than it had ~~done~~ before this spring & we had to ride six miles in the rain & then get off & pitch our shelter tents, though by this time it did not rain quite so fast. We went to the place where Lieut. Harmon[70] of Co. B. had been shot

---

68. Elliott Stedman of Howell, Michigan, enlisted in Granger's Company C, 5th Michigan Cavalry, as a bugler at age thirty-one on August 19, 1862, and was later promoted to sergeant. He was transferred to the Invalid Corps on January 15, 1864, and was finally discharged on July 3, 1865, from the 22nd Regiment, Veteran Reserve Corps. Soldier Records and Profiles; U.S. Civil War Soldiers.

69. Alexander Brown, age twenty-four, of Detroit, enlisted on August 15, 1862, in Company C, 5th Michigan Cavalry, and was mustered in on August 27, 1862. He remained with the regiment for the next three years. He was discharged June 19, 1865, at Fort Leavenworth, Kansas. Soldier Records and Profiles; U.S. Civil War Soldiers.

70. Allen M. Harmon, Northville, Michigan, originally enlisted on August 14, 1862, as a first sergeant in Company D, 5th Michigan Cavalry, despite being only nineteen years old. He received his commission as second lieutenant on December 15, 1862. He

Capt. Robert C. Wallace.
Courtesy of John Beckendorf.

dead a few days before by the accidental discharge of a rifle. While we were here Lieut. Bristol went into Fairfax to get the pay of the Company. I did not get paid as I have to go to Washington to get my accounts settled at the Adjutant General's Office. I shall have to be mustered out as Supernumerary & mustered in as Second Lieut. My commission is in Col. Gould's hands & I can get it whenever I want it, but the mustering

---

was accidentally killed by a gunshot in camp near Fairfax Court House on April 20, 1863. According to Sergeant Edwin B. Bigelow, Company B, as the lieutenant rode up, a rifle accidentally discharged and killed him. The rifle had been laying on a shed, when Pvt. William Perry, Company B, placed his weapon on top of it. His rifle caught the hammer of the other, which went off. The bullet struck the lieutenant in the head, killing him instantly. A cenotaph stands in his memory in Oakwood Cemetery in Northville, Michigan, but it is unclear whether his body was moved from Virginia to his hometown cemetery. Frank L. Klement, ed., "Edwin B. Bigelow: A Michigan Sergeant in the Civil War," *Michigan History* 38 (September 1954): 212–13, 217; Soldier Records and Profiles; U.S. Civil War Soldiers; "Lieut. Allen M. Harmon," memorial and gravestone at Findagrave.com, 55528784.

officer has gone to Washington & I don't know when I shall get my pay, but when I do, it will be up to the 1st of April so I shall have three months pay at once. I shall keep enough of this to get something to wear and to keep me from getting "dead broke" as I am now.

This is not a very good country for flowers as most of the woods here are all Pine. The flowers I do find are nearly all common in Michigan, Snow Drops, Spring Beauties, Adder Tongues, Blood Root, Anemonies, and Violets.

The only flowers I have yet seen which are new to me are a blossom of a kind of mint—some kind of blue flower very much like a forget-me Not and a peculiar species of Violet. Of the Forget-Me-Not I have pressed one or two specimens which I will enclose, trusting that they will reach you well preserved, as, at least, well <u>jammed</u> up. The Violets I did not find till today & though I put some of them into my pocket-book I doubt whether they will be worth sending, by the time I am ready to send this off, that is, if I succeed in getting this off at all. Week before last I commenced a letter to you & had succeeded in getting three pages of ~~an~~ most <u>interesting</u> matter written, after various interruptions, when I was called away a while & some fool employed his leisure in scribbling on the fourth page of my letter. Whew! Perhaps I went mad. My hard work for two days, every spare second devoted to that letter & all my labor rendered futile just by carelessness of some individual (fortunately for him) unknown.

Lieut. Bristol is very anxious to get a leave of absence as his wife is very sick, but I am afraid he will not succeed.

Your Brother
Ed.

❋ ❋ ❋

[LETTER 9]

Camp Near Fairfax Court House, Va.
May 20 1863 [Wednesday]

Dear Mother

I certainly thought I had written to you since I received your photograph, but if I had I should, of course, have spoken of it. I liked it very much indeed both as a picture and as a likeness.

CAMP LIFE AND PICKET DUTY   83

It looks as though you had a hard time to keep your eyes open long enough. My collection of photographs is getting to be so large that I shall have to get some kind of an album "when I get to Washington" if that ever happens. My mustering-out, and mustering-in, rolls are to be filled out this morning[71] and then all I have to do is to get a pass to Washington, where I expect to get paid; but I shall have to wait till the Commissary of musters has sent my rolls, or duplicates of them to the Adj. Gen. & he has sent them to the office of the Pay Master Gen. before I can get any pay.

You need not trouble yourself about my being "liable to be engaged in active service;" that is our least trouble now. We (Stahel's Division) are the only troops near Washington except two Regts. of Infantry at Chantilly whose time is up next month, and a small force of Infantry & artillery at Vienna, some six or eight miles North of Fairfax, so our chances, of standing Picket all summer, are most brilliant. Now Picket duty may be active enough but there is nothing dangerous about it, not even enough danger to relieve the monotony.[72] Heintzleman's whole Corps[73] which has, during the winter, had the honor of being the "Reserve Corps in Defence of Washington," has since the late battle[74] gone to reinforce Hooker—except, as I said before, our Division. There

71. Granger was referring to his official promotion to second lieutenant, effective April 1, 1863. It was not unusual for the effective dates of promotions and mustering to be quite different, depending upon the war's circumstances.

72. Robert F. O'Neill's book, *Chasing Jeb Stuart and John Mosby*, splendidly documents the dangers of picket duty facing the Union soldiers during this period of the war. Too, Granger's statement about the number of troops still near the nation's capital is inaccurate.

73. Maj. Gen. Samuel P. Heintzelman was graduated from the U.S. Military Academy in 1826 and saw action in both the Seminole War and Mexican-American War as well as in Indian conflicts in the West in the 1850s. Early in the Civil War, he rose to command the III Corps of the Army of the Potomac in the Peninsula Campaign, but despite his successes, he was soon eclipsed by such subordinate commanders as Joseph Hooker and Philip Kearny. After he was relieved from duty with the Army of the Potomac in late 1862, he commanded the Department of Washington, which was responsible for the defense of the nation's capital. He retired from the Army in 1869 after forty-three years of service and died in 1880.

74. The Battle of Chancellorsville, one of the classic engagements of America's Civil War, was fought April 30–May 6, 1863. Granger's 5th Michigan and the Michigan Cavalry Brigade saw no action, remaining on picket duty in the defenses of Washington, D.C.

is not a soldier in Washington or in any of the forts and encampments between here & the city, all of which used to be full last winter.⁷⁵

A few days ago, I was sent out in command of a detachment of the 5th and 6th Mich. Cav. to report to Lt. Col. Stagg⁷⁶ of the 1st Mich. Cav. with two days rations for men and horses. Col. Stagg's force consisted of portions of the 1st Mich., Eighteenth Penn. and the aforesaid detachment (54 strong).⁷⁷

We started late in the afternoon and halted that night at Chantilly which is about 5 miles out on the Pike.

Here we lay down with one blanket and an oil cloth under us and a blanket & Capt. Dodge's rubber coat over us &, in spite of a slight rain, slept soundly. It is strange how soon a person gets used to sleeping on the ground in any weather and without shelter. The next morning we resumed our journey about 5 o'clock and all day we wandered around without any apparent object except at keeping inside the pickets. We arrived safely that night at a point on the Alexandria and Leesburg

---

75. By his statement, Granger is likely more reassuring his mother than stating a literal fact. The Washington fortifications were always manned during the war, although the number of the troops varied, as the war's circumstances dictated.

76. Peter Stagg (1836–1884) was commissioned on August 22, 1861, as a second lieutenant in Company K, 1st Michigan Cavalry. During the war, he rose to colonel and commander of the regiment on August 17, 1864. He also was the last man to command the Michigan Cavalry Brigade. On March 31, 1865, he was brevetted brigadier general for gallant and distinguished service. He was mustered out on March 10, 1866, at Salt Lake City, Utah. "Peter Stagg," memorial and gravestone at Findagrave.com, 10470758; Soldier Records and Profiles; U.S. Civil War Soldiers.

77. This expedition is notable because it is the first documented instance of Lieutenant Granger commanding a larger body of troops in the field. Union intelligence had reported, inaccurately as it turned out, that as many as nine hundred guerrillas might be operating west of Leesburg and at Upperville, Virginia. Stahel ordered a force under the command of Lieutenant Colonel Stagg of the 1st Michigan Cavalry to search for the enemy. Stagg's troops may have numbered only as many as four hundred men, including Granger's fifty-four. The expedition commenced on Thursday, May 14 and returned on Friday, May 15, having failed to find evidence of any large enemy force in the area. A native of Hungary, Julius Stahel came to the United States in 1859. In 1861, he began his military career as the lieutenant colonel and colonel of the 8th New York (1st German Rifles). By March 17, 1863, he had been promoted to major general of volunteers. For his actions at the Battle of Piedmont on June 5, 1864, he was awarded the Congressional medal in 1893. After the war, he served in the U.S. consular service for many years in Japan and China. He died in New York City on December 4, 1912, at age 87 and was buried in Arlington National Cemetery. Warner, *Generals in Blue*, 469–70.

CAMP LIFE AND PICKET DUTY   85

Pike two or three miles inside of the lines and about 9 or 10 miles from Fairfax.[78]

That evening a squadron of the 1st went out on a scout and I was sent with my command to guard a ford, through which they had to pass, till their return. They got back about 9 P.M., having picked up several prisoners and horses. We returned to camp and passed the rest of the night in sleep. The next morning Col. Stagg sent in to Head Quarters for orders. Orders did not come and we lay there idle all day, the officers of the First "killing time" after a style that would have astonished the sedate and dignified officers of the Fifth.

Captains and Lieutenants scuffling just like the Privates & the Lt. Col. looking on and laughing. The officers tried to get up a game of cards but no two were willing to play the same game, and when, finally, one of them dealt they all commenced cheating so fast that they couldn't play at all. They tried pitching pennies with about the same luck. Then they got the Doctor to show them his case of surgical instruments and tell them the uses of the different ones. This was quite interesting, of course, as there was no knowing how soon some of us might have his lecture illustrated on ourselves if we continued our dangerous occupation of scouting inside the lines.

Not hearing from the orderly he had sent to Head Quarters for orders, Col. Stagg sent Lieutenant Maxwell[79] of the 1st and when he

---

78. Northern Virginia historian Debbie Robison provides interesting historical details about a number of pikes in Northern Virginia, including what Granger cites as the Alexandria and Leesburg Pike. According to her article, most of the early roads were abandoned or incorporated into modern county road systems. Remnants of the old roads still exist in places, and the article provides guides and photographs to them. Debbie Robison, "Middle Turnpike and Leesburg Turnpike: Remnants of an Early Road," *Northern Virginia History Notes* (historical blog), February 21, 2015, http://novahistory.org/MiddleTurnpike/MiddleTurnpike.htm.

79. This is likely Lt. George R. Maxwell, 1st Michigan Cavalry. At age twenty, Maxwell, of Monroe, Michigan, enlisted on August 15, 1861, at Trenton, Michigan, as a corporal in the 1st Michigan Cavalry's Company K. After promotions to sergeant and first sergeant, he was commissioned on July 30, 1862, as first lieutenant in Company E. He rose through the ranks to lieutenant colonel on October 24, 1864, and brevet colonel on March 13, 1865. He was wounded three times: July 4, 1863, at Monterey, Maryland; May 28, 1864, at Haw's Shop, Virginia; and April 1, 1865, at the Battle of Five Forks, Virginia, just before the war ended. On that occasion, his left leg was amputated. He was mustered out on August 4, 1865. In 1869, he moved to Salt Lake City, Utah, where he served two terms as register of the *(continued)*

came back without any definite orders, the Col. went in himself & returned with orders to report at Camp. By this time it was about dark & the man who led the column got lost and we wandered around till late at night, through all the mud holes &c. which could possibly be found near Fairfax. We finally arrived safe in Camp though slightly tired and hungry.

Yesterday I rode out to the Chantilly Battle Ground with Col. Gould, Mrs. Col. Gould, Mrs. Capt. Simonds and Mrs. Frasier.[80] Had a very pleasant time.

I have just been talking with Bob Wallace who has returned from a pleasant trip to Richmond where, he says, he was put up at the "Libby Hotel,"[81] a house much frequented by military men. Fortunately Bob will not be dismissed, as was feared he would, for he had not received the orders which were published the day he was taken, not to go into any house &c.

I don't suppose I will get much time to write, for after my return from Washington I shall probably have to go on Picket again though our 30 days have elapsed long ago.

E. G. Granger

Land Office and two terms as U.S. marshal. As a federal official he also battled the Mormon Church's leadership. He died July 2, 1889, in Salt Lake City. Soldier Records and Profiles; U.S. Civil War Soldiers; "George R. Maxwell," memorial and gravestone at Findagrave.com, 63164704. Also, see John Gary Maxwell, *Gettysburg to Great Salt Lake: George R. Maxwell, Civil War Hero and Federal Marshal among the Mormons* (Norman, Okla.: Arthur H. Clark, 2010).

80. A William A. Frazer (also Frasier or Frazier) is listed in the Soldier Records and Profiles as having enlisted at age thirty-eight as first sergeant, Company A, 5th Michigan Cavalry, on August 14, 1862. Born in New Jersey, he enlisted from Romeo, Michigan. On December 16, 1862, he transferred to Company K after he was promoted to second lieutenant. However, he was honorably discharged March 24, 1863, as a supernumerary second lieutenant. No other military or pension records list him with the 5th Michigan or any other army unit during the remaining period of the war.

81. Libby Prison was among the more infamous Confederate prisons during the Civil War. Located in a three-story brick warehouse on two levels on Tobacco Row along the James River waterfront in Richmond, Virginia, it was used primarily to house Union officers as prisoners. Wallace was quite fortunate to have been exchanged so soon after his imprisonment. For fuller details, see Wallace, *A Few Memories*, 20–27.

[LETTER 10]

Reserve Camp Out Post
June 7th, 1863 [Sunday]

Dear Mollie

The package Lieut Bristol brought from home to me was most welcome. I assure you. Having been unwell I could not relish a soldier's fare very much, and those pickles were the first things that had really tasted good to me. The dried fruit finds a ready market down here. Tell Aunt Lucy that I am very much obliged for the plums, and tell Uncle Edward[82] that those stockings came just in the nick of time for I had only one pair left and those I had worn over a month without any change.

The handkerchiefs were also just what I wanted, in fact, there was not much of anything that I did not want just then, but I have been to Washington since then and now am in want of nothing [illegible] money of which a soldier is always short. I have been paid at last and have sent to Uncle Charles $240.00, or rather I sent him $270.00 with a request that he send me $30.00 back.

When I was in Washington I had a dozen photographs taken for your benefit as I threatened to, but as I had just been sick I thought I looked bad enough without the extra effect of my hair, so I had it taken with my hat. The picture more than justifies my opinion, as it shows off my thin face to the best advantage but if it could only take off its hat to you, it would scare you out of your senses.[83]

You know I had not been paid the last time the Regt. was paid & I expected to have to go to Washington to get my pay. But the Regt. was paid off again a little while ago and as I had been mustered in, I got my 4 months pay. The day after the next I went to Washington.

I had been so long in the woods with "nothing to wear" that when I got on a clean suit I felt like a new man (or, rather, boy). I was in the City only forty eight hours, so I did not have much chance to go

---

82. As noted earlier, these individuals are his uncle Edward C. Walker and his wife, Lucy.
83. In his next letter, Granger reports that he was suffering from diphtheria. Other diseases commonly found in army camps or soldier ranks were typhoid fever, smallpox, measles, pneumonia, malaria, and tuberculosis.

anywhere, but I visited the Government green house for the first time. The collection of flowers is not very large, but there are a great many Tropical plants which were new to me. Palm trees of many different kinds, Bananna trees. There was one marked "Hybiscus" [Hibiscus] which had a beautiful blossom of the same shape as the blossom of our Hybiscus, but has layers of white and bright cherry red.

The night I was in Washington I went to Grovers Theatre to see Lucille Western[84] play Camille.

I was foolish enough to leave my pass at the hotel, and of course an officer came into the Theatre to look for passes. The consequence was, I was ordered to report, under arrest, at the corner of 19th & I Sts., at 10 A.M. the next day. Of course, when I showed my pass, the next morning, I was all right. This is the only time I have had the honor of being under arrest yet.

When I got back from Washington I reported out here for duty and last Monday [June 1] I was sent out on the Ox Road and Wednesday [June 3] we went out on Lawyer's [Lawyers] Road.[85] Here Bristol and I relieved each other every six hours, and just as I came out to relieve him at 3 A.M. Thursday while the relief was going round it was fired on by a party of Rebs, who were concealed in the bushes on our side of the road. Bristol and I were at post No. 5, about a mile from the place where the relief was fired on.[86]

---

84. Pauline Lucille Western was born on January 8, 1843, making her slightly older than Granger himself. She appeared for many years on the stage, but died early, at age thirty-four, on January 11, 1877, in Brooklyn, New York.

85. Precisely where Granger's duties took him is impossible to state today, but modern West Ox Road is State Highway 608 and intersects with Lawyers Road, State Highway 674, northwest of Fairfax, Virginia, in the vicinity of Herndon, Virginia. The site would be east of Dulles International Airport and south of the Dulles Toll Road, Highway 267.

86. One of Granger's enlisted comrades, Corp. James Avery, also reported on the raid in his own memoirs. He said only one man was wounded, while Granger reported three. Otherwise, their accounts are similar, to the point where both men criticize the detachment's overall commander, Colonel Gray. Avery states that Gray took too long to get his troops organized which allowed the raiding Confederates to escape. He said, "The only way to succeed in Cavalry is to work quickly, the more like lightning the better, for this is the true mode of mounted fighting." Gray had Granger's company and another from the 6th Michigan Cavalry with him. See Wittenberg, *Under Custer's Command*, 26. For more detail about the expedition itself, see O'Neill, *Chasing Jeb Stuart*, 207.

CAMP LIFE AND PICKET DUTY						89

The Rebs fired out one volley wounding two men slightly, killing one horse and wounding 3 others. All the men run to the next Post No. 2 except Sergeant Hobbs[87] of our Co. and Sergt. Bibbins[88] of Co. M.

These two rallied the men as soon as possible the men being, some of them, a little frightened and the horses still more so. They brought the men back to the scene of action and made them fire a volley, but the Rebs had run before this time.

At Post No. 5 we did not hear the fire of the Rebs at all, but as soon as we heard the firing of our own men we started ~~for~~ on the gallop and before we had gone far we met Sergt. Bibbins coming back on the run to tell us what was the matter. We then put our horses to the test of their speed and for the next two or three hours ~~the~~ we scoured the country in all directions but of course the Rebs got away as they knew the Country so much better than we did. After that all was quiet till 8 o'clock when we heard firing which I supposed to be our lines again. I started off with all the men I had in the Reserve and soon found that it was no where near our lines. When we had run two or three miles at a keen gallop, we saw a line of Cavalry, about 60 in number, which we supposed to be our own men, but were not sure. As we drew nearer we saw them dismount and prepare to receive us with their rifles.

By this time I could distinguish Maj. Ferry though they could not recognize us on account of the dust so I ordered my command to walk and presently the Maj. saw who we were and motioned us to come on. We again took the gallop and as we came near the line we saw that there had been something of a skirmish as we passed an officer's hat and a revolver in the road and could see a dead horse lying near the line. On coming up they told us that Mosby had just been there and chased the rear guard of the Sixth right into and through Co. F. of the

---

87. John E. Hobbs, of York, Michigan, enlisted at age forty-four in Granger's Company C, 5th Michigan Cavalry, on August 25, 1862. He was promoted to corporal on October 6, 1862, and later commissary sergeant. He was mustered out of the regiment on June 19, 1865, at Fort Leavenworth, Kansas. Soldier Records and Profiles; U.S. Civil War Soldiers.

88. Madison W. Bibbins, of Coldwater, Michigan, had enlisted as a sergeant in Company M, 5th Michigan, on August 16, 1862. On December 30, 1862, he was promoted to first sergeant. On March 4, 1864, he was commissioned as a second lieutenant and promoted to first lieutenant on August 10, 1864. By February 1, 1865, he was promoted to captain. He, too, was mustered out of the regiment on June 19, 1865, at Fort Leavenworth, Kansas. Soldier Records and Profiles; U.S. Civil War Soldiers.

Fifth, taking seven prisoners, wounding one man, killing the horse of Lieut. Sabine [Alvin Sabin][89] of Co. F. and wounding several more horses, without sustaining any loss but that of their surgeon. After we came up, the whole force under Col. Gray started in pursuit but they moved so slow that I soon became disgusted and returned to my Post. The rest were kept all day chasing (at a walk) the smartest man in this part of Virginia. Of course, they produced nothing.

In the attack on our Relief, Hobbs and Bibbins behaved splendidly. Though both of their horses were wounded the boys were so cool that they stopped them before they had run far and turned back immediately and rode up to the spot where they were fired on, though they did not know but the Rebs were still there and if they had been the boys would have been in a very dangerous place, as it was impossible to force a horse through the pine brush behind which the Rebs were concealed.

The boy whose horse was shot under him was a cool specimen. The horse was shot in the neck, bullet cutting the main artery, and he fell like a log catching the boy's leg under him. Reynolds[90] could not get out

---

89. Alvin N. Sabin enlisted as first sergeant in Company E, 5th Michigan Cavalry, on August 12, 1862. He was commissioned as a second lieutenant on May 28, 1863, and was wounded in action on July 24, 1863, at Newby's Crossroads, Virginia. He was promoted to first lieutenant, Company K, on March 5, 1864. On May 6, 1864, he was again wounded in the fighting at the Wilderness. He was promoted to captain of Company C on October 21, 1864, two months after Granger's death. Sabin received a promotion to brevet major on March 13, 1865, for gallant and meritorious services during the war. He was mustered out at Fort Leavenworth, Kansas, on June 19, 1865. Soldier Records and Profiles; U.S. Civil War Soldiers.

90. This was likely eighteen-year-old Polydore (sometimes Polodore) Milton Reynolds, of Ovid, Michigan. Born on December 9, 1844, in Penbrook, New York, he had enlisted in Company M, 5th Michigan Cavalry, on August 16, 1862, at Coldwater, Michigan. At some point he was promoted to sergeant and served throughout the regiment's time in the field. He was discharged June 19, 1865, at Fort Leavenworth, Kansas. Five other men with the last name of Reynolds served in the regiment, but Polydore, the youngest, more closely fits Granger's usage of the word "boy." Granger was only about twenty months older than Reynolds. After the war, Reynolds worked as an architect. Reynolds died on October 16, 1918, in Van Buren Township, Wayne County, Michigan, and was buried in Hillside Cemetery, Belleville, Michigan. According to his pension record, filed in 1875, he was also known as Fred M. Reynolds. After his death, his wife, Ellen Jane Reynolds (1866–1940), filed for a widow's pension. Soldier Records and Profiles; "Sgt. Polydore Milton Reynolds,"

and so he lay still and loosened his rifle which was fastened to his saddle. When the boys came up, they said he did not appear at all scared.

I have got to go out again in half an hour so I must begin to get ready.

Tell Mother that I will answer her letter as soon as possible but now we have to keep awake so much when we are on duty that we are too tired to write when we are in here.

Ed. G. Granger

I send a notice of our "fight" which I cut from the N. Y. Herald to show to you how near the truth such reports generally are.

E. G. G.

❋ ❋ ❋

[LETTER 11]

Reserve Camp Post Va. Near Fairfax
June 12 1863 [Friday]

Dear Mother

I received your letter of the 5th Inst this morning and though you are probably aware by this time that I am neither dead nor sick I thought I would write immediately as I don't know what infernal lies Keith[91]

---

memorial and gravestone at Findagrave.com, 61513499; Michigan, Death Records, 1867–1950, database at Ancestry.com, original data from Michigan Department of Community Health, Division for Vital Records and Statistics, Lansing, Mich. (hereafter cited as Michigan Death Records); U.S., Civil War Pension Index: General Index to Pension Files, 1861–1934, database at Ancestry.com, original data from National Archives and Records Administration, Washington, D.C. (hereafter cited as Civil War Pension Index).

91. This is William Keith, of Detroit, commissioned at age thirty as second lieutenant in Company F, 5th Michigan Cavalry, on August 14, 1862, the same day as Granger himself. However, as he was born on April 16, 1832, he was considerably older than Granger. Keith was promoted to first lieutenant on December 1, 1862. He served on General Custer's staff from July 1 to December 1863. On March 5, 1864, he was discharged on account of disability. On June 4, 1863, he married Anna F. Brewster. In the late 1880s, Keith worked as the Bay City, Michigan, comptroller. He died on December 2, 1904, in Bay City. Soldier Records and Profiles; Michigan Death Records; Civil War Pension Index; "William Keith," memorial at Findagrave.com, 73564338.

has been telling you. I heard that he said I had been sick ever since I left Washington &c &c. Now the truth is just what I have already told you. I never was unwell a moment till I was taken with the dipthaeria one Sunday morning. The Dr thought at one time that it was Quinsey[92] & I believe I wrote home to that effect but I know that it was dipthaeria. I was taken first with a chill and thought I had the ague & told Bristol that it was the ague, & I never thought to tell him that it was not, so that is the reason you heard I had the ague. The Monday afternoon after I was taken I went into Camp and into the Hospital where I received as good care and attention as I could have anywhere.

Our Company was out on picket, but one of my men who is in the Quartermaster Department, a rough sailor for whom I had obtained a furlough from Hunt eight or nine months ago, used to bring me all of the delicacies that I could eat as long as I was in the Hospital. I was very sick for a day or two but was well and out of the Doctor's care in less than a week. But this little sore throat took away my strength as thoroughly as the ague would have done, so I lay around Camp a good while "recruiting." But I staid much longer than I should have done, on account of my pay &c. As soon as I got back from Washington I came out here for duty, and have been on duty ever since and have even done double duty in the eating line. I am as well as I ever was, but no one would believe now, that I was ever a Gymnast. However I am playing base ball whenever I am off duty and am going to take sparring lessons to try and recover some of my lost muscle.

Now I hope you are satisfied in regard to the state of my health. but if you ever believe that I am sick when I say I am well on the word of any such fool as Keith, I won't condescend to contradict his report again. I have given Mollie a description of the attack on the pickets on the Lawyer's Road. The next day after I wrote to her we went out there again and while there one of the pickets said that he had seen a party of dismounted men just a little outside the lines. I started out to see whether I could find any thing of them, taking some men with me. As we had to pass through a pretty rough thicket there was soon only one man with me. When we emerged from the woods we were in sight of one of our pickets, though we could not see him. He didn't know that we were out, and commenced firing at us.

---

92. This is a form of tonsillitis.

CAMP LIFE AND PICKET DUTY

Lt. William Keith.
Courtesy of Paul Davis.

We were only about fifty-rods from him but, luckily, he was not a very good shot, still, by the time 3 balls had struck within a rod of our horses heels. I thought it time to commence a retreat which was accomplished in good order and without loss.

So you see I have been "under fire."

We are in a terrible state of anxiety [illegible] fear in this Camp at least [illegible] seems to expect Mosby here every day. Keeps us saddled (or rather our horses) all the time, and yesterday he kept the Brigade in line several hours, <u>waiting for orders</u>, which never came.

We have at last got a Colonel. He is Lt. Col. [Russell] Alger[93] of the Sixth. I have not seen him yet, and don't know any thing about him.

---

93. Colonel Russell A. Alger, born February 27, 1836, in Lafayette, Ohio, was one of the better-known officers in the 5th Michigan and the Michigan Cavalry Brigade. He entered the army on September 2, 1861, as captain of Company C, 2nd Michigan Cavalry. He was promoted to major on April 2, 1862. On July 1, 1862, he was wounded and taken prisoner at Boonesville, Mississippi, but escaped that day. On October 27, 1862, he resigned his commission in the 2nd Cavalry to accept a lieutenant colonelcy in the newly formed 6th Michigan Cavalry. As Granger states, on June 11, 1863, he was mustered in as the colonel of the 5th Michigan, with *(continued)*

Col. Russell A. Alger.
Courtesy of John Beckendorf.

I rec'd a letter from Uncle Charles Yesterday containing thirty Dollars. I will write to him as soon as I get another chance.

---

his rank backdated to February 28. Governor Austin Blair had selected Alger for the position over Lieutenant Colonel Gould and George Armstrong Custer, a young West Pointer and former aide to Major General McClellan. On July 3, 1863, Alger led the regiment at Gettysburg, but was wounded five days later at Boonsboro, Maryland. He remained out of action until September 13, 1863. At the Battle of Trevilian Station, he led a controversial cavalry charge that captured a large Confederate force, but took the regiment far beyond its support. On September 20, 1864, Alger resigned his commission. After the war, he gained success in the lumber business and in politics. In 1884, he was elected governor of Michigan. In March 1897, President William McKinley appointed Alger as secretary of war. However, Alger was criticized for the military's performance during the Spanish-American War and at the president's request, he resigned on August 1, 1899. However, as secretary, he took steps to ensure that his old enemy, Col. John S. Mosby, was unable to obtain a post in the McKinley administration. Alger enjoyed one more success in politics, when in 1902 Michigan's governor appointed him to fill a term in the U.S. Senate. Alger was subsequently elected to his own term in January 1903 but died in office on January 24, 1907. He was brevetted major general, U.S. Volunteers, on June 11, 1865, for gallant and meritorious services during the war. Soldier Records and Profiles; Michigan Death Records; "Russell Alexander Alger," memorial and photographs at Findagrave.com, 12646.

We shall probably go out again tomorrow, unless there is another alarm this afternoon or tomorrow morning.—I have just received an order to report to Capt. [David] Oliphant[94] with fifteen men at 1 P.M. today for duty on the Lawyer's road.

Tell Mollie to answer my letter soon as I am anxious to hear from her on a subject of great importance to me.[95]

E. G. Granger

---

94. David Oliphant of Detroit entered the service as a first lieutenant in Company B, 5th Michigan Cavalry on August 14, 1862. Promoted to captain on December 3, 1862, he was wounded at Brandy Station, Virginia, on October 13, 1863, and again on May 28, 1864, at the Battle of Haw's Shop, Virginia. He died June 4, 1864, in Washington, D.C. Soldier Records and Profiles; Michigan Death Records; "Capt. David Oliphant," memorial and gravestone at Findagrave.com, 54913450.

95. Unfortunately, we never learn what that issue of great importance was. We do not have Mollie's own letters to her brother. By the next time he writes home, he would be in the midst of the Gettysburg Campaign. By then, the issue seemingly had been forgotten.

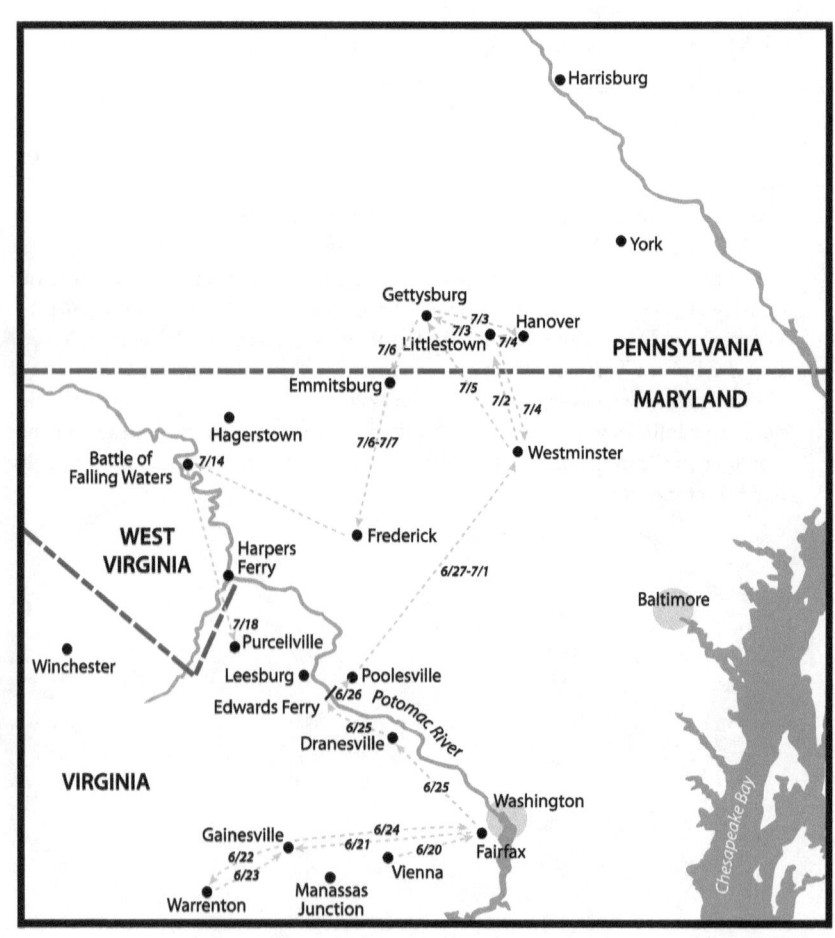

Granger's route during the Gettysburg Campaign, June 17–July 18, 1863. *Map by Gary Raham.*

CHAPTER 3

A SUMMER AND FALL OF CAMPAIGNING

Heretofore, Granger's writings have focused on camp life and the relative safety of picket duty. After some six months of, at best, minor military activity, Granger and his comrades in the 5th Michigan Cavalry Regiment were about to begin experiencing serious combat. In his first two letters in this section he recounts his experiences before, during, and after the important Battle of Gettysburg, July 1–3, 1863. The first letter, however, was written to his mother more than three weeks after his last one (at least that we have today), and two weeks after a second that is not included in the family's collection. He wrote it two days after the fighting at Gettysburg, Pennsylvania, had ended, when he finally had time to inform his family that he was all right. The letter also conveys a far different tone compared to his earlier ones. No longer did Granger see his army duties as some youthful grand adventure. Combat, he now realized, involved deadly business.

A few weeks before, as part of Stahel's cavalry division, now part of the Army of the Potomac, the Michiganders under command of Brig. Gen. Joseph Copeland had marched away from their long-term monotonous duties on the Washington, D.C., picket lines into Maryland and toward Gettysburg. The Union forces were pursuing the Confederate Army of Northern Virginia, which was believed to be on the advance in Pennsylvania. On June 25, 1863, Copeland's brigade forded the Potomac River, some men at Edwards Ferry and most at Young's Island Ford. However, after the river rose quickly, Stahel opted to leave his supply train on the south bank. Maj. Crawley P. Dake commanded a 5th Michigan battalion guarding the brigade train. Among his officers was Lieutenant Granger. The rest of the brigade marched on to Poolesville, Maryland.

On June 27, Copeland's troops camped on a farm near Frederick, Maryland. The next day he led the 5th and 6th Regiments on a reconnaissance toward Pennsylvania. Meanwhile, Maj. Gen. Joseph Hooker had been replaced by Maj. Gen. George Gordon Meade as commander of the Army of the Potomac. That change soon had a ripple effect across the army's cavalry units.

On June 28, the brigade rode into Gettysburg itself and stayed for several hours. Captain Safford reported, "The people gave us a great welcome. Flowers. A beautiful little girl gave me flowers. Food of all kinds & take us to their homes."[1] Enemy troops apparently had just departed the town. More important, Copeland had learned that Robert E. Lee's main body of troops from the Army of Northern Virginia was at Chambersburg, Pennsylvania, twenty-three miles west. Other Confederate troops were north and east of Gettysburg. Copeland dispatched couriers to carry the news to the headquarters of the Army of the Potomac.

During the early hours of June 29, 1863, as Copeland and his staff were riding toward Emmitsburg, a military courier stopped him with shocking news. Instead of receiving expected praise from his superiors for his successful scouting mission, the fifty-five-year-old Michigan officer had been relieved of command of the Michigan Cavalry Brigade. Stahel also was out at the division level. Replacing Stahel was Brig. Gen. Judson Kilpatrick, who reorganized the unit into two brigades. Cavalry commander Alfred Pleasonton also assigned three of his own staff members as newly minted brigadier generals. One was George Armstrong Custer, who would replace the capable but unlucky Copeland in leading the Michigan Cavalry Brigade.

In his first July letter, Granger failed to mention the changes in commanders. Given his whereabouts at the time, Granger's silence on the matter as he wrote his letter may have had more to do with his

---

1. Davis, *I Rode with Custer*, 31–32.

Brigadier General Custer and General Pleasonton
at Warrenton, Virginia, October 1863.
Courtesy of Little Bighorn Battlefield National Monument.

absence from the regiment. Granger and his Company C remained assigned to guard the wagon train for the Michigan Cavalry Brigade. Thus, he took no part in the regiment's sharp fighting that erupted at Hanover, Pennsylvania, on June 30 under its new brigadier general, or at the East Cavalry Field on July 3, when the brigade again encountered the cavalry command of Confederate major general J. E. B. Stuart. Custer did not appear in his writings until Granger's next letter.

Twice, however, while out on his own scouting missions apart from his brigade, Granger did venture onto the greater Gettysburg battlefield. Apparently on July 3, he found himself sheltered behind a ridge while the enemy's troops under Maj. Gen. George Pickett were storming the Union lines three quarters of a mile away on Cemetery Ridge. After the fighting ended and the Northern troops went in

Uncle Ferdinand and Aunt Elmira Walker. *Courtesy of Jim Adams.*

pursuit of the retreating Confederates, Granger was detailed to locate the brigade's wagon train. As a result of his lengthy absence, he and his small detachment were for a time reported as missing in action.

Granger did not write again to his family until July 18. The biggest news he had for the family concerned his assignment as commander of Company C serving as General Custer's provost guard and personal escort. That probably explains how he came to be added to Custer's staff the next month. The general would have become familiar with him and his abilities during this period. A staff appointment naturally would have followed.

In his series of letters home, Granger made clear that he also was corresponding with other members of the extended family. Most of those letters written beyond his immediate family apparently have been lost. However, one important exception surfaced late during the preparation of this book. Jim Adams of Peterborough, New Hampshire, provided the editor with a copy of a letter that the lieutenant wrote on August 22, 1863, to his eleven-year-old maternal first cousin, Emma Walker, from the brigade's camp near Falmouth, Virginia.[2] Because ownership of this letter is separate from the other forty-three extant letters that Granger sent home to Michigan, it is listed separately without a number, but it has been placed in its proper chronological position.

Young Emma likely had written to her soldier cousin in late July or early August 1863. Given her age, she undoubtedly was excited to receive word from him. She retained the letter for the rest of her life as well as two photos that Granger had given her. The materials have come down through the family line to Adams, who is Emma's great-great-grandson. After Granger was reported killed in action in August 1864, Emma, who would have been twelve by that time, must have been devastated.

Although that letter is one of Granger's shortest, it is important for two reasons. First, he confirmed the date, August 20, 1863, that he received his orders detailing him to Custer's personal staff. He also offered his first opinions about his recently appointed brigade commander. Another letter in his full series—letter 16, written to Mollie on September 3—reveals his personal excitement about Custer and his own new staff assignment. Granger's appointment to the staff was certainly important. It signified Custer's belief in the youth. While Granger served his commander well on the staff for nearly twelve months, the next August the position would cost Granger his life.

---

2. Emma Walker (1851–1926), the daughter of Ferdinand and Elmira Walker, was a first cousin to Lieutenant Granger. Her father was a brother of Granger's mother, Matilda. As she was born on November 5, 1851, Emma would have been only age eleven at the time she wrote to Edward Granger.

[LETTER 12]

Camp of Co. 5th Regt. Mich. Cav.
Guarding Train of Custer's Brigade
Kilpatrick's Division of Pleasonton's Cav.
Corp. Army of the Potomac, Gen. Meade
Westminster Md July 5 1863 [Sunday]

Dear Mother

At last I have a chance to write for the first time since the 21st of June [Sunday].[3] Two weeks ago today, in fact, it is longer than that, that we have been on the move.

About 3 or 4 weeks ago Lt. Col. Alger of the 6th was made Col. of the 5th and soon after the Regt. commenced moving from the place where we had been doing Picket duty, to Vienna a distance of about ten miles. We moved by Companies as fast as we were relieved. Cos. C and E were the last ones to move. We were relieved Monday afternoon [June 15] & expected to go that evening but Col. Gray was at Fairfax and we had to wait for orders. Tuesday, Col. Gray returned, but he was so drunk that he could give no orders. ~~and we~~ When he was coming through Fairfax he fell off his horse and got a black eye and a scratch on his face. Then he put spurs to his horse & rode through town at the top of his speed, covered with mud & his face all bloody. As Hooker was there with three of his Corps, of course the streets were full of officers. So Gray "cut a great swell."

That night at 10 1/2 P.M. we were ordered outside the lines on a scout from which we returned at 7:00 A.M. Wednesday [June 17]. After about an hour's sleep we finally recd. orders to go to Vienna. It was a very hot day and the dust was so thick that I could not see the second set of twos ahead of me, part of the time. Vienna was much better than Fairfax for a Picket post. We could get all we wanted to eat, and we only had to be on duty one day in three, while at Fairfax we were on almost two out of three days. But we had not long to enjoy our new position for Saturday afternoon [June 20] we had to return to Fairfax—not to the picket Reserve but to the camp of the Regt. We arrived at Camp at about dark and found all the tents down and everything packed, ready to go to Washington & we were informed that we were to join

---

3. No letter of that date remains in the family's collection.

the "Army of the Potomac." That night it rained right smart, as they say down here. I lay down among the tents and covered myself with one or two of them and slept soundly. Sunday morning [June 21] we could hear the roar of cannon, as we supposed in the direction of Bull Run. After waiting three or four of the longest hours I ever saw, the bugle sounded "to horse" every man started for his horse with a yell, and in a few minutes we were in the road.

The cannonading continued until 3 or 4 P.M. but we did not get any nearer to it. We camped that night 3 miles beyond Gainesville, at which place we saw the 2d Corps. The inhabitants here thought the firing was at Harpers Ferry but it proved to have been a fight between Pleasonton & Stuart at Aldie.[4]

The next day [June 22] we continued our march to Warrenton, where part of the force encamped while Scouting parties were sent in every direction.[5] As far as the Rappahannock one way & to the Blue Ridge in another. That night I had command of the Pickets at Warrenton. From one of my posts I saw the most beautiful scenery I have seen for many years. The next day [June 23] we returned to Gainesville and the next [June 24] to Fairfax where we lay one day and then started for the army. We went via Drainsville [Dranesville] to Edwards Ferry where we crossed forded the Potomac [June 26].[6] There was one pontoon

---

4. Granger is inaccurate here. Actually, the fighting had been farther west at Middleburg, well beyond Aldie. Aldie had occurred on June 17. On June 19, Pleasonton had made an effort with his Cavalry Corps to force his way across the Loudoun Valley by sending Brig. Gen. David Gregg's division through Middleburg to Ashby's Gap and Brig. Gen. John Buford toward Snicker's Gap. Pleasonton had little success in pushing Stuart's troops out of the area. The firing that Granger and his comrades heard on June 21 was probably from a battle at Upperville, Virginia, between Pleasonton's troops and those of Confederate general Wade Hampton. Stuart's ability to hold off Pleasonton's cavalry deprived the Union high command of the knowledge that Gen. Robert E. Lee was already moving his infantry divisions across the Potomac River into Maryland. O'Neill, *Chasing Jeb Stuart*, 225–28.
5. According to O'Neill, these troops were the 1st Michigan Cavalry under the command of Lt. Col. Peter Stagg. O'Neill, *Chasing Jeb Stuart*, 228.
6. Some members of the brigade and Stahel's cavalry division may have crossed at Young's Island Ford, a location some distance below Edwards Ferry. Rising water had made the crossing at Edwards Ferry more difficult, but Granger makes no mention of that. According to online articles by Craig Swain, the ford may be about a mile and a half to twelve miles below Edwards Ferry. Swain stated that it was one of several crossing points of the Potomac River in the vicinity *(continued)*

bridge just about where we forded the river, across which the infantry were marching four abreast in a column so long that during the two or three hours that we were near it we could see neither end of it.

They were building another bridge for the trains which filled every road we could see in every direction. That night we stopped near Poolesville, Md. and the next day [June 27] the Regiment went on, leaving our Battalion under Major Dake to escort the train when it should come up. Since that time we have been engaged in the honorable and <u>dangerous</u> business of guarding the train, while the Reg. is gloriously fighting at the front. At one time we got within a few miles of where our troops are now fighting the battle of Gettysburg but we immediately retreated to our present position 24 miles from any possibility of danger.

We arrived here Wednesday [July 1] about 3 P.M. & that same afternoon I was ordered to take 5 or 6 of my best men and go out & try to find the train of our Brig. of our Corps., which had left us some days before and of whose whereabouts nothing definite was known.

I took Fred Nims & 5 other boys & started out. That night we stopped a few miles from town & camped in an oatfield, which suited our horses very well. The next day [July 2] we met the Quartermaster of the Brigade of which we were in search, and gave him the order to report to the Corp./Quartermaster with his train. He said he had orders for the train to move to Hanover and that we might as well go directly to Hanover which was only 7 or 8 miles from where we then were. That just suited us, as it would give us a chance to go to the battle field and still be in Hanover before the train.

The road from Littlestown [Pennsylvania] to the battlefield was filled with those whose wounds were not ~~sufficiently~~ severe enough to prevent their walking. We must have seen at least a thousand men who were wounded in their hands or arms, and a good many who had slight wounds in the head. I forgot to say that soon after I got out of town the first night, we met a buggy full of wounded officers. It was

---

of Leesburg, Virginia. However, its place name has become obsolete and the historical record provides an imprecise description of the site. See Craig Swain, "Young's Island Ford," *To the Sound of Guns* (historical blog), September 13, 2009, https://markerhunter.wordpress.com/2009/09/13/youngs-island-ford/ and Swain, "Edwards Ferry—Cavalry Corps Crossing—Part 1," August 10, 2009, https://markerhunter.wordpress.com/2009/08/10/edwards-ferry-cavalry-corps-crossing-pt1/.

Maj. Gen. J. E. B. Stuart.
Courtesy of Library of Congress, 38003u.

pretty dark & I did not notice the officers very particularly but just as we had passed I was surprised to hear someone call me by name & going back I found that it was Gus Buhl who was wounded in the leg: The wound was evidently quite a severe flesh wound, but nothing serious at all dangerous. About 1 P.M. Friday [July 3] we arrived on the battle field.[7] The first we saw of the army was Pleasonton's Corps.

There comes an order to move in an hour so I must close. I will write again telling you what I saw of the battle. Suffice it to say I am all right & sure to stay for the rest of the war for it is almost impossible to get away from these trains when once attached to them. I saw Sam & Lycurgus the other day both well.

Ed. G. Granger

---

7. Interestingly, Granger fails to mention the severe fighting in which his comrades of the Michigan Cavalry Brigade were taking part at that very hour. Union cavalry brigades under Brig. Gen. David M. Gregg, including Custer's brigade, clashed with Confederate cavalry brigades under Maj. Gen. Jeb Stuart in what became known as East Cavalry Field, southeast of Gettysburg. For more details on this classic encounter, see Longacre, *Custer*, 121–65.

✳ ✳ ✳

[LETTER 13]

In Camp near Purcellville Loudoun Co. Va.
July 18 1863 [Saturday]

Dear Mollie

Lt. Keith says that Mother is very anxious to hear from me &c &c. I presume she has not recd. the letter I wrote in Frederick when she applied to Mrs. Keith for information as to my safety. There is no need of being alarmed about me because you don't hear, for if anything was the matter you would hear fast enough from Bristol.[8]

This is the first chance I have had to write since I left Frederick and will be very apt to be the last till the campaign is ended, & this letter may be cut short as the other was by an order to move.

I believe my last, ~~was~~ ended just as I was going to tell what I saw of the Battle of Gettysburg. We got on the field about noon [Friday, July 3] & the first thing that struck me was the coolness of every one near the field. The cavalry at Gen. Pleasanton's [Pleasonton's] Head Quarters was all dismounted and the horses unbridled and feeding while the men were cooking their coffee. We went over to the left of the Pike to try to get near the batteries but we soon met a crowd walking the other way just as quietly & coolly as though they were in Camp but at a pretty good rate. Many of them were wounded and we found out that the enemy were shelling a Hospital in that direction whereupon we retired in good order to the Pike. One of the men we met coming from the hospital had one arm shot off & he was leaning on one of his comrades & looking around as coolly as anyone apparently interested in everything that was going on.

When we got on to the Pike we went along to within about three quarters of a mile of Cemetery Hill where the Hardest of that day's (Friday July 3) fight took place. While we were here we witnessed the "grandest Artillery duel of the war," and though ~~the~~ the charge of Longstreet's Corps[9] was concealed from us by the Hill, we were

---

8. While Granger was seeking to reassure his sister, in the end things would not quite work out that way. When Granger was killed on August 16, 1864, Bristol had already been discharged for disability on July 5, 1864, from the army.

9. This charge is best remembered as Pickett's Charge, named after Confederate major

near enough to hear the yells of the Rebs as they charged. Then the prisoners began to pour in—we saw more than 3000 of them in one body. They had evidently been fighting well, for more than 1/3 of them were wounded. They seem to feel pretty well satisfied with their fate, however, in being taken and most of them were not very anxious to see any more fighting.

I obtained from one of them a Rebel postage stamp which I will enclose if I don't forget it as I did those flowers I was going to send you once. We left the battle field about 7 o'clock P.M. & to went to nearby Hanover where we expected to find the trains. The next morning [July 4] we went to the village but there was no train there & had been none the day before.

Then we went to Littlestown where I met Lt. [Samuel] Harris[10] of Co. A who told us that Maj Ferry was dead—shot in the head the day before, at Gettysburg. From Littlestown we went to Westminster where the we found the train all right.

The next night [July 5] the train and escort started for Frederick. As Bob had a sore back I rode a large grey mule which one of the men had picked up. After marching a little while I was ordered to go back to Westminster and taking the road to Gettysburg, to order all the teams of our train which I should meet to go to Frederick by the nearest road. When we had gone a mile or two on the Gettysburg Pike we turned in—getting a splendid bed on a barn floor, where we stayed till morning—while the Company was marching in a pouring

---

general George E. Pickett (1825–1875). His division, much to Pickett's frustration, had been the last to arrive on the Gettysburg field, but on the climactic third day, it was one of three divisions under the command of Lt. Gen. James Longstreet to participate in a disastrous assault on Union positions on July 3. His division was shattered, a result which haunted Pickett ever after until his death in 1875. In the closing days of the war, Pickett was defeated while in command of the Confederate troops at the Battle of Five Forks.

10. Samuel Harris of Rochester, Michigan, was born on September 15, 1836, in Hartford, Vermont and worked as a machinist. He was mustered into Company A, 5th Michigan Cavalry, on August 26, 1862, as a second lieutenant and on January 1, 1863, was promoted to first lieutenant. He was wounded in action on March 2, 1864, at Richmond, Virginia, and taken prisoner the next day at Old Church, Virginia. Exchanged on December 10, 1864, he was discharged on April 17, 1865, on account of his wounds received in action. Later in life, he moved to Illinois, where he married Sarah S. Harris. He died May 4, 1920, in Chicago, Illinois. U.S. Civil War Soldiers; Soldier Records and Profiles; 1880 U.S. Federal Census for Samuel Harris.

rain. The next day [July 6] we went on & got to Gettysburg before we met the last of our train. We had an excellent opportunity to see the Battlefield and we spent five hours on the field. All our dead have been buried but quite a number of Rebs still lay on the field where they had fallen in the grand charge of Friday. The city was full of wounded soldiers, every house being used for a Hospital.

We took the road for Frederick via Emmitsburg and about 6 miles from the field we came across the Michigan Fourth. Sam[11] was not with the Regt., but in the Hospital of the Division so I did not see him. I suppose of course you have heard that he is slightly wounded in the arm "just enough to give him a leave of absence" as an officer of the 4th, who had just seen him, told me.

I was slightly surprised to find the Army of the Potomac scattered along the road from Gettysburg to Frederick instead of being in "full pursuit" of the "flying foe" as all the newspaper correspondents had it, and I was still more surprised, on arriving at Emmitsburg Monday night [July 6], to find that the Rebs had only left that morning though Emmitsburg was the extreme left of our line of Battle & I suppose that the enemy had left in hot haste Saturday morning. The next day [July 7] we arrived at Frederick where we found that we had been reported captured and the Capt. was feeling terribly for the loss of his <u>mule</u>, which, I forgot to say, gave out with me the second day and I traded him off for a good one which a drunken Dutchman was trying to lead with such poor success that he was willing to trade for any thing. We laid around Frederick several days while the Regt. was distinguishing itself in six battles with Stuart's Cav., in five of which, they, (our Cav.) came off victorious and the manner in Kilpatrick's got them out of the other scrape gave his officers more confidence in their General than all the victories. On the 13th Inst. he joined our Regt. at Hagerstown and the same day we (Co. C) were detailed on a more ingloriously safe duty than guarding the train, i.e., Provost Guard to Gen. Custer (not Costar as the papers got it).

In that capacity we acted at the Battle of Falling Waters on the 14th & in that capacity we are acting now. We crossed the Potomac yesterday and to day are lying still but Capt. [Robert] Judson[12] says we

---

11. Sam Walker, Granger's cousin. See chapter 2, note 33.
12. Born on September 26, 1826, in Litchfield, Connecticut, Robert F. Judson was a lawyer from Kalamazoo, Michigan. He was commissioned on August 14, 1862, as the

Capt. Robert Judson.
Courtesy of John Beckendorf.

shall start soon. I suppose you know Capt. Judson is Chief of Staff to Custer who is now in command of the division. Bristol is also on his Staff as Commissary of Musters. Tell Mother our position in Battle is one mile beyond the reach of shell guarding prisoners, picking up

---

captain of Company L, 6th Michigan Cavalry. As a teenager, he studied four years at Yale University, and he then went to teach in Warrenton, Virginia, a town that he would frequently visit as a Michigan soldier during the Civil War. In 1853, he moved to Falls Church, Virginia, where he established a private school. In 1856, he moved again, to Kalamazoo, Michigan, where he completed his law studies and in 1858 was admitted to the bar. On April 7, 1863, he was appointed as the acting assistant inspector general at the brigade's headquarters. He was honorably discharged on October 7, 1864, on account of physical disability. He received a brevet to major on March 13, 1865, for gallant and meritorious service. Soldier Records and Profiles; "Robert F. Judson," memorial and gravestone at Findagrave.com, 30755765.

stragglers &c &c. I probably shan't have a chance to write again for a month or two if the army don't go into winter quarters.

Ed. G. Granger

I had to borrow ink & envelope & steal paper and I am sitting on the ground with a hard tack box for a desk.

E. G. Granger

✳ ✳ ✳

[LETTER 14]

Headquarters, 3rd Div. Cav. Corps
Warrenton Junction, Va. Aug. 3d 1863 [Monday]

Dear Uncle[13]

I have at last mustered courage to commence a letter, notwithstanding the terrible heat, which keeps everyone busy all day trying to keep cool, though all efforts to that end are vain.

We had begun to think that Virginia was no warmer than Michigan, but if this weather continues a few days longer that idea will be most effectually exploded. For three or four days it has been so hot that it is almost impossible to live except in the shade. Fortunately Co. C has nothing to do as our position of Provost Guard is nearly as useless as it is inglorious. Gen. Custer is still in command of Kilpatrick's Division so we are still acting Division Provost Guard though we only belong to the 2d Brigade.

There is a report that Kilpatrick is not to resume command of the Division, in which case, I suppose, Gen. Custer will retain it.

Lt. Bristol is Asst. Commissary of musters of the Division, and as Capt. Dodge is also on the staff by virtue of his position as Provost Marshal, I am in command of the company most of the time except when we are encamped,—as we stay at Head Quarters of course the Capt. is then in command.

---

13. Granger fails to confirm which of his uncles he was writing to, but Charles Walker seems to have been the more likely.

While we were at Amissville[14] I saw the first specimen I ever saw of a negro dance. The General had promised a pass to Washington to each one who would dance, and they all did their best, old and young, male & female. The fiddler was an old man with an enormous shock of grey wool, who seemed to enjoy the fun quite as much as any one. He was supported by a "likely nigger" of about thirty-five, whose hair stuck out from his head in all directions <u>in</u> little braids who "never made a practice of dancing" & therefore played the <u>bones</u> for his share in the entertainment. They danced for more than an hour and it was a most amusing sight.

We left Amissville last Friday [July 31] and I came to Warrenton Station where we now are and where I presume we shall stay till our horses are in much better condition than they now are. Though our Company has had so much less duty to perform than the rest of the Regt. even our horses will need good feed and rest for some days before they are fit for active service.

We were at Amissville five days without any grain for our horses, and, as we were also without rations, the horses had to be worked pretty well to keep the men from starving. When we came here we had a very hard looking set of horses, and though they have had plenty to eat here it will be a good while yet before they are in as good condition as when we reached Amissville and we thought then that they were used up.

It is impossible, from here, to form any opinion of what the army is about. Since we have been here, troops have been passing through here in the direction of Washington, nearly all the time.

Capt. Judson is well. He started for Washington yesterday, hoping, I believe, to get his pay. Capt. Judson dislikes Capt. Dodge very much & he told me the other day that he thought Dodge would be ordered to report to his Regt. soon. I hope he may as I dislike this place very much, though it is as easy as any place in the army. Any chance of promotion is of course out of the question as long as we are doing nothing and the Regt. is fighting, while there would be a chance if we were with the Regt. as I think there will be a general clearing out of

---

14. Amissville is an unincorporated community in Rappahannock County in Virginia, located on U.S. Route 211 about halfway between Warrenton and Washington, Virginia.

the Regimental Officers. Capt. Simonds' resignation has been accepted and I believe there are some other officers who will leave.

Major Trowbridge is in Washington (I believe) sick. Maj. Dake is sick, the Col. & Lt. Col. wounded & Maj. Ferry is dead so the Regt. is commanded by a Capt.

I have seen Henry Granger[15] several times. He has gone to Washington now.

Give my mother notice that she has owed me a letter for the past three months.

Yours
E. G. Granger

Fred[16] says it's <u>hotter</u> than ever.

E. G. G.

✳ ✳ ✳

[LETTER 15]

Headquarters Kilpatrick's Cavalry Division
Warrenton Junction—Va.
August 6th 1863 [Thursday]

Dear Mollie

I hardly know whether I am going to write a letter or not, but as I found a sheet of paper already dated, (with only 2 mistakes in the spelling

---

15. Henry William Granger was the much older first cousin of Edward and Mollie Granger. Henry had been born on April 4, 1823, at Champion, New York. His parents were Austin and Rhoda Granger. Austin was the brother of Edward Granger's father, Sylvester Granger. Henry had been commissioned a first lieutenant in Company K, 1st New York Volunteer Cavalry Regiment on August 12, 1861, but was promoted to major in the 7th Michigan Cavalry on December 20, 1862. In 1864, Henry assumed command of the 7th Michigan, but was killed in action on May 11, 1864, during a charge at the Battle of Yellow Tavern, Virginia. According to Findagrave.com, he was buried in February 1866 in Mount Hope Cemetery, Rochester, New York. Also see Soldier Records and Profiles; U.S. Civil War Soldiers; "Maj. Henry W. Granger," memorial at Findagrave.com, 32094629.
16. Undoubtedly, Granger is referring to his friend Fred Nims.

of the name of the Gen. then Comdg.) I thought I would take it to scribble on, & if I could make out to write any thing worth sending, without overexerting myself (the thermometer is somewhere about 100 degrees, or would be if there was ~~one~~ a thermometer in the country.) You will probably get it—on the payment of 6 cents as I have no stamp and, as Fred said on his letter the other day when he ran out, there's "not a d—d stamp in the Country." Guess <u>that</u> letter went.

I am in some doubt whether I owe you a letter, any way, as it seems such a short time since I wrote to you before, that I don't believe you had rec'd my letter before you wrote, & if you had you didn't say anything about it. Yours is the only letter I have rec'd from home since we left Fairfax on the 21st of June A. D. 1863, & I don't know how much longer, and Emma Walker is the only person who has written except, I beg his pardon, Don M. D.[17] who wrote me a most interesting letter, only it was in Latin & I couldn't read a word of it & didn't dare get any one to read it for me, as there was no knowing what was in it. I answered it in French, of which he knows as much as I do of Latin— By the way tell Miss Pollay,[18] that if she wants to find out any-thing about that bouquet, she must ask Don.

Poor Tite[19] is dead!

Tell Sara[20] she mustn't believe any-thing you say about Don.

When I wrote last we were at Amissville. We left that place last Friday [July 31] for our present Camp at Warrenton Junction, where we are likely to stay some time I guess though there is no such thing as knowing where we may be tomorrow.

We are but a little ways from Falmouth & it looks as though we were going to settle down into the old places for another year. It may be all right but I don't like it, especially as I know that Meade

---

17. Again, this is Donald MacDonald, who may or may not have been a male friend of his sister's at this time.
18. According to the city directory for Detroit in 1862, a Miss E. M. Pollay was the second assistant principal in the city's high school, which Granger attended. Granger's reference to Latin and French suggests that this might be a former schoolteacher whom he had in high school. *Detroit City Directory 1862*, 12.
19. This reference remains unclear.
20. This may be Sarah E. Granger (1830–1894), a first cousin to Edward and Mollie Granger. Sarah's father, Austin Granger, who had died the previous March, was a brother to the Grangers' own father, Sylvester.

was considered an out & out Rebel at the beginning of the war, & I heard Mrs. DeMill[21] say that he told her that he would resign if he was appointed to an active command, & it is said that he refused to take the oath of allegiance. The credit belongs to the defeat of Lee at Gettysburg I think is due Hooker, who was not relieved till the army was ready for the battle and with such a position victory was sure to be with our army. Since the battle the delays which are constantly occurring and for which we can see no reason are most wonderful to us who have seen the rapid movements of "Fighting Joe." Grant may have to come up here after all, when he has "cleaned out" the South West.

Bob has had such a sore back that I have not ridden him for a month till yesterday and of course he is in first-rate spirits after his long idleness. If he is inclined to think himself "master of the situation," so much as he used to be I shall probably have a pretty hard time to make him realize that I am his master.

Fred [Nims] is a personal friend of Gen. Custer and his chances will be first rate if there is any vacancy & as soon as he is an officer Custer will have him on his staff & Fred says he will need someone to take care of him more than ever then.

Custer is relieved of the command of the Div. by the return of Gen. Kilpatrick so we are now only Brigade Provost Guard.

There, that's all I'll write.

E. G. Granger

Love to Sara

Ed.

✳   ✳   ✳

---

21. According to the *Detroit City Directory 1862*, Peter Edward DeMill was secretary and superintendent of the Detroit Gas Light Co. He was married to Henrietta Marie Westbrook. Possibly Granger is referring to DeMill's wife. Ancestry.com; Rootsweb.com.

[Additional letter to
Granger's cousin Emma Walker]

Head Qrs. 2d Brig. 3d Cav. Div.
Aug. 22/63

Dear Emma

I am, at last, so situated that I can write with some comfort, till we go into active service again.²² The day before yesterday I received an order detailing me as an Aid de Camp on the staff of General Custer commanding the Michigan Brigade, consisting of the First, Fifth, Sixth and Seventh Regiments of Michigan Cavalry.²³ It is a very pleasant place indeed so far as I have yet seen it, but when in the field there is plenty to do. Just at present my duties consist in lying around, in wall

---

22. Granger's tone in this letter seems more appropriate for a person older than his young cousin. Granger does not indicate at the top of the letter where he is, but within the letter he reveals the brigade has been at Falmouth for about a week. Granger probably wrote this letter near Berea Baptist Church northwest of Fredericksburg. The church, built in 1852 and severely damaged during the war, still stands today on its namesake road off U.S. 17.

23. During the Civil War, senior field commanders had a staff structure, called either a general staff or a field staff. One portion was the special staff, responsible for engineers, ordnance, supplies, and transportation. In addition, commanders had a personal staff, responsible for keeping records and handling orders to subordinate units. In June 1861, a Congressional act authorized each brigade commander to have one assistant adjutant general and two aides-de-camp. As the war progressed, staff sizes increased at all levels, and personal staff officers became of increasing importance to lower echelon commanders, such as Custer. They collected information, prepared plans, developed orders, dispatched them to subordinates, and provided opinions or guidance to the commander. However, depending on the commander's own inclinations, staffers might have been no more than high-functioning office clerks. As R. Steven Jones has stated, "With no national general staff to help them, and with few War Department guidelines for staff work beyond the proper form for filling out reports, Civil War personal staff officers were adrift. Rather than reflect a national standard, staffs usually reflected the character of their commanding general and did as much—or as little—as he expected of them." While Custer has a historical reputation as a seat-of-the-pants commander, Granger's Civil War letters suggest he frequently relied on his aides, especially in carrying out his orders. See R. Steven Jones, *Right Hand of Command: Use and Disuse of Personal Staffs in the Civil War* (Mechanicsburg, Pa.: Stackpole Books, 2000), Kindle edition, 51–53, for more details on the use of staffs in that period.

tent all day, trying to keep cool, an almost impossible task, and eating my meals regularly when they are ready.—isn't this terribly hard upon a poor soldier? I have excellent company here and most of the time something to read—the greatest comfort of all, far worse than the want of food or sleep is the lack of something to read. The General is a <u>gentleman</u> as well as a brave soldier and a good officer. So you see how pleasantly I am situated now and I assure you that change is a most welcome one from my recent position in the Company, as I did not like my Capt. at all.[24]

I almost forgot where we were when I wrote you last, and I entirely forget whether you have answered my last, ~~and~~ but come to think of it I am inclined to think you have not, and if I had not commenced this letter under the mistaken impression that I was your debtor, I should'nt write at all—so you may credit this infliction to my mistake, if it is not your due.

Sunday Morning [August 23]. Last evening was so beautiful that it was impossible for me to resist the temptation to lay down my pen and give myself up to the laziness natural to the time and to me. This morning we are going to have services conducted by the Chaplain of the First Mich. ~~An~~ Mr. Hudson, who is a terrible bore.[25] I have'nt heard a decent sermon since I left Detroit. Chaplains in the Army are always men who were not fit to preach at home, which seems to be the only qualification necessary to obtain a position in the Army—Have been to meeting—exceeding edified, of course.

Since I wrote you last Co. C has been acting as Provost Guard, first for the Brigade, and then for the Division. During the first half of August we lay at Warrenton Junction, and such a steady spell of hot weather I never had the misfortune to see before.

About a week ago the Company was ordered back to the Regt. which was doing duty at Falmouth.

---

24. This was Capt. Horace W. Dodge.
25. Chaplain Jonathan Hudson of Trenton, Michigan, was born January 10, 1816, in Reading, Pennsylvania. Some sources list him as a prisoner of war in Richmond, Virginia. He entered the service on August 22, 1861, as the chaplain for the 1st Michigan Cavalry. He was mustered out at the end of his three-year enlistment on September 19, 1864. He died on January 7, 1876. Soldier Records and Profiles; "Jonathan Hudson," memorial and gravestone at Findagrave.com, 10603423.

The Rebs have a picket line across the River, but I think there is no large force across there. Last Friday they had a dress parade, which we could see from our post. The next day we went out on a scout and had a good time, confiscating all the peaches and watermelons we wanted. That night I received the order detailing me and here I am now with nothing to do & nothing more to write.

Your cousin Ed. G. Granger

* * *

[Letter 16]

Head Quarters 2d Brigade 3d Cav. Div.
Near Berea Church Va. Sept. 3d, 1863 [Thursday]

Dear Mollie

Your welcome letter was received this evening, together with one from Uncle Charles and; as I have nothing to do tonight and feel very much like writing, that is, for me; I will try to answer it to night. First and foremost, of course, as to my present brilliant position on the Staff of Brig. Gen. Custer[26]—It is a very pleasant position, indeed, as the

---

26. See "From the Michigan Cavalry Brigade," *Detroit Free Press*, Sept. 1, 1863. The report bore a dateline of August 26, 1863, and was written in Falmouth, Virginia. Capt. Jacob L. Greene was listed as the brigade's assistant adjutant general. Other appointments to the staff as aides from the 5th Michigan included Capt. Robert F. Judson, Lt. William Colerick, and Lt. Richard Baylis. Lt. James Christiancy, also mentioned by Granger, but a member of the 8th Michigan Cavalry, was among the other appointees. Officially only an aide, Granger would spend much of his initial period on the brigade staff as acting assistant adjutant general, or AAAG. As an aide-de-camp (often ADC) in a Civil War brigade, Granger was officially only answerable to his general and received orders only from him. An aide needed to enjoy the full confidence of his commander, whom he often represented. When communicating orders, whether written or verbal, the aide spoke with the commander's authority. Additionally, aides needed sufficient experience to understand the varying circumstances on a battlefield, the positioning of troops as well as the purpose of all orders issued by the commander. A staff adjutant general or an assistant had more well-defined administrative duties within the unit, including publishing orders, writing reports, and handling official correspondence. Effectively, he was the unit's administrative officer. Granger's appointment to the staff was important. It certainly signified Custer's belief in the youth.

General is one of the most perfect <u>Gentlemen</u> I have met in the Army, and I have the best men on the staff to mess with—Lieut. Colerick[27] and Capt. Judson. It is, when in Camp, a very easy position; but we have to make up for that when on the march. We or some of us, have to get up before anyone else in the morning to carry to the various Regiments the order to march, and at night we have to see that they know when to stop, &c &c. In battle, when we get into one, I suppose we shall have a chance to show the stuff we are made of as Gen. Custer is one of the "fighting Generals" of whom we read so much and see so little: but there is no doubt about his fighting qualities, for his command has not been in a single engagement in which he has not been under fire.

Per contra—The position is likely to be an expensive luxury, as the Staff both live and dress, in a style which is far ahead of that supported by most Line Officers. I am at present entirely out of clothing and am going to Washington tomorrow to replenish my wardrobe.

Perhaps you would like to know what kind of company I keep here—well if you won't tell Uncle Charles (who thinks I am inclined to criticize my betters rather too freely), I will tell you. First—The General is a young man of three and twenty, nearly six feet tall and well made, complexion red, eyes blue, hair yellow and hanging in curls on his shoulders, mustache & imperial of the same elegant color, dresses in velveteen with an indefinite number of yards of gold-lace on the sleeve of his jacket as an indication of his rank, but when dressed for review makes by far the most splendid appearance of any officer I have seen,—morals West Point—manners perfect—temperament lively

---

27. William Colerick (1827–1914) of Almont, Michigan, had enlisted at age thirty-four on September 6, 1861, as first sergeant for Company L, 1st Michigan Cavalry Regiment. He had been born on June 12, 1827, in Quebec, Canada. In 1846, he was appointed postmaster in Almont and kept a tin shop. He was promoted to second lieutenant on June 3, 1862, and to captain on December 4, 1864. Custer had named Colerick to his staff when he took command of the brigade in June 1863. Colerick was finally mustered out of the service on March 10, 1866, at Fort Bridger, Utah. He returned to Almont where he worked in the mercantile business. He died on December 14, 1914. Soldier Records and Profiles; "William Colerick," memorial and gravestone at Findagrave.com, 38663764; William Colerick biography, in *Portrait and Biographical Record of Genesee, Lapeer and Tuscola Counties, Michigan* (Chicago: Chapman Bros., 1892), 990.

& full of fun—Next comes Capt. ~~Judson~~ Green [Greene]²⁸ Assistant Adjutant General (but as he has not, as yet, his Commission; I am acting in his place—nominally my duties consisting of signing numerous documents of which I know about as much as you do, "By Order of Brig. Gen. Custer—E. G. Granger <u>Lt. & A.A.A.G.</u>"— you will have to get someone learned in military lore to give you my title). Captain Greene is a medium size man, fair complexion, eyes & hair & would look like a female but for a handsome beard—is a very pleasant, gentlemanly widower given to sentimental music. Capt. Drew,²⁹ Assistant Inspector General, is a splendid specimen of Napoleonic beauty, Complexion very dark & as "clear as mud" a nose

---

28. Jacob Lyman Greene was born August 9, 1837, in Waterford, Maine, and was graduated with a law degree from the University of Michigan. He became a lawyer in 1861 in Lapeer, Michigan, but soon after, in June 1861, he enlisted as a private in the 7th Michigan Infantry. Two months later, he was promoted to first lieutenant. Illness in January 1862 forced him out of the army for a year. For two months in the summer of 1863 he served as a volunteer aide on General Custer's staff, until his appointment as a captain in the 6th Michigan Cavalry was approved. Never mustered, Greene, instead, was commissioned as an officer in the U.S. Volunteers adjutant general department, at the rank of captain. He then served as assistant adjutant general on the Michigan Cavalry Brigade staff, until he was captured at Trevilian Station on June 11, 1864. He remained in Confederate prisons until he was paroled on December 9, 1864. On April 10, 1865, he rejoined Custer in the field now commanding the 3rd Cavalry Division. After the immediate end of the war, Custer was assigned to Texas as commander of the Cavalry Division of Texas; Greene, now a lieutenant colonel, served as his chief of staff. In the postwar years, Greene rose to become president of the Connecticut Mutual Life Insurance Company. He died at age sixty-eight on March 29, 1905. On February 9, 1864, when Custer married Elizabeth Bacon in Monroe, Michigan, Greene served as his best man. Greene himself had married Malvina Wood in 1859, but she died in 1860. On January 12, 1865, after his release from prison, Greene married a friend of Custer's wife Libbie, Annette Humphrey, but she died in 1868. In 1870, he married again, this time to Caroline Barrow. Soldier Records and Profiles; U.S. Civil War Soldiers; David Neville, "Custer's Best Man: Brevet Lt. Col. Jacob Lyman Greene," *Military Images*, May-June 2004, 23–31; Bill Ryan, "General Custer in the Corporate Archives," *New York Times*, April 14, 1996.

29. Capt. George A. Drew, 6th Michigan Cavalry, was named as the Michigan Cavalry Brigade's assistant inspector general and apparently temporarily the brigade's chief of staff at the same time as Granger's appointment, according to the *Detroit Free Press* article. Born March 15, 1831, in Mackinac County, Michigan, he enlisted as a captain on August 28, 1862, in the 6th Michigan. He was promoted to major on July 17, 1863, and to lieutenant colonel on June 6, 1864. He was discharged on October 11, 1865, at Fort Laramie, Dakota Territory, but was appointed on *(continued)*

which would rival Ed McGraw's[30] & Oh! such a lovely mustache of a beautiful black (that is, when lately dyed): Morals none—manners, keeping his morals company—temper "least said soonest mended" on that score. Then Capt. Judson whom you know, then Lieut. Colerick of the 1st Mich.—A.D.C. A gentleman in every sense of the word, about my size, grey eyes, fair complexion, mustache & long goatee, a brusk fellow & full of fun. Then "Jim" Christancy [Christiancy][31] of the 9th Mich. Cav. a young fellow not yet nineteen years old—a hand pet—but just as full of fun as he can live—he is the life of the Staff. Last but not least E. G. Granger Lieut. and A.A.A.G. who would be a very handsome youth if it were not for a horrible nose though his eyes are rather too small to look well and his complexion is poor and his teeth poorer—but his principal beauties are his hands and feet which are most delicately formed and of surpassing whiteness (especially the feet).

Day before yesterday the Div. went down the river about 25 miles to a place called Port Conway where we expected to find a large force of Rebs, but there were only about 50 there who crossed the river in a scow as soon as our advance Guard came up. We spent the day in shelling two gunboats which the Rebs took from us the other day & out of which they had taken the guns &c. Arrived safely at Camp this

---

May 15, 1866, as a second lieutenant in the Regular Army, serving in the 10th Infantry Regiment. In 1879, he was promoted to captain and retired as a major on March 15, 1896. He died on July 21, 1921, in Highland Park, Illinois, north of Chicago, and was buried in the Fort Sheridan Cemetery. Soldier Records and Profiles; U.S. Civil War Soldiers; "Col. George A. Drew," memorial and gravestone at Findagrave.com, 31046443.

30. This individual appears to be his friend Dr. Theodore McGraw. See chapter 1, note 5.
31. James Isaac Christiancy, eighteen, of Monroe, Michigan, enlisted on May 28, 1862, as a private in Company C, 17th Michigan Infantry and was promoted to sergeant major on August 26, 1862. He was appointed a second lieutenant on December 28, 1862, in Company D, 9th Michigan Cavalry. On October 10, 1892, he was awarded the Medal of Honor for his actions as a first lieutenant at the Battle of Haw's Shop, Virginia, on May 28, 1864. He died December 18, 1899, and was buried in Arlington National Cemetery. His father, Isaac P. Christiancy, was chief justice of the Michigan Supreme Court and later a U.S. senator. Isaac was one of Custer's chief political boosters and lobbied in Custer's behalf for the colonelcy of the 5th Michigan the previous spring. The *Detroit Free Press* article listing Custer's staffers shows James as a member of the 8th Michigan Cavalry. Soldier Records and Profiles; U.S. Civil War Soldiers; "James Isaac Christiancy," memorial and gravestone at Findagrave.com, 6164692.

morning having lost only one man Lieut. Percy S. Liggett [Leggett] of C.I. [Company I] 5th Mich. Cav.[32]

> Yours in haste
> Ed
> Direct Headquarters 2d. Brig. 3rd Cav. Div.
> Army Potomac

Don't direct to the A.A.A.G. but to E. G. Granger Lt. and A.D.C.

> Ed

Capt. Judson sends his kindest regards to Uncle Charles, Aunt Mary and the baby—Mr. Colerick sends his regards to you.

※ ※ ※

[Letter 17]

Kalamazoo Mich. Sept. 24th 1863 [Thursday]

Mollie

General Custer wished me to take my sister down to Grosse Isle to a pic-nic given, I believe, for the Gen's benefit, next Tuesday [September 29, 1863].[33] As I shall probably be away till Monday night or

---

32. Lt. Percival S. Leggett of Waterford, Michigan, enlisted as a sergeant in Company A, 5th Michigan Cavalry, on August 16, 1862. Born January 8, 1839, in New York City, he was commissioned on June 13, 1863, as a second lieutenant in Company I, and was killed in action on September 1, 1863, at Port Conway, Virginia. He was reportedly "Shot on the banks of the Rappahannock River while reconnoitering within the enemy lines on the evening of September 1st." He was buried in Oak Hill Cemetery in Pontiac, Michigan. Soldier Records and Profiles; U.S. Civil War Soldiers; "Percival Seaman 'Percy' Leggett," memorial, illustration, and gravestone at Findagrave.com, 44562170.
33. Three busy weeks had passed between Granger's previous letter and this one. As part of a general advance by the Union Army, on September 12, 1863, Maj. Gen. Alfred Pleasonton's ten-thousand-man Union Cavalry Corps moved from its camp near Warrenton, Virginia, and crossed the Rappahannock River intent on attacking the headquarters of Confederate major general J. E. B. Stuart at Culpeper Court House. Early the next morning, three Union divisions forded the Hazel River and approached Culpeper and forced Confederate pickets and skirmishers *(continued)*

Custer's brigade at Culpeper, Virginia, September 14, 1863.
Illustration by Edwin Forbes, *Frank Leslie's Illustrated Newspaper*.
Editor's collection.

Tuesday morning, I thought I would write, so that you might make

to retreat. About 1:00 P.M. September 13, 1863, during the fighting at Greenwood Hill during the Battle of Culpeper Court House, Virginia, Brig. Gen. H. Judson Kilpatrick, commanding the Union's 3rd Cavalry Division, ordered Custer's Michigan Cavalry Brigade to charge the main enemy defensive line. Custer seized the position as well as some one hundred prisoners and three artillery pieces. Eventually, the Confederates retreated toward the Rapidan River. In the fighting, Custer was wounded. He had personally led a charge on enemy guns that were creating havoc amid the lines of the 3rd Division. A bursting cannonball had killed the general's horse, and a piece of shrapnel tore through his boot and grazed his leg, leaving a nasty contusion. The wound failed to stop the general, who grabbed another mount and led several groups of his troops furiously through the Culpeper streets. The Confederates were forced to withdraw, but Custer had earned himself twenty days' leave. His staffers, including Edward Granger and Jacob Greene, took advantage of their general's absence to return to their own Michigan homes until about October 8. While on leave, Granger wrote this letter on behalf of General Custer to his sister, Mollie, inviting her to a picnic at Grosse Isle, Michigan, a large island in the Detroit River between Detroit and Lake Erie. Included with the letter was a poem by Granger to his sister. During the Victorian period in America, young people commonly wrote poetry to one another.

your arrangements to go, if you have any to make. It is only a small affair, I believe, but, of course aristocratic &c. &c. Some of the General's friends from Monroe are to be there and from some other small town, I forgot where.

All well. I write from Dr. Stones.

Yours
Ed

>Before Richmond
>To Molly
>This poem is respectfully dedicated
>
>Forward the Iron Brigade
>The pride of Old Michigan
>Charge to the Death—Wolverines
>The Staff of the Union
>
>"Follow your leader!" thunders Custer—
>The "Boy General" leads the van
>And by his side the Fearless Granger
>Natures Nobleman
>
>Down upon Treasons ramparts
>Bursts the wild northern blast
>Which bears from the free old Lake State
>To Traitors her bequest
>
>The golden locks of Custer
>As the rallying point afar
>As the gleaming crest of Henry—
>Of Henry of NaVarre
>
>The Glorious Eye of Granger
>Flashes grandly from his Soul
>His stern resolve to conquer
>Has by Freedoms side to fall
>
>His brave warm heart throbs purely
>For his father's flag of yore
>And he takes no step backward
>While its foe shall stand before

Oh God! Wilt thou protect him
In his dark hour of blood
And let not the tide of battle
Overwhelm him in its flood!

Then forward the Iron Brigade
The pride of old Michigan
Charge to the Death Wolverines
The Staff of the Union

✳   ✳   ✳

[LETTER 18]

Head Quarters 2d Brig. 3rd Cav. Div.
Near Cedar Mountain Va. Oct. 9th 1863 [Friday]

Mollie

We are safe in Camp again; and, though we had such a splendid time at home, it seems good to be back again.[34] I am not likely to find it very dull here, either as, on account of Capt. Greene's absence, I am again A.A.A.G. and this time in earnest. Of course, I have a clerk who knows what is to be done and how to do it, but he is not responsible for any-thing. So I have to see that everything is right, especially as I don't know if it is or not, till he tells me.

We stopped in Cleveland an hour & a half & I had just time to see Ada[35] a moment and bid her good-bye. The train on the Pennsylvania R. R. was delayed about an hour by some little accident and so we had to wait at every station almost, to let some other train pass. In consequence of this, we did not reach Washington till Wednesday afternoon [October 7], too late to leave for the front that day. That evening Colerick & I spent in keeping out of the way of Provost Marshals, Officers of the Day &c &c, while the General & Captain Judson went to the Theatre to hear Maggie Mitchell.[36] Don't you think we were to be pitied?

---

34. Lieutenant Granger's purpose with this letter was to let his family know of his return to the Michigan Cavalry Brigade.
35. He is again referring to his first cousin Adaline Walker.
36. Margaret Julia Mitchell (1832–1918), a popular American actress of the day, was born in New York.

A SUMMER AND FALL OF CAMPAIGNING

Culpeper's Main Street in 1862, about a year before
General Custer led a charge down the town's railroad tracks and city streets.
*Photographer Timothy O'Sullivan. Courtesy of Library of Congress,
LC-B811-0524B.*

The next morning we were to start for Culpepper [Culpeper][37] at ten o'clock. The General went off early that morning & said he would meet us at the cars. At ten we were all at the Depot with luggage enough for a Brigade, but the Gen. was not on hand. The train was just about to start when the Gen. came up in a carriage at a furious pace. Then there was a great scrambling to get into the baggage car in which we were to ride from Washington to Alexandria. The car was filled to overflowing already with passengers & baggage, but we all got in but Colerick and John,[38] the scout who went home with us, and they handed the luggage up to us; the last article was the General's trunk and they had just handed that up to us, and we couldn't get room for

---

37. Granger repeatedly misspells the name of the Virginia community, which is properly spelled as Culpeper.
38. John is unidentified.

it so we had to hold it in the door a moment & just ~~leaving~~ then the train started, leaving Colerick and John to climb on to the rear of the car as best they could.

We arrived at Culpeper at about 5 P.M. Thursday [October 8]. The orderlies were all there to receive us, and I assure you they were all glad to see the Gen. back. And Corser was there too with Bob, who, (Bob) was looking so much better than when I saw him last that I shouldn't have known him. At Head Quarters every one was delighted to see the Gen. Nothing had gone right since Gen. Custer had left.

Our Hd. Qrs. are about 9 miles from Culpeper at a beautiful place belonging to a man by the name of Slaughter.[39] It is about 5 miles from the Rapidan, along which River the Brig. is doing Picket duty.

Colerick says tell Mollie that I am well. Gen. says remember me to

---

39. This house where Custer had his October 1863 headquarters was located on the battlefield where a large engagement occurred on August 9, 1862, at Cedar Mountain, south of Culpeper. However, its ownership is hazy at best. The best candidate may be Col. John S. Slaughter (1732–1796), an officer in the Revolutionary War. According to information provided by Julie Bushong, a Culpeper Public Library researcher, this Slaughter's house, Meadow View, was located 7.4 miles southwest of Culpeper, then some two additional miles across roads that partially no longer exist or have been tied into modern country roads. Her information indicated the house was also known as the Mill Tract, or the Crooked Run tract because it was located along Crooked Run. It was constructed about 1817 and later was known more formally as Hilltop Farm. Although this Slaughter reportedly died in 1796, his heirs may have retained ownership until 1891. Who may have been living in the house at the time Custer took up residence is unknown. On October 22, 2016, my wife and I traced the combination of roads to Old Mill Road (also County Road 957), where it crosses Crooked Run on a culvert and becomes County Road 918. No roads or paths lead east into densely wooded private property east of Old Mill Road, but we concluded that John Slaughter's house must have been located to the southeast and north of that point along Crooked Run. As the crow flies, that was less than half a mile from General Winder Road (another portion of Country Road 957) to the concrete culvert that crosses Crooked Run on Old Mill Road. No roads today connect the two portions of CR 957. Michael E. Block, "The Battle of Cedar Mountain," *Blue & Gray Magazine* 32, no. 2 (2016): 6–26, 40–65; *Historic Culpeper: Bicentennial Edition*, 3rd ed. (Culpeper, Va.: Culpeper Historical Society, 2002), 95. Julie Bushong of the Culpeper Public Library provided pertinent data from the Virginia Works Progress Administration Historical Inventory Project sponsored by the Virginia Conservation Commission under the direction of the Division of History, April 16, 1937 (research by J. P. Thomson, Rapidan, Virginia). Interviews with Julie Bushong by phone and in person, October 2016.

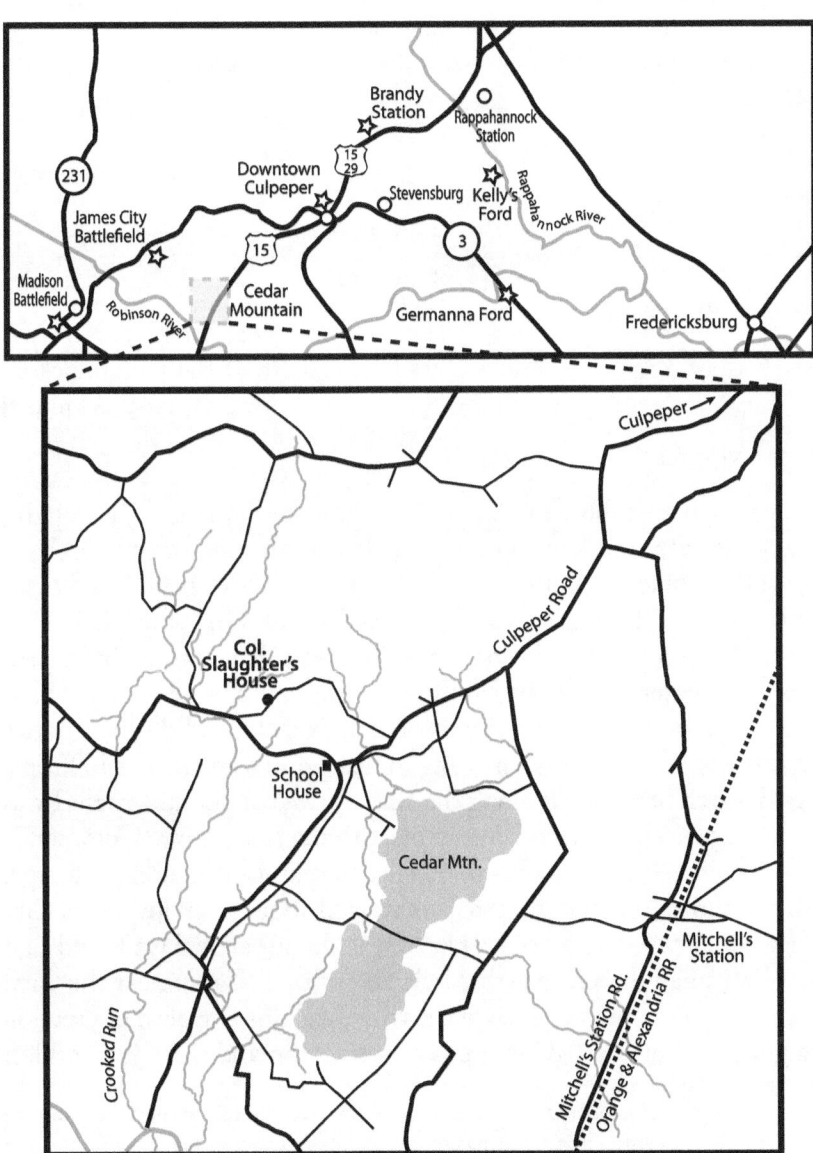

Area of Culpeper, Virginia, fall 1863–winter 1864.
Map by Gary Raham.

Miss Mollie & tell her that we have a piano & violin at Hd. Qrs. and if she were here we would have a quadrille every day.

I can't write, I am so nervous today & besides I have no time. Yours,

Ed. G. Granger

※ ※ ※

[LETTER 19]

Head Quarters 2d Brig 3d Div. C.C.
Near Kelly's Ford. North of Rappahannock R.
Oct. 12, 1863 [Monday]

Dear Mother

As you will probably hear, before long, of yesterday's battle, I thought, I would write, and let you know that I was safe, not, of course, that I was at all anxious to let you know that I had, at least been in a fight.[40]

To begin at the beginning. We arrived at Hd. Qrs. of our Brig Last Thursday [October 8] at about 7 P.M. as you have probably learned from the letter I wrote to Mollie the next day. Friday we lay still at Col. Slaughter's. That evening we rec'd, from Div. H'd Qrs.[41] notice that the enemy were seen moving in heavy force and orders to keep a good watch of the fords along the Rapidan. At about mid-night I was waked up on the rec't of orders to have all the Regimental Commanders draw three day's rations for their commands, & one day's forage. The next day [October 10, 1863] we started about noon for James City near which were Kilpatrick's H'd. Qrs. On our arrival we found that the Rebs. had driven the 5th Mich. out of their Camp near the City, capturing more than 20 men of the 5th. Gen. Custer placed our section (2 guns) of Battery "M" in a position to command the City, and left

---

40. On Monday, October 12, 1863, after a hectic few days, Granger took time to outline for his mother the most exciting combat action in which he had been involved so far during the war. He begins with the October 11 fight at Brandy Station, Virginia, although the day before the brigade had been engaged at nearby James City. Despite his seeming hesitancy to tell his mother about the battles and his near wounding and the wounding of his horse, Bob, he proceeds to outline the details for her.
41. He was referring to the 3rd Cavalry Division, commanded by Brigadier General Kilpatrick.

Officers of U.S. Horse Artillery, Culpeper, Virginia, September 1863. *(left to right)* Lt. Samuel S. Elder, Lt. Alanson M. Randol, Lt. C. K. Warner, Lt. A. C. M. Pennington, Lt. Rufus King Jr., Lt. T. Riley, and Lt. H. B. Read. *Courtesy of Library of Congress, LC-B817-7341.*

the 5th & 7th Mich. & part of the 1st Vt. to support it; and then took the remaining 4 guns of Battery "M" and the 1st and 6th Mich. & the greater part of 1st Vt.[42] about a mile and a half to the right (East) and cross the little "run" which separated us from the Rebs. The Gen. placed his Battery in position and then sent the 1st Vt. forward into a little piece of pine woods as skirmishers.

The woods in front & to the right of the 1st Vt. were full of Reb. sharpshooters & soon they commenced firing on our skirmishers. The firing was very brisk especially from the corner of the woods, nearest our line.

---

42. The 1st Vermont Cavalry had been assigned to the Michigan Brigade at the close of the Gettysburg Campaign and would remain with it until the next spring.

Gen. Custer told Capt. Pennington[43] to open his guns on their sharpshooters. Battery M is a Regular Battery and called the best in the service, but I don't believe it ever made a better shot than the first one it fired in obedience to this order. It burst just where it was wanted and after that not a shot was fired from the woods, though Pennington shelled them for some time. After a little while the Rebs opened on us with a Battery stationed in James City. You may understand the situation better by the aid of this illustration.

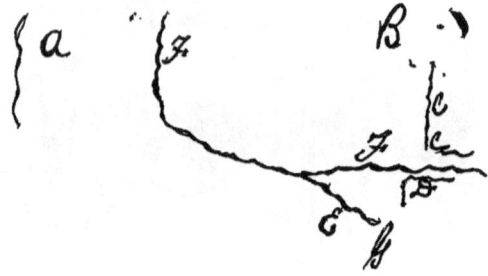

Granger's hand-drawn map of the action at James City two days before.

One section of the Battery with the 5th & 6th are at "A."
B is James City.

---

43. Born on January 8, 1838, Capt. Alexander Cummings McWhorter Pennington graduated from the U.S. Military Academy at West Point in 1860. He commanded Battery M, 2nd U.S. Artillery. The battery, named after him as Pennington's Battery, was attached to the Michigan Cavalry Brigade and played a significant role in the success of Custer and his brigade during the Civil War. Although a captain in the Regular Army, Pennington took a volunteer commission as the colonel of the 3rd New Jersey Cavalry on October 1, 1864. He commanded that regiment for the balance of the war and was mustered out on August 1, 1865. For his distinguished service during the war, he received brevet promotions to colonel in the Regular Army and brigadier general of volunteers. After the war, Pennington remained in the Regular Army, rising to colonel by the outbreak of the Spanish-American War in 1898. During that war he served as brigadier general of volunteers and retired on October 17, 1899, as a brigadier general in the Regular Army. Pennington died on November 30, 1917, and was buried in the Military Academy's Post Cemetery. Soldier Records and Profiles; U.S. Civil War Soldiers; "Alexander Cummings McWhorter Pennington," memorial, photograph, and gravestone at Findagrave.com, 3646.

C. C. Reb sharpshooters in woods.
D 1st Vt. Gen. Custer and Staff in two sections of Battery.
F. Crooked Run.
G. 6th Mich. supporting Battery.

One shell from this Battery exploded close by us, covering Capt. Judson, who happened to be nearest to it, with dirt, but fortunately injuring no one. Poor Bob was terribly frightened (we won't say anything about his master). While Pennington was replying to this fire Col. Alger sent word for him to be careful as the 5th was going to "Charge for the guns." We had an excellent view of the charge from the hill on which we stood. The Regiment came up in splendid style, Major Clark with his Battalion in advance and the other Battalions as reserve. They charged through the town, said town or City—consisting of one house, one old tavern (non occupied) one blacksmith's shop (out of repair) and the [illegible] of a pig-pen but, as the Rebs were behind stone walls & in the buildings, they could not accomplish any thing; however they rallied in good style & then Major Clark deployed his men as skirmishers and advanced again towards the City. When we saw the result of the charge the Gen. & Staff went over where the reserve of the 5th then was. The Rebs then turned their attention to the 5th & by the time we got to them (the 5th) there was quite a lively skirmish going on in front of the Regt. and the shells were flying on us pretty fast. Darkness soon came upon us, and then the effect of the explosion of the Reb shells was very fine. Most of them went into the woods just to the left of where we stood, and the noise of the explosions was five times as great as in the open plains & was accompanied by the crash of falling trees & branches oft.

Soon after dark we withdrew to our original position, or a little in advance thereof, leaving however these Regts. & Sections which were on the right, to remain where they were all night. We all went to bed that night expecting to be in a "big battle" the next morning, as so many of our battles are fought on Sunday. As the Gen. expressed it, "We will have Divine Service as usual tomorrow morning." At 2 1/2 A.M. Sunday the Gen. called us up & sent Judson & Colerick off with orders (as I am A.A.A.G. I don't have quite so much running to do as the other A.D.C.s have, except on the field.). At about half past five we commenced a movement to the rear, & we then found out that the whole Army was retreating & that the Mich. Brig. was to get as part of its rear guard. Till we reached Culpeper we did not see any thing of the enemy. Then they came on pretty fast driving the Brigade of Gen. [Henry] Davies[44] (the 1st Brig. of our Div.) before them. We took up a position on the East side of a small brook & planted our batteries on a hill to cover the retreat of the Infantry in our rear & our own.

From Culpeper to Brandy Station, a distance of 5 miles, we fell back disputing every hill till we were forced to abandon it to prevent being flanked, for they outnumbered us sufficiently to surround us entirely if we had given them the chance.

When we got near Brandy Station the Provost Guard & the Band; which were leading the retreat, were discovered coming back in much greater haste, even, than they had been going forward. They reported Rebs. in front of us, in between us & the River. Gen. Custer sent word to Pleasonton who came up & said that we must get through some way. Gen. Custer prepared to charge with his whole Brig. Sent for his tried friends of the First Michigan who came up on the trot with drawn sabers, he told them that the Rebs were between us and the River and he wanted them to follow him & drive them out. They gave three rousing cheers for their General in which they were joined by the whole Brig. & then we went on. We came to the top of a little rise of ground & there we saw a body of Cavalry on another hill just ahead of us and beyond them larger bodies all moving on the run to the right. We started to charge on those nearest us, when Kilpatrick stopped us stopped us & told us they were Buford's men. Then came one the grandest sights I ever saw. The Rebs had got between Buford & the River, but when they saw our Division coming they started on the run off to the right and Buford with his whole Division charged after them. Buford's men were going in a direction nearly parallel to

---

44. Henry Eugene Davies, a Harvard graduate and a lawyer, rose to the rank of major general during the Civil War. Davies began his service in 1861 as a captain in the 5th New York Volunteer Infantry Regiment and in August 1861 was appointed major of the 2nd New York Cavalry. By December 1862, he had been promoted to lieutenant colonel and in June 1863 to colonel. By September 1863, just before Granger wrote this letter, he was a brigadier general commanding the 1st Brigade in the 3rd Cavalry Division. He served with distinction in the Cavalry Corps, Army of the Potomac, in brigade and temporary divisional commands. On June 7, 1865, he was appointed to the rank of major general of volunteers, effective May 4, 1865. Soldier Records and Profiles; U.S. Civil War Soldiers.

the line of flight of the Rebs, & a few rods from them trying to cut them off. It was the most exciting sight I ever witnessed, far more exciting being out and unable to get into it, than it would have been to be there. Gen. Custer wanted to charge on a battery, which was shelling us from the right, but Pleasonton would not let him.

You never saw a man so excited as the General was. He was crazy to be in somewhere. It was not long before an opportunity—was afforded him, for we had not time to get our Battery in position, before the Rebs were down on us on the left on the rear. Gen. Custer prepared to charge on the Brigade in our rear when up came an A.D.C. from Kilpatrick saying that the woods to our left must be cleared—then the Gen. had to go and show him that the enemy in the rear was of the most importance & then he had to demonstrate the same fact to Pleasonton & by that time they would have been on us but for the Battery which had got to playing on them and which forced them to take to the woods on our right. Gen. Custer then got the 1st Mich. ready to charge on them & waited for them to come out of the woods which they soon did, driving part of the 1st Brig. at a great rate. Then the Gen. led the first and drove the Rebs back into the woods again where they rallied and commenced firing into us. As there was a Rail Road embankment between them & us & they were in the woods of course the First "retired to a better position" rallying, however, in grand style. The Rebs, of course, followed. Kilpatrick tried to lead the rest of the Mich Brig. to the rescue, but, as he afterwards said, himself, "he'd be d—d if they'd stir a step till he called Custer." Then Custer put himself at the head of the 5th Mich. and Kilpatrick led the 1st Brig. to the charge.[45] Kilpatrick was just enough ahead of us

---

45. As Custer wrote in a letter of October 12 to Libbie Custer's friend Annette Humphrey: "I gave the command 'forward!' And I never expect to see a prettier site. I frequently turned in my saddle to see the glittering sabres advance in the sunlight. I was riding in front, Captain Greene's sabre in my hand. Captain Judson and Lts. Colensis [Colerick] and Granger by my side, and behind me my new battle-flag so soon to receive its baptism in blood. Then came my orderlies, and behind them the regiments. "After advancing a short distance I gave the word 'charge!'—And away we went, whooping and yelling like so many demons.'" In his letter to Miss Humphrey, Custer also noted that "Lt. Granger's horse was shot, and his bridle cut close to the wrist." Marguerite Merington, ed., *The Custer Story: The Life and Intimate Letters of General Custer and His Wife Elizabeth* (New York: Devin-Adair, 1950), 66.

to get his Brig. broken in time to spoil our charge. We were doing a good work, had driven them into the woods & had just got almost to them, in perfect order, when the First Brig. broke and ran right into [illegible] that stopped us & gave the Rebel commander time to rally a few of his men & pour a hot fire in.

He was a splendid man that Rebel Gen. or Col. Comd'g a Brig. which ever he was—as cool as if he had no particular interest in what was going on. I was nearest to him of the Officers at the head of the column & I saw him take as deliberate aim at me with his revolver, as if I was there on purpose to be shot at. I gave Bob a hint that that wasn't a good place to stay in and, just as I got where the Gen. was a ball went through both my reins within two inches of my fingers & into Bob's neck. It went in just above his withers and this morning it was cut out of the other side of his neck and a foot nearer his head than where it went in. At the same time another ball struck him in the right shoulder & came out of the left side of his neck.

Neither wound is going to injure him, I hope. The General's horse was shot at the same time.[46]

As most of our force had retired by the time we returned from this charge, the Rebs followed us up till we came to a little ditch across which we rallied and chased them in turn—Here the Gen's 2d. Horse was shot—Just then, luckily for us, Buford came up back from his chase & he took up a position & allowed us to retire, which we did with good grace, for we were pretty well tired out by that time[.] Thus we made our way back to the Rappahannock as best we could, only stopping once to hold an eminence till Buford should get up. When we got to the River we had to wait some time for our turn to cross as there was only a narrow R.R. Bridge just wide enough to permit two horsemen to cross abreast, and you form some idea of the time it must have taken for all the Cavalry to cross that bridge when I tell you that a column of Cavalry containing one thousand men marching by twos is more than one a mile and a half long. When we finally did get across, we

---

46. On October 24, 1863, Custer wrote his official report of the operations of his command covering the period from October 9 to October 23, 1863. At the end of the document, Custer included Edward Granger among the officers whom he specifically cited. About Granger, he stated, "Lieutenant Granger, while heading a charge at Brandy Station, had his horse shot in two places." See *The War of the Rebellion: A Compilation of the Official Records of the Union and Confederate Armies*, series 1, vol. 29, pt. 1, 389–92. These documents are hereafter cited as *O.R.*

had a glorious time finding Kilpatrick as the whole Army was there at Rappahannock Station where we crossed. We finally found him and got into Camp at 8 P.M. after some 14 hours & some of us more than that. We were so busy all day that there was no time (except while) we were retiring which movement Pleasonton ordered us to make always at a walk, there was no time during the day when our horses were off of the Gallop for 15 minutes at a time & yet Bob was just as Plucky as ever at night, in spite of his two wounds.

I wouldn't give him for the best horse in the Brigade.

Last night (Oct 12/63) just before we got our supper an order came to get the Command ready to recross the River. Whew! Perhaps there won't [be] a mad set of men around H'd Quarters. Just as the Brig. was all ready to move an order came to picket the River on this side from Kelly's Ford to Hartwood Church. This was a great improvement, as we at H'd. Qrs. did not have to stir & only two of the Regts were put on duty.

This morning we came down here to be near our Picket line &, here now is the Mich. Brig. peacefully doing picket duty on the Rappahannock.

Rappahannock Station where we crossed the River is about 30 miles above Fredericksburg.

> Your son
> E. G. Granger

Excuse Abruptness haven't time to wind up properly, too sleepy.

> E. G. G.

✳ ✳ ✳

[LETTER 20]

> Head Qrs. 2d Brig 3d Div.
> Cav. Corps Oct. 22d 1863 [Thursday]

Dear Mollie

Your letter of the 12th was received on the 20th, so I presume that you had not received mine of the 9th before you wrote, though it should not take more than three days for a letter to go through. I also wrote to Mother on the 13th,[47] giving an account of the fight at Brandy Station, of which I have seen various accounts in the newspapers full of the most ridiculous statements & all evidently written by persons who were not on the field, for the nature of the Country is such that any one present could see the whole battle.

We left the place from which I wrote to Mother about 8 A.M. the next day [Tuesday, October 13, 1863]. When we arrived at Bealton [Bealeton] Station, on the Orange & Alexandria R.R., we found the Government buildings in flames, & heard that the R.R. bridge across the Rappahannock had been burned that morning. That day we marched past Warrenton Junc. and, just at night, getting behind the train of the second Corps, it took us three or four hours to go as many miles. The night was cold and we were all tired & hungry so you may imagine that we enjoyed the last part of that day's march.

To add to the pleasure of the ride Capt. Judson was very sick. That night we had to sleep almost without blankets, as the ambulance containing our bedding was with the Division train. Colerick & I had two oil-cloth blankets under us and one small horse-blanket over us.

Capt. Judson had two blankets over him, and when he had fallen asleep, Dr. Wooster[48] (of Grand Rapids, the Medical Director of our Brigade) took the blankets off of Capt Judson & spread them out for himself to lie on, though the blankets belonged to the Capt. J., who was sick.

---

47. His letter actually was dated October 12, 1863.
48. Dr. Samuel R. Wooster, who was born on April 22, 1830, was a prominent physician who settled in 1857 in Grand Rapids, Michigan. A Connecticut native, he studied medicine at Yale Medical College in New Haven. After his move to Grand Rapids, he built a highly successful practice. On August 19, 1861, he signed up as the assistant surgeon for the 8th Michigan Infantry Regiment, serving until February 1863. On April 11, 1863, he was commissioned as surgeon of the 1st Michigan Cavalry, remaining with the regiment until October 1864. For most of that period he was acting brigade surgeon on duty at Custer's headquarters. Mustered out on October 17, 1864, he was appointed as an acting staff contract surgeon engaged in field and hospital practice. After the war, he worked in Muskegon, Michigan, until 1871, when he returned to Grand Rapids. He died there on February 6, 1906. Ernest B. Fisher, ed., *Grand Rapids and Kent County, Michigan: Historical Account of Their Progress from First Settlement to the Present Time*, vol. 1 (Chicago: Robert O. Law, 1918), 426; Soldier Records and Profiles; U.S. Civil War Soldiers; "Samuel R. Wooster," memorial, photograph, and gravestone at Findagrave.com, 95581322.

The next day [October 14] we moved over to the Warrenton Pike which we reached at Buckland's [Buckland] Mills about 8 miles from Warrenton, and there went on towards Washington as far as the Bull Run Battle Field, where we lay two or three days expecting every moment a general engagement, especially as we could hear very heavy musketry & some cannonading for two days in succession.

I assure you we were very anxious, as the noise of battle on the second day was much nearer than on the first. But the result, on both days was very favorable to our side. Last Saturday [October 17] at about 4 P.M. our Div was ordered to move forward towards Warrenton. We started but were soon brought to a stand still, by night and Stuart. We went into Camp & the next morning [October 18] started again. Stuart had fallen back as far as Buckland's Mills where we had taken up a very strong position, with a little "run" between his forces & ours.

From this position he was driven by Gen. Custer, though he had much the best position for his guns & his sharpshooters were in the houses of the village. At a house near the village J.E.B. Stuart had breakfasted that morning & his name was engraved on one of the beech trees in the yard. Gen. Kilpatrick had been ordered to press forward towards Warrenton as fast as possible and so he went on with the first Brig, while Gen Custer stopped to let his Brig get their dinner. Gen. Kilpatrick sent back twice, ordering Gen. Custer to come on, but he was determined to hold on till he got his dinner, and it was fortunately for the Div. that he did.

Just as we were eating a report came that the enemy were coming down on our left. The General had been informed that Merritt's Brig. of Regular Cavalry, was coming in that direction & so he did not believe that the enemy were there, but he sent out the sixth to be safe. In about five minutes we heard a firing from the left, and soon found that the enemy were indeed there in force. Capt. Pennington brought his guns to bear on their line of skirmishers and very soon he was replied to by a Rebel battery situated in the woods, out of sight. After a brisk skirmish of about half an hour the Rebs. charged out of the woods still further to our left & rear & we discovered that we had been fighting a Division of Reb. Infantry [cavalry]. We only stopped there long enough to get our skirmishers mounted, and our Artillery safely across the run. One battalion of the Fifth commanded by Major Clark had been sent off, dismounted, by Gen. Kilpatrick without giving Gen. Custer any notice of its being detached from the Regt., & the Gen. supposed it was all safe with the Regt. till it was too late to give it any support. Only about 13 men & two officers got away out of the whole Battalion.

The last seen of Major Clark he was fighting his command splendidly. He is probably a prisoner.

The first Brig was cut off <u>entirely</u> & only escaped by going way around to the right.[49]

Since then we have been "lying around loose" and our prospects seem good for being employed in the same arduous service for some time to come. The army has moved out to Warrenton & we are at Gainsville [Gainesville] in the rear thereof.

General says he thinks that the pretty girls would have spoiled his appreciation of that dinner. He would rather not take them together.

E. G. Granger
Lt. & A.A.A.G.

❋ ❋ ❋

[LETTER 21]

Head Quarters 2<u>d</u> Brig. 3<u>d</u> Division
Cavalry Corps October 27<u>th</u> 1863 [Tuesday]

Mollie

The Rebs have all my writing paper and all of the <u>letter</u> paper of the

---

49. Granger surprisingly downplayed what was a serious engagement on October 19, 1863, for his brigade and the 3rd Cavalry Division. Confederate General Stuart effectively lured General Kilpatrick into an ambush and routed the Union forces, who were chased for five miles in an action that subsequently became known as the "Buckland Races." Kilpatrick's failure clearly irritated Custer, who did not easily accept the humiliation that came with defeat. On October 20, 1863, he wrote again to Annette Humphrey: "Yesterday was not a gala day for me. My consolation is that I was not responsible, but I cannot but regret the loss of so many brave men ... all the painful that it was not necessary." During the fighting Custer's headquarters wagon remained on the Confederate side of Broad Run and had been seized by the enemy. Since October 9, Custer's brigade had lost 214 men in killed, wounded, or missing. Gregory J. W. Urwin, *Custer Victorious: The Civil War Battles of General George Armstrong Custer* (Lincoln: University of Nebraska Press, 1990), 107–12; *O.R.*, series 1, vol. 29, pt. 1, 382–83; Merington, *Custer Story*, 68–69.

Brigade,[50] so I am compelled to use the best I can get, which is, as you see, a very poor quality of Fools cap.—however I shan't feel called upon to fill the sheet, especially as there has been nothing of any consequence going on since I wrote to you last.

Before I forget it. I will acknowledge the receipt of your letter.

Your letter of the 21st Inst. was received at about 3 P.M. yesterday [Monday, October 26]—there—are you satisfied that I have it.

I can't remember exactly when I wrote my last letter to the <u>family</u> but of course it was after the battle of Brandy Station. Your sympathy for "Poor Dodge"[51] was a little ahead of time—unfortunately he was <u>not</u> killed, isn't it provoking after you had wasted <u>so much</u> feeling too? He wasn't even wounded. The mistake arose from the fact that a private of "K." Company of our Regt. by the name of <u>Hodge</u>[52] was killed by a solid shot. You needn't swear at Hodge—poor fellow—he couldn't help it. One of the boys of our Company, who is in Hospital at Washington, saw the same paragraph which caused you so much grief, and he immediately wrote to Bristol <u>congratulating</u> him and the Company on the happy event. Dodge is not, I think, a coward. There are various opinions on the subject, though most of the officers seem to doubt his bravery.—but he behaved well at Brandy Station and I guess at Buckland's [Buckland] Mills.

If Bristol had had the chance, I doubt whether he would have taken command of the Company or not. His is such an excellent position on the Division Staff that I don't believe he would take a Captaincy in the Regt. In fact I should be very much puzzled what to do if I should have a chance to take a Captaincy—but unfortunately—or fortunately—I shall not be likely to be called upon to choose very soon. My present position is in every respect preferable to that of a Capt. in the Line, with the single exception that it is not one from which a man stands a very good chance of promotion. We are having good times here

---

50. That would have been due to the loss of the headquarters wagon during the Buckland Mills fighting.
51. Granger was referring to Capt. Horace W. Dodge.
52. This was Pvt. Milton Hodge, thirty, of Bennington, Michigan, who enlisted on September 2, 1862, in Company K, 5th Michigan Cavalry. He was killed in action on October 12, 1863, at Brandy Station, Virginia. His body may have been returned to his parents for burial in the Commerce Village Burying Ground, Commerce, Michigan. Soldier Records and Profiles; U.S. Civil War Soldiers; "Milton Hodge," memorial and gravestone at Findagrave.com, 11210093.

now, living in a house on the best the land affords, while Buford and Gregg are at the front doing the fighting—<u>Let 'em fight</u>—we had our turn from the tenth to the twentieth. During that time we were not quiet a single day, fought two battles; in each of which Stuart's whole Cavalry force was engaged and in the last, Buckland's Mills, some Reb. Infantry; besides several brisk skirmishes.

I don't know whether you will see the letter I wrote to Don,[53] the other day, or not—but, at the risk of repetition, I will state that on the 19th Inst. the 3<u>d</u> Div. C. C. started from Gainesville at day-light following up the Reb. Cav. under Stuart & Fitz-Lee. There was continual skirmishing along the road—but the enemy made no decided stand till they reached Buckland's Mills, a small village on the "pike" about three miles from Gainesville. Here the enemy posted his sharpshooters in the houses of the village which lies on the bank of Broad Run, a small stream crossing the "pike" at right angles. Our Brigade was in the advance, and when our advance guard halted, the General rode forward to see what was the matter. As we rode up to the top of the hill just this side of the Run, this Rebs opened on us from a battery which was concealed from our view by <u>something</u>, we did not stop to discover <u>what</u>, for the shell whizzed over our heads and struck a little behind us. The General turned off to the right of the road where he was sheltered by a piece of woods. He had hardly got out of the way of the battery when a minnie [minié] ball went through the crowd and struck in an old log house beside us. We "retired to a stronger position" & the General sent for the Artillery. The enemy had much the advantage of us in position, so our attempts to drive them were for a long time ineffectual, but when the 1st Brig. came up Gen. Kilpatrick put them in our place to keep the Rebs. busy while we flanked them on their left. While the General was reconnoitering their position, to see what disposition to make of his forces in this flank movement, the Rebs caught sight of him & his battle flag and opened on him with two guns. One of our orderlies lost his horse at this time but we speedily changed our base and no one was hurt. The Gen. soon got the Brigade around on their flank and then they had to leave on the double quick.

Stuart had to leave his breakfast and Col. Alger had the benefit of it. When they had left Buckland's we went into possessions and prepared

---

53. This letter is not contained in the Granger family collection, probably because MacDonald was not related to the Grangers.

to eat our dinners. Gen. Kilpatrick with Gen. Davies Brigade went on to New Baltimore about two miles along the Pike. Kilpatrick sent back orders for us to come along twice, but Gen. Custer stuck to his dinner, and it was lucky he did, for just as we were eating we rec'd information that the enemy were pressing us on the left flank, and they would have got in our rear if we had moved on. They drove us back & we took refuge behind our Infantry.[54]

I have just made up my mind that I have written all this to you once before. I don't care if it is your fault as your letter deceived me. You said you rec'd my letter just after you sent off your other epistle & I found that the date of that was Oct. 12 but, as the envelope was gone, I did not know when you had mailed it & I supposed that the letter you had rec'd was one I had written since the battle of Brandy Station & I don't think that was after the 19th & come to think of it, I don't believe I have written of this Battle before—if I have—I hope the two accounts may agree—at least, as well as could be expected under the circumstances—as my diary[55] is not in running order at present. Since we have been here, we have had music almost every night, although we have no piano to accompany our violin.

The General sends his Photographs one for you & one for Uncle Charles' <u>family</u> he said by which I suppose he meant his wife. The vignette is for you—the Carte-de visite, of course, for them.

Have you heard any-thing from my photographs from Grand Rapids. Remember me to Ella Gardner.[56]

---

54. With his comment, Granger effectively truncated the details of the fighting at Buckland Mills, probably because he expected his sister had already read his previous letter which covered the combat action there in detail. After the fighting, the Michigan Cavalry Brigade retreated to the safety of the Union's VI Corps line.
55. Many Civil War soldiers kept diaries of their wartime experiences. Granger, who frequently discussed his aversion to writing, may have written this reference tongue-in-cheek as nothing else suggests that he kept such a document. However, if he did, its whereabouts today are unknown.
56. Granger will mention Ella Gardner so often from this point on in his letters that we can reasonably conclude that he had a personal, if not a romantic, interest in the young woman. According to her death record on Ancestry.com, her name was actually Eloise Gardner and she was the daughter of Ransom and Olive Ann Gardner of Detroit. She was born July 10, 1844, making her fifteen months younger than Granger and about a year older than his sister, Mollie. In 1871, Ella, or Eloise, married William H. Dodge, and in 1874, they had a daughter, who also was named Eloise. Ella died on July 26, 1914, in Lansing, Michigan.

Tell Mother I won't write to her again till I hear from her.

From her dutiful Son & Your brother
E. G. Granger

Give my respects to "Cousin Mattie"[57] & my love to Jessie.[58]

Ed.

P.S. Don't get the messages in that last sentence mixed.

E. G. G.

Capt. Judson sends his regards to all friends.

❋ ❋ ❋

[LETTER 22]

Head Quarters 3d Div. Cav. Corps.
Stevensburg Va. Nov. 17th 1863 [Tuesday][59]

Mollie

I believe I am your debtor for two letters, but you will have to take one in pay't. of the whole debt. In answer to yours of the 4th Inst. I only acknowledge the receipt of your letter because Mother complained that I never did write as though I had rec'd any letters at all. I presume, by this time, you have heard of our being at Stevensburg; at least, I

---

57. Cousin Mattie is unidentified.
58. As cited in chapter 2, note 19, this is Jessie Rawson Walker (1859–1934), Granger's much younger cousin and the daughter of his uncle Edward Walker and his wife, Lucy.
59. This is Granger's first letter written from Stevensburg, Virginia, but it will not be his last from here. Stevensburg soon would be the brigade's winter home until early the next May. It is about seven miles east of Culpeper, Virginia. Earlier, on November 7, General Meade had tested Lee's Confederate forces below the Rappahannock River that forced Lee to fall back south to the Rapidan River, although the Union cavalry had little to do at that time. For the next two weeks Union cavalry, including Custer's 3rd Cavalry Division with him in temporary command, probed the enemy's lines.

intended you should hear of it when I told Hunter,⁶⁰ the other day, that Gen. Custer was relieved from command of the Brigade. A little after noon of the day I wrote to Hunter, the Gen. came into the room where Capt Judson, Colerick & I were sitting and told us that he had been relieved & ordered to report at Washington. Before we had had time to realize what a calamity had befallen the Brigade, the General had left the room and gone up stairs. For a while we sat staring at each other in dismay & then Colerick led the way up to the General's room. There we found the General packing up. He said he did not know for what he had been relieved, so we had nothing for it but to wait and see what was the trouble. You never saw a bluer set than we had around this house that afternoon. Col. [Charles H.] Town was put in command of the Brigade, and Baylis [Lt. Richard Baylis],⁶¹ the Brig. Provost Marshal is a most bitter enemy of Col. Town, so Baylis was sure of being sent to his Regiment: & Capt. Judson was afraid of the same fate: and we all felt very sorry to lose the General. T'was several hours before we found out that Gen. Custer was relieved of the command of the Brigade to take command of the Division: Gen. Kilpatrick having been ordered to Washington.⁶² I assure you there was a general brightening up when we found how we had been sold. Like a good boy, I resolved to give you, at home, the benefit of the joke, so I opened a letter which I had just sealed and put in a P.S. the statement that the Gen. had just been relieved, hoping that Hunter would show it to Uncle Charles, if he did not publish it. The General said he hoped it would get into the papers & get out to Monroe.

60. This is Granger's friend Hammond Hunter. See chapter 1, note 8.
61. This soldier's last name is variously spelled as Baylis, Bayliss, or Bayles. Even the *Detroit Free Press* article of September 1, 1863, listing the names of Custer's staff appointees, misspells his last name as Bayliss. However, it appears that Granger's spelling is correct. It matches what appears on the man's grave marker in Mount Rest Cemetery in St. Johns, Michigan. Born on November 22, 1830, in Ovid, Michigan, Richard Baylis was commissioned in the 6th Michigan on August 26, 1862, as a staff officer. On June 29, 1863, he was appointed as acting assistant adjutant general for the brigade. A year later, on June 12, 1864, he was wounded in action at the Battle of Trevilian Station, Virginia. Mustered out on November 17, 1864, he received the brevet rank of lieutenant colonel in 1865. He died on September 14, 1886. Soldier Records and Profiles; "Richard Baylis," memorial and gravestone at Findagrave.com, 69130337.
62. On November 13, 1863, Kilpatrick had been ordered to appear as a witness at a court-martial in Washington, D.C. Longacre, *Custer*, 192.

Last Saturday night [November 14] it rained very hard here, & about 2 A.M. Sunday the General routed up Colerick & Jim & sent them with dispatches to the two Brigades to be ready at daylight for reconnaissance in force.

The first thing in the morning [Sunday] I was waked up to carry an order to Col. Town. The Gen. told me to get my breakfast first, & by the time I had eaten that, he was ready himself so I started off with him.

It was raining very hard and there was wind enough to drive the rain down my neck, in spite of my coat collar, & in a few moments we were pretty well soaked. You may imagine what a jolly ride we must have had, none of the Staff but me being up, it was a great addition to the enjoyment of the ride to think how comfortably they were housed at home while they ought to have been with us, out in the rain.

Arrived at the Fords of the Rapidan, we found them too deep to be crossed, and so, after some artillery firing on both sides, we returned, having accomplished our object by ascertaining that the enemy held the opposite bank of the Rapidan in heavy force. The General sighted one of the guns several times and made the best shots that were made that morning & Battery M is one of the best in the service as far as good shooting goes.

This afternoon several English Officers who had been visiting at Gen. Meade's H'd. Qrs. are down here to see Gen. Custer and are now reviewing the Second Brig. They are accompanied by Maj. Gen. Warren[63] & Staff & portions of the Staff of Gen. Meade.

Among the latter is the young Lieut. about whom I asked Mother, whom I did not recognize. Who do you suppose it is? Charley Bissell.[64] You would never know him. I never saw more improvement in the personal appearance of any-one in the same amount of time.

---

63. Maj. Gen. Gouverneur K. Warren (1830–1882) was a Union Army general and civil engineer during the Civil War. He served heroically during the war, including at Gettysburg, but in the waning days of the war, he was relieved of his command of the V Corps on April 1, 1865, by Gen. Philip Sheridan during the Battle of Five Forks. Warner, *Generals in Blue*, 541–42.

64. Charles T. Bissell was commissioned as an officer in Company D, 5th Michigan Infantry, on December 18, 1862, but was mustered out on July 16, 1864. About two weeks later, on August 3, 1864, he was commissioned a first lieutenant in the 1st Michigan Cavalry. Thus, Bissell and Granger would have served together for about two weeks. Soldier Records and Profiles.

Capt. Greene wishes to be remembered to Miss Durant & "to your sister," Jim to the latter & I to the former. Colerick sends his respects to you. The Gen. wishes you to ask Miss Dunn[65] whether she ever came down to the Exchange that night or not. If she did, you are to make all due apologies for him as you know he had no time that evening.

He also says he certainly expects her down here this winter with a party of young Ladies to come down with Col. Kellogg.[66]

Give my respects to Carrie & Mattie—I don't believe it does any good to send any message to Ella Gardner, as she is not likely to get it. If you do see her, however, give her all you can think of to pay for what you have not delivered heretofore.

~~When~~ I wanted your photograph Mollie. I should have asked you when I was home but I was hard up.

Have you rec'd any photographs from Grand Rapids for me?

I have to go to the picket line.

Goodbye
Ed. G. Granger

❋ ❋ ❋

[LETTER 23]

Head Quarters 2nd Brig 3d Div. C.C.
Stevensburg Va. Nov. 20th (or 21st I don't know which) 1863
[Friday/Saturday]

Dear Mother

It is a beautiful day to write letters, that is, our winter rains have just set in, and, if appearances don't deceive us, forty-eight hours more will leave the Army of the Potomac stuck in the mud for another three months. With the Rapidan in our front & the Rappahannoc[k] in rear, a movement in either direction does not look very feasible just now. So, in harmony with the weather & the prospects, we are getting very comfortably settled.

---

65. Miss Dunn is unidentified.
66. Congressman Francis W. Kellogg (1810–1879) was a U.S. representative from Michigan during the Civil War and Alabama during Reconstruction. Early in the war, he was instrumental in organizing the 2nd, 3rd, and 6th Michigan Cavalry regiments and was appointed briefly as the colonel of the 3rd Michigan.

Captain Judson left this morning for Washington on a 20 day's sick leave—the <u>leave</u> not the <u>Capt.</u> being sick. He intends to visit Connecticut &, I believe, to return <u>via</u> Detroit & <u>Monroe</u>. He went off this morning while I was away. I guess I will apply for a certificate from the Surgeon—my nerves are in a terrible condition this morning, as my handwriting will bear witness.

Kilpatrick has got back, so Gen. Custer is again in command of the Brigade.

We hope, however, that Kil (as he is reverently styled by his own Staff), will get his other Star soon, within a week <u>he</u> says. If he does, Col. Town <u>ought</u> to have the command of the 2<u>nd</u> Brig., but I am afraid that Col. Alger of the 5<u>th</u> will get it.

If Col. Alger does get the appointment of Brigadier it will very much improve my ~~opportunity~~ chances of ever getting any promotion in the Regt., as the only way to get promotion from Alger is to pay him for it, &, of course, I never would do that.—Indeed my present position is preferable to a Captaincy in the Regt. with any such man as Col. Alger in command.

N.B. <u>This</u> letter, at least, must be kept at home. I heard from <u>Monroe</u> a criticism on <u>one</u> of my letters.

I don't think the First Mich. will go home to recruit this winter & even if it does, Col. Town says that he does not want to go to Michigan again this year, but would stay down here with his new Battalion, which would have to be drilled by someone.

I should think they have enough Officers there now to take care of this battalion without keeping Alexander[67] who must be very anxious to rejoin his Regt. Does he appear to be <u>very</u> Sick?

Capt. Dodge is doing very well & seems to enjoy himself much better than I thought he would <u>after death</u>. He is in command of a battalion nearly all of the time, and part of the time in command of the Regt. Indeed he is one of the best Officers that are left in the Regt., and I should not be surprised to see him made Major if Col. Alger gets out.

George Martin[68] has got the appointment & commission of a Second

---

67. This is undoubtedly Granger's cousin Alexander Caskey. See chapter 1, note 1.
68. This appears to be George H. Martin, eighteen, of Grand Rapids, Michigan, who enlisted as a commissary sergeant on January 12, 1863, in Company I, 7th Michigan Cavalry. On some unknown date, he was mustered out as a quartermaster sergeant, apparently to accept an officer's appointment. He was commissioned a

Lieut. in the Seventh, & though he can't be mustered in just yet, the General asked me this morning to find out whether George wished to come up here to H'd Qurs. before he got mustered in. If he does, we will have a good time up here.

I don't know whether I have ever written home that my Orderly, Corser, was killed while we lay at Gainesville. After his death I received several letters from his wife, directed to him, before she rec'd my letter telling her of her Husband's death. She seems an excellent, though uneducated, woman and her letters to him were terrible to read, knowing that the next letter, for which she was so anxious would contain the news of her husband's death.

I tell you, if I had ever had any intention to commit matrimony those letters would have been <u>very discouraging</u>.

There is nothing going on for me to write about, and in fact that's the reason I got time to write.

Write soon
E. G. Granger

P. S.
Mollie

The General has had his hair cut off and he says "tell Miss Dunn that I too, have lots of locks" and that he will trade on any reasonable terms. I don't know whether I wrote to you that Fred Nims was a Second Lieut of Co. M. of our Regt and that he was going, or rather, has gone home. He promised to call & see you before he returned.

I have a strong impression that I have written that once before.

Lieut. Keith is Capt. of Co. F.

I think it would be a good idea for you to write to me in French, once in a while, at least,

From your
Brother Ed

---

second lieutenant on October 1, 1863, but was transferred to the 14th Independent Battery, Michigan Light Artillery, and was recommissioned on February 11, 1864. He resigned February 20, 1865. He was born in 1845 and died January 14, 1905. Soldier Records and Profiles; U.S. Civil War Soldiers.

P. P. S.

I shan't write again till I feel in a better mood for writing than I do now. I don't think it is as good a day as I gave it credit for being.

E. G. G.

❋ ❋ ❋

[LETTER 24]

Head Quarters 3d Div. Cav. Corps.
Near Stevensburg Va. Dec. 4th 1863 [Friday]

Mollie

Since I wrote to you last, the Army of the Potomac has made a grand move which has been a grand failure, and we are again where we were a week ago.[69]

About midnight of the 23d ult. [November] Colerick was routed out to carry the order to be ready to march at 6 A.M. the next morning. The next day, however, it rained & so we did not march, but lay around the house all day "ready to march at a moment's warning" which means nothing at all, except that every-one is perfectly miserable—waiting for orders which never come. Every thing is packed up just enough so that you can't get a single article you want, the fire goes out, for lack of an ax to cut wood to burn, you don't get any dinner because the mess chest is locked, your nigger don't do any thing right and your horse has a shoe off & the blacksmith can't put one on because we are "ready to march at a moment's warning."—And yet when the order to march does come, it takes just as long to get off as it would have taken if we had not been ready at all.

Just imagine our crowd lying around in this style after one wet miserable day. Wednesday, the [November] 25th, was a pleasant day & we began to hope again for orders.

About ten P.M. that night I had to get up & carry the wished for orders to Gen. Davies, & to the Div. A.Q.M. & A.C.S.

---

69. In this letter to his sister, Mollie, Granger will be providing extraordinary detail about the Battle of Mine Run, a Union failure fought on November 26, 1863. For more information about this engagement, see Urwin, *Custer Victorious*, 112–13, and Longacre, *Custer*, 192–94.

It took me so long to find the latter that I did not get back until 2 A.M. Thursday [November 26]. We started at about 6 A.M. of the 26th and marched to Morton's Ford[70] where we waited patiently till nearly noon, when we heard guns on our left which was the signal for us to open. We then opened the ball by shelling their rifle pits. Our role was to make such a demonstration as to make the enemy think that our whole Army was intending to cross at Morton's and Raccoon Fords, but we were not to attempt to cross. We succeeded perfectly. They kept a heavy force of Infantry in the rifle pits and fortifications opposite us & at least six batteries at Morton's Ford, for they opened on the General with that number while he was riding along the road. Jim [Christiancy] ran his horse into the woods & Capt. Greene was in such a hurry that he rode way ahead of the General, though the shells did not come very near us.

This was when we were going over to where we supposed our wagons were, to get our dinner. When we got there we found that the wagons had not left Stevensburg so we had to go back to the Ford. Here, however, we found a Thanksgiving dinner ready for us. Our dinner, like most of our meals now-a-days, was more remarkable for quantity than variety. Consisting of about a bushel of turnips—in which-ever style the diner liked, that is, that washed, or unwashed—being be very hungry at first, most of us prefered the latter style, at least, until we had eaten one or two.

Our feint so completely deceived Lee that the whole of our Army crossed at Germania [Germanna][71] & other fords without the slightest opposition and reached the line of the enemy's rifle pits along Mine Run while they were occupied by a part of one Corps of Lee's Army.

Now, Friday Morning [November 27], was the Golden opportunity, which Meade may never get again, and now commences to be seen the cursed jealousy of Corps Commanders. Warren with the Second

---

70. The sites of both Morton's and Raccoon Fords are along the Rapidan River between Orange and Culpeper counties.
71. The fords are also along the Rapidan River. This ford's proper name is Germanna. For an extensive background on Germanna Ford and some of the other related fords, see Erik Nelson, "Historic Crossings of the Rappahannock and Rapidan Rivers That Played Critical Roles in Fredericksburg Area Battles," *Blue & Gray Magazine* 32, no. 3 (2016): 6–26, 46–51; and a related tour article, "Historic Crossings of the Rappahannock and Rapidan Rivers," 52–65.

Corps ~~was~~ is the only one yet up, and [William H.] French[72] with the 3d Corps is only 5 miles in the rear. Gen. Meade sends an A.D.C. to hurry French up. French replies that there is no road & that he is going into Camp where he is.

The Aide replies that he has just come back along the road & that it is a good clear road running straight to where French is wanted. Still French goes into camp. Aide after Aide is sent with positive orders for the 3d Corps to move on, but with the same result: & on Saturday morning Lee occupies the entrenchments in force.

This is the story as I heard it from [Henry C.] Christiancy,[73] Jim's brother, who is a personal A.D.C. to Gen. Humphry [Andrew A. Humphreys][74] Meade's Chief of Staff & I suppose it is the story that

---

72. William H. French was an 1837 graduate of the U.S. Military Academy at West Point, New York, who rose to be a corps commander during the Civil War. Unfortunately, his military reputation was effectively ruined when after the Battle of Mine Run, General Meade blamed French for being slow to move his corps into place. He was removed from command and mustered out of volunteer service on May 6, 1864. Granger provides insight into the reasons for his loss of his corps command. While French remained a colonel in the Regular Army, he was assigned to desk duty in Washington, D.C., for the balance of the war. He served in the postwar army, commanding military posts, including Fort McHenry in Baltimore. He retired in 1880 and died in 1881. Warner, *Generals in Blue*, 161–62.

73. As Granger states, Henry Clay Christiancy, born September 6, 1841, was the older brother of Lt. James Christiancy. Both men were the sons of U.S. Senator Isaac P. Christiancy. Henry enlisted at age nineteen on April 20, 1861, as a private in Company F, 1st Michigan Infantry, but was commissioned as an officer on August 17, 1861. He was promoted to captain on April 28, 1862. He received brevet promotions to major and lieutenant colonel, and he was mustered out on January 20, 1866. After holding government jobs for many years, he died on May 18, 1925, in Detroit, Michigan. Soldier Records and Profiles; U.S. Civil War Soldiers; Michigan Death Records for Henry C. Christiancy, May 19, 1925; "Maj. Henry C. Christiancy," memorial at Findagrave.com, 154716343.

74. Andrew A. Humphreys (1810–1883) was a career army officer, a civil engineer, and a general in the Civil War. He graduated from the U.S. Military Academy at West Point, New York, in 1831. After brief service in the Seminole War of 1836 in Florida, he spent the next two decades as a highly regarded engineering officer. He helped to determine the most practical route for a transcontinental railroad. After the Civil War broke out, Humphreys rose quickly and was soon promoted to command a division as a brigadier general. He performed well in the Battles of Antietam and Fredericksburg in late 1862. When General Meade assumed command of the Army of the Potomac, he wanted Humphreys as his chief of staff, but the latter wanted to

Meade will tell. On the other hand the friends of French say that the grand blunder was made on Monday by Warren, & that French was on time always, though I have not heard anyone of them attempt to explain the delay of Friday.

Monday morning Warren had twenty eight thousand men, half of the Army, under his command: & was placed on the left of the line. French was on or near the right & was to open at 8 A.M. & after a cannonade of an hour the attack was to be made along the ~~lines~~ whole line.

At the appointed time, French opened & then started his corps for the enemy's rifle pits. He had crossed the run and was within 150 yards of the pits when Warren sent word that he "could not attack successfully."

The attack was suspended much to the disgust of French, and after going in person to the left, Gen. Meade seemed satisfied that Warren could not reasonably have made the attack. Meanwhile our Div. under Gen. Custer had not been idle.

On the morning of Friday the 27th we found that the enemy had left his entrenchments on the other side of the Rapidan & so we crossed. We stayed on the other side till three or four P.M. when the Rebs advanced on us from the direction of Raccoon Ford. We had no orders to fight them[,] Gen. Meade not even knowing that we were across: so we retired slowly & in good order to this side. From prisoners we learned that the force opposed to us was ~~part of~~ [A. P.] Hills[75] Corps which had been lying at Orange C. H. but had left that place early that morning.

---

retain his division. Just after Gettysburg, he agreed to be chief of staff. In November 1864, he assumed command of the II Corps, which he led to the end of the war. In the postwar army, he was appointed as a permanent brigadier general and chief of engineers. He retired in 1879 and died in 1883. Warner, *Generals in Blue*, 240–42.

75. Ambrose Powell Hill (1825–1865), better known as A. P. Hill, was a Confederate Army general, who was killed in action in the closing days of the war. A native Virginian, Hill served in both the Mexican-American War and the later Seminole War, but chose to join the Confederacy in 1861. He quickly became one of Gen. Thomas "Stonewall" Jackson's ablest division commanders. After Jackson was wounded in May 1863 at Chancellorsville and subsequently died, Hill assumed command of the Confederate III Corps. Illness sidelined him for periods in 1864–65, but he returned to action on April 1, 1865. He was killed in action on April 2, 1865, at Petersburg, Virginia. Ezra J. Warner, *Generals in Gray: Lives of the Confederate Commanders* (Baton Rouge: Louisiana State University Press, 1959), 134–35.

Saturday morning the Rebs had again retired from the River & again we crossed. It rained most of this day so we remained in a house till pretty near dark & were just making preparations to put up our tents when we were surprised by the report of a gun in the direction of Raccoon Ford & the explosion of a shell in our immediate vicinity. Again we betook ourselves to the River but the rain had nearly spoiled the Ford & when we got there we found one of our guns stuck in the mud on one side of the River & one wagon in each of the two places of exit on the other side. Fortunately for us it was so dark that the enemy had no idea how small a force we had or they might have made sad havoc in our little Div. just then—but we held them in check till all got over safe. Bob not being very tall got into a hole where the water was over his back & he had to swim to get out. Of course, I got my boots full of water & then had to go off to Gen. Davies' Brig. with an order, so that it was two or three hours before I could get my boots off.

Sunday [November 29] we lay still by order of Gen. Pleasonton. Monday [November 30] we received intelligence from several sources that Lee was planning to retreat, & Gen. Custer sent me with the news to Gen. Pleasonton. Though we were on this side of the River & it was uncertain where the two Armies lay, the shortest way to Meade's H'd Qrs. was on the other side & there was quite as much danger of being "gobbled" by Mosby if I went down on this side, as there was of running into the Reb. lines on the other side, so I took the shortest route. I set out with five orderlies, none of us knowing anything about the way, more than the general direction. As soon as we crossed the River we saw a Reb picket fire about half a mile from us, but we kept well out of sight behind hills woods &c. & went on.

At every house we passed there had been "soldiers" (the negroes did not dare to say Rebs. for fear we were "of that ilk,") within an hour or two. However we got through safely without seeing a single Reb. The first Picket we came to, we surprised, not knowing to which Army he belonged we made him <u>tell us</u> to which side he belonged instead of <u>telling him</u> who we were. We arrived at Gen. Pleasonton's H'd Qurs. just about 6 P.M.—just in time for me to get supper with part of the Staff, which suited me exactly as I had come off without my dinner (Being invited out, too, to a dinner of turkey and Oyster soup—Hang the luck!).

Gen. Pleasonton wanted me to wait till he could find out what orders Gen. Meade wished him to send to Gen. Custer, so I stayed there that night, and the next day [December 1], about noon I started off with the news that the Army was going to fall back that night.

When within about a mile & a half from Morton's Ford I saw something suspicious looking ahead just in the edge of the woods. I started up & got there just in time to capture a Reb. cavalryman before he could get on to his horse. He had been scouting around the country with one companion who had got so much the start of us that we couldn't catch him.

We took our prisoner and made the best possible time for the River which we reached all right.

That night the Army retreated to the old position & we are here near Stevensburg again, though not the same house. The Cavalry-man I captured had a splendid mare & the General said I might keep her, but Capt. Greene and Maj. Drew were both anxious to get her, & immediately a muss was raised about "captured property." The <u>Poor Innocents</u> it hurt their consciences that Uncle Sam should be cheated out of a horse! Drew has sold at least one captured horse, that I know of, and Greene is riding one for which he promised the man who captured him five Dollars which promise he has never fulfilled.

The last mentioned model of all the virtues, lived in style, while home, on $400 <u>which a private soldier sent home to be deposited for the benefit of a sick wife</u>. However I euchred 'em both on the horse game—if I can't have the mare myself I've put [it] out of their reach.

Give my love to all the Girls—I haven't time to distribute it into smaller parcels for its bed-time & I'm cold.

E. G. Granger

Custer and his staff, circa March 1864, at his Clover Hill headquarters in Stevensburg, Virginia. *Courtesy Little Bighorn Battlefield National Monument.*

CHAPTER 4

CAMP LIFE, WINTER 1863–1864

※ ※ ※

For most of the next five months, Lieutenant Granger focused on the downtime experiences of the Union Army's winter encampment in the vicinity of the crossroads community of Stevensburg, Virginia. Today, Stevensburg sits astride State Route 3 at Stevensburg Road (Culpeper County Road 663), about seven miles east of Culpeper, Virginia. But in the winter of 1863–64, both north and south of Route 3 today, the Union Army's II Corps and its Cavalry Corps, including Custer's Michigan Cavalry Brigade, set up a huge winter encampment in that vicinity. The dominant geographical feature is Hansbrough Ridge, which stretches between a mile to a mile and a half north from State Route 3 and east of Stevensburg Road. In front of the ridge and along Mountain Run is Lenn Park, part of the modern Culpeper County park system. Between the park and the ridge lay mostly farm fields. With Mountain Run at the foot of the ridge, it is easy to see why the area was chosen as part of the Union Army's winter camp system.

Modern State Route 3, known as the Germanna Road in the Civil War era, divides the encampment area. Much of the Union Army wintered north of Route 3 along Hansbrough Ridge. The Michigan Cavalry Brigade's campsite actually was located south of Route 3 and east of County Road 663. The camp stood generally in front of a high ground known today as Stony Mountain or Stony Point.

Custer's headquarters and living quarters were located about a mile west in a mansion known as Clover Hill. That property, north of Route 3, today includes both a modern farm and the historic house used by Custer as his residence that winter of 1863–64. Unfortunately, that building is not being properly maintained and is badly deteriorated. The decaying house is still visible from Highway 3, although the public is not allowed on the property. The house particularly became important after Custer married Elizabeth Bacon of Monroe, Michigan, on February 9, 1864. The newlyweds returned to Clover Hill, where they honeymooned the rest of that winter into the spring.

In his multiple letters of that winter, Edward Granger makes no specific mention of that house. Whether it served a dual purpose as Custer's personal residence and his brigade's headquarters is unclear.

5th Michigan Cavalry encampment, Stevensburg, Virginia, near Culpeper, winter of 1863–64. Likely this is the place where Lieutenant Granger had his winter hut built. *Courtesy of John Beckendorf.*

However, period photographs do show the staff with Custer on the porch or standing in front of the house that winter.[1] None appear to include Granger in them.

---

1. According to *Historic Culpeper*, 112, the frame plantation house was built circa 1775. It was sided with twelve-inch tongue-and-groove boards, English in style with a foreign saw pattern. The unusual boards are similar to those on George Washington's house at Mount Vernon. Clover Hill has a steeply pitched gabled roof with false dormers. Windows are arched, and some are double. Reportedly, at the time of the war, James Barbour (1828–1895) owned the property. A lawyer and planter, he was a delegate to both the 1860 Democratic National Convention and the 1861 Virginia secession convention. He served as a major on Gen. Richard S. Ewell's staff in the Confederate Army during the Civil War, but resigned January 30, 1863, after a dispute with Ewell. "Maj. James Barbour," memorial and gravestone at Findagrave.com, 8684957.

Most of Granger's comments in his winter letters focus on mundane camp matters, including at the outset an elaborate description of his planned winter quarters, made out of pine logs, that enlisted men will build for him. In late January, he traveled home to Michigan to visit his family about the time that Custer married Elizabeth Bacon (more familiarly known as Libbie). Granger did not attend, but sadly, his trip would be his final visit to his Detroit home and family.[2]

※   ※   ※

[LETTER 25]

Head Quarters 3d Div. Cav. Corps
Stevensburg Va. December 11th 1863 [Friday]

Mollie

I attempted to answer your last two letters several days since, but failed ignominiously, for lack of anything to write or the ability to write about nothing: and I am afraid the present trial may have a like disastrous end, as I have received no great accession to my stock, either of facts or brains since the aforesaid attempt was made.

Your two letters of the 25th Ult. & the 2nd. just were handed to me on the night after the 5th. The General's birth-day, you remember.[3] We—i.e., Jim[4], Colerick & I were in the sitting room waiting for the arrival of a number of Officers who were coming over to help

---

2. Edward G. Granger, Compiled Military Service Records. In a letter written from Detroit on January 26, 1864, to the Headquarters, Cavalry Corps, Army of the Potomac, and found in his military records, Granger asked for an extension of fifteen days for his leave of absence that he previously had been granted on January 19.

3. Custer was born December 5, 1849, in New Rumley, Ohio. His parents were Emmanuel Custer and his wife, Maria. His siblings included brothers Nevin, Thomas, and Boston and their sister, Margaret. Maria's two children from her first marriage, David Kirkpatrick and Lydia Ann Kirkpatrick, also lived with them. George, Thomas, and Boston would all die on June 25, 1876, at the Battle of Little Big Horn in then Montana Territory. Additionally, Lydia's son Autie Reed and Margaret's husband, Lt. James Calhoun, would be killed in action that day. See Sandy Barnard, "New Rumley, Ohio, Custer's Birthplace," in *Shovels & Speculation: Archeology Hunts Custer* (Terre Haute, Ind.: AST Press, 1990), 54–60; and Charles B. Wallace, *Custer's Ohio Boyhood: A Brief Account of the Early Life of Major General George Armstrong Custer* (Cadiz, Ohio: Harrison County Historical Society, 1987).

4. This is fellow staffer Jim Christiancy.

Brigadier General Custer and his staff at Clover Hill, circa February 1864. Custer is seated in the chair on the porch. Below him is Capt. Jacob Greene, whom Edward Granger often criticizes. Custer's servant, Eliza, is sitting at the base of the steps. Granger himself is not identifiable in the photograph. *Courtesy Little Bighorn Battlefield National Monument.*

celebrate the day—or rather night. We had a splendid time, tho I could not appreciate either of the three attractions of the evening—music, dancing & whiskey. Will Perkins' singing was the only thing I could enjoy, except watching the performances of the others.[5] Some of the Officers of the 7th Mich. Infantry stayed till 2 A.M.

---

5. William Henry Perkins, who was born May 10, 1842, in Montreal, Quebec, Canada, was commissioned on August 22, 1861, as a first lieutenant in Company E, 1st Michigan Cavalry. He was promoted to captain on August 23, 1863, and was mustered out on October 15, 1864. In civilian life, he worked as a millwright, bookkeeper, and dry goods merchant. He died March 17, 1907, in Detroit and was buried in Elmwood Cemetery. Soldier Records and Profiles; U.S. Civil War Soldiers; 1870, 1880, and 1900 U.S. Federal Censuses for William H. Perkins, "William Henry Perkins," memorial, photograph, and gravestone at Findagrave.com, 119212149.

Last Monday we had a review of the Div. by Gen. Custer—Gen. Kilpatrick being still away on leave. There were several Staff and Officers from the 2nd Corps. (Infantry) with the General and when he went around "inspecting" the two Brigades, which merely means riding around them, the General went at a pretty good gait & when we halted the "Dough-boys"[6] had to tuck their pantaloons into their boots, and one of them said to me: "that was a pretty smart ride for an Infantry man." They always ride just about as George Sheley[7] used to, if you remember how that was. Since then every thing has gone on smoothly at Head Qurs. Though the next day the First Mich Cav were badly beaten—in a horse-race by the second Corps, but the General has given up betting, so we don't patronize races "as much as we did."

Last night the General brought from Head Quarters A. P. some large photographs of himself & General Pleasonton & as we had ordered some, he advised Colerick & I to go up today & get them before Pleasonton's Staff got at them so as to get our pick. Accordingly I went off to Brandy Station, some four or five miles off but when I got there the artist had gone to deliver some pictures, & after hunting for him an hour or two I returned minus the pictures & plus an "awful" cold for it has been a bitter cold day.

Some time ago Capt. Dodge was ordered to go to his quarters under arrest, by Maj Dake. Dodge replied in a most impudent manner, cursing the Maj, accusing him of stealing horses &c. &c. in the presence of nearly all the Officers of the Regt. Now Maj Dake is the meekest of men,[8] Moses "wasn't a circumstance" to him, but he had before been insulted by Dodge several times, and his patience was exhausted, so he "finally puckered up courage & went" and filed charges against our doughty Capt. This was more than Dodge had bargained for & he offered to apologize but the Maj was bound to push his charges through so Dodge has sent in his resignation. Whether his resignation will be accepted or not is yet to be seen—we can only "wait and pray."

I like your photograph very much—as a work of art, of course, I

---

6. "Doughboys" was a familiar nickname for infantry troops in the Civil War and in the nineteenth-century U.S. Army. They often marched on dusty roads, which gave them an appearance similar to the flour-covered doughboys who assisted bakers.
7. For more about George Sheley, see chapter 1, note 38.
8. For more information on Crawley P. Dake, see chapter 2, note 12. This seems an odd way for Granger to describe Dake, given that the major would become a U.S. marshal in Arizona some fourteen years later.

mean. The General liked it too, but all the rest said "it was not so good looking as the original." I don't know whether they said so from a desire to be complimentary, or from ignorance.

The General says he wants one of your photographs.

Isn't Miss Dunn going to trade?

Greene is sick poor dear! I have that mare now in spite of them all, but I don't know whether I shall be able to keep her. (Dec. 12) she ran away last night and can't be found.

Can't keep up my correspondence with you let alone writing compositions but—you are welcome to my old ones if you find any that will do you any good.

Are you reading Shakespear of or Shakespeare? Maj Ferry had a brother but he went in the Army too, I believe.

Yours

Ed G. Granger

Greene sends his respects to Miss Dunn. He don't appear to be so sick as he was. I guess he was only drunk.

E. G. G.

Charlie Safford is going home if he can get a leave & I guess he can.[9] He promised to come & see you if he goes home. Have you seen any thing of Fred[10] yet? He had to stay in Mich. awhile to recruit for the Regt. If I don't seal this letter pretty quick I am afraid I shall be tempted to write a P.S. & that would be girlish you know.

Tell Carrie she promised me one of her photographs as soon as she had any taken and I want one, as soon as she can spare time from her charitable labors at the <u>Asylum</u> to write to me. I wish I had been home on the 25<u>th</u> to administer the regular punishment which you so much needed that day.

Au Revoir
Ed

---

9. Granger also invited Captain Safford to "pass the evening" with the headquarters staff on December 12, according to Safford's entry for that date in his journal. Davis, *I Rode with Custer*, 83.
10. Granger is likely referring to his friend Fred Nims.

✳ ✳ ✳

[LETTER 26]

Head Quarters 3d. Div Cav. Corps.
Stevensburg Va. December 20th 1863 [Sunday]

Mollie

Yours of the 15th Inst was received last night with one from Uncle Edward of the 14th. At the time you wrote that letter, you evidently had not received my last. I presume you have that, by this time: but in case you have[n't] I can give you a summary of its contents. First, it contained every thing that your letter suggests that it ought to contain, that is; a receipt for your photograph & an expression of the proper amount of admiration therefor; and a requisition for Carrie's Photograph, properly approved & signed. Secondly, it contained an application for your photograph from General Custer. It seems to me that you ought to have received the aforesaid document before the 15th but perhaps I may be mistaken as to its date.

There has been nothing of very great moment going on in the Army lately, though of course our daily life here is one of suffering, privations and romantic adventure. We become so accustomed to this that we scarcely ever think of it, still ~~less~~ write home about it, especially as we know that our friends at home are sufficiently uneasy without any such unnecessary harassing of their feelings. However I am tempted to night, to overstep this practice & give you a <u>true</u> description of the life we lead. One day will serve as a sample of all. In the first place my troubles begin early in the morning, for Colerick always insists on getting up before the proper hour, & so I am "broken of my rest" for two or three hours before the usual time for our <u>reveille</u> (9 A.M.). Then my "nigger," Sam, never gives me notice in time to get dressed before breakfast so the toast is always cold, or, at best, only warm. And such a breakfast as we are waked up, at such an abnormally early hour, to eat. No fresh meat except beef, and occasionally a chicken, turkey or duck; potatoes (Irish at that) and hot toast or biscuit, & butter, with coffee (milk & sugar), & applesauce. After breakfast we adjourn to our tent but if it happens to be a very windy day our stove smokes and we have to go out in the mud or cold & fix the pipe. Then we have nothing to read except Jomini's Art of War[11] or some other dry military work till the newsboy comes (about an hour) & then very likely he hasn't got the paper you need, or if he has it's all wet & you have to spend half an hour in drying it, before it can be read. About 4 P.M. comes a summons to appear at once at the dinner table. This meal is but a repetition of the other with the addition of apple dumplings or pudding (rice, plums or apple) by way of desert. Then we are compelled to listen to the band for half an hour or so, and just as we are settling down for a quiet evening in our tent an orderly announces that the General wishes to see us in his room & we go up & play euchre or whist till nine or ten P.M. & then retire to our tent & wrap ourselves up in a blankets (we have only <u>eleven</u> between us).

Now Mollie don't you pity us? It's rough I tell you!

Capt. Keith[12] is really very unwell though his disease is one peculiar to this climate & one which would not alter <u>his</u> appearance much. I think it would be visible on ~~any~~ one of my complexion, except Keith's.

Capt Judson has no extension of leave, having omitted to send an application ~~of~~ for extension, with his surgeon's certificate. I'm afraid it may make him trouble. An order has been issued returning him to his Regt. when he returns.

Does Uncle Charles think Capt. Judson stands any chance of getting the Colonelcy or Lt. Colonelcy of the Regt. in case Col. Alger gets his star?

You want to know what you can do for me [for] Christmas. I don't know unless you can mend my pantaloons which are sadly torn, as usual, & will probably remain so, unless you repair them, by mail or in some other way. I thought I was going to have a chance to bring them home myself as the General was intending to be home Christmas & New Years & promised to take us with him, but that project fell through, so you will not probably have the honor of seeing me again till this "cruel war is over" or till I can get sick, which latter alternative

---

11. Antoine-Henri Jomini (1779–1869) was a military theorist and a Swiss officer who served as a general in the French and Russian armies. His works were influential in military circles during the eighteenth century. Prior to the Civil War, his theories were the only ones taught at the U.S. Military Academy at West Point.
12. See chapter 2, note 91 for more on Capt. William Keith. He was discharged on March 5, 1864, on account of disability.

you would think the worst of the two if you could see me just now. I'm as fleshy as Lig Taylor,[13] & getting worse every day. I didn't know that George Chester[14] was in the Army but I did know that he was a clerk in the Q.M. Dept. in Washington if that is what you call "the Army."

The General says don't forget that photograph.

Remember me to Carrie. My "Cousin Mattie" & Mattie Guthrie, as well as to C. I.

Your brother E. G.

P. S. I hear you are taking singing lessons of Mr. Dance. I would recommend for your careful consideration the enclosed extract.

E. G. G.

Bribate Dictionary
Presence—not presance
Too—an adverb to
Chemistry—Chymistry is obsolete
Mean not meen

Respectfully submitted
E. G. Granger
Lt. & A.D.C.

※ ※ ※

[LETTER 27]

Head Quarters 2nd Brig. 3d Div.
Cavalry Corps. January 3d 1864 [Sunday]

Mollie

Having nothing whatever to do, I have taken myself to my dernier resort, writing though I am about as short of any-thing to write as of any-thing to do.

---

13. This individual is unidentified.
14. This individual is unidentified.

Colerick went off yesterday with his Regiment which has gone to Michigan as a Veteran Regiment, more than three fourths of the men having re-enlisted.[15] The men have thirty-five days furlough and then the Colonel reports with his Regt. to the authorities of the State. You see this leaves me "alone in my glory" for the greatest part of the winter, at least, to say nothing about my anticipations of a good time when Mrs. Town should come out here.

Don't you pity me? I expect to be very lonely pretty soon—haven't the time just at the present. This morning I commenced making preparations to build. I hope my mansion will be completed by Tuesday night. It is to be of pine logs, twelve feet by nine, with a board roof & a floor. It will be built on to the rear of my wall-tent, which will be ripped open for convenience of communication. The tent will serve for a parlor & the house for sitting-room, bed-room &c. &c. I have a nice front door from for my residence, but shall be forced to have it at the rear. I expect to be able to secure a window from some neighbor who will be so kind as to lend me one for the winter, for which I may ask him in the Spring, if I don't forget it.

This matter of quarters occupies my time pretty well now, but when I get settled down I don't know what I can find to do with myself. Colerick gone, & I don't have any-thing to do with the rest of the Staff, scarcely seeing any of them more than once a day, and the General keeps so close that black Eliza[16] says "Do all you northern men act so

---

15. The 1st Michigan Cavalry's enlistment period expired in 1864. Some 370 of its veterans reenlisted during the winter of 1863–64. They were allowed to return to Michigan on thirty days' leave after the reenlistment. The regiment also recruited some eight hundred new men to fill out its ranks.

16. Eliza Brown Davison was the Custers' black cook. A short, stocky woman, about age twenty-five or twenty-six, she had run away from the plantation of her owner, Robert Pierce, after she learned of the Emancipation Proclamation. In August 1863, she met Custer, then commanding his cavalry division, when it was encamped near Amissville, Virginia. At that time, Granger was commanding his company as the division's provost guard and likely encountered the former slave. Custer asked her to work as his cook and maid. After his marriage to his wife, Elizabeth, in February 1864, the two women "fashioned an arrangement that lasted for five years," according to historian Shirley Leckie. At the disastrous battle of Trevilian Station on June 11–12, 1864, Eliza was captured by the enemy but soon escaped. In 1869, she was dismissed by Libbie Custer for being insolent. Shirley A. Leckie, *Elizabeth Bacon Custer and the Making of a Myth* (Norman: University of Oklahoma Press, 1993), 40, 48, 122.

Maj. Smith Hastings at Stevensburg winter encampment.
Courtesy of John Beckendorf.

when you are going to be married?" (Poor fellow! he can't be blamed, it's the last chance he'll ever have to enjoy a few days in quiet.)

For reading matter I have an old number of the Atlantic which I read through once a week—it being so dry that it only takes that length of time to forget it all—Harper's for January which is so much worse than the other that I have not been able to read it once, yet: and a "Staff Officers' Manual"—a compilation differing from a dictionary in this, that it contains nothing that a person don't know already. I do have not seen a newspaper in so long that I don't know whether [James] Longstreet[17]

---

17. James Longstreet (1821–1904) was a prominent Confederate general during the Civil War and one of the most trusted advisers to Gen. Robert E. Lee. A West Point graduate, he achieved a record for bravery during the Mexican War. During the Civil War, he rose to the rank of lieutenant general. After the war, his ties to Republicans made him a controversial figure among his fellow Southerners. Warner, *Generals in Gray*, 192–93.

CAMP LIFE, WINTER 1863–1864   167

is running from [Ambrose] Burnside[18] or vice versa or whether Averrill [William W. Averell][19] has returned or not.[20] Our Head Quarters are out of the way and the newsboy never comes here. I have had one letter within a month & that was yours of the 15th ult. Now the Holidays are passed I suppose you will have time to write, again.

Tell Don that he owes me a letter. By the way, have you seen anything of Lieut. Ros. Holmes[21]—a cousin of Don's, from the Seventh

---

18. Ambrose Burnside (1824–1881), an 1847 graduate of the U.S. Military Academy, followed a number of careers in his life besides the army: railroad executive, inventor, and industrialist. In politics, he was elected governor of Rhode Island and its U.S. senator. During the Civil War, he compiled a mixed record as an army officer. He led successful campaigns in North Carolina and Tennessee, but as commander of the Army of the Potomac, he led it in the disastrous defeat at Fredericksburg in December 1862 and was replaced the next month. Although ill-suited for higher command, he led the IX Corps for much of the rest of the war. However, on July 30, 1864, after he authorized what became known as the disastrous Battle of the Crater, Gen. Ulysses S. Grant relieved him of command on August 14, 1864. Not given another assignment, Burnside resigned his commission on April 15, 1865. Warner, *Generals in Blue*, 57–58.
19. William Woods Averell (1832–1900) was a career army cavalry officer and a general during the Civil War. Graduating from the U.S. Military Academy in 1855, he joined the U.S. Army Mounted Rifles as a second lieutenant. By September 1862, he had risen to the rank of brigadier general of volunteers. By February 1863, he commanded a division of cavalry, but soon was relieved of command by Maj. Gen. Joseph Hooker because of his purported slowness during a Chancellorsville raid. He regained his reputation later that year in the Department of West Virginia. Early in 1864, he performed admirably in actions in the Shenandoah Valley, but later that year, under Gen. Philip Sheridan, he was again removed from command after the Battle of Fisher's Hill. He later resigned his volunteers commission and his Regular Army commission. After the war, he involved himself in business and politics until his death in 1900 in Bath, New York. Warner, *Generals in Blue*, 12–13.
20. Granger's statement about these episodes is interesting. In the fall Union forces under Maj. Gen. Ambrose Burnside controlled Knoxville, Tennessee, while Confederate Lt. Gen. James Longstreet besieged the city with his own forces. The siege ended when Maj. Gen. William Tecumseh Sherman reinforced Burnside's troops. Longstreet ended his siege on December 4, 1863, and headed for winter quarters. As for Averell, in November and December 1863, he had successfully led his Union cavalry on raids against the Virginia & Tennessee Railroad's depots and supply garrisons.
21. Roswell H. Holmes was born November 25, 1838, in Holmesville, New York. Before the war, he was a salesman in Detroit. He was commissioned on September 12, 1862, at Detroit as a second lieutenant in Company E, 7th Michigan Cavalry. The next August he was promoted to first lieutenant. On October 19, 1863, he was *(continued)*

Cav.? He told me that he was going to accompany Mrs. Clift from Syracuse to Detroit & I told him to call over & see you if he had the time. I presume you will see some of the officers of the First Cav. as several of them will stay in the City most of the time of their leave. They are a first rate set of officers & very gentlemanly fellows. Colerick promised to call while in the City.

If he comes after you receive this, tell him that Lieut. [Dallas] Norvell[22] is all right, the order came down last night. The same order contains Dodge's acquittal of all the charges preferred against him by Maj Dake.

Henry Gale,[23] one of the Sergeants of Co. C returned from Michigan yesterday. He says that Fred Nims is out at Grand Rapids & can't get away, having had only two days at home since he has been in Mich. How I pity him! I would, if I could, offer myself a "living sacrifice" <u>in his place</u>, to save him from the horrors of his position.

> taken prisoner at the Battle of Buckland Mills, but escaped two days later. He was promoted to captain officially on March 1, 1864, but had received a battlefield appointment August 1, 1863, for gallantry in action. Owing to ill health, he resigned on March 28, 1864. Soldier Records and Profiles; U.S. Civil War Soldiers; John Robertson, comp., *Michigan in the War* (Lansing, Mich.: W. S. George, 1880), 851; Lee, *Personal and Historical Sketches*, 194; *Detroit City Directory 1862*.
>
> 22. Lt. Dallas Norvell was a younger brother of Col. Freeman Norvell, the 5th Cavalry's early commander. He was promoted to first lieutenant on January 6, 1863, but was discharged for disability on October 10, 1863, likely due to chronic diarrhea. As a member of the 5th Cavalry, he may have served on Custer's staff, although that is uncertain. *Michigan in the War* lists him as assistant quartermaster on General Copeland's staff in December 1862. He was born July 28, 1825, in Philadelphia and died March 5, 1888, in Amerstburg, Ontario, Canada. Before the war, he had attended the University of Michigan. For a time after the war, he served as deputy postmaster of Detroit. Soldier Records and Profiles; U.S. Civil War Soldiers; Robertson, *Michigan in the War*, 573; "Lieut. Dallas Norvell," memorial, photograph, and gravestone at Findagrave.com, 17714467.
>
> 23. Henry D. Gale, from Monroe, Michigan, enlisted on August 22, 1862, as a corporal in the 5th Michigan Cavalry. As a sergeant, he was mortally wounded by a gunshot through the left shoulder during the Battle of Yellow Tavern on May 11, 1864, and died June 20, 1864. According to David Ingall, "Henry was cared for tenderly by a Virginia family who wrote a touching letter back to his family telling them that he had died in their care and even though they were enemies, that he was a good son and brother." He is buried in Woodland Cemetery in Monroe. David Ingall, "David Ingall's Speech for Civil War Monument Dedication," Monroenews.com, posted May 28, 2012; Soldier Records and Profiles; U.S. Civil War Soldiers; "Henry D. Gale," memorial and gravestone at Findagrave.com, 77900028.

Remember me to all friends (of the female persuasion, of course),

Ed. G. Granger

P. S. In the above truthful & heart rending account of the sufferings a soldier is called on to endure for his "bleeding Country" (at $112.00 a month). I forgot to state that my stovepipe keeps tumbling down & I have to run out in the cold & "fix it," (Don't let Miss Pollay see that,) & it always falls when I have my coat and boots off.

From Your Afflicted Brother Ed.

[LETTER 28]

Head Quarters 2nd Brig. 3d Div. C. Corps.
My New House January 8th 1864 [Friday]

Mollie

I have a new house and now if I could only get a fifteen days' leave, I would come home and try to make the little arrangement you speak of in yours of the 30th ult. I suppose if Colerick was at our house he told you that I was intending to put up a mansion for winter-quarters, and if so, he probably laughed at the idea of my accomplishing that, or any other task. However the house is finished & I am going to give you a history & description thereof, to night, the first evening I ever spent in a house of my own, though as you can see for yourself I am so nervous I can hardly write, even now, & there is no knowing whether the last part of this epistle will be legible or not.

Colerick left last Saturday [January 2], & Sunday morning I had some men detailed to come & work for me. They have been from that time to 4 P.M. Friday, Jan 8th in erecting the building which is the subject of this letter. It (the house not the letter) is built of pine logs & covered with a sort of stucco composed of a mixture of water & the "sacred soil." The roof & floor are made of boards obtained by tearing down the granary of our next neighbor. The house is built just in rear of my tent with which communication has been opened by ripping the seam in the back of the tent, open, so the tent is my parlor, & the log part my sitting & bed room. This latter is nine feet wide and twelve feet long, & seven logs high. At the rear end of the room is a large fire-place & a door. The fire place is built of stone and mud.

Last night when the men quit work & went to the Regt. my stove was out of doors, my tent was ripped open so I could not sleep in that & the chimney to my fire-place was not built, and the night was evidently going to be a very cold one. I thought at one time my chances of freezing were better than they had ever before been in any one year's soldiering. However the boys brought the stove in to the house & stopped up all the holes that were more than two feet square, so I managed to sleep quite warm till most morning though I certainly did not suffer from lack of fresh air. There are still some slight cracks, through which the wind comes in rather too freely for comfort, so that I have to leave my writing once in a while & thaw myself out by the fire; but expect to be all right in a few days, & it is much better than a tent now.

I wish I could have been home to help trim Church for Christmas this year. I did not even <u>go to Church</u> on Christmas, in fact I haven't been inside of a Church, or heard a sermon since I returned from Michigan. Chaplains are about "played out," as the boys say, There are two in our Brig. but all that I have heard from them lately is that the Chaplain of the Seventh[24] is a first-rate man in a fight, & that [S. S. N.] Greely[25] of the Sixth can't be beat at drinking whiskey.

---

24. Charles P. W. Nash, of Muskegon, Michigan, was born March 16, 1831, at Clarkston, New York, and died in January 1913. According to an inscription on his tombstone, he was a Universalist minister for more than fifty years. He was buried in Lakeside Cemetery in Holly, Michigan. His enlistment date is given variously as September 6, 1863, or October 2, 1863, and he was mustered out November 7, 1865, or December 15, 1865, at Fort Leavenworth, Kansas. According to one account he may have been the tallest chaplain. He was described as "a monstrous big man," standing six feet, six inches tall. In an address in October 1901, fellow 7th Cavalryman Asa B. Isham referred to the "tall forms" of Nash and another soldier. In a sketch in Lee, Nash briefly describes some of the action he saw, including at Yellow Tavern and Front Royal. Lee, *Personal and Historical Sketches*, 70–71; Robertson, *Michigan in the War*, 156; Mark Haynes, "Chaplain's Corner," *Sons of Union Veterans of the Civil War: Picacho Peak Camp No. 1 Newsletter*, January 2008, 2–3; Soldier Records and Profiles; U.S. Civil War Soldiers; "Charles P. Nash," memorial and gravestone at Findagrave.com, 44486505.

25. The Rev. S. S. N. Greeley, a Congregational clergyman, began pastoring First Congregational Church in 1858 in Grand Rapids, Michigan. He remained until

Gen. Custer had on a shirt with a regular sailor's collar except that there was no star in the corner,—blue flannel, about 4 inches wide (the collar I mean), when that picture was taken.

Did I ever tell you that just after he had his hair cut, the General sent home to his intended a picture; which he cut out of a U.S. Report of the Japan Expedition, representing the most hideous specimen of humanity ever created—a bald headed Japanese Priest—and labeled "The boy General with the golden locks."

The General wished me to say to you that he was very much obliged for your Photograph.

Tell Don that Maj Purdy lost the book he (Don) sent me by the Maj. Also tell that young gentleman, that if he thinks that he is going to get a letter out of me for any such note as that enclosed in yours, he is mistaken—he owes me a letter yet.

Tell Carrie B. Hawley[26] that I want that Photograph and a letter under pain of receiving another as dull as the last from me if she don't write.

Dodge has been honorably acquitted, so there is no chance of my having to refuse a 1st Lieutenancy as I should certainly do if one were offered me, on condition of returning to the Regt.

> about 1862. On October 15, 1862, at age forty-two, he was commissioned as chaplain for the 6th Michigan Cavalry and served until he was discharged on June 21, 1865, at Fort Laramie, Dakota Territory (today's Wyoming). He was born on January 23, 1813, in Gilmanton, New Hampshire, and died on September 25, 1892, in the same community. He graduated from Dartmouth College in 1835 and studied in Gilmanton Seminary from 1836 to 1838. Ordained in 1839, he pastored churches in New Hampshire, Massachusetts, and Michigan until 1862. After his wartime service, he served a church in Oswego, New York, until 1873. Ill health caused him to move back to Gilmanton, but he still headed a church in Pittsfield, Massachusetts, while living in Gilmanton. He continued to preach until shortly before his death. *Historical Collections: Collections and Researches Made by the Michigan Pioneer and Historical Society*, vol. 35 (Lansing, Mich.: Wynkoop, Hallenbeck, Crawford, 1907): 658; "Rev. Stephen Sewell Norton Greeley," memorial and gravestone at Findagrave .com, 117610917; *Record of Service of Michigan Volunteers in the Civil War, 1861–1865*, vol. 36, *Sixth Michigan Cavalry* (Kalamazoo, Mich.: Ihling Bros. & Everard, 1905): 61; Albion H. French, "Old Gilmanton Matters," *Granite Monthly* 41, no. 8 (August 1909): 258.

26. Little is known about Carrie B. Hawley, other than what Granger says about her in his letters. Whether she was anything more to him than a friend of his sister's remains unclear.

When is Ella coming home?

You need not have stated that your paragon was homely—the fact that any girl <u>could</u> like her is sufficient warranty for that. You know "The only sin one woman can <u>never</u> forgive another is the sin of being handsome."

Yours
Ed. G. Granger

✳   ✳   ✳

[Letter 29]

Head Quarters 2<u>nd</u> Brig. 3<u>d</u> Div.
Cav. Corps. A. of the Potomac Jan. 17<u>th</u> 1864 [Sunday]

Mollie

Yours of the 11<u>th</u> Inst. was received night before last. I had almost given up expecting any letters from anyone, but they all seem to write at once, as I have received four letters this week, (unless, today is Sunday, as I was told that is—but my informant did not seem very positive on the subject, and I don't believe that it is), and you know that I have not many more than four correspondents; to hear from.

Four or five days ago Sam Walker and a Captain [William H.] Loveland[27] of the 4th came down here from Bealeton, where the Regt. is stationed.

I went down to Brandy to meet them and took two pretty smart horses down for the "Hoofers" to ride. Captain Loveland was on a

---

27. William H. Loveland of Adrian, Michigan, was a highly experienced officer at the time he made his visit to Granger. He enlisted on June 20, 1861, as a sergeant in Company D, 4th Michigan Infantry. On January 10, 1862, he was promoted to sergeant major, and on September 10, 1862, he was commissioned as a first lieutenant. According to his military records, that same day he was promoted to captain for Company B. On May 4, 1864, Loveland was wounded during the Battle of the Wilderness and died of his wounds on May 31, 1864, at Alexandria, Virginia. He was buried in Carroll Hill Cemetery in Fairfax, Vermont. He had been born in 1841 in Vermont, but according to the 1860 U.S. census, his residence was in Sylvan, Michigan. Soldier Records and Profiles; U.S. Civil War Soldiers; "Capt. William H. Loveland," memorial and gravestone at Findagrave.com, 19414196; 1860 U.S. Federal Census.

citizen's saddle and it was all he could do to hang on. I would start up Bob and run past the Capt. whose horse, not wishing to be out run would try his best to keep up, the Capt. holding back with all his might, but to no purpose, the horse <u>would</u> run, in spite of his rider.

Before we reached Stevensburg the Infantry men were pretty well covered with mud, and not very anxious for much further equestrian exercise that day. However I got paid in my own coin the next afternoon. "We all," went down to Culpeper in the morning. Bob was a little lame from running over the rough ground the day before, and I was riding him with a snaffle bit. I knew, of course, that if he got to running I couldn't hold him with that bit, but as he was lame, I did not intend to let him run any. Coming home Capt. Loveland's horse started to run & Bob started after him. I tried to hold him in, but 'twas <u>no go</u>. I could only keep him far enough behind to get pretty freely spattered with mud, so I resolved to pass the Capt. and was closing up for that purpose, when, just as I had got near enough to get the <u>most possible</u> mud in my face, I had to hold up for a bad hole in the road. This set me way back again & the second time I was stopped in the same manner and when I finally did pass him we were home & a worse looking specimen than I was just it would have been hard to find. Perfectly covered with mud from head to foot, & my mouth and one eye effectually closed for the time being.

This was bad enough but the day the "Mud-crushers" left we got in deeper than that. Lieut. [George S.] White[28] of our Regt. is a cousin of this Capt. Loveland, and White & I went down to the Station to see them off. The regular passenger train had gone when we got down to the Depot[.] there was a train of open cars coming along which we got on to. The brakeman said the train was not going just yet—was "only going to run down there a little ways to switch off." White &

---

28. George Snow White of Ann Arbor, Michigan, was born on February 15, 1838, in Ann Arbor and died March 21, 1909, in Jackson, Michigan. He enlisted as first sergeant of Company K, 5th Michigan Cavalry, on August 30, 1862, at Detroit. On November 25, 1862, he was commissioned as a second lieutenant and on July 3, 1863, as a first lieutenant. On March 5, 1864, he became the regimental quartermaster. He was brevetted a captain on March 13, 1865, for gallant and meritorious services during the war. White was mustered out on June 22, 1865, at Fort Leavenworth, Kansas. Soldier Records and Profiles; U.S. Civil War Soldiers; "George S. White," memorial and gravestone at Findagrave.com, 18660234.

I staid on till the train got under good headway & then found that it was not going to stop. We rode some three miles and had to foot it back. You can imagine the abuse we had to take while we were riding with Sam & Capt. Loveland, but you can't imagine our sufferings while marching back to Brandy, in the mud. After running out of our way to catch a wagon, we found that it was not going to the Station & we double quick it for about a half a mile further to catch another wagon, in which we rode the last mile of the ~~road~~ way. To add "insult to injury," just as we arrived at Brandy the train came in, on which we might have ridden all the way back, if we had waited a few minutes.

I had a very pleasant visit ~~from~~ with Sam ~~indeed~~ while he was here. His Regt, (or part of it) had re-enlisted and Sam is expecting to go home about the last of this month or the first of next. He says Lillie[29] writes that Uncle Ed is quite sick. You have said nothing about it, I hope that he has recovered? That interrogation point is meant to refer to his recovery.

As I have not yet received Colerick's letter, I presume he did not write. Do you know whether he rec'd any pay while he was in Washington?

I heard this morning that Col. Town was in Washington again. Did he not take his wife home when the Regt. went? If he did, have you seen her? The Officer Col. Town left in command of the remains of his Regt. is under arrest for a quarrel with Drew—begun continued & ended by the latter—as far as it is ended. Have you seen any of the Officers of the First yet? If you do see any of them I advise you to get acquainted with them as they are best set of fellows in the service. All hard cases, though.

Tell Carrie to hurry & find that Photograph.

Give my respects to Cousin Mattie[30] and Mattie Guthrie.

Ed. G. Granger

You don't say when Ella is coming home. Do you know that you didn't tell me the name of the young Lady you have found? Is it any one I ever saw? From your silence on the subject I'm inclined to think you must have recovered from your severe attack of admiration for her. Has she cut you out; or has some boy pronounced her pretty?

---

29. Lillie is unidentified.
30. Cousin Mattie and Mattie Guthrie have not been identified.

Tell Don to give my respects to Miss Strong,[31] the next time she calls to see Mrs. Clift.

Write soon Ed.

※ ※ ※

[LETTER 30]

Head Quarters 2nd Brig.
3d Div. Cav. Corps. Feb 23d 1864 [Tuesday]

Mollie

For the first time since my return to my log palace, I have a few minutes of leisure, and without any one in my house but myself I have to set out to reduce as much as possible the pile of unanswered letters lying before me.

I found <u>eight</u> letters awaiting me. More than I had received in two months before I left. Of course, like a dutiful brother, I commenced by answering yours.

My journey through Pennsylvania was the most exceedingly pleasant one, the trains failing to connect at every opportunity.

As a preparation for the trials of "lying round" Pittsburgh and Harrisburgh [Harrisburg], I stopped three hours at Toledo, which place my stay was rendered peculiarly interesting by the shape of the weather, it being so cold that I could not stir out of the Depot.

In Cleveland I met Hobart[32] who is trying to get into the service of the Government as a clerk in the Quarter Master's Department. Maria[33] was at school, so I did not see her. As I only had from 9 P.M. Wednesday till 1 P.M. Thursday to stay of course I could not make much of a visit at Canfield's, though I called there. Ada was busy getting ready for the Sanitary Fair.

I arrived in Washington Saturday [February 20], just too late to take the train for the front that day. Gen. Custer was not at Washington as I expected he would be, nor I believe has he arrived there yet.

I have no ink & that which I borrowed to write with, tonight, has been taken away again during my temporary absence, so I thought I

---

31. Miss Strong remains unidentified.
32. For more about Hobart Walker, see introduction, note 24.
33. See chapter 1, note 17 for information about Maria Louisa Caskey.

would finish my letter with a lead pencil, but my pencil is a very poor one and I can't make it work well, so I guess I'll let it rest till tomorrow.

I've got another pencil now which goes better & so I guess I'll finish the letter tonight after all.

When I got to Brandy Station Sunday there was no one there to meet me, & so I had to foot it more than half the way to Head Quarters. The rest of the way I rode in an ambulance which happened to be going that way.

Yesterday I spent in calling on the Regt. &c. &c. There have been a lot of Gentlemen and Ladies from Washington out here at Div. Head Qrs. for the last few days.

The Mich. Senators & delegates & their wives & daughters & various others of the upper ten of the nation. Senator [John P.] Hales's daughters[34] & Vice President [Hannibal] Hamlin's[35] (If her father has inherited her voice he is just the man to preside over the Senate in these stormy times). Ham Howard[36] & Fred Delano[37] are here too, the former resplendent in plug hat & all the etceteras.

---

34. John P. Hale (1806–1873) was elected twice U.S. senator from New Hampshire and was appointed to fill out another term. His two daughters were Elizabeth (1835–1895) and Lucy (1841–1915). Lucy was reportedly secretly engaged in 1865 to John Wilkes Booth, the assassin of President Abraham Lincoln. Booth had a picture of Lucy Hale with him when he was killed by pursuing federal troops on April 26, 1865. Lucy eventually married William E. Chandler, who later became a U.S. senator.
35. Hannibal Hamlin (1809–1891) was the fifteenth vice president of the United States (1861–65) during President Lincoln's first term. His daughter Sarah was reportedly present at Ford's Theater the night Lincoln was shot in April 1865.
36. Ham Howard may actually have been Alfred Howard. According to the *Detroit City Directory 1862*, he was a clerk with Root, Johnson & Barbour. More important, he boarded at 93 Fort Street West. Granger himself was listed as boarding at 99 Fort Street West. However, a number of other apparently young men with the last name of Howard also appear in the directory. No one by his name appears in Civil War unit records.
37. Fredrick M. Delano (sometimes Frederick) of Detroit was a first lieutenant in the Brother Jonathan Zouaves and a director on the board of the Brother Jonathan Base Ball Club, according to the *Detroit City Directory 1862*. An endnote in a book about early baseball in Michigan, *Baseball Fever*, indicates Delano played first base for the club and later became a stockbroker. He himself was not otherwise listed in the directory, but Sarah E. Delano, identified as a widow, was. The 1860 U.S. census lists a seventeen-year-old Frederick Delano, born in 1843 and living in Detroit's Ward 7 with his family, including his mother, Sarah. The 1880 U.S. census

Today we had a grand review of our Div. and the Second Army Corps. The reviewing Officers were Gens. Meade & Warren & Pleasonton with their respective Staffs. They made a grand show themselves. Almost a Regiment of Commissioned Officers including four Major Generals (Meade, Pleasonton, Warren & General Humphreys, Meade's Chief of Staff).

There was a great crowd of Ladies from Army H'd Qrs. to see the performances & indeed I believe the Review was gotten up for their benefit.

All this was very nice, of course, but there was one part of the review of which I could not see the beauty—i.e.—staying out from 11 A.M. till 3 or 4 P.M. without anything to eat, when I had had a very early breakfast.

I forgot to say that I met Col. Alger in Washington. He was going to Fortress Monroe on special service, peddling the "Amnesty Proclamation" to the Rebs. Long life to him—in his new position!

Dodge & Co. have had Maj. Dake before an Examining Board—& he passed a splendid examination.

No more time, paper, news or nonsense so Good Bye

Ed.

Tell Carrie B. Hawley that I have her letter and photo & will receipt for the same in due time.

How are Mrs. [illegible] children?

Love to all (scil the girls)[38]

Ed.

---

also lists him at age thirty-seven living with his mother, who was seventy-three herself. He died on May 29, 1935, at age ninety-two. A death record for him lists his birth date as Sept. 1, 1842, or about seven months before Granger's birth. His occupation was given as an investment banker. His obituary in the *Detroit Free Press* indicates he served in Battery A, 2nd Michigan Artillery. Unfortunately, he was not listed in the usual Ancestry.com databases. Michigan Death Records; Peter Morris, *Baseball Fever: Early Baseball in Michigan* (Ann Arbor: University of Michigan Press, 2003), 283; Fredrick Delano obituary, *Detroit Free Press*, May 31, 1935.

38. "Scil" or "scilicet" is a Latin term meaning literally "one may know." It essentially introduces a clarification of the speaker's remarks.

* * *

[LETTER 31]

Head Quarters 2nd Brig. 3d Div. Corps
Army of the Potomac March 4th, 1864 [Friday]

Mollie

Your letter No. 1 of the latter part of Feb. was received tonight. I had about given up expecting it at all. Who directed it? I never saw the hand-writing before, I think. Your letters directed by some one else used to be a source of great disappointment to me, but I am getting to be suspicious of them now.

Day before yesterday, or rather Tuesday night [March 1] at twenty minutes of 12 the command of Gen. Custer returned from a grand raid of which you have probably seen an account before this reaches you.[39] We rested Wednesday & Thursday & this morning we started off again, that is the Gen. & Staff—we did not have the same command but another part of Brig. & Division. We only went on a reconnaissance to Ely's Ford[40] to see whether the Rebs. held it in force, or not. They did not and we returned after driving in their Cav. Pickets, making the trip of thirty two miles, including stopping from 10 A.M. to 6 P.M.

---

39. This is Custer's expedition toward Charlottesville, Virginia. Granger's passing mention of Custer's own march toward Charlottesville in the west may suggest that he himself did not accompany the general on the raid, although that does not seem likely. The more historically controversial raid on Richmond, Virginia, was led by General Kilpatrick. Kilpatrick's goals in proposing his raid to the Union higher command were to destroy Confederate infrastructure and free Union prisoners of war. On February 28, 1864, Union Col. Ulric Dahlgren and some 460 cavalrymen crossed the Rapidan River at Ely's Ford. Separately, Kilpatrick led a force of 3,500 cavalrymen, including some 500 members of the Michigan Cavalry Brigade, toward Richmond, but without Custer in command. Kilpatrick viewed Custer as a rival and purposely relegated him to a secondary role, as outlined by Granger in his letter. Author Bruce Venter refers to Custer's participation "as a sideshow, spawning internal conflicts in the 3rd Cavalry Division that may have figured in the raid's outcome." Bruce M. Venter, *Kill Jeff Davis: The Union Raid on Richmond, 1864* (Norman: University of Oklahoma Press, 2016), xvi.
40. The site of Ely's Ford is west of Fredericksburg and north of Chancellorsville on the Rapidan River.

There's nothing to write here. The weather that <u>dernier resort</u> of all unlucky letter writers, is beautiful. Since our return the sun has shown most all the time (day-times) & the mud is getting pretty well dried up.

I have erected a vaulting bar in the yard just next to my shanty and spend the greatest part of my time in exercising, & enjoying the attempts of the boys to follow suit.

We have been off so much & have been so large a part of the time while here trying to recover from the effects of our various journeys that I haven't seen much of Mrs. Custer yet.[41]

I like her very much, so far, as I have become acquainted with her. Lib goes out riding every day with the Gen.—don't you wish you were here?

Another reason I don't see much of Mrs. Custer is that my bar takes so much of my time. You can't imagine what a comfort it is. Then too, she has Greene to keep her in company & Jim, & Jim is really one of the oddest mortals I know, & when he is good natured & <u>sober</u> as good company as can be easily found down here.

They have put a surgeon in my tent with me, for a while—I don't know how long. He is a very estimable member of society if I may judge from his appearance—I don't know him personally. He is about 5 feet 2 inches in his boots and weighs somewhat less than 200 lbs: his face is covered with a beard very much like that of Mr. Rexford,[42] only it isn't red, & his hair is combed in the same style as mine & about as often, i.e., once a month.

Dodge has just returned from a leave & he is putting on more old

---

41. Granger would come to know Mrs. Custer well during the next few months, but he likely was merely one more member of the Michigan Cavalry Brigade to her. In none of her own books, written later in the nineteenth century after the death of her husband, does Mrs. Custer mention Granger; her books of course, focused more on the Custers' lives on the plains. In 1950, Marguerite Merington published heavily edited excerpts of the correspondence between the Custers. See Merington, *Custer Story*. Three references to Granger appear in letters written by the general to his wife (66, 67, and 100), but none by Mrs. Custer. Two other major books about the general's wife herself fail to mention Granger, although they do mention a concussion suffered by Custer in a carriage accident that involved Granger. See Leckie, *Elizabeth Bacon Custer*, and Arlene Reynolds, *The Civil War Memories of Elizabeth Bacon Custer* (Austin: University of Texas Press, 1994).
42. Rexford is unidentified.

lace &c &c than you have ever seen. Individual—at least, since the days of the lancers.

I am very glad that Sam Walker got home—you didn't tell me how it happened.

Poor Samuel & Aurelia, how terribly the loss of Jason must affect them![43]

Tell Don—if ever I get any-thing to write about I'm going to write to him, mean while he will undoubtedly hear from me often through Carrie.

Give my love to Miss Walton & tell her I would have been at Church that night if I had received her message before I had promised to stay home.

Hope you like the style of the writing but I knew if I did not make the most of what little I could write, I shouldn't fill my sheet, and I did not write because I had anything to say but merely to send the enclosed X out of which you may get that picture of the two Generals framed & the change I presume you can get rid of some way.

Ed.

If I meet "any nice young man" who has a sister at home I will let you know, as it only seems fair to you that you should be always the medium of communication between your brave brother & the girls without ever having a chance yourself to use any of yours & of theirs in the same way.

E. G. Granger

Glad to see that you are learning to build a fire—I won't do any thing of that kind now.

Oh I forgot to tell you that on our raid my orderly confiscated a citizen's saddle for me, & I rode in it to day & Bob would trot & I wasn't used to the saddle & the consequence is that the saddle & the horse's back are very sore tonight—of Course, I ain't.

Ed.

---

43. Granger appears to be referring to his cousin Samuel G. Walker, but historical information about his marriage to Aurelia or the birth or death of a son named Jason is unconfirmed. See chapter 2, note 33 for more information about Samuel Walker.

[LETTER 32]

Head Quarters 2nd Brig. 3d Div.
Cav Corps A. P. March 16th 1864 [Wednesday]

Mollie

Yours of the 4th (inst. No. 2) was not received till the evening of the 10th, and I have not yet rec'd. my answer to mine of the 4th.

I have delayed writing till I could get a photo having disposed of all I had. The enclosed was taken from life though you may not recognize it. I don't like the looks of the pictures any better than I did my last. Of the resemblance to the original of course, I am not a good judge: but I should hope it is not very striking. Tell Ella that if I ever do get a good looking picture of myself, I will replace this one, but, the artists in the Army are not apt to be very successful in the taking of any-thing but money.

I was told that night that Ella was at Miss Pullings, and I thought that was somewhere in Washington. If I had yet known she was so near home I should certainly have seen her.

Should Frank and Helen[44] still be in Detroit, and after seeing this specimen, the least of the lot still wish one of my photographs—you may inform them that I don't give one of those articles to any one without a good prospect of an immediate return in kind. I forgot to tell you that you are not to give Ella this one till you have one of hers in exchange.

I have a splendid photograph of the General which I shall probably send home if I have an opportunity. The General came pretty near getting killed yesterday.[45] There was to be a race on the track in front of our Head Quarters and we all went out to see it. Finding that there was a quite a crowd of Ladies out there, the General sent me to tell Mrs. Custer that if she wished to see a horse-race she would probably never get a better chance. She consented to go and I had her side saddle put on my mare, but Beauty was not used to a lady rider, and behaved

---

44. The identities of these two people are unknown. They do not appear to be members of Granger's extended family. Granger Family Tree, Ancestry.com.
45. Historians Jeffry Wert and Shirley Leckie are among the authors who interpret Custer's injury as a likely concussion. Jeffry D. Wert, *Custer: The Controversial Life of George Armstrong Custer* (New York: Simon & Schuster, 1996), 142; Leckie, *Elizabeth Bacon Custer*, 42.

so badly that Mrs. Custer did not dare to ride her. Then the General had his two horses hitched to a carriage and the Gen & wife and Jim & I got in and the General drove around the track in great style. Our team was composed of two of the handsomest horses on the ground. After the race was over the Gen. started, his horses in on the run—the horse of one of the men got frightened and backed into the road so that the front wheel of the carriage struck him, stopping the carriage on the spot. The General and Jim being on the front seat were thrown out, and Mrs. Custer was thrown forward onto the front seat, & I staid where I sat. The Gen. struck on his head and shoulder and was insensible when picked up. We carried him as far as Maj Drew's house and laid him on the bed. He recovered the use of his tongue just as we reached the house; but, though perfectly sensible as to what was going on around him, he had no memory last night. Just before morning he went to sleep and when he waked up was perfectly sensible and all right, except a head ache and a little general weakness. Jim was only hurt a very little.

The horses were broken loose from the carriage by the shock, and they ran to their quarters, upsetting an ambulance on the way.

Talking of races, I expect to see the greatest show in that line tomorrow that the Army affords. The Irish Brigade, formerly Gen. Meagher's[46] is going to celebrate St. Patrick's day by a grand horse race. The

---

46. Thomas Francis Meagher (1823–1867) was an Irish patriot who led the Young Irelanders in the Rebellion of 1848. Convicted of sedition and sentenced to death, he was eventually sent to Van Diemen's Land (today's Tasmania) in Australia on a life sentence. Escaping in 1852, he came to New York and gained renown as a lecturer. Almost immediately after the breakout of the Civil War, Meagher joined the Army and eventually rose to brigadier general. His most notable achievement was recruiting the Irish Brigade, composed almost completely of Irishmen in regiments from New York, Massachusetts, and Pennsylvania. The brigade gained a reputation as one of the fiercest fighting units in the Union Army, especially in such battles as Antietam and Fredericksburg. Meagher resigned in May 1863 when the army refused to let him recruit new men for his now-battered brigade. He briefly returned to duty later in the war. After the war, he was appointed first as secretary of the Territory of Montana and later as its acting governor. His stint was controversial, but came to an abrupt end on July 1, 1867, when he fell overboard from the steamboat *G. A. Thompson* into the swift-running Missouri River. His body purportedly was never recovered. Because of its nature, his death has always been viewed suspiciously. See Timothy Egan, *The Immortal Irishman: The Irish Revolutionary Who Became an American Hero* (New York: Houghton Mifflin Harcourt, 2016); and Paul R. Wylie, *The Irish General: Thomas Francis Meagher* (Norman: University of Oklahoma Press, 2007),for more information about Meagher.

(left) Bvt. Maj. Gen. George A. Custer.
Courtesy of Library of Congress, LC-DIG-ppmsca-39810.

(right) Elizabeth Custer, 1885.
Courtesy of Little Bighorn Battlefield National Monument.

race track, which is just a few rods from our Head Qrs. is a mile long and is crossed by three hurdles about three feet & a half high and 3 ditches, about six feet wide (or less). The riders are to be officers of the Irish Brigade. Yesterday I saw one of the officers who were going to ride, jump his horse over one of the hurdles. They both jumped pretty well, the horse striking on his head, and the officer doing the same, some distance beyond the horse. Last year one Lt. was killed at the race. Generals Custer & Kilpatrick had thought of trying their "luck," but the Gen. will not be very apt to try any thing of the kind very soon, I guess.

Our Brig. has not yet returned, though some of the officers have, Col. Gould among the rest. The Brigade has lost about one hundred and seventy five men. Our Regt. 56, or about that. "C" Company as usual is one of the lucky Companies. Only one man lost, and he got drunk and straggled from the command. The Company has only lost two men, killed so far, including my orderly. One company of the Regt. lost 10 men out of fourteen.

Bristol has got home safe, in fact there is only one officer of the Regt. lost—captured I should say, for he is certainly no <u>loss</u> to any one here.

You may give my respects to that "member of St. John's"; but I wish you would be a little more explicit in your descriptions though I have no doubt I know who you mean.

Remember me to all my friends, and tell them they all owe me letters for they do—nearly all of them.

If you had not pleaded a headache, I should have sent [multiple words are blacked out and cannot be read].

Send that photograph as soon as possible.

E. G. Granger

Do you know where Col. Town is; what he is doing; and when he expects to get back to the front? His regt. is still in Washington—can't get horses, they say. The capture of Lt. Col. [Allyne C.] Litchfield[47] of the 7th Mich. leaves Henry Granger the only Field Officer in the Regt. If he chooses to come out to the front, he may very likely, get the Colonelcy of the Regt. He is at present in command of dismounted Camp in or near Washington and, of course, Laura[48] would not wish him to take the Colonelcy even if he could get it; but, from what I hear

---

47. Allyne C. Litchfield was born July 15, 1835, in Hingham, Massachusetts. He was commissioned as captain of Company B, 5th Michigan Cavalry, on August 14, 1862. On November 14, 1862, he was promoted to lieutenant colonel of the 7th Michigan Cavalry Regiment and on March 20, 1864, as its colonel. On March 1, 1864, during Kilpatrick's Raid on Richmond, Virginia, he was among the members of the 7th Michigan who were seized as prisoners. He was held until March 1, 1865. On March 3, 1865 he received a brevet as brigadier general for gallant and meritorious service. In 1871, he was appointed U.S. consul general in Calcutta, India. Litchfield died of pneumonia on May 16, 1911, in Erie County, Pennsylvania, and was buried in Marshfield Hills Cemetery in Marshfield, Massachusetts. A lengthy personal account of his capture appears in Lee, *Personal and Historical Sketches*. Also see Soldier Records and Profiles; U.S. Civil War Soldiers; "Allyne Cushing Litchfield," memorial and gravestone at Findagrave.com, 100098869.

48. Maj. Henry W. Granger had married Laura E. Thompson (1827–1907) in 1847. They had one daughter, Anna, who was born in 1852 and lived until 1921. Granger Family Tree, Ancestry.com.

of a friend of his say when I was home, I think he would take it. He is pretty good at figuring, I guess, he is a good fighting man when he gets fairly into a fight—but—he don't seem to like to get there very much.

This weather continues very fine much to our disgust as, if we don't get rain and mud enough to prevent horses, Old Lee may make some movement while our Cavalry is used up by Kilpatrick's late Raid. If we have to move, within a month, this Division won't do much service, I'm afraid; unless they give us new horses, and horses seem to be pretty scarce.

Write soon.
Ed

[Letter 33]

Head Quarters 2nd Brig. 3d Div. Cav. Corp
Army of the Potomac March 18th 1864 [Friday]

Mollie

I had just finished the heading to this letter when I was interrupted by a visit from an officer and before he left I rec'd. an invitation to come up into the General's room where I remained till a few moments since. It is about 11 p.m. now, but I guess I'll finish your letter tonight.

Yours of the 12th (no. 3) was received yesterday.

In my last, written day before yesterday, I told you of the preparations for a grand horse race, by the Irish Brigade. Yesterday, St. Patrick's day, was a very fine day for the sport; the sun shining brightly but the day not being too warm for the exercise. The first performance was the hurdle race. Officers of the Irish Brigade being the competitors: and riding their own horses. They were dressed in jockey style, with riding pantaloons, and no their shirtsleeves. They wore variously colored shirts, and altogether they made a brilliant appearance. One Captain was thrown from his horse in attempting to jump the 1st hurdle. He was not seriously injured, however. After the race came all sorts of Irish games, which you will find described in Adam Bide[49]—climbing a greased pole, catching a pig by the tail; that appendage to the pig

---

49. Granger is referring to the character, carpenter Adam Bede, in author George Eliot's first full-length novel, *Adam Bede,* published in 1859. It remains a major work in nineteenth-century English literature today.

in question being scarcely visible to the naked eye—the sack race—boxing—a mule race &c. &c.

The games were superintended by Gen. [Joshua T.] Owen,[50] who commands a Division in the Second Corps, I believe, & every thing passed off very pleasantly as far as the "main show" was concerned; but at one of the side races an officer of General Caldwell's staff was thrown from his horse and stunned, so that they sent over here to get an ambulance to take him home in. I have not heard since that whether he was seriously hurt or not.

The General has so far recovered from his fall as to be down stairs and out of doors this morning. He is pretty lame yet—a sort of general lameness;

"Nothing local as one may say," and his head aches some what.

I told you that Mrs. Custer got on to my mare the other day but did not dare to ride her. Wishing to get the animal accustomed to a lady's riding dress, we tried to get Eliza, the General's cook, to ride her, as Eliza is used to riding. But Jordan, my "colored man," having a very strong interest in the fair Eliza, persuaded her not to make the attempt. Of course we could not give up on any such slight disappointment and so Billy Carroll,[51] my Orderly, was rigged up with a dress, riding skirt, Lowave basket, hair net and riding cap, with a black veil to conceal his face, which is altogether too good-natured to pass for the phiz[52] of one of the "softer sex."

---

50. Joshua T. Owen's (1821–1887) military career could be best described as unsuccessful. In 1861, he was commissioned as colonel of the 69th Pennsylvania Volunteer Infantry, but his time with it was controversial. He commanded the regiment during the 1862 Peninsula Campaign and the Battles of Second Bull Run and Antietam and was promoted to brigadier general in November 1862 with command of the Philadelphia Brigade. However, after Chancellorsville in May 1863, he was arrested and relieved of his command, although the reasons remain unclear today. Later, he was restored to the brigade's command and led it at the Battles of the Wilderness, Spotsylvania Court House, and Cold Harbor in May and June 1864. However, Gen. John Gibbon relieved Owen of command after Cold Harbor for disobeying orders to support another brigade. He was mustered out in July 1864. Soldier Records and Profiles; U.S. Civil War Soldiers; "Joshua Thomas Owen," memorial, photograph, and gravestone at Findagrave.com, 21881.

51. William Carroll enlisted in Company C, 5th Michigan Cavalry, at age twenty on August 21, 1862. He was mustered out on July 25, 1865, at Detroit. Soldier Records and Profiles; U.S. Civil War Soldiers.

52. This is an old usage formed by shortening and altering the word physiognomy, which refers to the face or countenance as an indication of character.

Billy came out on to the race track yesterday in this costume, escorted by one of the orderlies, who was very attentive to the fair damsel. <u>She</u> (Billy) attracted considerable attention by <u>her</u> daring horsemanship. A crowd of officers were admiring the ease with which ~~she~~ retained her seat while the mare jumped hurdles and ditches. [Sparling D.] Predmore[53] <u>her</u> escort, was going to enter his "Lady" for the purse if they had any Ladies riding, as they expected to have.

Billy says he will have his picture taken in that costume, some of these days, on the mare. If I can get one I will send it home.

The day before the race Billy was riding "Beauty" (the mare) barebacked around the track to teach her to jump. She went over the first hurdle and the first ditch in fine style and when she came to the second ditch, which was the widest of all, Billy was prepared for a grand jump. Beauty came up to the ditch <u>on the run</u> and stopped just on the edge—Billy came up to it <u>on the move</u> and stopped just in the bottom of the ditch, which was 4 feet deep. He landed safely on his head. Beauty ran home and Billy had to walk.

To day I found the first wild-flowers I have seen this season, except a kind of chickweed which blossoms any warm day in the winter. The flowers I found to-day, were; a little blue starshaped flower, very common at Fairfax last Spring, and two very small and very pretty specimens that I do not know.

I also found near the ruins of a sesesh mansion some blossoms of the myrtle, and a daffodil and a hyacinth in bud. Capt Dodge sent me, the other day some jonquils, so I have a bouquet in which yellow predominates most decidedly.

I was congratulating myself the other day on not being at home on my birth-day, but I am afraid I was not half thankful enough—certainly not half so much, so as I should have been had I known of the change in the fashion you mention.

I had almost forgotten to tell you about Jordan's pies. The last he made, before these, he worked conscientiously for an hour and a half,

---

53. Sparling D. Predmore, about age twenty, of Pontiac, Michigan, enlisted in Company D, 5th Michigan Cavalry, but not until February 20, 1865. That was long after Granger had been killed in action. No one else of that last name appears in Civil War records for the 5th Michigan. This Predmore is listed in some sources as dying of disease on July 6, 1865, at Fort Leavenworth, Kansas. A possible second Sparling Predmore, without a middle initial, is also listed as serving with the 1st Michigan Cavalry until September 1, 1865, but they likely were the same man.

rolling the crust. Eliza told him that <u>rolling</u> the crust made it tough & (I think she spoke the truth), so this time Jordan doesn't roll it all & brings the pies on to the table with an inch thick & about a quarter of an inch of apple. I did not like to refuse to eat the pie, as it would, of course, hurt the old fellow's feelings, so I had to make the best of it. I ate the last of it before dinner this morning but have not yet recovered from the effect thereof.

Give my love to all the girls, who want it; and, if you haven't already sent it, hurry up with that Photo.

Your Brother
E. G. Granger

Don't you wish you could write such a regular hand as your brother? Look at this <u>page</u>! I can't tell which is my handwriting I wrote it all; and the rest as it came handy. I have written the letter in less than 2 hours, while it usually takes me all day to write as much & it is not proportionally any.

E. G. G.

❋ ❋ ❋

[LETTER 34]

Head Quarters 2<u>nd</u> Brig. 3<u>d</u> Div.
Cav. Corps A.P. Mar. 26<u>th</u> 1864 [Saturday]

Mollie

Your letter No. 4, dated Mar. 18<u>th</u>, but not sent from Detroit till the 23<u>d</u>, was received this after noon.

Easter Sunday March 27<u>th</u> 1864. I had progressed so far in answering the said letter, last night, when Jim Christiancy wanted me to go into the house & play cards, so here I am this morning, preparing to put an end to this document. I was slightly surprised to find that you had not received mine of the 16<u>th</u> when you wrote. It seems an age since I wrote it.

The General and Bride have just started off for Washington and Baltimore. The Ladies are all leaving the Army and so the General thought he might as well take Mrs. Custer in now, when he could get a sick leave. His head is good for 20 days yet. The only trouble he has now, from his fall is a severe head-ache. If the Army moves within the 20 days he will return, but if not he will stay till the expiration of his leave. When he comes back Mrs. Custer will stop in Washington at the same boarding house with Mrs. Colonel Grey [Gray] and Mrs. Sheldon.

The other evening when I was in the house the General gave me the enclosed photograph of his wife "to send to your Sister." Mrs. Custer said that if I sent that she wanted me to tell you that she was a great deal prettier than the picture—which is the truth. (E. G. G.) I asked her if she was ready to certify to that fact & she said "Yes." I wrote out the certificate on the back of the card and she signed it. Then the General wanted to put an endorsement on the document. Mrs. Custer stood over him to see that he did not make any improper statement, so he omitted the word "handsome" till he had written the rest. She tried to prevent his filling up the blank but did not succeed. Then he tried to scratch out the title which she had affixed to her name, but she prevented that. The picture is very natural, but is not nearly as pretty as the original. In fact, I don't think a photograph is ever very flattering to any one who has a good complexion & light eyes.

Jim Christiancy went with them to Washington this morning. It is likely to be quiet enough around these Head Quarters for the next twenty days, especially as Col. Sawyer, who is commanding the Brig. has his Hd. Qurs. at Stevensburg. While the General is gone I shall have nothing at all to do—a great change. However, our Regts. have just adopted the "double rank" drill, and I shall have occupation enough for some time yet in studying tactics. This drill is much more complicated than the "single rank" and I don't like is [sic] as well, but it was necessary to have some uniformity, and the majority of the Regts. in the service used the "double rank" so we had to follow suit.

There's nothing whatever going on down here that would be of any use interest to you. There have just been a lot of promotions made in my Regt. among others, three officers, who were originally enlisted men, have been made First Lieutenants.

Gen. Pleasonton has been ordered to Missouri, as, of course, you know. This is bad for General Custer as Pleasonton was one of his warmest personal friends. Who will get the command of the Cavalry Corps now, I can hardly guess. General [David McMurtrie] Gregg[54] is, temporarily, in command, but, as he is no more of a friend to Meade than Gen. Pleasonton was, he stands no chance of getting it permanently. Before his late "Raid," Kilpatrick would have been sure to get it in case of a vacancy: but he is virtually dead, if one can judge by the feeling in the Army, which is unanimously in favor of adding "ed" to the first syllable of his name. Gen. Merritt[55] commanding the First Div. is probably a good officer but he has never had a chance to show his ability to handle troops. Gen. [Robert Byington] Mitchell of Island No. 10 fame is spoken of, as well as Gen. Averill [William W. Averell].[56]

54. David McMurtrie Gregg (1833–1916) graduated from West Point in 1855 and served initially in the West. In January 1862, he took command of the 8th Pennsylvania Cavalry and distinguished himself during the Peninsula Campaign that spring. In December 1862, he was promoted to brigadier general and commanded a brigade in General Pleasonton's division. After the cavalry was reorganized in early 1863, Gregg found himself commanding the 3rd Cavalry Division. He led his division at both Chancellorsville and Brandy Station in May and June 1863 respectively. During the Gettysburg Campaign another reorganization gave Gregg command of the 2nd Cavalry Division. On July 3, 1863, Gregg's troops and Custer's brigade clashed with Jeb Stuart's Confederate in the significant East Cavalry Field fight three miles east of Gettysburg. Early in 1864, in the interim between Pleasonton's departure and Gen. Philip Sheridan's arrival, Gregg commanded the Cavalry Corps. Gregg's division took part in all the major engagements of the Overland Campaign in May and June 1864. Warner, *Generals in Blue,* 187–88.
55. Wesley Merritt (1834–1910) was born in New York City and was graduated from West Point in 1860. In his assessment of Merritt, Granger is revealing his ignorance, as Merritt was already recognized as one of the finest cavalry officers in the Union ranks. His early assignments were as aides to Generals Philip Cooke and George Stoneman, both of whom commanded the cavalry of the Army of the Potomac. On June 29, 1863, he was promoted to brigadier general of volunteers just before Gettysburg. From that point until the end of the war, he commanded a brigade and then a division of cavalry in the Union Army. By the war's end, he had been promoted to major general. After the war, he served as the lieutenant colonel of the 9th U.S. Cavalry, colonel of the 5th U.S. Cavalry (1876), brigadier general (1887) and major general (1895). With the outbreak of the Spanish-American War in 1898, Merritt, then age sixty-five, was given command of the first Philippine expedition. Along with Admiral George Dewey, Merritt forced the surrender of the Spanish forces. He retired from the army on June 16, 1900, and died December 3, 1910. Warner, *Generals in Blue,* 321–22.
56. Both Generals William W. Averell and Robert Byington Mitchell were competent officers, but, as Granger suggests, they probably had little chance of being elevated

If any Gen. from this Army gets the other star Gen. Custer seems to stand as good a chance as the rest, though these things are terribly uncertain.

General Custer stands higher with the fighting Generals of the Army than any other Cav. General but his friendship for Pleasonton may operate against him.

I received a Chicago Tribune day before yesterday containing a brief notice of Eugene's death.[57] Melvin, Ben, and Gene! It seems as though all the best of those of our family who had gone to the war were the only ones killed.

I did not know that to day would be Easter till I received your letter. I wish I could be home, just for to day.

---

to the cavalry commander's post. Mitchell had been born in Ohio and served in the Mexican War as a lieutenant with the 2nd Ohio. In 1856, he had moved to Kansas Territory, and at the outbreak of the war, he had been appointed as the colonel of the 2nd Kansas Infantry. By the Chickamauga Campaign of 1862, he acted as chief of cavalry for the Army of the Cumberland, but was not as well known in the east. Averell, on the other hand, was a West Point graduate and had served in the southwest where he was wounded in fighting Indians in 1859. Early in the war, he was appointed colonel of the 3rd Pennsylvania Cavalry and served admirably in many engagements for the Army of the Potomac. Having been advanced to brigadier general in September 1862, Averell led his 2nd Cavalry Division to a significant victory for the Union cavalry in March 1863 at Kelly's Ford, Virginia. Warner, *Generals in Blue*, 12–13, 328–29. Also, see chapter 4, note 19, for more information on Averell.

57. Granger's extended family is a microcosm of the tragedy that was the Civil War for Americans on both sides. Granger's remarks here about the loss of "the best of those of our family" are poignant, given his own fate in just a few months. Granger himself was one of six extended family members who were killed during the war. A number of others were wounded or had at least served, including Samuel G. Walker and Lycurgus Granger. The Eugene that Granger referred to here was Eugene E. Walter, also a maternal first cousin in another branch of his extended family, who had been killed in action on March 5, 1864, while serving as a lieutenant in Company C, 3rd U.S. Colored Cavalry Regiment, at Yazoo City, Mississippi. Another maternal first cousin, Hobart M. Walker, as mentioned earlier, died in March 1865 in the sinking of the SS *General Lyon*. Maj. Henry Granger, a paternal first cousin, was killed in action on May 11, 1864, while leading a charge of the 7th Michigan Cavalry at Yellow Tavern, Virginia. A maternal first cousin, Corp. Melvin C. Munson, 9th Michigan Infantry, was killed in action on February 22, 1862, at Elizabethtown, Kentucky; his brother Sgt. Benjamin G. Munson, 10th Michigan Cavalry, was killed in action on February 25, 1864, at Burnside Point, Kentucky, and buried in the Mill Springs National Cemetery, Nancy, Kentucky. Granger Family Tree, Ancestry.com.

Friday, I found some snow drops on Pony Mountain,[58] the first I have found this year, though not the first wild flowers. The weather is more variable than it was two weeks ago, but still most of the time we enjoy a more beautiful weather than you often see up North.

I have been making inquiries in every letter I have written as to whether Aunt Polly[59] is in Detroit yet &c. &c. but I have not heard a word on the subject yet. Also about Col. and Mrs. Town I would like to hear something.

Are those photographs of Bryant and Jessie[60] of such a size that they can be sent in a letter? If they are I would like one very much.

Give my love to Miss Walton, and my respects to Miss Hutchins, and anyone else that wants them.[61]

E. G. Granger

If you have not already attended to getting that photograph before you get this letter, I hope you will not trust to "meeting Ella in the street within a month or two."

Ed.

[LETTER 35]

Head Quarters 2nd Brig. 3d Div. C.C.
Army of the Potomac Mar. 31st 1864 [Thursday]

Mollie

<u>You're a Brick!</u>

Yours of the 24th—27th was received to day. That photograph of Jessie

---

58. This hilltop at the end of Hansbrough Ridge was also called Signal Hill. Both the Union and Confederates used the site as an important signal station in the Culpeper area.
59. This was Granger's maternal aunt Polly Walker. She was born November 5, 1797, in Johnstown, New York, and died on June 13, 1886, in Syracuse, New York. She was about thirteen years older than Granger's mother, Matilda Walker. Granger Family Tree, Ancestry.com.
60. Bryant Walker, then age seven, and Jessie Walker, then four, were the children of Granger's maternal uncle Edward Carey Walker and his wife, Lucy Bryant Walker. See introduction, note 29. Granger Family Tree, Ancestry.com.
61. Neither of these women has been identified.

and Bryant is the most beautiful picture I ever saw. Tell Aunt Lucy I am very much obliged to her for it. Jessie looks so natural that I almost expect to be <u>pinched</u> when I look at her.

Tell Helen[62] I am sorry I have no better picture to send her in return for hers, which is very good, indeed, but I spoilt the best one I had in endeavoring to remedy one of the worst of its many defects. The artist <u>did not</u> do justice to my <u>moustache</u>, which, in the original, is, 'pon honor, distinctly visible. In attempting to supply this deficiency my pencil slipped, ruining the picture and so discouraging me that I did not dare to try the experiment again; so Helen will be obliged to take my word for the moustache, though, if necessary, I can obtain certificates from Gentlemen of undoubted veracity "in proof of my assertion."

As for sending you one, I won't do it—I don't intend to have any more than I can help of this edition issued, and I hope, that no very distant day, to call in the circulation. You always think the last one best, and I am inclined to think that you only say so, this time, to use your own expression, "to make it go down."

Ella's photograph is excellent, and, though I don't suppose there is much use of sending her any message through you, if you do see her tell her I am much obliged. I'm sorry she is going to leave Detroit, and I can't get out to Kalamazoo, I'll let her know when I get Home again.

The only <u>very exciting</u> topic I can scare up down here is the weather. The day before yesterday General Grant was going to review our Div. but before the appointed time it commenced to rain so the review was postponed. ~~It~~ By 6 p.m. it was raining in a style that a young Lady would call "awful." Fortunately, I had stretched the fly of my tent over my "shanty" some days before, but after a while the big drops began to find their way through roof & fly both, and to make the situation more interesting, my chimney commenced to draw the wrong way. After enduring the smoke till forbearance ceased to be a virtue, I went out in the rain and found a board which I wanted to brace up over my fireplace, in hopes that that would help the matter. It took me half an hour to get my board in its place, as I had to work just over the fire ~~and~~ the smoke made me almost blind. There the board was supplied with several broken pieces of nails on which I scratched

---

62. Whether this woman was Helen L. Oakley, who in 1868 married Granger's cousin, Jerome Walker, is unconfirmed. However, Oakley was born January 11, 1841 in New York, which placed her close in age to both Edward and Mollie Granger. Thus, she could have been their mutual friend in 1864. Granger Family Tree, Ancestry.com.

my hands most delightfully. Finally my board was up, and the smoke went up the chimney, at least, half the time. This was a great relief and I immediately went to bed, so as to be ready to make the best of any extra long interval between the fits of smoking by going to sleep. I thought once or twice, I should have to get up and open the door or smother to death, but my firmness (and laziness) carried the day, or, rather the night, and I finally went to sleep.

The next morning I found that the First Mich. had come out from Washington the night before, and had to lie right down in the mud & rain, wherever they could find a place solid enough to hold them. I tell you it was "<u>jolly</u>" to think how much worse off those fellows were than I had been, though I thought I was seeing <u>some</u> of the beauties of soldiering very plainly. All the sleeping room there was to spare in the Brig. was seized immediately upon their arrival, by the Veterans of the First, and the Recruits all had to sleep outdoors. They thought it was a pretty rough introduction to Camp life.

The pay of the 1st is stopped on account of a riot in which they were engaged in Elmira N.Y. on their return from Michigan.[63] One of their Officers, Lieut. [Edward L.] Negus,[64] is under arrest at Elmira with pretty grave charges against him.

---

63. According to the *New York Times* of Thursday, February 25, 1864, the First Michigan Cavalry had arrived in Elmira, New York, on that morning on their way back to Washington, D.C. Some fifty or sixty of the soldiers "commenced a raid on various bars and eating-saloons." Troops from the Invalid Corps intervened to restore order. The paper reported that "most of the ringleaders were arrested and lodged in the guard-house."

64. Among those charged was Lt. Edward L. Negus, who later was sentenced to be cashiered from the army, according to the *Army and Navy Journal* of October 15, 1864. He had been charged with "conduct prejudicial to good order and military discipline (resisting the provost guard), exciting mutiny, and joining in mutiny." Civil War records list him as a captain at the time of his ouster. According to Civil War pension records, he filed for a pension in 1884 from Michigan. He had enlisted from Chelsea, Michigan, on April 29, 1861, as a private in Company D, 1st Michigan Infantry, a three-month unit. That August, he was promoted to sergeant, but almost immediately mustered out to accept a commission as second lieutenant in the 1st Michigan Cavalry. Negus, who was born in 1840, was promoted to captain on October 25, 1864, and mustered out of the regiment on November 7, 1865, with an honorable discharge at Fort Leavenworth, Kansas. Records indicate he was cashiered on May 21, 1864, but recommissioned as a first lieutenant on September 27, 1864. According to the *History of Washtenaw County, Michigan*, Negus

Capt. Alexander[65] is in Washington, I believe.

Since the General went away I have been relieved from the many and arduous duties of an A.D.C., as I have nothing to do with the Brig. when Gen. Custer is not with it. Therefore I spend my time in reading, attending horse-races and riding around the country.

I wish Ella were here to ride Beauty but I rather doubt whether she would dare to ride her. The little animal has taken a notion that she is a fast horse, and when she wants to run it is hard work to hold her.

Billy was offered a good horse and a hundred dollars "boot" for Bob the other day.

When we were home last, General Custer was in Detroit but once, & then he did not see Miss Drew. Instead of Capt. Greene's being the General's "favorite" he is the laughing stock of the staff, and Jim & Drew never neglect a chance to "trot him out" in the General's presence and the Gen. enjoys it as much as anyone.

I believe, Ed. Sumner[66] is in Ypsilanti recruiting.

I have not seen anything of the letter you say "Carrie is writing to you."

This afternoon Black Eliza told me that one of the men, who has been an ambulance driver ever since he has been in the service, read to her, a letter which he had just rec'd. from his wife, saying, "It makes me mad every time I think you are down there fighting for the niggers."

---

was operating Chelsea Planing and Cider Mill about 1870 with his father-in-law, Curran White, which he did so for many years until the mill was destroyed by fire. According to the 1870 and 1910 federal censuses, he was married to Balina W. Negus. In 1877, he served as captain for Company I, First Regiment, Michigan State Troops. Negus died in 1918, according to a list of individuals buried in Chelsea's Oak Grove Cemetery that was compiled in 2000. According to her headstone in the cemetery, his wife died in 1917. Barbara J. Feldkamp Burns, "Oak Grove Cemetery, Chelsea, Lima Township, Washtenaw County, MI," Rootsweb, August 2000, www.rootsweb.ancestry.com/~miwashte/cemoge.html; Robertson, *Michigan in the War*; Civil War Pension Index for Edward L. Negus; *History of Washtenaw County, Michigan*, 772; *Michigan Argus* (Ann Arbor), October 5, 1877; Nina Belle Wurster, "History of Chelsea," *Washtenaw Impressions* (Ann Arbor, Mich.) 10, no. 1 (February 1953): 5; 1870 U.S. Federal Census for Chelsea, Mich.; 1890 Veterans Schedules for Edward L. Negus, Ancestry.com; Michigan Genealogy on the Web, migenweb.org (for listing of veteran's burial sites); Soldier Records and Profiles; U.S. Civil War Soldiers. See Longacre, *Custer*, 203, for more information on this episode, which also involved Capt. James Cullen, Company A.

65. His identity is unknown.
66. His identity is unknown.

Eliza said: "Tell her, for me, that if no one did more <u>fighting</u> for the darkies than <u>you</u>, the sesesh would not be very much scared."

Was I "vamosed." That's just about the way all the southern women write to their husbands.

I had not heard of Capt Judson's[67] marriage & don't think that he is informed of it yet. However, I'll ask him the next time I see him. I'm very sorry to hear that Don & Mrs. Clift are sick. Ros Holmes is going to leave for Mich. tomorrow—resigned on a/c of ill health.

Give my love to cousin Mattie & tell her that if she'll send me her photo & will send her mine—when I get a decent one taken.

E. G. Granger

There's no use of my telling you that "I direct my own letter for I don't believe anyone else could get that up-hill slant in the direction of a letter so regularly as I do."

Ed.

---

67. Judson had been twice married and widowed. See chapter 3, note 12. In October 1865, he married a third time to Elizabeth George of Alexandria, Virginia.

CHAPTER 5

CAMPAIGNING IN THE SPRING AND SUMMER OF 1864

ON APRIL 28, 1864, LIEUTENANT GRANGER WROTE HOME for the first time in nearly a month. In his opening, he expressed his irritation to his mother about how few letters he had recently received from home. However, he told her that with so little going on with the army at present, he, too, was not disposed to write. He concluded by threatening to "just quit writing entirely."

For the next couple of months he expected to be too busy to correspond with his loved ones. The renewed combat he soon would experience would be savage, the most violent he had faced during the war. The Michigan Cavalry Brigade had recently been transferred from the Cavalry Corps' 3rd Cavalry Division to the 1st Cavalry Division. In addition, the 1st Vermont Cavalry had been reassigned from the brigade to the 3rd Division. Such changes once again had upset Custer's staff, who feared the general himself might be reassigned, putting their own cushy positions at risk.

A few days later, on May 3, he wrote similarly to his sister, Mollie. Several leisurely months in winter camp were about to end, with his brigade about to take the field. He expected his letters would become less frequent. With the war returning for the Michigan cavalrymen and their comrades in the Army of the Potomac, soon the names of such battlegrounds as the Wilderness, Yellow Tavern, Haw's Shop, and Trevilian Station would become all too familiar for the violent combat experienced by soldiers of the competing armies.

That also would soon become evident to Granger's extended family. On May 15, 1864, Edward Granger wrote hurriedly to his mother with the sad news that his first cousin, Maj. Henry William Granger, the son of her late brother-in-law Austin Granger and his wife, Rhoda, had been killed in action on May 11, 1864, at Yellow Tavern, Virginia. In so quickly dashing off his message to his mother, Edward omitted news of the Michigan Cavalry Brigade's serious combat during the previous ten days in General Grant's Overland Campaign to take Richmond. After breaking camp, Custer and his Wolverines had marched in the Union Army's rear, protecting its lengthy supply train. On May 5, 1864, the two armies collided in the tangled underbrush of the Wilderness near Spotsylvania Court House, Virginia, fighting for two days to a bloody stalemate. All that first day the cavalry sat in the rear. After midnight of day one, Custer's and Thomas C. Devin's[1] brigades were called on to protect the Union's left from Confederate general J. E. B. Stuart's two challenging cavalry divisions. The Michigan Brigade occupied the junction formed by the Brock Pike and Furnace Road, where a gap existed between David Gregg's cavalry and the II Corps. At one point Custer sent Granger to Gregg at Todd's Tavern to obtain artillery support. He returned with two guns.

Once in position, Custer was concerned about the ends of his lines, both of which seemed unprotected. With his staff, he rode repeatedly along his picket line checking for the enemy's whereabouts. About 5 o'clock the early morning's silence was broken by the sounds of an enemy charge. Custer responded, and soon the brigade's Spencer rifles nullified the enemy's numerical superiority. Unfortunately, Custer was denied permission to pursue the startled Confederates.

The next morning, May 7, Custer's brigade fought its way two miles down the Brock Pike to Todd's Tavern to link up with Gregg's men.

---

1. Thomas C. Devin (1822–1878), a highly successful Union cavalry officer during the Civil War, began as a captain in the 6th New York Cavalry and rose to command the regiment as its colonel. In December 1862, he served as a brigade commander at the Battle of Fredericksburg. In 1863, he fought with distinction at the Battles of Chancellorsville, Brandy Station, and Gettysburg. After that, he served as a brigade and a division commander, receiving brevet ranks as brigadier general and major general. Warner, *Generals in Blue*, 123–24.

Meanwhile, Custer's superior, Maj. Gen. Philip Sheridan,[2] was irate at what he considered the interference of army commander Gen. George Meade in the Cavalry Corps' activities. During their clash, Sheridan demanded that he be allowed to cut loose from the Army of the Potomac and draw Stuart's cavalry after his Union cavalry. Sheridan planned to move around Robert E. Lee's left and aim at Richmond. He figured that Stuart would have to face him in an open pitched battle. General Grant approved the mission.

About 6:00 A.M. Monday, May 9, Sheridan's ten thousand cavalrymen, riding in ranks of four and stretching back thirteen miles, headed out with Richmond as their goal. Custer's brigade made up the vanguard. As sunset approached, Custer's men were close to Beaver Dam Station on the Virginia Central Railroad. First, the Michigan Brigade rescued 378 Union prisoners as they were about to be loaded on trains to take them to POW camps. In addition, the 1st and 6th Michigan regiments seized two locomotives and three trains full of supplies. Custer then burned the entire complex, including the trains, the station, and the remaining supplies.

---

2. Philip H. Sheridan (1831–1888) was one of the most celebrated Union Army generals of the Civil War, standing with Ulysses S. Grant and William T. Sherman. He graduated from West Point in 1853. Although he had served on the frontier for eight years, when the Civil War began, he was still a second lieutenant. By May 1862, he led the 2nd Michigan Cavalry as its colonel and was promoted to brigadier general in September that year. In March 1863, he was promoted to major general of volunteers and commanded the 3rd Division of the XX Corps. At the Battles of Chickamauga and Missionary Ridge, his outstanding performance brought him to Grant's attention and led to his appointment as the commander of the Army of the Potomac's Cavalry Corps the next spring. In August 1864, he was appointed commander of the Army of the Shenandoah, responsible for destroying the Shenandoah Valley's usefulness as a major Confederate supply source. Having accomplished his mission, with Custer's considerable assistance, he was made a major general in the Regular Army in November 1864. After returning to the Army of the Potomac, he led troops at Five Forks and Sailor's Creek that forced large segments of Lee's Army of Northern Virginia to surrender to the Union Army. In 1869, after General Grant was elected president and General Sherman replaced him, Sheridan was boosted to lieutenant general. He would play an instrumental role during the later Indian wars, including the Great Sioux Campaign of 1876–77 that led to Custer's death at the Battle of Little Big Horn on June 25, 1876. In 1884, when Sherman retired, Sheridan became commanding general of the army. He later received the full rank of general. He died on August 5, 1888, and was buried in Arlington National Cemetery. Warner, *Generals in Blue*, 437–39.

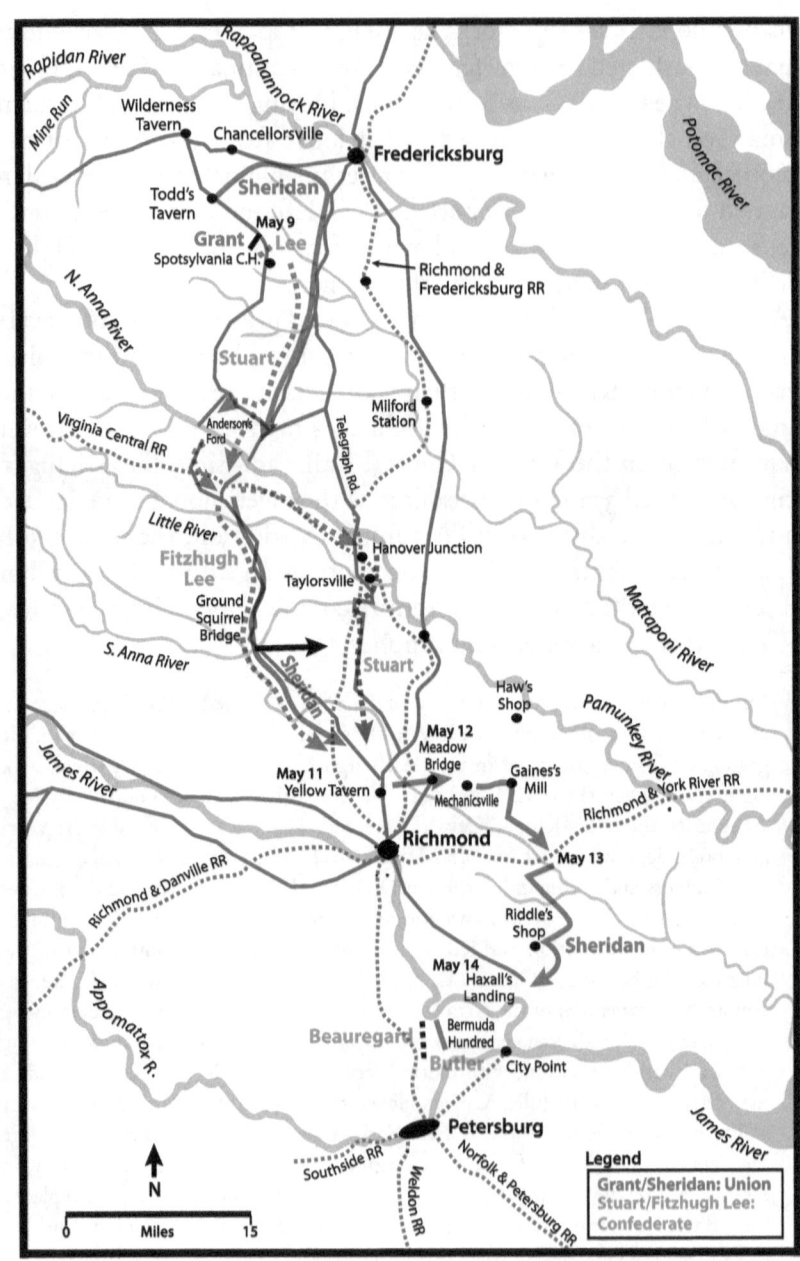

Sheridan's Richmond raid, May 9–14, 1864.
Map by Gary Raham.

On May 10, the Yankee raiders covered eighteen more miles to Ground Squirrel Bridge. Heretofore, Stuart's men, believing the Union troops merely intended to outflank Lee's army, had nibbled at the Union's rear and flanks. Suddenly, Stuart realized that Sheridan's actual destination was Richmond itself.

By midday on Wednesday, May 11, 1864, Custer's brigade had been replaced in the lead by brigades led by Colonels Alfred Gibbs[3] and Thomas Devin, who found Stuart's troops lined up in their front. Brig. Gen. Wesley Merritt, the division commander, positioned Devin's brigade to Gibbs's right and Custer's to the left. Sheridan then directed the 3rd Cavalry Division and one of Gregg's brigade to form a grand battle line on the left.[4]

While the other units were taking their positions, the 5th Michigan under Col. Russell Alger moved out too eagerly and found itself in trouble. The 6th Michigan came to the aid of their comrades, but a Confederate battery had been raising havoc among the brigade's units. Custer successfully sought Merritt's permission to launch a saber charge on the battery and assigned the task to the 1st Michigan.

According to Urwin, "Every Northern witness was impressed by the utter fearlessness of Custer's charge."[5]

---

3. Alfred Gibbs (1823–1868) graduated in 1846 from the U.S. Military Academy and was wounded twice during the Mexican-American War. In 1857, he was wounded a third time while fighting Apaches in the southwest. While largely uncelebrated, Gibbs found himself leading brigades at crucial times during the Civil War, including in May 1864, which placed him in line with Custer's own brigade on the Richmond raid. After the war, he remained in the army as the senior major in Custer's 7th U.S. Cavalry, but because of poor health, he was largely relegated to desk duty. In the summer of 1867, after Custer himself had been suspended from command of the regiment, its junior major, Joel H. Elliott, held field command through early October 1868. The second-ranking major, Wickcliffe Cooper, had committed suicide in June 1867. On November 27, 1868, with Custer again leading the 7th Cavalry, Elliott was killed in action at the Battle of the Washita in Oklahoma Territory. At age forty-five, Gibbs himself died of "congestion of the brain" on December 26, 1868. Warner, *Generals in Blue*, 172–73; also, see Sandy Barnard, *A Hoosier Quaker Goes to War* (Wake Forest, N.C.: AST Press, 2010) for more on Gibbs's time with the 7th U.S. Cavalry.

4. Much of this section is based on Urwin, *Custer Victorious*, 131–49; Longacre, *Custer*, 195–217; and Gordon C. Rhea, *The Battles for Spotsylvania Court House and the Road to Yellow Tavern, May 7–12, 1864* (Baton Rouge: Louisiana State University Press, 1997), 197–231.

5. Urwin, *Custer Victorious*, 142.

While the charge broke the Confederate line and demolished the battery, the Southerners fell back only about four hundred yards to regroup and to counterattack. Custer met the challenge by ordering the 7th Michigan Cavalry, commanded by Maj. Henry Granger, to repulse them. Despite the regiment's bravery, the terrain played havoc with its charge and horses and men were jammed up in exposed positions, forcing them back. However, the 7th was soon joined by other Union forces in a successful charge on the Confederate position.

Tragically, after the fighting ceased, Maj. Henry Granger's body was found by Sgt. David B. Rose, Company C, 7th Michigan Cavalry. In a reminiscence, Rose wrote, "On this field I saw a black object lying. . . . I hastened to the spot and found, as I feared, a dead soldier. Dismounted, and found that it was our loved Major, still and cold in death."[6]

Henry Granger apparently had been shot in the heart and head and cut by sabers. Rose was instructed to carry the body to the rear. Before he could do so, Custer himself rode up and asked Rose whose body he had.

"My answer to him was Major Granger."

The major's death touched Custer himself, who reportedly exclaimed, "My God, is Granger dead; can it be?"

Rose pointed out the major's remains to Custer. According to Rose's story, the general continued: "I sat just where I could see every move made by the major at the time of the charge, and I never saw a man go more gallantly about the work before him than he did. He was a splendid man; too bad, too bad."

After Custer instructed Rose to convey the major's body to the rear, he and other men set about the task. Shortly, Custer returned with his whole staff, presumably including Lieutenant Edward Granger, based on the latter's letters to his mother and sister.

Rose concluded his reminiscence with the following: "As he rode up, he said, 'Sergeant, I am back again; please let these gentlemen see the Major.' Again I uncovered his face and every one drew up to his side and took a long, last look. All spoke words of praise, and regretted the great loss we had sustained in his death."

Granger's letter 38 to his mother and 39 to his sister are unique, as

---

6. David B. Rose, "Major Granger's Death," in Lee, *Personal and Historical Sketches*, 125–26.

they are the only times the young officer reveals any significant emotion about the battlefield carnage he has witnessed in his twenty-one months of service. All his other comments about a fallen comrade usually were stated in matter-of-fact language.

Custer's modern critics often blame him for the high casualties his commands sustained during the war. Of course, his later defeat in 1876 at the Little Big Horn, which cost the lives of about a third of his regiment, provides further fodder for such criticism. But, as Urwin stated, "The Wolverines had witnessed ample instances of Custer's skill and courage many times before, but at Yellow Tavern they discovered he also had a heart."[7]

In his report of the battle at Yellow Tavern, Custer paid tribute to the fallen major. "Major Granger, like a true soldier, placed himself at the head of his men and led them bravely up to the very muzzles of the enemy's guns, but not withstanding the heroic efforts of this gallant officer, the enemy held their position, and the Seventh Michigan was compelled to retire, but not until the chivalric Granger had fallen. Pierced through the head and heart by the bullets of the enemy. He fell as the warrior loves to fall, with his face to the foe."[8]

Henry Granger was not the only officer of significance to fall at Yellow Tavern on May 11. During the fighting one of Custer's Michiganders mortally wounded Confederate General Stuart, who died the next day. Colonel Alger of the 5th Michigan credited Pvt. John A. Huff, Company E, with the kill shot, but the enlisted man died in action later that month. Thus, controversy about who shot Stuart has existed across the years.

With the major fighting over, Sheridan had to abandon his plans to take Richmond. He realized he lacked sufficient troops to hold the city. Over the next two days, his Cavalry Corps successfully fought its way south toward the Union Army of the James.

Later that month and well into June, Lieutenant Granger would write his last few letters home. While Sheridan's Cavalry Corps had been engaged at Yellow Tavern and elsewhere, General Grant had been continuing his Overland Campaign with the inconclusive fighting at the North Anna River between May 23 and 26. After that, Grant had

---

7. Urwin, *Custer Victorious*, 143.
8. *O.R.*, series 1, vol. 36, pt. 1, 818.

Lt. Henry W. Granger first saw combat in the 1st New York "Lincoln" Cavalry. As a major in December 1862, he transferred into the 7th Michigan Cavalry. He was killed in action on May 11, 1864, at age forty-one, while leading the 7th Michigan at the Battle of Yellow Tavern, Va. *Courtesy Mike Hogle.*

decided to move his troops widely around the Confederate left flank, relying on the Pamunkey River to screen his army from Confederate lines positioned on the southern banks of Totopotomoy Creek.

In these last letters, Granger filled in numerous gaps in his recitation of the brigade's activities that month. That included engagements on May 27 north of Salem Church and on May 28 at Haw's Shop, Hanover County, Virginia (variously Hawes Shop or Enon Church). On May 27, Custer's troopers had scattered Confederate pickets at Dabney's Ford on the south side of the Pamunkey and followed that up with fighting Maj. Gen. Fitzhugh Lee's cavalry, including troops from Maryland and North Carolina, north of Salem Church. Uncertain of Grant's own intentions, Lee had dispatched Maj. Gen. Wade Hampton's cavalry on an intelligence-gathering mission, or reconnaissance in force, on May 28. Instead, Hampton clashed with Union cavalry under Brig. Gen. David Gregg. With the outcome in doubt, two brigades from Torbert's division and Custer's Michigan Brigade joined in the fray. Sheridan claimed victory when Hampton withdrew, but the latter already had the information Lee wanted and opted to pull back. A bloody engagement, however, had already taken place. The fighting had begun three miles west of Hanovertown and a mile beyond a large blacksmith shop called Haw's Shop, when Gregg's men encountered Hampton's at Enon Church. About 4:00 P.M. Custer's brigade deployed as if they were infantrymen. Heavy rifle and artillery fire cut down at least forty-one of his Michiganders in the ensuing fighting. In his letter, Granger reported on a number of his friends who were either killed or wounded in the severe combat. However, the Confederates believed that Union infantry units were preparing to enter the fray and Hampton again withdrew west of Totopotomoy Creek.

The end to the fighting would prove only temporary. In just two days, on May 30, the two armies would fight a second time in that vicinity in the Battle of Old Church, or Bethesda Church. During that fighting Granger would be struck and likely bruised by a spent ball. Another move to the rear followed this encounter, thereby removing the Michigan Brigade from the action for just a day. On May 31 and June 1, the brigade again joined in a significant fight, this time at Old Cold Harbor, Virginia.

A newspaper dispatch captured just how involved Granger was in all of this fighting. According to a correspondent for the *Detroit Advertiser and Tribune*, during the Haw's Shop fighting, "Captain Green[e] was actively engaged in urging forward the line as also were Lieuts. Baylis, Granger, Norris and Stranahan." He filed similar comments about the June 1 fighting at Cold Harbor: "Capt. Greene and Lieuts. Baylis, Granger and Stranahan cheered the men on, and by their personal daring, as well as the efficiency of the line officers, kept them up to the works and held the ground."[9]

On June 3, the infantry of both armies would clash at Cold Harbor in a wide-ranging, bloody battle. During the midst of this fighting,

---

9. *Detroit Advertiser and Tribune*, June 4, 1864. From the personal sentiments the writer often expressed, he likely was an officer associated with the brigade.

the Union cavalry moved repeatedly about the country between Bottom's Bridge and New Castle Ferry until June 6. On June 7, the Cavalry Corps and its Michigan Brigade moved out again, crossing the Pamunkey River. For three days they marched toward Gordonsville, where on June 10, they camped within two miles of Louisa Court House. The next morning, the Confederates launched an attack on the Michigan Brigade, setting off the two-day Battle of Trevilian Station.

The resulting letter, number 42, is both Granger's last major letter home as well as arguably his most important. Unfortunately, its first page and an accompanying map were lost at some time. Without the first page, we cannot be sure when he actually wrote it, but date references late in his text strongly suggest he penned it on June 14, if not June 13. According to historian Eric Wittenberg, Sheridan's cavalry camped on June 14 at Shady Grove Church, three miles from Todd's Tavern.[10] In this letter Granger provided his sister with probably his most lengthy and detailed observations about any battle. This classic cavalry engagement, the Battle of Trevilian Station on June 11 and 12, 1864, has often been labeled as "Custer's First Last Stand." He mentions both his own heroic actions as well as Custer's in what is often viewed as the general's most serious failure during the war.

Of perhaps greater personal significance, not only did he and Custer lose their personal belongings when the brigade's wagons were overrun by the enemy, but his faithful horse, Bob, also was captured. The experienced animal had carried Granger throughout his previous twelve months of combat. Without Bob, in two months Granger would be forced to ride a different, highly uncontrollable mount at the Battle of Crooked Run with fatal consequences. As Granger's letters 40, 41, and 42 are all written in pencil, not in ink, that likely means he lost his writing supplies as well. Additionally, if Granger had retained any letters from friends and loved ones as well as a possible diary he may have kept, they, too, likely disappeared into the hands of Confederate soldiers.

After this letter of June 14, 1864, Granger would write only once more, on July 17, 1864. At least only one has survived. That seems odd, given that, after their return from Trevilian Station, the brigade and the Cavalry Corps enjoyed several weeks of more modest activity

---

10. Eric Wittenberg, *Glory Enough for All: Sheridan's Second Raid and the Battle of Trevilian Station* (Washington, D.C.: Brassey's, 2000), 224.

compared to the serious combat of the previous six weeks. Granger usually had been more prolific during his unit's downtime, despite his frequent complaints about the hard task of expressing himself in writing. Perhaps any additional letters he wrote to his family during his final weeks were lost across the years.

If Granger needed a reason to write home on that July day, it probably had to do with his long-awaited promotion to first lieutenant. According to his military records, he succeeded Lt. Myron Hickey, his friend with whom he had signed up two years before. Hickey had been promoted to captain, opening a vacancy for Granger. On the next day, Granger completed an affidavit before Colonel Alger, commander of the 5th Michigan Cavalry, and First Lt. Frederick Pistorius, the adjutant of the 1st Michigan Cavalry.[11]

For a final letter, the contents of his July 17 writings were not remarkable. His comrade, Lieutenant Bristol, was heading home, so Granger planned to send a draft of $50 with him. Inasmuch as he mentions having sent $100 to his Uncle Charles "the other day," that suggests he wrote at least another letter home in July. He wanted the $50 to be divided between his mother ($30) and Mollie ($20).

His closing remarks loom more poignant, because of what history tells us would happen to him in a few short weeks. He chastised Mollie, stating he would not write again until she returns the favor. From his remarks, it appears she had been remiss recently in writing to her brother. He closed with the observation that General Custer had returned to Washington and soon would be in Michigan.

---

11. Early in the war Frederick Pistorius had been commissioned on July 21, 1861, as a captain in the 23rd Indiana Infantry Regiment. He was mustered out on October 8, 1862. On February 20, 1864, he had been commissioned as a first lieutenant and the adjutant of the 1st Michigan Cavalry, but, again, was mustered out quickly, this time on September 11, 1864. According to a Findagrave.com entry, he may have been born October 15, 1836, in Germany and died October 21, 1911, in Ann Arbor, Michigan, with burial in Forest Hill Cemetery. The 1894 Ann Arbor City Directory lists his occupation as "attorney at law, real estate, insurance and steamboat agent." In 1860, he may have earned a law degree from the University of Michigan, according to *The Semi-Centennial Celebration of the Organization of the University of Michigan, June 26–30, 1887* (Ann Arbor: University of Michigan, 1888), 311. Soldier Records and Profiles; U.S. Civil War Soldiers; "Frederick C. M. Pistorius," memorial and gravestone at Findagrave.com, 43390423.

✳ ✳ ✳

[LETTER 36]

Head Qurs. 1st Brig. 1st Division
Cav. Corps A.P. April 28th 1864 [Thursday]

Dear Mother

Yours of the 11th inst. was duly rec'd. and would, probably, have been answered before this if I had not happened to feel somewhat provoked at the irregularity of my letters from home, & thought I would try and see how you like the style of corresponding you practiced. It is very easy for me to get along without writing just now as there is nothing whatever going on here now to furnish material for letters, and I like the idea so well that if my correspondents don't "come to time" hereafter, I shall quit writing, entirely.

Tell Mollie that the last letters I have rec'd. from her are numbered 6 & 8, and dated respectively April 12th and 20th. Should there have been one in between them?

The weather has been delightful here for a long time, and Grant seems to be very anxious, I can't think with what though—I never can lest Lee should make some move. Yesterday a scouting party of the 1st Mich. was sent out beyond our right to Robertson's River.[12] I went with them. We went through James City and within a mile and a half of Madison Court House, the largest place in this part of the country. Captain [George R.] Maxwell,[13] who commanded the party, was ordered to find out whether the Rebs. held the North side of Robertson River.

We scared up a picket post of about 20 men on the other side of the river, but found none on this side. We had a very pleasant ride of about 35 miles. Speis Warren[14] was with us. Did you know that he is a

---

12. The river is actually the Robinson River, but period maps apparently listed it as Robertson's. The river is a thirty-four-mile tributary of the Rapidan River in Madison County, Virginia. It starts in Shenandoah National Park and flows southeast to its confluence with the Rapidan. See R. P. Tollo and T. K. Lowe, "Geologic Map of the Robertson River Igneous Suite, Blue Ridge Province, Northern and Central Virginia," U.S. Geological Survey, no. 2229, 1994, http://pubs.er.usgs.gov/publication/mf2229.

13. For more about George R. Maxwell, see chapter 2, note 79.

14. Robert Spies Warren enlisted in 1861 as a private in Company K, 1st Michigan Cavalry, and later was promoted to first lieutenant. Reportedly, he was commanding his

second Lieut. in Gus Buhl's Company of the 1st Mich. Cav.? I didn't till I saw him over with the Regt. the other day.

This morning, before daylight, a stronger reconnaissance started off with orders to go to Madison Court House, a mile and a half beyond the Robertson River. The force sent out was composed of Col. Devin's Brig. and the 5th & 6th Mich. This party proceeded as far as the river without seeing any Rebs. and the few who were between the river & the Court House left without making any resistance.[15]

I don't think that we are going to make any advance from here till some movement from some other direction shall have compelled Lee to leave his entrenchments or, at least to send away part of the force he has in our front.

The other night the First Vermont was ordered to leave our Brigade and join the 3d Division from which we had just been transferred.[16]

At the same time General Custer received an order to report in

> company in June 1864 at the time of the fighting at Trevilian Station, Virginia. The first day's fighting occurred on June 11, but on June 12, action resumed to the west. The Confederates in a strong defensive position repulsed seven attacks. Warren was killed in action during one of them. In his report on Trevilian Station, Custer cited Warren's death. *Portrait and Biographical Album of Hillsdale County, Mich.* (Chicago: Chapman Brothers, 1888), 367; *O.R.*, vol. 38, pt. 1, 824; Wittenberg, *Glory Enough for All*, 91n.

15. On this occasion, Granger apparently remained in camp.
16. In early March 1864, Lt. Gen. Ulysses S. Grant had been promoted to that rank and assigned as "General-in-Chief of the Armies of the United States." He opted to remain in the field and to accompany the Army of the Potomac, even as General Meade retained command of that army. Grant's goals were to capture Richmond and to destroy Lee's Army of Northern Virginia. He also made wholesale personnel changes, including dispatching both Generals Pleasonton and Kilpatrick to the West. In Pleasonton's place, he appointed Maj. Gen. Philip H. Sheridan, who would play a significant role in Custer's future army career. Too, as Granger reported, the Michigan Brigade was shifted to the 1st Cavalry Division, giving Custer the most prominent one-star position in the Cavalry Corps. His immediate divisional superior was Brig. Gen. Alfred T. A. Torbert. Custer had expected to receive command of the 3rd Cavalry Division, but Grant, instead, appointed James H. Wilson, an engineering officer on his staff in the West, but who had never commanded Cavalry troops. Both Custer and General Meade were outraged. Custer had been the senior officer under Kilpatrick in the 3rd Division, plus he outranked Wilson, whom he did not respect. To alleviate tensions, Meade transferred the Michigan Brigade to the 1st Cavalry Division. Urwin, *Custer Victorious*, 124–25. Also, see Gregory J. W. Urwin, "Custer: The Civil War Years," in *The Custer Reader*, ed. Paul Andrew Hutton (Norman: University of Oklahoma Press, 2004), 21.

person to the Adjutant General in Washington. Of course the only supposition on which we could account for such an order, was that he was going to be relieved. That night there was a "blue" crowd around these Head Qurs, you may believe. However I was soon told that the General was only going to Washington to try and get the First Vermont ordered back to his Brig. and then I had the fun of seeing those of the Staff who did not know the truth, lament their approaching end.

Greene did not find out the true state of the case till after he had gone to bed.

Lieut. Stanahan [Farrand S. Stranahan],[17] of the First Vermont, was the Officer who told me. He has just been detailed as A.D.C. to the General and he tents and messes with me. His father came from Cooperstown, N.Y. Did you ever know him? He—Mr. Stranahan is acquainted with Mr. Diller and family, having lived some years in Brooklyn with an aunt of his by the name of Chapman, I believe. He lived on Clinton Avenue. Isn't that the Street Uncle Ferdinand lives on? Lieut. Stranahan is a brother-in-law of Governor Smith of Vermont. He appears to be a very gentlemanly fellow, indeed, and his Colonel says he is a very good fighting man—but (Poor Mollie!) he is married.

The General returned from Washington to night. General Burnside and staff were on the same train with him. Burnside brought reinforcements of forty thousand men to the Army of the Potomac a few days since.[18]

---

17. Farrand Stewart Stranahan was born on February 2, 1842, in New York City and came from a well-to-do family. In 1859 he moved to Vermont where he married Miranda Aldis Brainerd. His sister-in-law Ann Brainerd was married to J. Gregory Smith, president of the Central Vermont Railway and the state's governor. Stranahan enlisted on August 15, 1862, as first sergeant of Company L, 1st Vermont Cavalry. He was commissioned a second lieutenant on January 18, 1864, and promoted to first lieutenant, effective February 28, 1864, As Granger indicates, Stranahan served several months as a Custer aide. He resigned on August 28, 1864, but on October 19, 1864, Stranahan was one of the pursuers of the fleeing Confederates who had participated in the St. Albans Raid in Vermont. For much of his postwar life, Stranahan worked in railroading and banking. In the 1880s, he served one term as Vermont's lieutenant governor. He died on July 13, 1904. Soldier Records and Profiles; U.S. Civil War Soldiers; "Farrand Stewart Stranahan," memorial, photograph, and gravestone at Findagrave.com, 23780745.

18. After his disaster at Fredericksburg as commander of the Army of the Potomac in late 1862, Burnside had been sent to East Tennessee, where his success in the fall of

Received a letter from Will Colerick last night saying that he had been appointed Assistant Provost Marshal in Lapeer County [Michigan] but that some of his enemies had published in the Advertiser the history of his dismissal from the Army, and he expected that Col. Hill would deprive him of his position. I hope he will not be removed. Col. Town & Lt. Col. Stagg both say that Colerick shall ~~have~~ fill the first vacancy that occurs in the First, and the General will do any-thing in his power to get him back. General says the other day that there wasn't a better staff officer in the Army than Colerick.[19]

Col. Alger is in Washington & is coming out tomorrow, I believe. Lt. Col. Gould is in command of the dismounted men of the Division, a larger command than any Regt. in the Brig. Fred Nims got back to day. Maj Dake is soon to be tried by Court Martial. I sent some money to Uncle Charles on the second of this month & wrote the same day asking him to acknowledge the rect [receipt] or write if he did not receive it. I have not yet heard from him. Tell Mollie, I'll write, if I ever get any thing to write about.

E. G. Granger

1863 in holding Knoxville while facing Lt. Gen. James Longstreet partially restored his reputation. The next spring he returned to the eastern theater with his IX Corps acting for a time as an independent command; at the time he outranked General Meade. However, Burnside brought something more than twenty thousand troops with him, not the forty thousand that Granger claimed. In May 1864, Burnside agreed to serve under Meade. That summer, when troops under Burnside failed at the Battle of the Crater at Petersburg, Grant relieved Burnside on August 14. He never regained a command and resigned his commission on April 15, 1865.

19. Colerick had been court-martialed on April 8, 1863, found guilty, and sentenced to be dismissed from the service, arising from a series of incidents in February and March 1863. On March 25, 1863, near Stafford Court House, Virginia, he reportedly had been drinking with enlisted men, and refused an order from another officer to go to his quarters. Earlier, he reportedly was absent without leave from February 25 to March 1, 1863, from his company at Stafford Court House. On March 29, according to another specification, Colerick absented himself from the company on the march and became drunk again, while sharing his liquor with enlisted men. The court found him guilty on three of the five specifications and sentenced him to be dismissed from the army. He was dismissed, effective June 30, 1863, although Custer's report for Gettysburg listed Colerick in action. The date of his return to the service is unclear. General Order No. 199, June 30, 1863, in General Orders of the War Department, 1863, U.S. Adjutant General's Office, Washington, D.C.

Direct Head Qurs. 1st Brig. 1st Div. Cav. Corps A. P.

Washington, D.C.
E. G. G.

✳ ✳ ✳

[LETTER 37]

Head Quarters 1st Brig. 1st Div.
Cav. Corps. A. P. May 3d 1864 [Tuesday]

Mollie

As there is no knowing when I may have another chance to write I will make the best of the last evening of our "Camp life," for the present at least. We take the field in the morning. I suppose, Our position will probably be in the rear, for the movement is to be by our left flank and this Brigade is on the extreme right of the line. The Infantry are moving to night and we don't start till nearly noon tomorrow. The Army is to cross at Germania [Germanna] Ford and the Fords below; but before you get this you will probably know more than I know now of our movements.

The last letter I have rec'd from you is dated April 20th and numbered 8, but I have not yet recd No. 7. I presume it will be some time before we get any more mail. You need not expect to hear from me again till the Army makes a halt somewhere unless we happen to get into a fight, in which case, I will report as soon as possible thereafter.

Col. Alger came out from Washington tonight so we finally have a commander for our Regt. Lt. Col. Gould is in command of the dismounted men of the Brig. & the Regt. has been under Capt. [William T.] Magoffin,[20] one of the poorest Officers in it. Fred Nims came

---

20. The historical record offers no support for Granger's contention that Capt. William T. Magoffin was a poor officer. Born March 6, 1827, in Clarence, New York, Magoffin served in the Mexican War after enlisting in the Light Battery K, 1st U.S. Artillery, according to his obituary. On August 27, 1861, while living in St. John's, Michigan, Magoffin was commissioned as a first lieutenant in Company B, 3rd Michigan Cavalry, but resigned March 29, 1862, because of poor health. On August 14, 1862, he was commissioned as captain of Company G, 5th Michigan Cavalry. During the fighting at Trevilian Station, Virginia, on June 12, 1864, he was thrown from his horse and injured. He was discharged on August 1, 1864, on

back a few days ago and is coming up here in the morning. We'll have a good time I expect, this summer. Fred and Stranahan & I shall mess together, probably.

The General just saw me writing & asked me if I was making my will. I told him I was writing to Mollie & he said "Give her my love." He says he is just as hard up for something to write about tonight as I am—rather strange, as he has not written since last night. Last night we had a grand spree in our tent. A sutler had given the General a basket of Champaign, and as the General don't drink he sent an orderly to bring the wine into our tent where he was playing euchre with Greene, Balis [Baylis] & [Pharo] Gray.[21] After the wine was gone, Some whiskey was brought out, and Capt. Greene and Drew got pretty drunk. While Greene was feeling very happy Drew induced him to drink a large dose of Stoughton bitters. You may not know the exact nature of this composition; but it is somewhat like boneset tea "only more so." There is a little fellow by the name of Walker staying around Head Qrs. who was pretty merry, too. He sleeps with Jim & after they had gone to bed the General & Maj Drew let their tent

---

a surgeon's certificate of disability. By 1870, he was living with his wife and son in Akron, New York. He died May 1, 1910, in Akron and was buried there. According to a family genealogical website, he returned home to Akron where he engaged in the grocery and drug business. He also served as postmaster for thirteen years and superintendent of Indian Schools for twelve years. See Ralph Manning Magoffin, "The Magoffin Record," *Magoffin Hinshaw Family*, http://www.magoffin hinshawfamily.com/Media/Magoffin%20Record.pdf, 20–21. According to the *Annual Report of the Superintendent of Public Instruction for the State of New York*, vol. 29 (Albany, N.Y.: Weed, Parsons, 1883), 127, Magoffin was school superintendent on the Tonawanda Indian Reservation in 1882. A photograph of Magoffin appears in "Photos of Civil War Soldiers," Michigan Genealogy on the Web, http://www .migenweb.org/michiganinthewar/photos/magoffin.htm. 1860 U.S. Federal Census and 1870 U.S. Federal Census; Index to Pension Files of Veterans Who Served Between 1861 and 1900, Michigan, Fold 2, by Ancestry.com; Soldier Records and Profiles; U.S. Civil War Soldiers.

21. Born March 24, 1843, in Douglas, Michigan, Pharo Gray, age nineteen, enlisted on August 20, 1862, in Granger's Company C, 5th Michigan Cavalry, and was later promoted to sergeant. On January 12, 1864, he was commissioned as a second lieutenant and on November 16, 1864, as first lieutenant. He was mustered out as a captain on June 23, 1865, at Fort Leavenworth, Kansas. He died December 24, 1893, in Milwaukee, Wisconsin. Soldier Records and Profiles; U.S. Civil War Soldiers; "Capt. Pharo Gray," memorial and gravestone at Findagrave.com, 122991977.

down onto them. Jim got up & tried to straighten matters & Walker seized a pail of water & ran out &, thinking he had caught the rogue, poured his pail of water on Jim, who turned around, grabbed Walker by the shirt collar & threw him so that he rolled down the hill in front of the tents. This morning, of course there was a brilliant set of fools around Hd. Qurs.

Has Professor Boise[22] moved into the City yet? He was to move the 1st Inst. If he has—have you seen Miss Alice[23] yet? She said she expected to go to the High School. Of course, you won't like her, she isn't your style—to judge from the "model of all the virtues" you expected me to be <u>stuck with</u> last winter. I don't think much more of your choice than I do of Don's. <u>Chacun a son gout</u>.[24]

It's most time for me to quit, as I have various rents in my nether garments to repair before I am ready for the coming campaign. Oh dear! <u>Why didn't you</u> send me a wife when I applied for one? I feel the evils of a bachelor's life, to night, but not half so bitterly as I shall before I get those unfortunate breeches mended, my only needle is rusty as an old crowbar & about as sharp; besides being bent a little.

That Major [Daniel H.] Darling,[25] I know but little of, and that little is decidedly <u>not</u> in his favor.

Remember me to Carrie.

Tell Mrs. Clift and Don that they owe me letters.

E. G. Granger

Please send me fifty P. O. stamps when you write & keep the change.

Ed.

---

22. He remains unidentified.
23. She remains unidentified.
24. *Chacun à son goût* is French for "each to one's own taste."
25. Born on June 8, 1836, Daniel H. Darling enlisted on November 1, 1862, as a captain in Company C, 7th Michigan Cavalry and later was promoted to major on March 22, 1864, and lieutenant colonel on May 26, 1865. He was mustered out on December 1, 1865, at Jackson, Michigan. In the 1890s he filed for a pension from Illinois. He appears to have died July 15, 1909, in Joliet, Illinois, but was buried in Painesville, Ohio. Soldier Records and Profiles; U.S. Civil War Soldiers; "Daniel H. Darling," memorial and gravestone at Findagrave.com, 132364425; Civil War Pension Index.

✳ ✳ ✳

[LETTER 38]

Head Qurs. 1st Brig 1st Div.
C. C. Malvern Hill, May 15th 1864 [Sunday]

Dear Mother

Henry Granger is dead. I saw his body.

Everybody else that you know in our Brig. is all right. I saw Sam Walker the day before the C. C. left the A. P., i.e., May 8th. He was well then. Bristol is well. All well here.

Gen. Custer has done more than all the other Brig's in the Corps on this raid.

Yours in haste

E. G. Granger

✳ ✳ ✳

[LETTER 39]

Head Quarters 1st Brig. 1st Div.
Cav. Corps A. P. Near Chesterfield Station
May 25th 1864 [Wednesday]

Mollie

Just returned from "Sheridan's Great Raid."[26] Can't get this letter off, just at present, any way, but may be able to, by the time I get it written.

Don't know how long we shall stay here—don't know any thing, except that Grant is whipping Lee thoroughly <u>and following up his victories</u>.

I wrote to you the night before we started from Culpeper May 3d, [Tuesday] & to Mother from Malvern Hill on the 15th Inst. Have not yet rec'd any acknowledgement on the rec't of the letter to you.

Your letter No. 9 reached me on the Battle-Field in the Wilderness

---

26. By the afternoon of May 14, Sheridan's Corps had reached Malvern Hill, where it spent three days refitting and resupplying at the Bermuda Hundred base camp occupied by the Union Army of the James under Maj. Gen. Benjamin F. Butler.

& to day I found Nos. 10 & 13 the intervening numbers I have not yet seen.

On the morning of the 4th Inst. the First Div. broke camp, and about noon left Culpeper. We were on the extreme right of the Army, & the movement across the River was by the left flank, so our Div. was the rear guard. We encamped at Stony Mt. that night, & the next morning crossed the Rapidan at Ely's Ford & marched to Chancellorsville Battle Field, where we bivouacked that night [May 5]. That evening we could hear the sound of the guns of our Infantry. The next morning [May 6] we marched five or 6 miles before daylight to Todd's Tavern.[27] This was on the extreme left of our line. Then after stopping to get breakfast we marched back about a mile and a half to a cross roads, which Gen. Custer was ordered to hold with his Brig.[28] While marching to this place, we met the 1st Vermont Cav., which had been transferred from our Brig. to Wilson's Div. just before the Army moved. The Div. they are in had been badly whipped the day before they saw we met them by one Brig. of Fitz-Hugh Lee's[29] Cav. & they were all very mad at

---

27. Today Todd's Tavern is an unincorporated community in Spotsylvania County, Virginia. It was the site of the May 7, 1864, cavalry battle. The tavern was located at the intersection of Brock Road and Catharpin Road. The intersection retains the name today.
28. This was the intersection of Brock Road and Furnace Road. Today, the National Park Service labels the road as Jackson Trail East, as it was part of Jackson's route during his famous movement during the Battle of Chancellorsville in May 1863.
29. Fitzhugh Lee (1835–1905), the nephew of Robert E. Lee, was both a Confederate general during the Civil War and a U.S. Army general during the Spanish-American War. A graduate of West Point in 1856, he served in the army until his resignation in 1861 to join the Confederate forces. By July 1862, he had been promoted to brigadier general and enjoyed success during a number of engagements, notably at Kelly's Ford on March 17, 1863. At Gettysburg, his brigade fought unsuccessfully in the action on East Cavalry Field, which involved Custer's Michigan Cavalry Brigade, but General Stuart still praised him as one of the finest cavalry generals. In the Overland and Petersburg Campaigns of the spring and summer of 1864, Lee served as a divisional commander. In the Shenandoah fighting of later 1864, he fought heroically until severely wounded. In the last two weeks of the war in 1865, Lee commanded the cavalry forces of the Army of Northern Virginia. He led the last charge of the Confederate cavalry on April 9, 1865, at Farmville, Virginia. After the war, he returned to farming, but was also involved in politics. He served as governor of Virginia from 1886 to 1890. President Grover Cleveland appointed him in 1896 as consul general in Havana, Cuba. He served until the sinking of the USS *Maine*. With the outbreak of the Spanish-American War, Lee was

[James H.] Wilson.[30] When they saw Gen. Custer they greeted him with hearty cheers which were kept up while we were passing the whole Regt. Some of the Officers asked Maj. Drew if he could not get them "a pair of Custer's old boots"—for they should have more confidence in them than they had in Wilson. This feeling seems to be shared by Gen. Sheridan; for on his Raid he kept Wilson in the center all the time except, one morning, when he—Wilson—being put in the advance lost his way—ran into the fortifications of Richmond & was driven back: giving the Rebs time to destroy Meadow Bridge and erect breast works in the road which he should have taken. The result was that our Div. was put in the advance & Wilson returned to his safe position in the center, where he has been ever since.[31]

---

one of four ex-Confederate general officers appointed major generals in the U.S. Army. He commanded the 7th Army Corps, but took no part in any military operations. After serving as the military governor in Havana and commanding the army's Department of the Missouri, he retired in 1901 as a brigadier general. He died four years later. Warner, *Generals in Gray*, 178–79.

30. James H. Wilson (1837–1925), born in Illinois, was an 1860 graduate of West Point. Early in the Civil War, he worked as a topographical engineering officer. He later joined Gen. Ulysses S. Grant's staff in the western theater, but even with a promotion to brigadier general, he largely remained on staff duty handling engineering tasks. In 1864, he found himself as chief of the Cavalry Bureau in Washington, D.C., but in early May, Grant had him assigned to command the 3rd Cavalry Division under Sheridan. While he was a rival of Custer's and Granger wrote critically of him, Wilson performed well. In October 1864, he was transferred back to the West as Gen. William T. Sherman's chief of cavalry, effectively operating at the same level as Sheridan in the East. He showed his administrative and combat abilities by leading some seventeen thousand Union cavalry in November and December 1864 in defeating the Confederates at the Battles of Franklin and Nashville, Tennessee. The next spring, he defeated Union Army nemesis Brig. Gen. Nathan Bedford Forrest at Selma, Alabama. He then launched a final wide-ranging attack through the southern states and defeated remaining Confederate forces before him. He reached Macon, Georgia, on April 20, 1865. Wilson later was brevetted a major general. After a brief stint as an engineering officer in the postwar army, he resigned in 1870 to involve himself in railroad enterprises. At the outbreak of the Spanish-American War in 1898, Wilson returned to the army as a major general in Puerto Rico and Cuba. He also took part in the Boxer Rebellion in China. He finally retired in 1901 as a brigadier general. Warner, *Generals in Blue*, 567–68.

31. Still just a youth himself, Granger may have been parroting the beliefs of more senior officers, especially Custer himself. As a divisional commander, and one who had little experience in commanding cavalry, Wilson likely had the misfortune of holding a post that the ambitious Custer may have believed should have been his.

To go back to my story. We had been at the aforesaid cross road an hour or two when an order came <u>from Gen. Meade</u> that <u>Custer's Brig.</u> should proceed to feel out & check Gen. Longstreet's Corps, which was reported to be marching down the Brock Turnpike to turn our left. It was certainly very flattering to the Brig. to be thus specially designated for such a difficult & dangerous, duty, but it was a most unpleasant compliment. The Gen. was just preparing to obey the order, when a very brisk fire was heard a few rods in front of us & our pickets were seen coming in faster than they usually retire. The Gen. gave the band orders to play "Yankee Doodle" and started for the scene of action. He found the pickets very close to the field in which we had been resting and retiring before a charge of the enemy.[32] The Gen. rode out beyond our retiring line & rallied them checking the Rebs till the 1st Mich. could get mounted and ready for the fight. Then the Regt. charged & drove the Rebs. back across an open field where the latter took refuge behind their battery. We had no artillery and so the Gen. sent me to Gen. Gregg for some guns. Gregg was at Todd's Tavern which was on our left as we now stood. He sent back one section (two guns) with me. When I got back with the guns, I found the Brig. drawn up in line in a hollow just in the rear of the field across which the 1st had charged, while the Reb. battery was in a plowed field beyond and was shelling at our line, which was out of sight. The shelling was pretty good though most of the shells exploded a few rods in front of the line. One shell exploded in the midst of my Regt. killing & wounding several horses & wounding two or three men but the boys did not mind it at all. They closed up the gap & then stood still as though nothing was less probable than that the next shell would strike in that neighborhood.

The Rebs. still had the advantage of us both in numbers of men & guns, so I was sent back to hurry up Col. Devin with the 2<u>nd</u> Brig. of our Div. which had been ordered by Gen. Torbert[33] to support us. When Devin came up, his battery opened on that of the Rebs. & the

---

32. Today, the brigade's position and the area on both sides of Brock Road are largely wooded.

33. Alfred T. A. Torbert (1833–1880), for a brief time, was an officer in both the Union and Confederate armies. A native of Delaware, he had graduated from West Point in 1855 and served at various times in Texas, Florida, Mississippi, Utah, and New Mexico. On February 25, 1861, he was promoted to first lieutenant, but was on leave until April 17. On March 16, he had been appointed as a first lieutenant in the Confederate Army. Instead, he mustered recruits for the 1st New Jersey Infantry Regiment and was

CAMPAIGNING IN THE SPRING AND SUMMER OF 1864

Gen. Alfred T. A. Torbert and his staff with Lt. Robert Wallace *(top step, far right)* and Capt. Marcus A. Reno *(bottom step, middle right)*. In 1876, then-major Reno was Custer's second-in-command at the Battle of Little Big Horn. *Courtesy of John Beckendorf.*

5th and 6th Mich. were sent to drive the Rebs out of the woods on our

> appointed its colonel in September 1861. During the war's first three years, he held infantry assignments, fighting in many of the major engagements of the Army of the Potomac. On November 29, 1862, he was appointed a brigadier general of volunteers. In April 1864, he was appointed to command one of Sheridan's cavalry divisions and continued in the position through the summer and fall. Originally Sheridan's chief of cavalry during the Shenandoah Campaign, Torbert performed admirably in the Battles of Tom's Brook and Cedar Creek in October 1864. He ended the war as a brigadier general and was mustered out in January 1866 from the volunteer service. He reverted to his Regular Army rank of captain, but was offered no higher position when the army was reorganized that summer. Apparently upset by the snub, he resigned on October 31, 1866. Later, he held several minor diplomatic posts and engaged in business in Mexico. On August 29, 1880, he lost his life when the steamer he was on wrecked off Cape Canaveral, Florida. Warner, *Generals in Blue*, 508–9.

right front & thus flank their battery. This was accomplished though with considerable loss on our side, & more loss to the enemy.

Lee made up his mind he wasn't wanted there & left. We had positive orders not to follow him so we held the position for the rest of the day & in the afternoon we opened communication with Gen. [Winfield Scott] Hancock's[34] [II] Corps on our right, & then we had a perfect line connecting with the Infantry on our right & with Gregg on our left—Gregg had also been fighting with portions of Fitz Lee's Div. The force opposed to Gen. Custer's command was composed of the Brigades of Gens. [Pierce M. B.] Young[35] & [Thomas L.]

---

34. Winfield Scott Hancock (1824–1886) proved to be one of the Union's more significant generals during the Civil War. After graduating from West Point in 1844, he spent two years in Indian Territory and took part in the Mexican-American War. He also was the quartermaster during the Utah Expedition against the Mormons. In September 1861, he was appointed a brigadier general in command of a brigade. At Antietam, he commanded the 1st Division of the II Corps after Maj. Gen. Israel B. Richardson was mortally wounded. In November 1862, he was promoted to major general. One of his more significant achievements occurred on the first day of Gettysburg on July 1, 1863, when he took command of Union forces after Maj. Gen. John Reynolds was killed in action. He anchored the federal line on Cemetery Ridge. However, after turning over command to General Meade, Hancock was wounded on the battle's third day as his troops repulsed Pickett's Charge. Later that year, he reassumed command of the II Corps and made it one of the more dependable forces in the Union Army until combat and casualties wore it down in 1864. In the postwar army, he served as a major general. In 1866, he assumed command of the Department of the Missouri, covering Missouri, Kansas, Colorado, and New Mexico. In the spring of 1867, he botched negotiations with the Sioux and Cheyenne and ordered the burning of an abandoned Cheyenne village in Kansas. Among his subordinates was Lt. Col. George Armstrong Custer, then commanding the 7th U.S. Cavalry Regiment. After Custer abandoned his regiment in the field, Hancock preferred charges against him. A court-martial led to Custer's suspension from command for fifteen months. In 1880, the Democrats nominated Hancock for president, but he lost the election to Republican James A. Garfield. Warner, *Generals in Blue*, 202–4.

35. Pierce M. B. Young (1836–1896) was a Confederate major general during the Civil War and later a four-term U.S. congressman from Georgia. He attended West Point, but was among those who resigned before graduation after Georgia's secession. His rise initially was slow, but after he switched to the cavalry, his prominence increased in the Confederate Army. Promoted to brigadier general in October 1863, he played an important role in the 1864 Overland Campaign. After Stuart's death at Yellow Tavern, Young assumed command of a division. Young was engaged in 1864 in defending Savannah, Georgia, during General Sherman's march across Georgia and was promoted to major general in December 1864. Later in 1865, he continued to fight Sherman in battles across South and North Carolina. Warner, *Generals in Gray*, 348.

Rosser,[36] both of whom had been at West Point with Gen. Custer. We took the Adjt. of White's Battalion prisoner[37] & killed the Lieut. who was acting as A.A.G. to Gen. Rosser, the Capt. & one Lieut. of the Battery & one or two other Officers. We found on the field a dispatch which the Medical Director of the Div. wrote to the M.D. of the Corps stating that he had over 60 wounded for whom he wished transportation.

One of the prisoners captured by the 5th told them they thought they had got hold of the same Div. they had whipped the day before (the 3d) till "we heard your d—d band, & then we knew it was that curly-headed devil."

About dark we rec'd an order stating that Hancock's left had been turned & therefore ordering us to fall back to the furnace—about half way to Chancellorsville. We knew that Hancock's left had not been turned as we connected with it, but the order had to be obeyed, so we fell back. The next morning Meade found out his mistake & we were ordered to occupy the same position we had held the day before.

Col. Devin's Brig. took the advance & drove the Rebs. from the position & then we came up, but they did not allow us to hold it long in peace. The enemy came down from Todd's Tavern on our left flank. The General put part of the 1st. Mich. in the woods on each side of the road dismounted, and one squadron mounted, commanded by Billy Brevoort[38] & Gus Buhl charged down the road. We drove them back where they came from though they had a heavy force of dismounted

---

36. Thomas L. Rosser (1836–1910) was a highly capable Confederate major general during the Civil War and frequently faced his former West Point roommate, George Custer, in battle. That included at Gettysburg, Trevilian Station, and numerous engagements during the Shenandoah Campaign of 1864. The two men later renewed their friendship on the frontier when Custer commanded the 7th U.S. Cavalry and Rosser was chief engineer for the Northern Pacific Railroad building across Dakota and Montana territories. In 1898, Rosser returned to the U.S. Army as a brigadier general of volunteers during the Spanish-American War. Warner, *Generals in Gray*, 264–65.
37. This was Lt. John W. Watts, 35th Battalion Virginia Cavalry.
38. After Capt. William M. Brevoort (1842–1864) of the 1st Michigan Cavalry was killed in action on June 1, 1864, at Cold Harbor, Virginia, Col. Russell Alger called him "one of the bravest and best officers in the brigade." Born on April 27, 1842, Brevoort, a Detroit resident, joined the 1st Michigan on August 8, 1861, as a second lieutenant. On August 22, 1861, he was promoted to first lieutenant and appointed the regiment's adjutant. He was seized at Winchester, Virginia, and taken prisoner on May 25, 1862. On May 1, 1863, he was promoted to captain. After his death, he was buried in Cold Harbor National Cemetery. Soldier Records and Profiles; U.S. Civil War Soldiers; "William Macomb Brevoort," memorial at Findagrave.com, 127568952.

men & one gun. This fighting you must remember was all done in the Wilderness, a place most appropriately named. The woods are so full of underbrush that a man is invisible at the distance of two rods. While we were here a shell struck a branch of a tree just over the head of Fred Nims covering Fred with dust & splinters. Fred reached up & touched the branch with his hand. The Rebs. seem to be perfectly satisfied that they could not make any thing out of our Brig. so they let us alone for the rest of the day. However they were treated just as badly by the Regular Brig. with which they [were] fighting all the afternoon & till after dark. This was one of the most hotly contested Cavalry fights I ever heard of & the Rebs were handsomely repulsed, though with great loss of men & officers on our side. The gallant Capt [Joseph P.] Ash[39] who was with Gen. Custer on his Charlottesville raid was killed here, & one U.S. Regt. lost 6 out of 12 Officers.

The next day, Sunday May 9th [8th], the Brig. marched to within a mile or two of Spotsylvania C. H. where we found the 5th Corps Gen. Warren engaged with the enemy. We started back, as we have no inclination to get mixed up with the family quarrels of the Infantry. On

---

39. Joseph P. Ash, a member of the 5th U.S. Cavalry, had been with Custer's forces on his raid toward Charlottesville earlier that year. At one point on February 29, 1864, during a skirmish at the Rio Mills Bridge over the Rivanna River, Custer ordered Ash to lead sixty men of his 5th U.S. Cavalry across the river and attack the Confederate camp from the east and south. Custer's main force would attack from the north and west. A Confederate artillery officer had his men pretend to be arriving Confederate cavalry. The bluff worked and confused Custer's attackers, including Ash and his men. Custer's men retreated after burning the bridge. Ash was killed in action on May 8, 1864, during the Wilderness fighting. Ash was born in Philadelphia on July 4, 1849. His initial heroics during April 1861 gained him an appointment as a second lieutenant in the 2nd U.S. (later the 5th) Cavalry. He performed admirably until he was wounded on November 8, 1862, at Warrenton, Virginia. When he returned to action the next September, he had been promoted to captain and commander of the regiment's Company A. He frequently received praise from his superiors, including Custer, whose report of the Rio Mills skirmish noted that Ash "drove the enemy back very gallantly" (*O.R.*, series 1, vol. 33, 162). He was killed May 8, 1864, while trying to rally an infantry regiment near Todd's Tavern during Spotsylvania Court House. His commander noted that "he died nobly in the discharge of most important duty; a heroic, patriotic, intrepid cavalry officer, a noble martyr in his country's services." Donald C. Caughey, "Fiddler's Green: Joseph P. Ash," *Regular Cavalry in the Civil War* (historical blog), April 16, 2009, https://regularcavalryincivilwar.wordpress.com/2009/04/16/fiddlers-green-joseph-p-ash/; *O.R.*, series 1, vol. 36, pt. 1, 812; Soldier Records and Profiles; U.S. Civil War Soldiers.

our way back we met the 6th Corps. with Gen. Sedgewick [Sedgwick] at its head, marching to what I suppose was his last battle; for I am not sure that he was killed that day not having seen any account of his death. The favorable impression I had received of him before was fully confirmed by his bearing on that day. The Brig marched that afternoon to a place near Fredericksburg, called Silvers.[40] Here the whole Corps was gathered together that night preparatory to starting off for the rear of Lee's Army. On the morning of the 9th the Cavalry Corps cut loose from the Army of the Potomac and marching around the right of the Rebel Army got into their rear. The Michigan Brigade was in the advance. In the afternoon we halted at Chilesburg[41] a small village a few miles from the R.R. Here there was a consultation of the Generals. Most of them thought it advisable to wait till night before advancing on Beaver Dam[42] the station at which we expected to strike the R.R.

---

40. According to articles by Eric Mink, Isaac Silver, a New Jersey native, had moved to Spotsylvania in the 1850s and owned a farm along the Orange Plank Road in the Chancellorsville area. During the war, he was a Northern sympathizer who worked as a "Union scout." He kept the Union informed about Confederate troop strengths and movements, especially during the 1863 Chancellorsville Campaign. Troops of both sides swirled around his farm during the fighting. He also claimed to have been a guide for General Sheridan during the Battle of Spotsylvania Court House in May 1864. On May 8, 1864, Sheridan's cavalry divisions were gathered around Silver's farm on Orange Plank Road, as Granger suggests. Mink cites a dispatch from Sheridan's headquarters sent on the afternoon of May 8 that stated the general would be at Silver's that night. The following morning Sheridan led his command away toward Richmond and the Battle of Yellow Tavern. In early 1865 the Confederates apparently grasped what he had been up to and sent Silver to the Salisbury, North Carolina, prison camp for the war's final months. In 1870, Silver moved his family to Stafford County, Virginia. He died in 1901 at age ninety-one. Eric Mink, "'I Was in the Secret Service of the Army of the Potomac . . .'—Isaac Silver of Spotsylvania County," pts. 1 and 2, *Mysteries & Conundrums, Exploring the Civil War–Era Landscape in the Fredericksburg & Spotsylvania Region* (historical blog), October 7 and 8, 2010, https://npsfrsp.wordpress.com/, provided to the editor by John Hennessy, chief historian at Fredericksburg and Spotsylvania National Military Park, August 26, 2016.
41. Today Chilesburg is an unincorporated community in Virginia's Caroline County.
42. Today Beaver Dam is an unincorporated community in Virginia's Hanover County. The then station along the Virginia Central Railroad proved strategic during the Civil War for both sides in moving soldiers and supplies. The original station dated to at least 1840, if not earlier, but it was destroyed at least three times. The current station remains historic, but was rebuilt in 1866. It is listed on the National Register of Historic Places.

but Gen. Custer told them if there was anything worth getting there it would be run off before night. General Sheridan acted on this suggestion & we started on again. Just as we reached the North Anna River the Capt. of the 1st who was in command of the Advance Guard reported that there was a train of ambulances in front of him. The 1st was sent forward with orders to charge for the train. As we followed the Regt. we found several ambulances containing wounded Rebs. which the 1st had captured & left in the road. The Regt. continued on the charge and presently we could tell by their cheers that they had come across something. We put spurs to our horses & in a moment were in the midst of some 350 men of the 5 & 6 Corps who had just been re-captured by the 1st. I never saw any men so delighted as these were when they knew that they were free and safe. They were within half a mile of the Station, where a train was waiting to convey them to Richmond, when the advance guard reached them. The 1st pushed on & got to the station in time to stop the train of cars.

May 3d, Newcastle, Va. [June 3—Actually New Castle Ferry on the Pamunkey River.][43]

At the station we found a train of 47 cars loaded with commissary stores, besides a very large stock of the same which was in & around the depot. There was bacon by the cord, ham, fish & sugar by the hogs head & rice by the ton, and hundreds of barrels & bags, of flour. There was one Locomotive attached to the train & another came up while we were there & tried to back out again, but was stopped by Lieut. [Warner H.] Pierson[44] of the 1st. In an hour after our arrival locomotives, trains & stores were all in flames.

---

43. In his haste, Granger wrote down the wrong date when he resumed his letter and he also truncated the name of the site where the Michigan Cavalry Brigade was resting. His reference in this letter to the death in combat of Captain Brevoort is a clue to the date. Brevoort was killed on June 1, or two days before, as Granger indicates. The fighting that claimed Brevoort had been severe, but the cavalrymen managed to hold their line against charging Confederate infantrymen. Fortunately, later that day, infantry troops from the Union VI Corps replaced the Michiganders in the line, who then fell back to Old Church, Virginia, near both Totopotomoy Creek and the Pamunkey River. The Army of the Potomac spent much of that time fighting Lee's troops along the Cold Harbor lines, but the cavalry lingered for several days resting and picketing from its base at New Castle Ferry to Haw's Shop to Old Church, according to Longacre.

44. Warner H. Pierson enlisted in Company G, 1st Michigan Cavalry, on August 15, 1861, as a sergeant. He was later promoted to first sergeant and then to second lieutenant

CAMPAIGNING IN THE SPRING AND SUMMER OF 1864   225

About 11 o'clock the Staff "went to bed" in the front yard of a house near the burning depot, the General being at Div. Head Quarters some distance off. We hadn't been asleep long when we were waked up by the noise of fighting in our front. We were all so sleepy that it was some time before we could make out what was going on, & the whole command seemed to be in the same predicament. For a few minutes it looked as though there would be a stampede, as every one seemed to think that it was poor policy to stay near the fire, but the picket of the 1st which was attacked soon repulsed the enemy, and the General's appearance restored order. The Gen. then took the Brig back a little ways, out of the light of the conflagration & bivouced [bivouacked] till morning.

On the [May] 10th we marched to the South bank of the South Anna, crossing the River at Ground Squirrel Bridge.[45]

About day light the next morning we were waked up by the sound of artillery & small arms. The Rebs. had a gun in such a position that they threw a shell into Gen. Gregg's camp, and at the same time the pickets of the Regular Brig. of our Div. were attacked. The Sixth Michigan were ordered to dismount and march through the woods in rear of our camp, just beyond which the Regular Brig. was skirmishing.

When the Regt. got out there the Col. in command of the skirmish line asked Maj. Kidd to take his Regt. to the right of the line, which the Maj. did. When we came to move, I was sent out to find the Sixth. I went through where the 6th had been ordered, & found there the 1st N.Y. Dragoons of the Reg. Brig., the Maj of which Regt. knew nothing about the orders his Col. had given Maj Kidd. This Maj said there was no Mich Regt. on his right & he knew of none in his front. He didn't seem to know what was in his front, so I thought the 6th might be there. Two of our horses with saddles on, stood out in the field & I went up to see what they were. Just before as I came near one of them, I saw a puff of smoke rise from among the tall grass with which the field was covered. I knew what that meant & as I wheeled my horse a ball whizzed over my head. The fool had shot at me, if he had aimed at

---

    on May 18, 1863. On June 14, 1864, he was promoted to first lieutenant and on October 25, 1864, to captain. He was mustered out of the regiment on November 7, 1865, at Fort Leavenworth, Kansas. Soldier Records and Profiles; U.S. Civil War Soldiers.

45. Ground Squirrel Bridge is about eighteen miles below Beaver Dam Station and crosses the South Anna River. After his entire Cavalry Corps crossed the bridge, General Sheridan directed that the bridge be destroyed. As Granger suggests, the troops made camp, had supper and tried to sleep.

the horse he couldn't have missed him as he was not more than 5 rods off. Before I got out of range several more balls passed uncomfortably near me. I didn't hunt for the 6th in that part of the field, any longer.

Some time about noon, I should think, of the 11th, Stuart came down on our left flank just as the advance had arrived at Yellow Tavern, at the junction of the Telegraph Road & the Brook Turnpike.[46] Col. Gibbs, commanding the Regular Brig., had the advance & our Brig. was in rear of the Div. After Gibbs had been fighting some time without accomplishing any thing, Gen. Merritt who was in command of the Div., ordered our Brig. to go in. Gen. Custer ordered the 5th & 6th to dismount and drive the Rebs from a position in the edge of a piece of woods. The Regts. obeyed as they always do, but it was a hard task and they lost pretty heavily. They had to charge dismounted, across two plowed fields while the Rebs were in the woods, & behind a fence. Sergeant Gale[47] of 6th Cav. was mortally wounded and Corporal Comte[48] killed.

---

46. The tavern itself was abandoned. It was located about six miles north of Richmond. The Union cavalry column had been traveling down the Mountain Road toward the Yellow Tavern area. Stuart's troops had been deployed to the left of the Union troops and east of the Mountain Road, astride the Telegraph Road itself. In the vicinity of the tavern, the Mountain and Telegraph Roads merged to form the Brook Pike. As Granger indicates, Custer advanced his 5th and 6th Michigan regiments through the fields to the left. The two regiments cleared the woods and exchanged fire well into the afternoon.

47. Granger may be mistaken about this soldier's regiment. No soldier named Gale from the 6th Michigan was killed at Yellow Tavern. However, Sgt. Henry D. Gale, Company C, 5th Michigan Cavalry, was wounded and died May 11, 1864. The twenty-four-year-old soldier was buried in Woodlawn Cemetery, Monroe, Michigan, next to his brother Franklin Gale, who had been killed in action on July 1, 1862, at the Battle of Malvern Hill, Virginia. "Henry D. Gale," memorial and gravestone at Findagrave.com, 77900028; David Ingall and Karin Risko, *Michigan Civil War Landmarks* (Charleston, S.C.: History Press, 2015), 98–99; Soldier Records and Profiles; U.S. Civil War Soldiers.

48. Victor E. Comte, age twenty-eight, enlisted in Company A, 2nd Michigan Infantry on May 25, 1861, but was discharged for disability on August 17, 1861. A year later, on August 27, 1862, he mustered into Company C, 5th Michigan Cavalry, but died of his wounds at Yellow Tavern on May 11, 1864. French by birth, he wrote some fifty letters home to his wife, Elize, back in Detroit, that are on file in the Bentley Historical Library, University of Michigan. A biographical article, "Detroit's Little French Corporal," citing Comte's letters, was published by F. Clever Bald in *Michigan History* 46 (1962): 126. Comte, a French-speaking Swiss native who immigrated to Detroit, was born in 1833 in Bern, Switzerland. According to his entry

Ask mother if she remembers the two women who came to her to ask about their husbands, when I was home last fall. One of them was dead when I returned to the Army, & Comte was the other. Capt. Axtell[49] of the 5th was wounded so badly that he will never be fit for service, though Rebel prisoners captured on the 27th say he is alive. We had to leave all our wounded who could not ride, except a very few, as we had no transportation except the Reb. ambulances & wagons we had captured. While the 5th & 6th were fighting on the left there was a Rebel battery farther to the right which was doing considerable execution. The firing from this battery was the best I ever saw the Rebs do. As the column could not move till that battery was out of the way, Gen. Custer made preparations to charge it. When the 5th & 6th had driven the Rebs. from their first position, those two Regts. marched through the woods & commenced firing at the battery.

The General had the 1st drawn up ready to charge, mounted when "old Tom Howrigan"[50] came up & asked the Gen. if he might take

    in Findagrave.com, he is believed to have been buried in a mass grave with other fallen soldiers from Yellow Tavern. U.S. Civil War Soldiers; "Victor E. Comte," memorials and photograph at Findagrave.com, 138207874 and 112245044.

49. Granger probably did not realize how badly wounded Benjamin F. Axtell (1838–1864) actually was. According to author John Peter Beckendorf, Axtell not only had to be left with other Union wounded at a private house, but he later died on July 15 in Libby Prison in Richmond. On September 2, 1862, Axtell had been commissioned as the first lieutenant of Company L, 5th Michigan Cavalry. On February 5, 1864, he was promoted to captain of Company A. His Findagrave entry indicates he died of disease on July 15 while a prisoner of war at Libby Prison. He is buried in Richmond National Cemetery, Virginia. John Peter Beckendorf, "The CDV Album of Major Robert C. Wallace, 5th Michigan Cavalry," *Military Images* (Export, Pa.) 26, no. 6 (May–June 2005): 8; "Capt. Benjamin Axtell," memorial at Findagrave.com, 87301155; U.S. Civil War Soldiers; Soldier Records and Profiles.

50. Thomas M. Howrigan (1824–1879) was commissioned at age thirty-eight as an officer in Company H, 1st Michigan Cavalry, on August 8, 1861. He was promoted to major on March 1, 1863. Howrigan was mustered out on June 19, 1865, at Fort Leavenworth, Kansas. He apparently stayed in the Kansas City area, as he and his family are buried in Mount St. Mary's Cemetery, Kansas City, Missouri. Given Howrigan's age, it is understandable why Granger referred to him as "old." At Yellow Tavern, according to Colonel Alger, Howrigan led a gallant charge against the Confederate guns, just before Major Granger led his ill-fated charge of the 7th Michigan Cavalry. U.S. Civil War Soldiers; Soldier Records and Profiles; "Thomas M. Howrigan," memorial and gravestone at Findagrave.com, 9069646.

his battalion & lead the charge. The Gen. gave him permission & Howrigan's battalion was transferred from the rear to the front of the Regt. The Gen. then sent me through the woods to tell Col. Alger, commanding the 5th & 6th, that the First was going to charge for the guns, & to order Alger to do the same, dismounted. When I got back the Gen. had started across the field with the 1st. It was a ploughed field at least half a mile broad with several ditches & fences to pass and the battery was pouring canister into the column as fast as possible. But the glorious old Regt. never faltered, Howrigan led the Regiment as well as ever men were led, and no men ever followed their officers better than the men of the 1st followed Howrigan.

Before I could get to the head of the Regt. a cheer, louder than any that had preceded it, told that, the guns were ours. When I came up the General was rallying the men to be ready to repel any attempt the enemy might make to retake the guns, or to pursue him if necessary.

We captured two guns in this charge!

Maj Howrigan was slightly wounded in the arm—just a scratch, another ball passes through his clothes & a third struck his saddle bags.

The 5th & 6th met a more obstinate resistance on the left where one gun of the battery was posted in a piece of woods, and the 1st & 1st Vt. were sent to their assistance as soon as possible. The Rebs. ran off their gun, but the woods were still full of sharp shooters & they held a strong position in the road.

I was sent to ~~bring~~ hurry up the 7th, which had been left back supporting our battery. Henry [Granger] was in command and I gave him the order—the last time I ever spoke to him. He brought the Regt. up on the trot, & Gen. Custer ordered him to charge up the road. As he started to obey the order the Gen. said, "If the Regt. will only follow him, it will be all right." He went in gloriously at the head of the Regt. but as soon as he fell the 7th broke, having no other commander in whom they had any confidence. The position was finally carried & we found his body nearest the enemy. He was shot through the heart & just over the right eye. His death was evidently painless. I never saw the face of any one killed in battle look more quiet & natural than his looked. He was buried on the field before the fight was over, Capt. [James G.] Birney[51] & Dr. [George R.] Richards[52] of the 7th taking

---

51. See introduction, note 36 for Birney's background.
52. Dr. George R. Richards (1841–1895) was born in Ireland and came to Michigan

charge of his burial. His pockets had been plundered by the Rebs. before we found him. His death is a great loss to the Brig. as there is no officer of the 7th here capable of commanding the Regt.

After losing this position the Rebs retreated across the Chickahominy, & kept up an artillery dual [duel] with our battery till dark. Just before the firing ceased it commenced raining.

In this battle J. E. B. Stuart was mortally wounded & Col. H. Clay Pate,[53] of Border Ruffian notoriety, killed.

After the rain was over, we fell back a little ways, & formed the command in columns of squadrons & lay down for a little sleep.

Some-time in the night we were routed up & commenced our march again. Our Div. was in the center, Wilson having the advance. As I have told you, Wilson lost his way & ran into the Reb. Militia, occupying the second line of fortifications in front of Richmond. Then we had to take the advance, and cross the Chickahominy at Meadow Bridge, which the blunder of Wilson had given the enemy time to destroy. The road running through the swamp at this place is for about half a mile, just about wide enough for a column of Cavalry marching "by fours" with an impassable morass on either side. Meadow Bridge is nearly in the center of this piece of road.[54] The General set a party

---

as a child. He graduated from the University of Michigan in 1861. He enlisted as the regiment's assistant surgeon on February 5, 1863, and was mustered out on November 7, 1865. However, he immediately joined the 1st Michigan Cavalry and was finally mustered out on March 10, 1866, at Salt Lake City, Utah. "Dr. George R. Richards," memorial and gravestone at Findagrave.com, 87446243; William Page Johnson, "The Skirmish at Arellton and the Michigan Cavalry Brigade Hospital at Fairfax Court House," *Fare Facs Gazette* 11, no. 4 (Fall 2014): 8–9, 16–17; Soldier Records and Profiles; U.S. Civil War Soldiers.

53. H. Clay Pate (1833–1864) was a Confederate colonel who was killed May 11, 1864, at Yellow Tavern just before General Stuart was mortally wounded. Earlier in his life, he was a newspaperman in Kansas and Ohio. A proslavery sympathizer, he joined others in tracking down militant abolitionist John Brown, but was taken prisoner by Brown. In 1860 he returned to Virginia, but recruited a company of cavalry after the war began. Eventually, he was a lieutenant colonel under Stuart's command, but quarreled with both Stuart and Rosser. "Col. Henry Clay Pate," memorial, photograph, and gravestone at Findagrave.com, 5373786.

54. Granger spent more of his letter discussing his own exploits during the Meadow Bridge actions, but the engagement was more serious than he makes it out to be. On May 12, General Sheridan had found himself nearly boxed in between the swollen river on his left and Confederate cavalry to his rear. He had already decided to bypass the city, figuring he could not hold it without infantry support. *(continued)*

of pioneers at work on the bridge & was at on the bridge himself superintending operations, when suddenly, without any warning, a canister burst just over the bridge. Every man there but the General & [Alexander] Walker[55] left the bridge in a hurry, expecting that the shot would be followed by others. I am happy to say I wasn't there, nor were any of the rest of the Staff. If I had been there I should have hated to stay on the bridge & should have hated to leave the General there. Walker was in that fix, but he has first rate grit & he stayed.

However the Rebs. threw no more canister and the Gen. got the men working again very soon. Soon after, when we were all in the road, the Rebs. threw a few shells at us, which caused us to get out of the way till the bridge was finished. Then the Gen. sent the 5th, 6th, & 7th into the woods on both sides of the road and they moved through to the edge of the open field, on the other side of which the Reb gun was posted. The Rebs. had been building breast works of pine trees while we were repairing the bridge, but our sharp shooting soon made them run their gun out of the way. Then the Gen. sent back to Gen. Merritt for some more Regts. to give us force enough to charge the breast works, dismounted. General Merritt sent two Regts. of the Regular Brig. & two of Col. Devin's Brigs. Then the Gen. sent me forward to order Col. Alger forward. I was told that Col. Alger was on the right of the R.R. track, which runs parallel with the road, & to the right of it. I had to cross the track & as the bank is very steep my saddle slipped back onto Bob's hips, & he commenced kicking with all his might just

---

> To get across the Chickahominy River, he needed the nearby severely damaged railroad bridge repaired to enable his troops to cross to safety on the far side of the river. He assigned Custer's brigade to restore the bridge for use and to gain a foothold on the other side of the river, while the rest of his command held off the threatening Confederates to the rear. The 5th and 6th Michigan suppressed the enemy's fire and made their away across the damaged railroad bridge to clear the far banks and secure positions there. By midafternoon, Merritt's division was able to cross the bridge and drive the enemy back to Gaines's Mill. The rest of Sheridan's command soon were safely over the river as well. Longacre, *Custer*, 215–17.

55. This was likely Maj. Alexander Walker, twenty-seven, of the 7th Michigan Cavalry. He had been commissioned the captain of Company A, 7th Michigan Cavalry, on October 1, 1862. Wounded at Gettysburg, he was promoted to major on February 14, 1864. When Lt. Col. Melvin Brewer was wounded at Trevilian Station, Walker assumed command. Walker commanded the regiment from May 26 to July 4, 1864. He was mustered out on disability on November 28, 1864. He is buried in Greenwood Cemetery in Rockford, Illinois. Soldier Records and Profiles; U.S. Civil War Soldiers.

as his front feet reached the top of the bank. Fearing that he might fall down the bank, I rolled off his back as quick as I could consistently. He ran down into the road, kicking all the way, and at first started for the enemy's lines, but he soon stopped, & looked around a moment as if thinking which way he had better go. Fortunately he resolved to come back. As soon as I saw him caught by one of our men, I went on, dismounted to give Col. Alger the order to advance. After looking for him some time I found that he was on the left of the road.

It was very hard walking, & by the time I had got back to the R.R. the Regulars had commenced to advance in splendid order. I found Maj Dean [Charles W. Deane][56] of the 6th at the R.R., and ordered him forward. Then I crossed & gave the same order to Col. Alger. The whole line advanced under a very hot fire, and drove the Rebs. from their breastwork.

The Reb. right was turned by the left wing of the 5th or it might have been a more difficult position operation to drive them from the position. This was the most brilliant charge of dismounted Cavalry over an open field I have seen, & there have been several in this campaign.

Here the Reb. Gen. [James B.] Gordon[57] was mortally wounded. [Williams C.] Wickham's Brig.[58] also was here.

---

56. Charles W. Deane of Pentwater, Michigan, was mustered into the 6th Michigan Cavalry at age twenty-five as the captain of its Company I on August 25, 1862. He was promoted to major on November 11, 1863, and was mustered out on January 5, 1865, at Camp Russell, Virginia. Soldier Records and Profiles; U.S. Civil War Soldiers.
57. James B. Gordon (1822–1864) enlisted at the outbreak of the war in 1861 and was appointed a major in the 1st North Carolina Cavalry Regiment. By November, serving under J. E. B Stuart, he had been appointed a colonel of cavalry. In the aftermath of the Battle of Gettysburg, he defeated Union troops at Hagerstown, Maryland, which helped the Army of Northern Virginia escape into Virginia. That September, he was appointed a brigadier general and assigned command of the North Carolina Cavalry Brigade. When Stuart was killed on May 11, 1864, at Yellow Tavern, Gordon replaced him in command and in defending Richmond. During the fighting on May 12, 1864, at Meadow Bridge, Gordon was mortally wounded. He died on May 18, 1864, and was buried in St. Paul's Episcopal Churchyard in his native Wilkesboro, North Carolina. "James Byron Gordon," memorial, photograph, and gravestone at Findagrave.com, 10877; Warner, *Generals in Gray*, 111.
58. This brigade was commanded by Brig. Gen. Williams C. Wickham, a Virginia native, who was a lawyer before the war. In 1861, he voted against the articles of secession, but opted to serve his native state when Union forces threatened Virginia. He was commissioned a lieutenant colonel of the 4th Virginia Cavalry in 1862 and later a colonel. He fought in such major battles as Chancellorsville, Brandy *(continued)*

We met with no further opposition that day & that afternoon, we encamped at Gaines's Mill. Before reaching the latter place, we passed through Cold Harbor—a place we have visited since. The next day May 13th [Friday] we marched to a place near Bottom's Bridge where we went into camp. Today June 3d [Friday],[59] we are encamped just across the road from that place, & Then we were 40 or 50 miles from our Army—today our Army is on our right, & we are guarding its flank. On the 14th May [Saturday], we passed over the ground of several of the seven days battles, & towards evening, reached Malvern Hill. There were several gun-boats in the River, when we came in sight, & we were not sure whether they were ours, or the enemy's. Our uncertainty was not rendered very pleasant by the gratuitous gift of several 9 inch shells from said gun-boats. However we soon succeeded opening communication with them & found that they were Union.

Lieut. Gray[60] is going to the White House this P.M. & as I may not have so good an opportunity to send off this letter again, I'll send this now, especially as I have carried the Cav. Corps safely to the James River & shan't have so good a place to stop, in some time.

I shall continue this interesting epistle as I find time & send it off as I get a chance.[61]

Station, and Gettysburg. On September 9, 1863, he was promoted to brigadier general and given command of a brigade in Fitzhugh Lee's division. As Granger indicates, Wickham's brigade fought against the Michigan Cavalry Brigade at Yellow Tavern and Meadow Bridge on May 11 and 12, 1864. In August, the two forces would meet again at Front Royal, the battle in which Lieutenant Granger himself would be killed. Wickham resigned in October 1864, after having been elected to the Second Confederate Congress. He was involved in efforts to end the fighting. After the war ended, he was elected president of the Virginia Central Railroad, which had been severely damaged during the war. He spent the rest of his life as a significant figure in the railroad business in Virginia. He also held various political positions. He died on July 23, 1888. Warner, *Generals in Gray*, 335–36.

59. On May 13, Sheridan's cavalry command had remained on the far bank of the Chickahominy River and eventually recrossed at Bottoms Bridge. On May 14, the command had reached the James River near Malvern Hill. Union gunboats shelled the column until the cavalrymen revealed their identity by draping the American flag from the roof of the house. Sheridan then negotiated with the supply base personnel of Maj. Gen. Benjamin F. Butler's Army of the James for assistance and new mounts. Butler's command was away to the north near the Richmond defenses. Longacre, *Custer*, 219.

60. This is Lt. Pharo Gray. See chapter 5, note 21.

61. Granger's dateline suggests he began this letter May 25, but this paragraph and

I wrote you a note from Milford some time ago.

Jim Christiancy has rec'd. a severe flesh wound in the thigh. The rest of us are all well. Capt. Brevoort of the 1st Mich. was killed day before yesterday & Hazlett [William M. Heazlit][62] wounded—Maxwell[63] was wounded the same day Jim was. Geo. Hill[64] of the 7th who used to be Q. M. Sargt. of "C" Co. is missing since the 11th ult.

Capt. Judson has just come out from Washington where he has been since we were on the James.

Remembrance to all the friends.

E. G. Granger
Lieut. & A.D.C.

---

the reference to June 3 two paragraphs previous clearly reveal he did not finish it or mail it that day. Supporting that belief is his reference to Captain Brevoort's death on June 1.

62. William M. Heazlit of Dowagiac, Michigan, was commissioned at age twenty-one on August 12, 1861, as a second lieutenant in Company M, 1st Michigan Cavalry. He was promoted to captain on November 12, 1862, long before Granger refers to him as a lieutenant in this letter. Col. James Kidd refers to Heazlit as wounded in East Cavalry Field at Gettysburg on July 3, 1863. Heazlit was mustered out on October 30, 1864. In 1905, the commissioner of pensions denied a pension claim of Melissa D. Heazlit of Dowagiac. She claimed to be the captain's widow, having married him in 1864. But Lottie E. Heazlit claimed to have married Heazlit on March 28, 1883. The pension decision hinged on the validity of a divorce petition rendered February 3, 1883, in Bent County, Colorado. Eventually, the bureau decided in favor of the second wife, Lottie, ruling that the divorce was valid. John W. Bixler, ed., *Decisions of the Department of the Interior in Appeals Pension and Bounty-Land Claims*, vol. 15 (Washington, D.C.: Government Printing Office, 1905), 553–56; Soldier Records and Profiles; U.S. Civil War Soldiers.

63. For more about Maxwell, see chapter 2, note 79.

64. This may be former Sgt. George W. Hill, who joined Company C, 5th Michigan Cavalry, as quartermaster sergeant and later was appointed a second lieutenant in Company G, 7th Michigan Cavalry, on December 3, 1862. He was born April 21, 1839, at Ypsilanti, Michigan, and enlisted on August 16, 1862, in the 5th Michigan Cavalry. He was taken prisoner at Yellow Tavern and was held until he was exchanged on March 1, 1865. That May 24 he was promoted to first lieutenant. On November 7, 1865, he was transferred to the 1st Michigan Cavalry and remained with the regiment until he was mustered out on March 10, 1866, at Salt Lake City. According to Hill's pension records, he successfully applied for a pension in July 1900. He died September 3, 1901 and was buried in Ypsilanti. Soldier Records and Profiles; U.S. Civil War Soldiers; Lee, *Personal and Historical Sketches*, 244; Robertson, *Michigan in the War*, 849.

(left) Lt. George Hill. *Courtesy of John Beckendorf.*

(right) Capt. William Brevoort, 1st Michigan Cavalry. Brevoort was killed in action on June 1, 1864, in Cold Harbor, Virginia. *Courtesy of Paul Davis.*

✳ ✳ ✳

[LETTER 40]

Head Quarters, 1st Brig 1st Div.
Cav. Corps. A. P. Milford Va.
May 26th 1864 [Thursday]

Mollie

All well. No time to write. Returned from our Raid yesterday & march again this morning at 10 o'clock. Don't know where we are going.[65]

The General & Staff are all right. No one that you know in the Regts is hurt. Henry Granger is dead. Geo. Hill is missing.

---

65. Granger is referring to the Richmond Campaign that resulted in combat action at Yellow Tavern and Meadow Bridge. The new movement would take the brigade into even greater combat and danger than before, eventually resulting in the Battle of Trevilian Station on June 11–12, 1864.

Am writing a letter as I get time, & will send it as soon as possible.⁶⁶

Yours
E. G. Granger

※ ※ ※

[LETTER 41]

Head Qurs. 1st Brig 1st Div.
Cav Corps A. P. June 6th 1864
Near New Castle Hanover Co. Va.

Mollie

There is a mail going out at 8 P.M., so I thought I'd just write a line as I intend to do whenever we get a chance to send a letter.

We are all well except Maj. Drew who is (we all hope) soon going to be sick enough to get to Washington. He's trying pretty hard at any rate.

We've heard from Jim up to the time he left White House. He was in good spirits & his wound was doing as well as could be expected.⁶⁷

Maxwell will not lose his arm I hope nor will Charlie Osborne⁶⁸

---

66. Here he is referring to his letter No. 39 that he will not complete for a week, June 3, or until he has a break at New Castle Ferry.
67. Jim Christiancy had been wounded on May 28, 1864, at the Battle of Haw's Shop, Virginia. As stated in chapter 3, note 31, he would receive the Medal of Honor in 1892 for his actions at that battle. Because the Custers were good friends with his family, Libbie Custer insisted that he stay at her boarding house, because the crowded hospital was "unbearable because of the horrible odor." The young officer was later taken home to Michigan by his father to recover. White House, Virginia, is today an unincorporated community in New Kent County. In 1862 and again in 1864, nearby White House Landing was the site of a major Union Army supply base. Leckie, *Elizabeth Bacon Custer*, 48.
68. His military records give his name variously as Charles Y. Osborn or Osborne. On August 30, 1862, the Owosso, Michigan, resident had enlisted at age twenty in Company K, 5th Michigan Cavalry. He was promoted to sergeant major on February 28, 1863, and was commissioned as a second lieutenant in Company H on August 18, 1863. He was promoted to first lieutenant on November 2, 1863. As Granger states, Osborn was wounded May 28, 1864, at Haw's Shop. On August 9, 1864, he was promoted to captain, but was discharged September 28 on account of wounds he had received in action. He died at age forty-nine of heart failure on February 4, 1892, and was buried in Oak Hill Cemetery in his hometown. Soldier Records and Profiles; U.S. Civil War Soldiers; "Charles Y. Osborn," memorial at Findagrave.com, 88275003; Michigan Death Records.

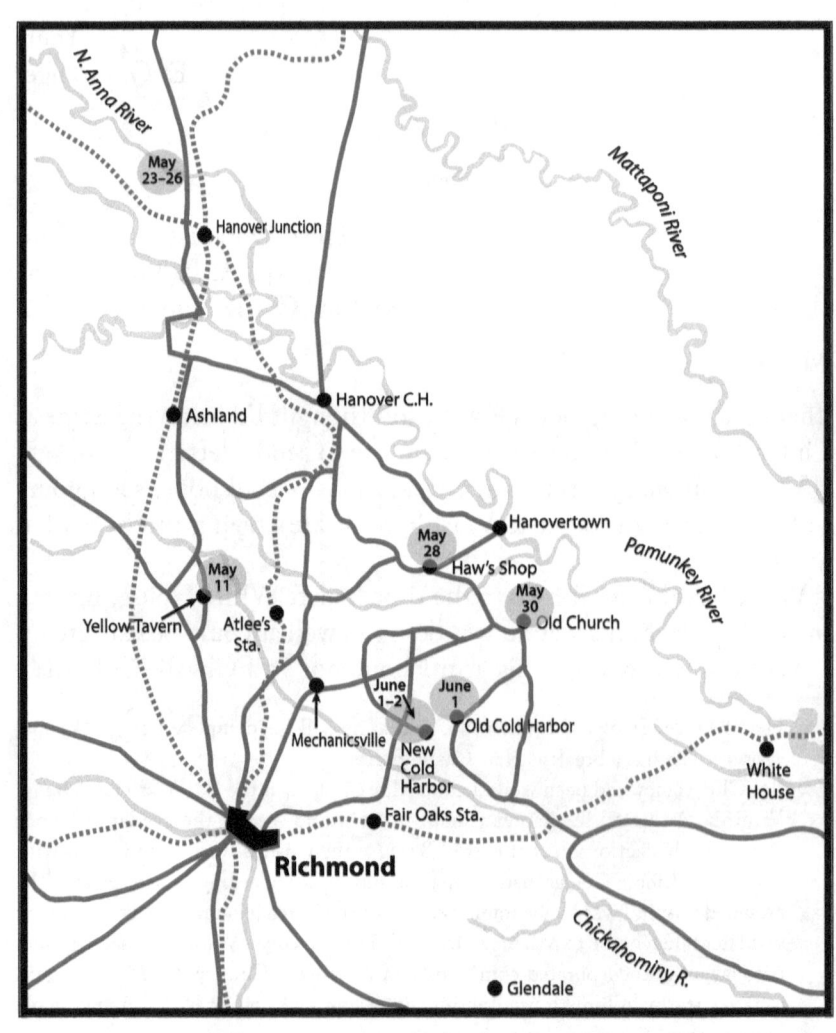

Union cavalry actions, May 28–June 1, 1864.
Map by Gary Raham.

lose any of his fingers though all the knuckles of his left hand are spoiled. Col. Gould who gave us this information says that Hobbs[69] will probably die & he is afraid Capt. Oliphant[70] will, also.

I have not rec'd. any letter from you later than the 20th No. 14 Rec'd. Carrie's of the 26th a day or two since, & yesterday I rec'd. a note from Don in reference to a letter which he is supposed to have written at some indefinite past time, but of which I have seen nothing.

Our Div. has retired from the fighting list & tomorrow we expect to go off some-where—where there is no fighting &, probably some foraging, to be done. So you must not be surprised if you don't hear from me again in some time.

The statement in the Advertiser of the 25th, which Uncle Edward sent me, that Henry Granger was captured & then killed is <u>a lie</u>. He was shot through the heart, at the head of his Regt. and <u>the Rebs did not get at his body till his feet were so swollen that they could not unbuckle his spur straps</u>, which they had evidently tried to do.

Sent off the first 18 pages of a letter, which I am writing as I get time, the other day.

Write often so that I may get some letters at least.

Ed.

Excuse the paper—I left my valise lying out doors the other night &, of course, it rained that night, and the valise being open my personal property became slightly damaged.

E. G. G.

I enclose a Magnolia leaf which I picked from a tree growing on the place where stood the house in which Patrick Henry was born.

---

69. This was Sgt. Levant Hobbs, age twenty-two, of York, Michigan. He had enlisted on August 15, 1862, as a sergeant in Granger's Company C, 5th Michigan Cavalry. He died on June 6, 1864, at Washington, D.C., of wounds received in action. He was buried in Arlington National Cemetery. Soldier Records and Profiles; U.S. Civil War Soldiers; "Sgt. Levant Hobbs," memorial and gravestone at Findagrave.com, 16890206.

70. See chapter 2, note 94. According to Findagrave.com, Oliphant was buried in Oakwood Cemetery in Saline, Washtenaw County, Michigan. "Capt. David Oliphant," memorial and gravestone at Findagrave.com, 54913450.

✳ ✳ ✳

[LETTER 42]

EDITOR'S NOTE: *As pointed out in the introduction for this section, the first page of this letter and an accompanying map have been lost. Thus, we cannot be certain when Granger actually wrote it, but textual references suggest either June 14 at Shady Grove Church, three miles from Todd's Tavern, or June 13, 1864.*

[May 27, 1864: north of Salem Church, Hanover County, Virginia][71]

... short range, with his Spencer Rifles. The Rebs belong to the Maryland Line, troops who had seen but little fighting, and, as green troops very often do, they stood fire splendidly. But the General soon bro't up the 7th & sent them around to charge on the right flank of the enemy. As soon as the Rebs saw the 7th, they broke, with the cry "we're flanked." The Marylanders claimed that the Georgians were the first to break, but however that was, there was soon a general stampede. The 7th charged after them for more than a mile, capturing some 38 prisoners, & killing & wounding several of the enemy. About the time the 7th were following up their "flying foe" we began to see the results of the work of the 1st & 6th. The road along which those Regts. were advancing was filled with Rebs. who were even more demoralized than those we had been fighting. Gen. Custer said he had never seen a more perfect route in any battle of the war. At least one large Brig. passed down that road just as fast as their horses could carry them running from our two Regts. dismounted. If the Gen. had had another Regt. to send in at that moment, we could have cut them off & captured a large number of prisoners, but our men were all busy.[72]

---

71. On May 27, 1864, Union cavalry forces had established a bridgehead at Dabney's Ford on the south side of the Pamunkey River. Custer's brigade chased Confederate cavalry that had been picketing the site. Union engineers erected a pontoon bridge over the river. Custer's men engaged Fitzhugh Lee's cavalry north of Salem Church, including the 1st Maryland. The Confederates soon withdrew.

72. For further details about this fighting and the various maneuvers of the Michigan Cavalry Brigade, see Gordon C. Rhea, *Cold Harbor, Grant and Lee, May 26–June 3, 1864* (Baton Rouge: Louisiana State University Press, 2014 reprint), 27–60.

[May 28, 1864: Haw's Shop/Enon Church][73]

We slept that night on the battle field. At noon the next day [May 28] the advance of our Infantry came up and we moved [to] Hawes' Shop. Here we found Cav. Corps Head Quarters. Gen. Gregg had been fighting all the morning at Enon Church about a mile from Hawes' Shop. He had a very heavy force opposed to him, but had held his position with the tenacity for which Gregg is so well known. General Sheridan himself ordered Gen. Custer to take his Brig. in and "fight it for all it was worth." When the Gen. came near Enon Church he dismounted all of his Brig. except the 1st which he left back for a reserve. He then put the 5th & 7th on the left [south], & the 6th on the right of the road [north]. The Rebs. were in a piece of thick woods and they made such a desperate resistance that the 6th could not advance. The Gen. sent me back for the 1st, which coming up dismounted went in with a yell and the whole line advanced at once, the Rebs falling back, when once started, without stopping at all. But they made a desperate fight before they broke & the loss of the Brig. was heavier, in proportion to the number of men we had, than in any other fight we were ever in. Capt. Maxwell of the 1st was shot through the arm, but is not going to lose his arm. Jim Christiancy had the end of his thumb shot off & received, also, a severe flesh wound

---

73. Troops under Maj. Gen. Wade Hampton, the senior Confederate cavalry leader in the wake of the death of General Stuart, launched a reconnaissance as the Army of the Potomac approached Richmond. Maj. Gen. David McMurtrie Gregg at the same time was probing west with his federal cavalry division searching for the Confederate left flank. Three miles west of Hanovertown and a mile beyond the shop of blacksmith John Haw, called Haw's Shop, Gregg clashed with Hampton's troops near Enon Church. As both sides looked for an edge, General Sheridan sent in two cavalry brigades from Torbert's division. Eventually Custer's four regiments were thrust into the fight. Because of the wooded terrain, Custer dismounted his troopers to fight as infantrymen. The fighting was both severe and bloody. The Michigan Brigade lost at least forty-one soldiers, including Pvt. John Huff, who reputedly had fired the fatal shot at General Stuart earlier in the month at Yellow Tavern. Both sides withdrew, but this was merely an opening engagement to the bloodbath that would mark fighting at Cold Harbor, Virginia, in the coming week. As Granger states, veterans considered this battle their most severe of the entire war. Wittenberg, *Under Custer's Command*, 79; *O.R.*, vol. 36, pt. 1, 821 contains Custer's account. Also, see Rhea, *Cold Harbor*, 61–91.

in the thigh. He is now in Washington staying with Mrs. Custer & enjoying himself immensely.

Capt. Oliphant of the 5th was wounded in the shoulder and has since died of his wound. Lt. Osborne [of the] 5th was wounded in the left hand while urging the men on. Capt. Dodge was slightly wounded in the leg. The Dr. told him that after a few days in the Corps Hospital he would be fit for duty, but Dodge "couldn't see" this Hospital, & reported for duty again that night, a little lame but able to ride. The force we fought here was the whole Reb. Cav. Corps. & the particular Brig. opposed to ours was Butler's Brig. composed of 7 full Regiments of S. Carolina Mounted Infantry, who had never been in a fight before.[74] They fought better than any other portion of the Reb. Cav. we ever met.

I never saw dead & wounded men so thick as they were lying in those woods. The S. Carolinians did not know enough to surrender when they were fairly taken, but said they "had no orders to surrender." The woods through which we drove them were so full of fallen trees & under brush as to make it very hard work to get through them, even without any opposing enemy. But our Spencer Rifles[75] are terrible weapons. The Reb papers in their account of the battle of Enon Church (Hawes' Shop, they call it) say that their forces had the better of us all day till our "infantry (estimated at 2 Corps) came up." The 2 Corps

---

74. Granger is incorrect here in his numbers. The units under then–brigadier general Matthew C. Butler (1836–1909) were only the 4th, 5th, and 6th South Carolina Cavalry regiments, which were newly arrived and inexperienced. Butler's troops fought bravely at Haw's Shop and a few weeks later at Trevilian Station. Butler himself later was promoted to major general; in 1898, he was appointed major general of U.S. Volunteers during the Spanish-American War. While he saw no field duty, he ably supervised the withdrawal of the defeated Spanish Army troops from Cuba.

75. The Spencer repeating rifle originally carried by Custer's regiments was a manually operated lever-action, seven-shot rifle that was produced between 1860 and 1869. It was adopted by the U.S. Army and its use increased during the Civil War. It proved both popular and reliable during the war, because of its rapid-fire capabilities and because its ammunition was waterproof and long-lasting. During the winter of 1863–64 Custer's troopers were rearmed with seven-shot Spencer repeating carbines that were lighter and eight inches shorter than the rifle version. They could be operated much more easily by troopers in their saddles. All of Custer's regiments carried these Spencer carbines by the start of the Overland Campaign in May 1864. Longacre, *Custer*, 198.

of Infantry was our little Brig. of Cav. The General had a horse shot under him while riding along the skirmish line where the firing was so hot that brave officers who were dismounted [illegible] were lying down on the ground.

[May 30: Battle of Old Church at Matadequin Creek]

After the fight we were relieved by the Infantry and fell back a few miles going into camp at 2 A.M. the 29th [Sunday].[76] We lay in camp, with only one move of a few miles till afternoon of the 30th, when we were ordered out to Old Church Tavern. About a mile beyond the tavern, the Reserve Brig was fighting and we were ordered to support them.[77] The General went in with the 5th on the right of the [Bottoms Bridge] road while the 1st & 7th went in on the left. The General formed a line, dismounted, behind a hill. Just as the line was ready to advance, my saddle commenced slipping back, & I had to get off & adjust it. Then I rode up on the hill to get up with the General. When I got on top of the hill, I found that the General & staff, &, in fact all the men, had gone into the woods on my right as the open field where I was was too hot to hold any one. I turned to ride down where the others were & just as I reached the edge of the woods a spent ball struck me in the breast. I think the ball must have struck

---

76. Custer's brigade had been relieved by Union infantry after dark on May 28 and fell back to the Pamunkey River. Its camp was about a mile from the mouth of Totopotomoy Creek. On May 29, as Granger indicates, the brigade moved again, this time across the creek to New Castle Ferry, where they rested until noon on May 30. Longacre, *Custer*, 225.
77. The infantry of the North and South were engaged in the Battle of Bethesda Church on May 30, when General Sheridan was asked to assist on the Union's left flank. Eventually Devin's brigade from Torbert's division was dispatched forward and established a position at the Barker's farm. Regiments from Butler's brigade pushed Devin's troops back, but a counterattack restored the original line. A second attack by the Confederates brought Merritt's Reserve Brigade into the fray. Finally, Custer's brigade entered the fight. As Granger states, the 5th Michigan deployed on foot to the right of Bottoms Bridge Road with the 1st and 7th dismounted on the left. The 6th remained mounted in reserve. The Michiganders forced Butler's men to flee. A counterattack failed, because the Southerners could not overcome the Michigan Brigade's firepower with its Spencers. Butler eventually corralled his men at Old Cold Harbor, while Torbert's cavalry bivouacked about 1.5 miles northeast of the intersection. Longacre, *Custer*, 223–26; see Rhea, *Cold Harbor*, 132–39.

a tree before it reached me as I was too near the Reb. lines for a ball to have lost its force—no thanks to my good intentions, however, as I wouldn't have gone there with my eyes open. The ball merely broke the skin & had no serious effect, though it has left just as good a scar as if it had really been a wound.[78] The General soon pushed his line through the woods & then advanced across the short open space between the woods & the Rebel line, which was posted behind a fence & in a piece of small pines.

The 5th advanced across this open space & the Rebs. left in a hurry. I could see Charlie Safford, who was made conspicuous by the white hat which he wore, far ahead of his men charging into the aforesaid clump of pines, which was pretty well filled with Rebs. Charlie ran down one man and took him prisoner. The Rebs did not make another stand, and the field was soon our own. The 1st Michigan, on the other side of the road, met with more determined resistance but they were equally successful, though with more loss.

It was Butler's Brig. that we fought there, but they did not do as well as they did at Enon Church. They had learned to retreat. We moved back that night and went into Camp again at Parsley's Mills [Mill] on the Totopotomoi [Totopotomoy] Creek.[79]

[May 31: at Old Cold Harbor, Virginia]

At about 3 P.M. of the next day [May 31], we moved out of camp in the direction of Cold (or Coal) Harbor.[80]

---

78. On May 31, 1864, Custer wrote to his wife, Libbie, to let her know that he was safe and well. He also told her that "Lt. Granger received a slight wound in the shoulder." He also listed the injury in his official report of July 4, 1864. Merington, *Custer Story*, 100.

79. Granger is inaccurate here. The mill was on Parsley's Creek, south of the Old Church fighting of May 30. Totopotomoy Creek was two to three miles to the north.

80. By the afternoon of May 31, 1864, Maj. Gen. Fitzhugh Lee's Confederate cavalry was in position at Cold Harbor. Fearful that Lee intended to resume his previous day's attacks, Torbert and Custer were determined to attack first. They met at Custer's camp near Parsley's Mill and set a plan for a two-pronged attack along Cold Harbor Road. Custer would follow Brig. Gen. Wesley Merritt's brigade in the main assault along Cold Harbor Road. Colonel Devin would launch a near-parallel attack along Black Creek Road. Rhea, *Cold Harbor*, 182–87.

At some distance from that place we found the reserve Brig.[81] engaged with the Rebel Cav. Corps. As I was sent off to the 6<u>th</u>, which was on another road some distance to our left, several times during the early part of this fight, I can't pretend to give any very accurate account of the battle.

When I finally rejoined the General, the Brig. (except the 6<u>th</u>) was near Cold Harbor. By this time the Reb. Cavalry was relieved by a Division of Infantry, which held a very strong position in the Harbor. The road which we were following to the place, ran up a hill, on top of which, the Rebs had a strong barricade. On the right of this barricade was a tavern[82] & several out houses, & on its left a fence which the Rebs used as a breastwork. The fire from this barricade was about as hot as any I ever was under & it was hard work to get the men up, but finally the General led the 1st up to the charge on a side road. The dismounted men pushed forward at the same time & I don't know which reached the works first as I had just been sent back to bring up

---

81. On May 31, Merritt's troops were serving as Reserve Brigade, when it became engaged with Fitzhugh Lee's division at the critical crossroads at Cold Harbor. Custer sent in regiments one after another, but the Confederates still retained their breastworks. Flanking fire by the 5th Michigan and a charge by the 1st Michigan again failed to dislodge the enemy. Surprisingly, Custer discovered, as he readied another attack, that the enemy had pulled out, but enemy infantry loomed ahead of the two Union cavalry divisions. However, Sheridan's orders from Meade required the cavalry to hold the position that night.
82. As noted earlier, Merritt and Custer had pushed their brigades along Parsley's Mill Road and then Crown Hill Road toward where the latter intersected with Rockhill Road and Cold Harbor Road. Devin advanced south of them along Rockhill Road, or Black Creek Church Road. Devin's route angled closer to that of the other two commanders and facilitated communication among the advancing columns. To connect them, Custer dispatched the 6th Michigan across the interval between the roads. By his own words, Granger accompanied the 6th. The Confederates had constructed strong breastworks of logs across each of the roads. Severe fighting ensued, but the Union commanders were concerned about taking heavy casualties by attacking directly, even though the three commands were aligned. Torbert devised a plan for a flanking movement, which ultimately proved successful in dislodging the Confederate defenders. One key action involved a saber charge by Col. Melvin Brewer with a battalion of the 6th Michigan. That undoubtedly included Lieutenant Granger of the brigade staff. As the Michigan Brigade itself reached the intersection, the tavern would have been to its left, but as Granger came in from the southeast with the 6th Michigan, the tavern was on his right.

the 5th, which was on the left. Certain it is that the Rebs. were driven out of their position; & that Cold Harbor remained in the hands of the 1st Div. Cav. Corps. This was a very important position for Grant's plans, & Sheridan rec'd. orders that night from Meade to hold it, at any cost, till relieved by the Infantry.

[Defense at Cold Harbor—June 1, 1864]

That night, our Brig. fortified their position as well as possible & the next day, early in the morning [June 1] we were attacked.[83] The attack was principally on our right wing where the 1st & 7th were posted. Our men were behind breast works, but the Rebs. could get pretty close to the works, in the woods, & the firing was at very close quarters. The Reserve Brig [Merritt's] was on our right but they didn't connect with us as they should have done. Lt. Col. Stagg[84] com'd'g the 1st saw this, & took the responsibility of closing up the gap. He was just in time to prevent the Rebs. turning the left flank of the other Brig. (I'm not sure but it was the 2nd Brig.). We soon drove the Rebs. back & formed the connection, with the other Brig. The General rode along the whole length of the lines under pretty hot fire part of the way. It is almost impossible to keep him from exposing himself needlessly, but it can hardly be called needless exposure either, as it not only incites the men to "deeds of noble daring," but <u>it keeps him posted on the exact position of his men</u> and when I hear the orders which are often sent by Gen. Officers who don't know their exact position & that of the enemy, I think it would be better if more of our Gens. exposed themselves as he does himself.

About 15 minutes after the Gen. had been riding along the line of the 1st, Capt. Brevoort was killed. Gen. Custer's description of Brevoort is endorsed by all who knew him. "A perfect Gentleman & no better

---

83. Leading the June 1 Confederate attack was an inexperienced colonel, Lawrence M. Keitt, an ardent secessionist and defender of slavery, according to Rhea. He had arrived just a few days earlier at the head of the 20th South Carolina Cavalry regiment. Once arrived, he assumed command of its parent brigade. He would lead the attack against Torbert's Cavalry, including Custer's Michigan Cavalry Brigade, but would be mortally wounded. Fitzhugh Lee had ordered the attack, as he hoped to retake the important crossroads before additional Union troops arrived on the battlefield. Rhea, *Cold Harbor*, 198–206.

84. For more about Peter Stagg, see chapter 2, note 76.

Officer in the Cav. Corps." No Officer in the Brig. had more, warm friends, in the Army; and in the Regt. there was no one so popular as Billy Brevoort though a better lot of Officers was never in one Regt. than there is in the 1st Michigan. Capt's [Andrew W.] Duggan[85] and Heazlit were slightly wounded in the action. After a spirited attack of about three hour's duration the Rebs. gave up in disgust, & soon after we were relieved by the 6th Corps.

[Post–Cold Harbor]

From this time to the 6th of June [Monday] we occupied the time in marching around the country—to Bottom's Bridge, from which place I wrote you a note, & back again to New Castle.[86] On the 7th we were routed out pretty early in the morning to cross the Pamunkey. After we were across, we had to wait till nearly dark for the forage train of Gen. Merritt's Brig.

For the next three days we marched towards Gordonsville.[87] On the night of the 10th we camped within 2 miles of Louisa Court House.[88]

---

85. Andrew W. Duggan was born on November 11, 1832, in Michigan and commissioned on August 25, 1861, as a first lieutenant in Company B, 1st Michigan Cavalry. On July 5, 1862, he was promoted to captain, and on October 25, 1864, to major. After the war, but while the regiment remained in federal service, he was promoted to lieutenant colonel on December 4, 1865. He was mustered out on March 26, 1866, at Detroit. He died on May 4, 1921, in Cañon City, Colorado, and was buried in Lakeside Cemetery. Soldier Records and Profiles; U.S. Civil War Soldiers; "Andrew W. Duggan," memorial, photograph, and gravestone at Findagrave.com, 33211942.
86. One of Granger's 5th Michigan Cavalry comrades, James H. Avery, stated in his memoirs that the brigade moved to Paisley's Mills after the fighting ended on June 1 and only moved to Bottoms Bridge on June 2. The troops remained there on June 3, and on June 4, they moved to Old Church. On June 5, they went on picket duty at Anna Church and repulsed the Confederates who tested their lines. On June 6, the brigade again returned to Old Church. Orders came down that day for Custer's troops to prepare for yet another raid on June 7. See Wittenberg, *Under Custer's Command*, 82.
87. According to historian Wittenberg, Gordonsville was a strategic point at the intersection of the Virginia Central and Orange & Alexandria railroads. Supplies from the important Shenandoah Valley were moved through this point. Wittenberg, *Under Custer's Command*, 82.
88. Founded in 1742, Louisa Court House saw its future assured when the Central Virginia Railroad reached the town in 1838. However, that also made it a prime target of the North's army during the Civil War, as the railroad was also vital to the Confederate supply lines.

The next morning our pickets were attacked by a Brig. of Reb. Cavalry. They ~~Brig.~~ did not press very hard & we moved out according to orders, though not till about two hours after we were ordered to start. Our Brig. was about a mile in advance of the rest of the Div., & were ordered to march to Trevilian Station on a road leading to the right from our camp while the other 2 Brigades went on a road straight across from their camps to Trevilian, a much shorter route than the one we took. Gregg's Div. followed the other Brigs of our Div. The force of Reb. Cav. in our rear troubled us some what, from the moment we started, but the 1st was in rear, Gus Buhl commanding the Rear Guard; and the Rebs. didn't make much out of him. Trevilian Station was about 5 miles from our camp of the night before.

When we got within about a mile & a half of the Station, the advance Guard (Capt. [Smith] Hastings[89] again) reported that there was a wagon train in front. The General ordered Col. Alger to charge for the trains. The Col. charged two or three miles capturing some hundred wagons, five caissons & over a thousand led horses. But the Rebs were perfectly panic stricken when the 5th charged them, collected together as soon as the Regt. passed and charged down on the rear & flank, and as there was a whole Brig. of them, they soon succeeded in cutting the 5th off. The General sent the 6th in to the support of the 5th as soon as possible.

Part of the 6th was captured including the two Majors, who were immediately recaptured. The General went to hurry up the 7th & 1st but the pack train & wagons were in the way so that it was some time before they could get up. To add to the pleasant excitement, the Rebs in our rear became more earnest in their attempts to drive the 1st on

---

89. Smith Hastings was only age eighteen when he enlisted as a private in Company C, 1st Michigan Infantry, on May 1, 1861. Born on December 27, 1843, at Quincy, Michigan, which made him about nine months younger than Edward Granger, he was mustered out of the regiment on August 7, 1861. A year later, he was mustered into Company M, 5th Michigan Cavalry, on August 14, 1862, as a first lieutenant. On December 17, 1864, he was promoted to colonel and command of the 5th Michigan. He was mustered out June 22, 1865, at Fort Leavenworth, Kansas. He was awarded the Medal of Honor for his actions commanding his company at Newby's Crossroads, Virginia, on July 24, 1863. He died on October 13, 1905, in Denver. Soldier Records and Profiles; U.S. Civil War Soldiers; "Smith H. Hastings," memorial, photograph, and gravestone at Findagrave.com, 7117443.

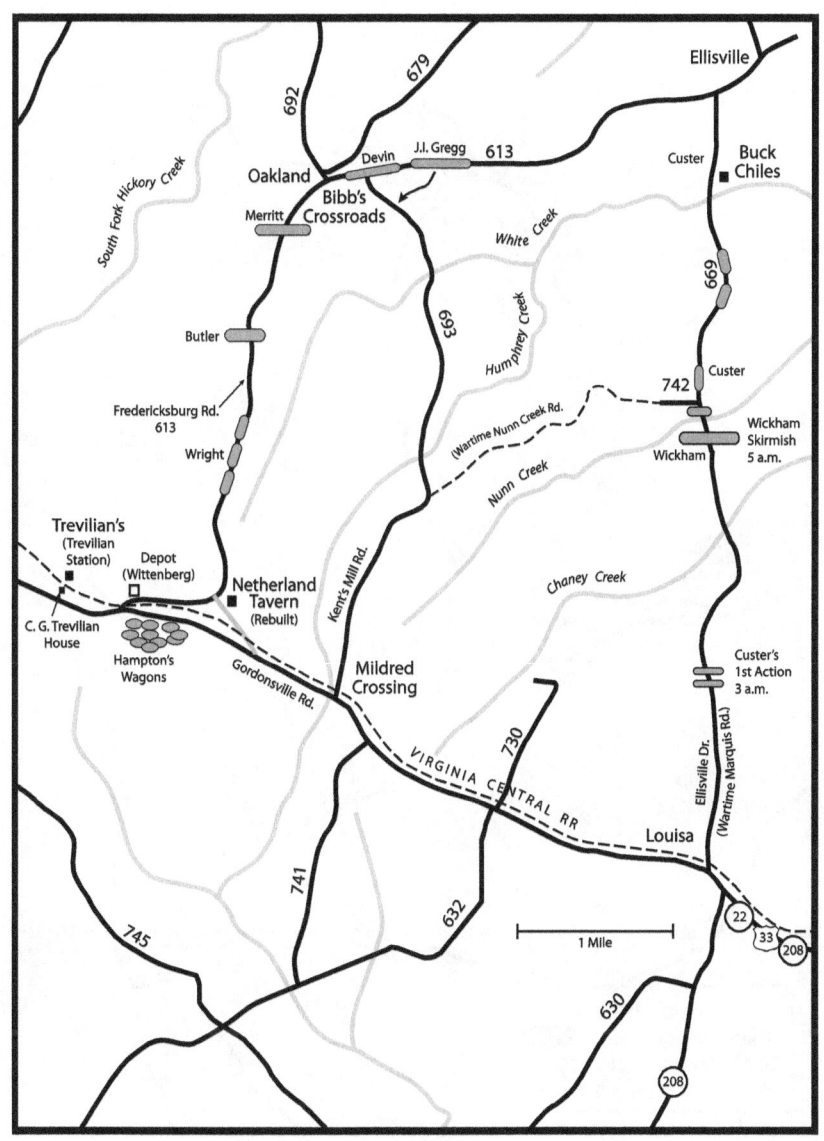

Battle of Trevilian Station, Virginia, June 11, 1864.
Map by Gary Raham.

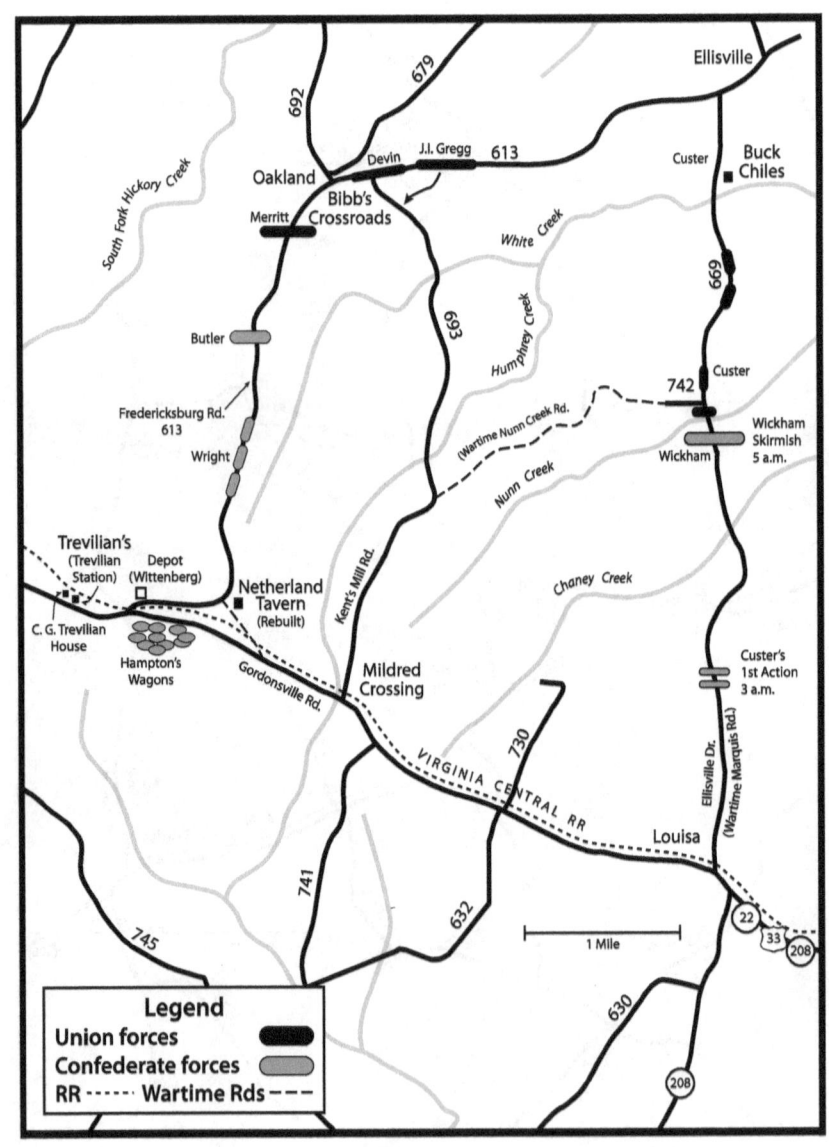

Early morning opening action at Trevilian Station, June 11, 1864. *Map by Gary Raham.*

to the rest of the Brig but they did not succeed. As soon as the 7th came up, the General moved on to the Station, but Col. Alger had gone on & we could hear nothing from him.

We were at Trevilian Station but not ordered with the rest of the Div. [illegible] was there, as he was to have been. Instead of our Div. there were one or two Divisions of Reb. Cavalry. The Gen. selected one body of Rebs. who were in an open field just beyond the Station & made preparations to drive them out of their position.

It would be impossible to make any thing like an accurate map of the battle even if one man could have seen it all which was scarcely possible as we were fighting on all sides at the same time & all the time: so you will please regard my account, not as a description of the battle, but of what I saw of the battle. The sketch I enclose may help you to form some idea of "the situation." The body of Rebs of which I spoke were posted at the place marked A and the Gen. to drive them out sent Maj Brewer, with the 7th, down the Main Road just beyond the Station with orders to charge across the field (B) & the R.R. as soon as he heard our guns open from the Station. Then he sent back for the battery to have two guns sent up into the Station, & to Col. Stagg to come up into the field (C) in rear of the Station. Col. Stagg tried his best to come up, but he had his hands nearly full tending to the force in his rear, so that he made but slow work getting up. Meanwhile the General had selected a position for one of the guns in rear of a small building at the Station (D). In getting to this position the gun had to be for a moment exposed to view of the Rebs.—just as it was crossing the R. R. The General had left his Staff & flag in the Station when he went to this position, but when he saw a gun going over there with Pennington's brilliant flag we thought we shouldn't attract any more attention that way so we followed—flag & all. The Gen. immediately sent us back and we took up a strong position with a house (E) in front & a small body of Cav. in our rear. But the Rebs had seen the gun, or the flag and immediately sent out a force of dismounted men to take the place. As these men moved along the edge of the woods (W) we could not see them from our position. The Gen. having no support for his gun (the 1st not having yet come up) run it out of that place as quickly as possible through the field (L). He was the last man to leave, and came near being taken. All this time we were ignorant of our danger & knew nothing of it till a man from the battery came down & told us that the Rebs. were right on us.

The Lt. commanding the Section of the battery which was in the Station, came after his remaining gun, just about the same time. This gun was near the body of the Cavalry, I have spoken of, and there was a pretty lively race between the gun & Cavalry to see who should get to the road first. It was all the officers could do to prevent a collision. Lt. Eagan [William Egan],[90] of the Battery, was struck by a ball which just took the skin off the top of his head. He lost the three men who limbered up his piece.

When we got opposite the end of the long building marked (F) the Rebs were along the end of it, & not two rods from us, why they did not hit more of us. When we got into the Main Road, we all turned to the right. There I found Capt. [George] Drake[91] of the 5th trying to stop the Cavalry to give the gun a chance to get off. I stopped to help him & we succeeded in getting some of them to make a stand till the gun [was] out of the way. This was made much easier by a diversion in our favor made by the advance of two squadrons of the 1st dismounted, which made the Rebs keep pretty close in the Station. Pennington, also, had already got the Battery into position & was shelling them well. After some maneuvering the Rebs prepared to charge up the road. The Gen. had the 1st dismounted & put behind a barricade which was very soon thrown up across the road & to the right of the road (G). The Rebs. came up till a few of our men fired & then they halted

---

90. William Egan began his service as a sergeant with the 5th U.S. Artillery in the western theater of the war. He transferred to the eastern theater, along with Battery K, 5th U.S. Artillery, sometime between the Battle of Murfreesboro and the Battle of Gettysburg, after having been promoted to lieutenant. After Gettysburg, he transferred to Battery M, 2nd U.S. Artillery. He was the battery's commander by the end of the war. Robert J. Trout, ed., *Memoirs of the Stuart Horse Artillery Battalion*, vol. 2 (Knoxville: University of Tennessee Press, 2010), 217n245.

91. George Drake, twenty-five, of Farmington, Michigan, enlisted in Company H, 5th Michigan Cavalry, as first sergeant on August 23, 1862. He was commissioned a second lieutenant on January 11, 1863, and promoted to captain on October 24, 1863. On May 17, 1865, he was promoted to major. He was mustered out on June 19, 1865, at Fort Leavenworth, Kansas. He died March 28, 1900, in Lenawee County, Michigan. Soldier Records and Profiles; U.S. Civil War Soldiers; "George Drake," memorial and gravestone at Findagrave.com, 27674147; Beckendorf, "CDV Album," 8.

out of range & ~~came no further~~, after a while fell back. Soon after this Capt. [David W.] Clemmer[92] of the 1st reported some movement of the enemy & I went with him to see what was going on. We went along the left side of the R.R. Clemmer, ahead towards the Station. Before we had gone far I saw the Capt. coming back & looking in the direction in which he pointed I saw several Rebs just across the R. R. from us in the edge of the woods. We immediately responded to the General & he ordered Mr. [Carle] Woodruff[93] to open with his two guns on the woods with canister. The result was a great stampede of the Rebs. who had a large force in the woods unknown to us. Then the Gen. ordered the 1st to take the Station, and the Regt. advanced across the open field, dismounted, & took the Station driving the Rebs out and capturing some prisoners. Capt. [Craig] Wadsworth[94] of Div Staff & I went with the 1st, or, rather, with the part of it which went to the Station.

92. David W. Clemmer, twenty-four, of Dowagiac, Michigan, enlisted on August 12, 1861, as first sergeant of Company M, 1st Michigan Cavalry. Clemmer was born in Cincinnati, Ohio. He was promoted to first lieutenant on November 12, 1862, and to captain on May 2, 1863. He was discharged December 14, 1864. He died sometime after 1880, as the Lansing City Directory for 1888 (viewable at Ancestry.com) lists his wife, Philena, as a widow. Soldier Records and Profiles; U.S. Civil War Soldiers.

93. Carle Woodruff (1841–1913) turned out to be a career soldier in the U.S. Army, rising to the rank of brigadier general. During the Civil War, he was awarded the Medal of Honor for his gallantry as a section chief on July 24, 1863, in a battle at Newby's Crossroads, Virginia. Born in Buffalo, New York, he was commissioned in 1861 as a second lieutenant in the 2nd U.S. Horse Artillery. After the war, he remained in the Regular Army as an artillery officer. He died in Raleigh, North Carolina, in 1913. Soldier Records and Profiles; U.S. Civil War Soldiers; "Carle Augustus Woodruff," memorial, photos, and gravestone at Findagrave.com, 7817641.

94. Craig W. Wadsworth was commissioned a second lieutenant in the 25th New York Infantry Regiment on September 19, 1861. His father was a well-known New York politician and businessman, James S. Wadsworth, who served as a brigadier general in the Union Army and had been mortally wounded a month before leading his division at the Battle of the Wilderness on May 6. He died two days later. The younger Wadsworth was born in 1841 and received a brevet as a brigadier general while serving as a Torbert staff officer. Wadsworth was mustered out on July 16, 1864. He died on January 1, 1872. Soldier Records and Profiles; U.S. Civil War Soldiers; "Gen. Craig Wharton Wadsworth," memorial and gravestone at Findagrave.com, 167939876.

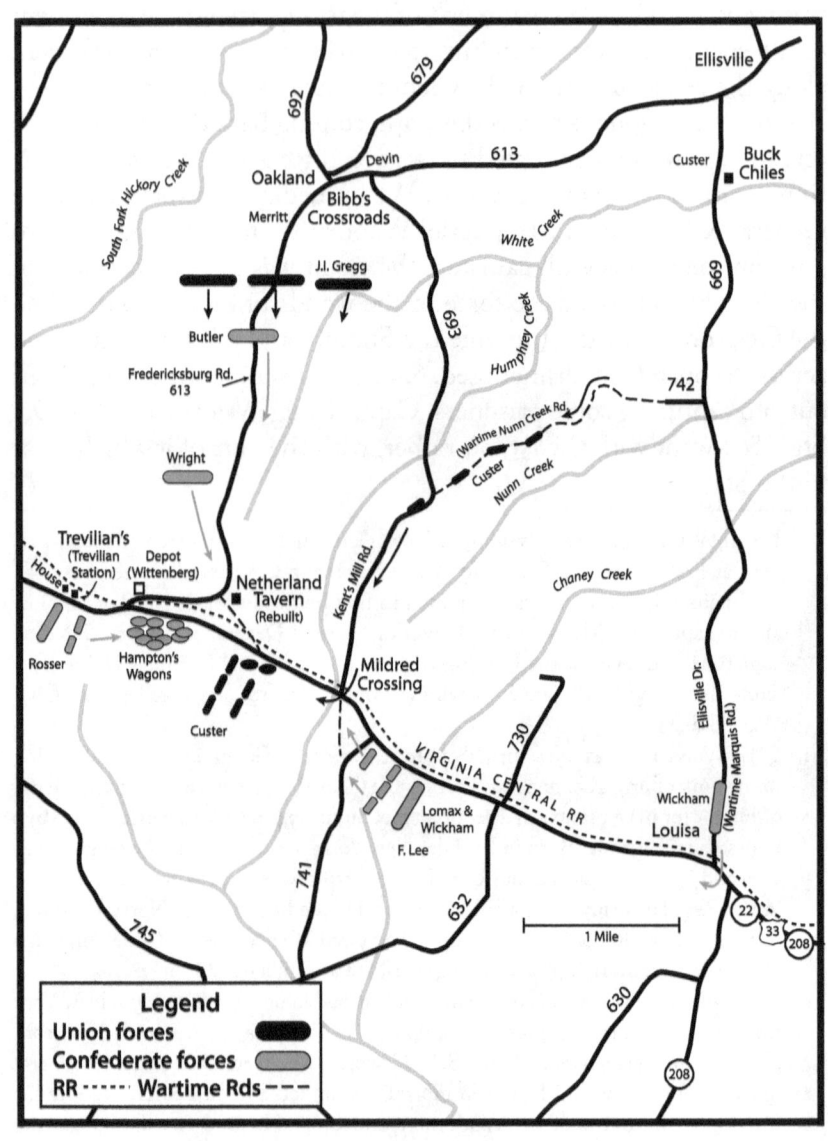

Later action at Trevilian Station, June 11, 1864.
Map by Gary Raham.

Then we turned around, Wadsworth & I, & were going back where the General was when we noticed the led horses of the Brig. moving in the direction indicated on the sketch. We saw that they were getting out in plain sight of the Reb Battery (at A) which was then playing on the Station. I went over to turn the horses back, but when I got down there I saw the cause of their trouble way over in our <u>rear</u> I saw Cavalry charging & recharging from one hill to another. (H)

I hastened over there & found the General charging for a gun & trying to get a few scattered men to follow him. He didn't succeed very well for he was 20 rods ahead of any other man when he reached the gun, but the men finally came up and the gun was ours. The General stopped at the gun, & I went on & tried to get the men along but there were not many Officers with them, & there was no organization so they did not get along very well. Fred [Nims] was with me & if we could have got a dozen men together we would have made a rush for a flag—the most beautiful one I ever saw in the Reb. ranks. There was a large ditch the Rebs had to cross and there were not more than 30 Rebs. behind the flag when it came to the ditch. However the men could not be got to come along, which was not very strange as the Rebs had ten men to every one we had on that hill there. When some of our men came up we followed the Rebs. some distance but did not get up with them. I found out afterwards that the gun we were charging for was one of Egan's Section which the Rebs had taken while Woodruff's Section was at the barricade, playing on the Station. As soon as Pennington told the Gen. that the Rebs had one of his guns, the Gen. started for the place & hastily collecting about 100 men, of no one organization, but from every Regiment in the Brig. he charged & retook the gun, it was again taken from him & again he retook it. The Rebs held the ground 3 times before they were finally driven off. The force of Rebs engaged was Wickham's entire Brig. except one Regt. which was engaged at that time in capturing our Head Qurs. wagons & Pennington's caissons. If it had not been for the personal exertion of the Gen. our gun never would have been retaken. At the same time this fight for the gun was going on, the Brig. of Georgia troops formally commanded by Gen. Young came down on Col. Stagg's line (J) they were beautifully repulsed & with the loss of some 30 prisoners.

After this the General made a charge at the head of the 7th Mich. after our wagons, but did not succeed in taking them, as they were out of the way. Lieut Baylis was wounded in this charge & our Colorbearer was wounded, mortally.

While the Gen. was in the charge Capt. [Amasa G.] Dana,[95] Div. A.A.G. came up & announced the arrival of Gen. Torbert at the Station.

The Rebs. had taken advantage of a good position to hold Torbert in check with two Brigades while the rest of the Reb. Cav. Corps devoted its attention to us. All the troops who were fighting our Brig. thought that our whole force was opposed to them.

After Gen. Torbert came up there was but little fighting done—the Rebs. leaving very unceremoniously & we being too tired to follow.

There was fighting on all sides of our Brig. all the time—but, as I only saw the above portions of the fight I shan't say any more about it.

Greene was captured with the wagons. I lost Bob & all my traps.[96] My personal property that mainly consisted of: One hat, well worn, one blouse, which I've had since last August, one velvet vest; one shirt, dirty one, pair of pants, ragged, one pair drawers, stolen; one pair boots, holy & run over at the heels; one pair stockings, soiled; two handkerchiefs, one stolen; one photograph Album; one memorandum book; 3 P.O. Stamps; one pocket book, empty; one mare, stolen, one saber C.S.; one Revolver U.S. & one belt & one pair spurs, C.S.[97]

---

95. Amasa G. Dana of Cherry Valley, Illinois, was commissioned on September 10, 1862, as a second lieutenant in Company E, 8th Illinois Cavalry, and was promoted to first lieutenant on December 5, 1862. Promotion to captain followed on April 20, 1864, but he was mustered out that day to accept an appointment in the U.S. Volunteers adjutant general department. On November 12, 1864, he was promoted to major and to brevet lieutenant colonel on March 13, 1865. He was mustered out May 25, 1865. Born in New York, he was buried in Belvidere City Cemetery, Belvidere, Illinois. Soldier Records and Profiles; U.S. Civil War Soldiers.

96. Granger mentions his loss of Bob only in passing, as he could not know how important that incident would prove to be for him in two months at Front Royal, Virginia. On that occasion, Bob's successor would prove unmanageable and cost the twenty-one-year-old lieutenant his life.

97. Custer's own loss was even more substantial. Among some of the many Custer items captured were a very fine presentation officer's sword, scabbard, sword belt, and rosewood storage box by Tiffany Company of New York City, a pair of riding boots that probably belonged to Libbie Custer, an old valise, his tent, a fine saddle, uniforms, and other personal items. In a June 21, 1864, letter Custer wrote

Since then I have managed with the assistance of my orderly, to pick up a pretty good mess kit, a valise, & a fair stock of clothing. Am now dressed in sailor's rig purchased on one of the gun-boats, in the Pamunkey. On the 12th Sunday, our Div. made an attempt to proceed on the road towards Gordonsville, but the Rebs. were in strong intrenchments and we could not drive them out, though the 1st drove them out of the one part of their works. Our loss in killed & wounded was greater than the day before but we lost no prisoners. I forgot to say that Col. Alger & all his Officers got in safely on the night of the 11th but with very few of his men. Our loss (the 5th) in prisoners is about 18, though we have heard of a squad of 25 men who went way around to Alexandria, safely.[98]

I have already written to you that Spies Warren was killed on the 12th. Poor boy! he died bravely, remaining on the field when he had a good excuse for going back.

The night of the 12th we commenced to fall back & reached this place last night. We had a tough time getting here, &, if I don't have any thing better to write about next time I write perhaps I'll tell you of it, but it is time for me to close this letter as I don't know whether I have P.O. Stamps enough to carry what I have written.

Your two letters of the 13th & 15th both numbered (15), came last night after I had commenced this letter.

I return the card with my autograph. If Uncle Charles has any money of mine in his hands please draw from him & subscribe my share & yours towards the present to Jones.

Tell Carrie that I shall be glad to hear from her as often as she gets time & when she does write, I hope to hear of her interview with Don. I'll write to her as soon as I get time. By the way you might as well get money enough from Uncle to get me some stamps—id est[99] if you want to hear from me again.

---

to his wife from White House Station, Virginia, he lamented that the enemy had captured from him "everything except my toothbrush." Among the other items captured was his commission as a general, which he had received only a few days before, and a packet of his wife's love letters. Merington, *Custer Story*, 104; Urwin, *Custer Victorious*, 164.

98. See Wittenberg, *Under Custer's Command*, 88–94, for the extraordinary account left by Corp. James Henry Avery, Company I, 5th Michigan Cavalry, of their week's journey and their efforts to avoid capture and reach safety.

99. Latin phrase for "That is."

Give my love to my cousin Mattie.
Write soon.
Enclosed a Reb. letter captured at Beaver Dam.[100]

E. G. Granger

If you don't like the length of this letter I'll do better next time.

E. G.

※ ※ ※

[LETTER 43]

Head Qurs. 1st Brig. 1st Div.
Cav Corps A. P. July 17th 1864 [Sunday]

Mollie

As Lieut. Bristol is going home within a few days I thought I would impose the opportunity to send you the enclosed draft of $50.00.

I sent a hundred dollars to Uncle Charles the other day from which, of course mother can draw as long as it lasts; but I thought she might like to have a little loose change where she need not have to draw from it. When you get the draft cashed please give mother thirty dollars, and keep the other twenty for your own use.

I won't write to you till I hear from you. This writing all the time and not getting any letters at all don't suit me. So you had better get about half a dozen letters down here as soon as possible, for you are at least so many behind.

The General has gone to Washington & will soon be in Mich., I suppose.

All well
E. G. Granger
1st. Lieut. "B" Co. 5th Mich. Cav.
and A.D.C. to Gen. Custer

---

100. Such a letter is not contained in the family's collection.

Mollie Granger later in life.
Courtesy of Lisa Mower Gandelot.

P.S.
You can get the Draft cashed at Butler's by writing your name on the back of it.

Ed.

My commission has just been rec'd, and Col. Alger said I may be mustered into "C" Co. instead of "B," as Bristol's resignation creates a vacancy in that Co. so I am 1st. Lieut. of "C" Co. If I can get mustered before Bristol goes home I will send my commission home by him.

E. G. G.

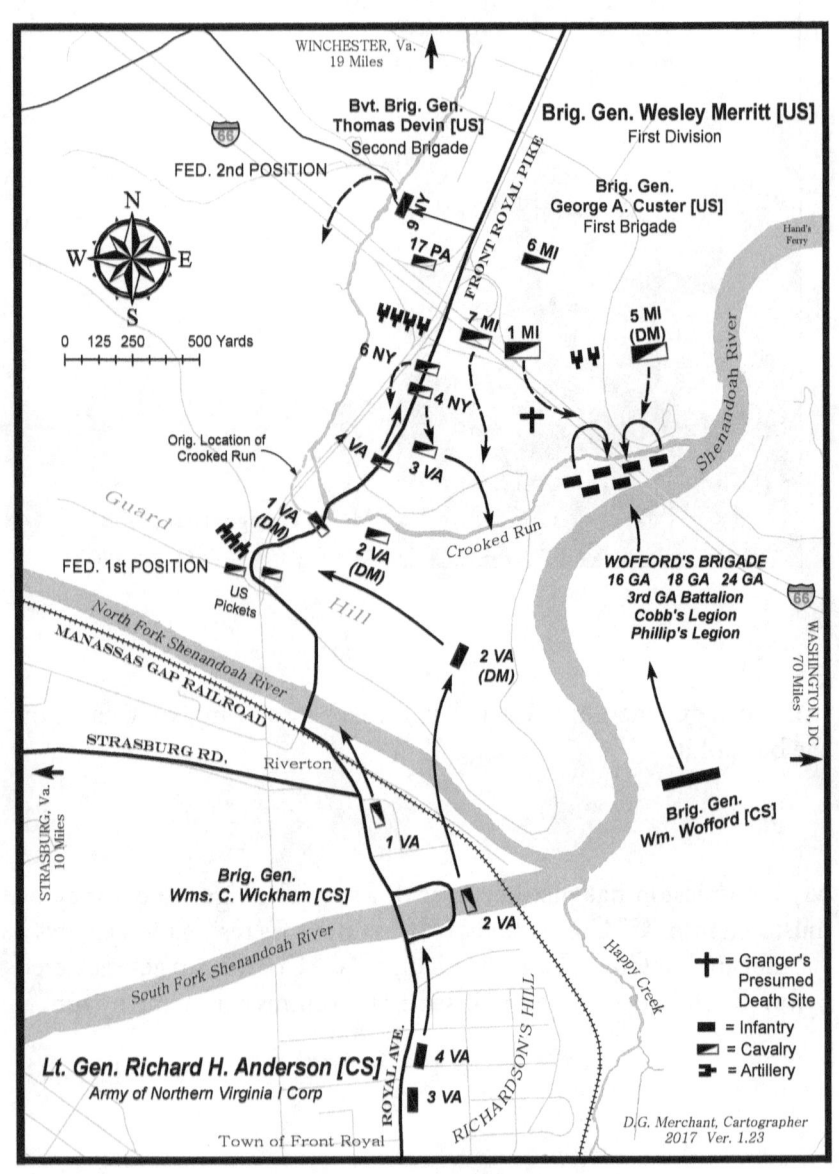

Battle of Crooked Run, August 16, 1864.
Map by Darryl Merchant.

EPILOGUE

DEATH ON A HOT AUGUST DAY

DEATH CAME SUDDENLY FOR LT. EDWARD G. GRANGER late in the afternoon of August 16, 1864, at the Battle of Crooked Run, north of Front Royal, Virginia. Granger had received orders from General Custer to carry to the commanders of the 1st and 7th Michigan Cavalry who were to charge the staggered enemy. As he was wont to do at such moments, Granger rode between the two regiments of onrushing cavalrymen. This time was different. Granger disappeared into the maelstrom of men and horses. Clouds of smoke from guns and artillery enshrouded the battlefield and made it difficult to discern exactly what was happening.[1]

Frequently during Granger's two years in the 5th Michigan, officers from his regiment and brigade had returned to Detroit on leave and stopped by the family's house to visit. Perhaps that is how Mrs. Matilda Granger and her daughter, Mollie, learned of their son's and brother's disappearance at Crooked Run. Or, maybe one of Charles or Edward Walker's numerous political and military friends had alerted them to

---

1. Unfortunately, General Custer's report of Crooked Run did not make the *O.R.*, but Maj. Gen. Wesley Merritt's report of the 1st Cavalry Division's actions between August 9 and October 20, 1864, appears in *O.R.*, series 1, vol. 43, pt. 1, 439–40. He referred to the action as the Battle of Cedarville, named for a small community about a mile north of Crooked Run. He made no mention of Granger's loss, but praised Custer "for the masterly manner in which he handled his command."

259

Lt. Edward G. Granger,
5th Michigan Cavalry, circa 1863.
Courtesy of Jim Adams.

Edward Granger's fate. Definitive word certainly came to the family several days later in a letter written to Charles Walker on August 20, 1864, by General Custer, who outlined what he had observed about the circumstances leading to his young aide's disappearance. However, the roots of Granger's final chapter actually go back about two months, to June 13, 1864, when General Lee sent his II Corps, commanded by Lt. Gen. Jubal A. Early, on a unique mission.

Early had been operating in the Shenandoah Valley with Confederate infantry and cavalry. Following Lee's directions, Early's troops that June traveled down the valley without opposition and bypassed Harpers Ferry, West Virginia, before crossing the Potomac River into Maryland. At the Battle of Monocacy on July 9 near Frederick, Maryland, he defeated a Union force, commanded by Maj. Gen. Lew Wallace, which fell back toward Baltimore. Wallace's efforts sufficiently delayed Early's move against the nation's capital and allowed Union reinforcements to reach Fort Stevens on the city's northwest outskirts. For two days, July 11–12, Early's troops skirmished with Union forces. Early's attack greatly alarmed Washington's officials, but reinforcements under Maj. Gen. Horatio G. Wright and the fort's own strong defenses convinced the Southern general not to launch full-scale attacks. At one point, President Abraham Lincoln personally observed the fighting. By late on July 12, Early withdrew. On July 14, he again crossed the Potomac River at White's Ferry into Leesburg, Virginia, and returned to the safety of the Shenandoah Valley.

But Early's success, as mixed as it may have been, angered the Union top command. The Shenandoah Valley had long played a dual role for the Confederacy, serving as a natural supply depot and a relatively secure base from which to launch operations. General Grant decided the time had finally come for him to destroy the valley's usefulness to the enemy. Numerous Union generals, most recently David Hunter, had proven unsuccessful at the task, but Grant this time turned to his favorite warhorse, Philip Sheridan.[2]

On August 6, 1864, Sheridan assumed command of the newly formed Middle Military Division, which combined three earlier elements into one fighting force—the Army of the Shenandoah. Of note, Torbert's 1st Cavalry Division was added to the mix of troops, including, of course, Custer's Michigan Cavalry Brigade.

Sheridan's orders were also unique and marked another turn in what had become a vicious war for all concerned. Sheridan should go up the valley and "nothing should be left to invite the enemy to return." His soldiers should take whatever provisions, forage, or stock they needed. Otherwise, "such as cannot be consumed, destroy."

Of interest, Sheridan was not to destroy the buildings of valley residents. At the same time, Southerners should realize that the Union forces would launch further raids if enemy combatants chose to live among them. In other words, not only were the armies at war, now the people who supported the enemy would feel the pain. A new term in the lexicon of warfare became familiar to all—total war.[3]

On August 1, Torbert's cavalry boarded steamers on the James River and sailed up Chesapeake Bay and the Potomac River to Washington, D.C., where they arrived August 6. From there, they marched two days to the new army's camps at Harpers Ferry. Sheridan designated Torbert as his chief of cavalry, which moved Brig. Gen. Wesley Merritt up to command the 1st Division. Maj. Gen. William W. Averell

---

2. Longacre, *Custer*, 241.
3. Urwin, *Custer Victorious*, 168–69.

took command of two brigades in a newly designated 2nd Cavalry Division.

The Army of the Shenandoah moved out on August 10, but General Early kept his distance from the Union force advancing against him. Custer's brigade, in the lead on August 11, skirmished with Early's men before Winchester, but the Confederate leader kept withdrawing his troops deeper into the valley. At Fisher's Hill, Early dug in, stretching his infantry breastworks across a narrow valley between the Massanutten and North Mountains. Before he attacked the uninviting Confederate defensive positions, Sheridan opted to wait for reinforcements sent by Grant to arrive.

On August 14, Sheridan learned that Gen. Robert E. Lee was sending both infantry and cavalry reinforcements to Early. That evening, Sheridan dispatched Devin's brigade beyond Front Royal and into Chester Gap to look for these additional Southern troops, commanded by Confederate major general Richard H. Anderson. These troops included Maj. Gen. Fitzhugh Lee's cavalry division and Maj. Gen. Joseph Kershaw's infantry division.

On August 15, Custer's brigade, sent out to join Devin's men in that effort, reached them early in the afternoon near Front Royal. They were encamped a mile above Crooked Run on the east of the Winchester and Front Royal Pike. Today, the North and South Forks of the Shenandoah River merge with each other just northeast of the city at Riverton to form the main river channel, which flows on toward Harpers Ferry as a major tributary of the Potomac River. The city is bounded on the east by the Blue Ridge Mountains and on the west by the Massanutten Mountains. The major modern roads through the town are U.S. 522 on the east and U.S. 340 on the west. They merge on the northern edge of town and U.S. 522 continues north, crossing the river forks of the Shenandoah and passing through the enlarged gap between Guard Hill on the west and Round Top Hill on the east.

About halfway between the gap and Interstate 66, the historic Crooked Run, a deep stream with steep banks, crosses underneath the highway bridge. It has meandered south some ten or twelve miles from its headwaters just above Lake Frederick, Virginia, toward the gap at Guard Hill. Just as it did it in the Civil War era, it suddenly turns sharply east, flowing under the highway bridge for a distance before twisting northeast to complete a wide U across the valley north of the two hills. The stream rambles about another two thousand feet before it enters the Shenandoah River itself.[4]

As one travels north through the Guard Hill gap on Highway 522 out of Front Royal, much of the quarry that destroyed the fighting ground on the east over which Custer's men fought remains. Modern hotels and restaurants have been built west of Highway 522. North of the I-66 interchange, or exit 6, shopping malls have further altered the once historic landscape where Custer and Devin maneuvered their Union brigades to clash with their Confederate enemies.

With Custer taking overall command, the two Union generals prepared for any eventuality on August 15, even though no enemy troops had yet appeared. However, the Confederates were in the area and preparing for the Yankees themselves. Kershaw deployed pickets on the south bank of the South Fork of the Shenandoah River and on the road leading out of the town.[5] Fitzhugh Lee's cavalry was also present, but Anderson opted to remain idle in Front Royal, pending further word from Early, even though his troops likely could have seized the fords over the two rivers that day.

The next day, August 16, Anderson sent Fitzhugh Lee to see Early to coordinate their plans for an attack on Sheridan on the 17th. In his absence, back at Front Royal, action quickly developed. Just north of the town, a much more narrow Front Royal and Winchester Turnpike crossed both the North and South Forks of the Shenandoah River and ascended Guard Hill. From the high ground, artillery could dominate the approaches from the north as well as the river fords below and to the south. Pickets from the 9th New York Cavalry of Devin's brigade, however, controlled the road and blocked any southern advance.

Anderson dispatched two brigades, one of cavalry under Brig. Gen. Williams C. Wickham and one of Georgia infantry led by Brig.

---

4. At the time of the battle, the creek actually approached much closer to the gap between the hills before it turned east under the road. In modern times it has been diverted much sooner under the highway before it reaches the passage in the hills.
5. The remains of the historic bridges and the roads leading to the fords can be viewed east of the modern multilaned U.S. Highway 522 bridge. I am indebted to Joe Whitehorne of Front Royal, who gave me an excellent tour and summary of the battle and the landscape on September 25, 2015.

Gen. William T. Wofford, with orders to open the fords and to seize the high ground. Supporting federal forces from Devin's and Custer's brigades were encamped a mile or so farther north approaching Cedarville. Between the pickets and their reinforcements was the imposing obstacle of Crooked Run.

Custer had posted his brigade east of the road, amid ridges and ravines that gave his men cover. He dispatched 150 men of the 6th Michigan forward as pickets. Unfortunately, as noted, the battlefield at Crooked Run has been severely altered by development. Foremost was the digging of the quarry, sandwiched today between the hills to the south that overlook the river forks and to the north the roadbed of the east-west Interstate 66. At one time the quarry extended farther north across the modern interstate area, but portions were later filled in for development. That allowed for the interstate's construction, including its bridge over the Shenandoah River. Some eight stories of fill dirt reportedly were used in building the river segment of the road in the Front Royal vicinity. Today, the area where Custer's brigade waited for action, and over which they made their repeated charges, is covered with parking lots and the buildings for Lowe's Home Improvement, Walmart, and other stores. Shopping centers dominate both sides of Highway 522 where the Union brigades once stood.

About 3:00 P. M. August 16, the Southerners launched their attack with the 1st Virginia Cavalry and the 2nd Virginia Cavalry. While the New Yorkers on the picket line did their best to hold their position in the gap of the old highway, the Confederates soon forced the Northerners back toward Crooked Run, which historian Scott C. Patchan has called "the defining geographic feature of the developing battle."[6]

In an article reporting on the battle for the *New York Times*, writer E. A. Paul, its cavalry correspondent, aptly described the run:

> [It] makes a bend something in the general shape of a horse-shoe, the toe pointing toward Front Royal, the pike passing through it longitudinally a little to the right of center; just across the run, and to the left of the pike, is a small cultivated hill 75 feet high, called in the locality Round Top. Still further to the right, and also beyond the run, is the spur of a hill running in a southern direction approaching within 40 rods of Round Top. The

---

6. Scott C. Patchan, "The Battle of Crooked Run: George Custer's Opening Act in the Shenandoah Valley," *North & South* 11, no. 2 (December 2008): 76–83.

right bank or opposite side of the creek is a high bluff, except immediately at the toe where the hill gradually recedes and the whole of it is covered with a small growth of trees sufficiently large however to partially conceal the movement of troops unless marching directly to the run. The ground between the position occupied by our two brigades, between the heels of the shoes and the run, is broken and rolling, with limestone cropping out on every hand, and the view only obstructed here and there by a locust-tree.[7]

Wickham's brigade quickly gained a foothold on Guard Hill. This not only gave him control of the valley of Crooked Run below but allowed him to deploy several guns from a battalion of the Stuart Horse Artillery on the summit of Guard Hill. With the New York regiment in retreat, Wickham's men fired at will from the heights upon the brigades of Merritt's Division encamped in the distance back from Crooked Run.

However, at the run Capt. Daniel Lapham's retreating New York pickets soon joined with Capt. Timothy Hanley's dismounted squadron in reserve. Hanley and Lapham posted their troops at the southern end of the bridge over Crooked Run. They also took up positions on the high ground on either side of the road and fired upon the advancing enemy. Still, outnumbered, the Union troops fell back slowly over the run, all the while continuing to fight.

Meanwhile, word reached Custer about Wickham's advance and the retreat of the Union pickets. Within ten minutes, he had the Michigan Cavalry Brigade ready for action as he himself stood on a piece of high ground surveying the then rugged battlefield before him. Granger and his other staff members would have been with him. He sent a full squadron of the 6th Michigan forward to join his earlier dispatched pickets from that regiment. He also deployed Capt. Dunbar R. Ransom's battery of the 3rd U.S. Artillery to the center of the ridge near him. Soon the artillery from both sides were measuring each other with shot.

Two of Custer's regiments, the 1st and the rest of the 6th, stood somewhat hidden behind the Union guns. The 5th Michigan's troopers were positioned on Custer's left flank near the Shenandoah River. On the right, next to Devin's brigade, waited the 7th Michigan, commanded by Col. Melvin Brewer.

---

7. E. A. Paul, "The Cavalry Engagement at Crooked Run," *New York Times*, August 25, 1864.

Back at the gap between Round Top and Guard Hill, an annoyed Wickham decided Hanley's New Yorkers needed to be forced from their position. The 3rd Virginia Cavalry broke the Union line and were soon joined by the 4th Virginia Cavalry in chasing the retreating New York cavalrymen.

Devin unhesitatingly responded by ordering the 4th New York into the fray. The remaining squadrons of the 9th New York charged upon Wickham's left flank. Devin's artillery also opened up. Soon the 6th New York and the 17th Pennsylvania entered in support of his other regiments. Devin ordered a charge by the 4th New York, which pushed the Confederates back across Crooked Run. Wickham's efforts against the Union troops had been repulsed.

The lull that grew on that side of the field seemingly ignited the fighting anew in Custer's front. Custer's new assistant adjutant general, Capt. Levant W. Barnhart, spotted Wofford's brigade crossing the Shenandoah River itself in two columns at a downstream ford.[8] Custer repositioned his 5th and 1st Regiments, but kept them hidden from the view of Wofford's Confederates at the river crossings. He also tantalized Wofford by dangling a section of Ransom's battery in plain view, seemingly unsupported by any other Union troops.

Wofford took the bait and sent his 16th and 24th Georgia regiments after the battery. Ransom's guns failed to slow the onrushing Georgians, but as they neared the crest, Colonel Alger advanced his 5th Michigan into view of the suddenly stunned Southerners. The 5th's seven-shot Spencers ripped apart the Confederate lines.

Custer himself had moved close to the action, when he suddenly seemed to grab at the side of his head. Fortunately, a Confederate bullet had merely clipped off one of the general's golden ringlets, dropping it to his shoulder. About that time, the repositioned 1st Michigan, commanded by Maj. Angelo Paldi, charged on the right of the 5th Michigan into Wofford's left flank. As Patchan wrote, "The devastating onslaught of Custer's Wolverines shattered Wofford's advance."[9]

His troops scampered back toward Crooked Run where they joined other troops seeking to make a stand. But the 5th Michigan followed them and continued to pour a murderous fire into the Confederate ranks

---

8. Barnhart had replaced Jacob Greene, who had been captured at Trevilian Station.
9. Patchan, "Battle of Crooked Run," 80.

with their Spencers. A bullet felled Wofford's horse, slamming the general violently to the ground. He managed to flee on foot and swim to safety across the run, but his injury effectively ended his military career.

Devin spotted Wofford's rear column moving toward the action and he responded. Troops from the 4th and 6th New York pitched into the enemy and drove them into the run. Numerous enemy were captured. Back on the right, Wickham tried again to resume his offensive, personally leading the 4th Virginia Cavalry into the gap after Devin's troops had focused elsewhere on the field. Unfortunately for him, two squadrons of the 6th New York remained hidden in a ravine west of the road. First, they fired volleys at the advancing enemy, then drew their sabers and charged. Once again, the 4th Virginia was knocked back to the banks of Crooked Run. Wickham again rallied his troops and charged anew with the 3rd Virginia Cavalry.

Custer saw that the 3rd Virginia's advance was threatening the Union forces on that side of the field. Passing orders to Lieutenant Granger to carry to the commanders of the 1st and 7th Michigan Cavalry, Custer sensed the time had come for a dynamic blow at the weakened enemy. Commanding the 7th was Colonel Brewer, while at the head of the 1st was none other than Granger's Detroit friend Capt. Gus Buhl.

According to reporter E. A. Paul, the two regiments "charged up handsomely under a terrible artillery fire, now coming from the Round Top. . . . As the men started on this charge, the enemy's mounted cavalry commenced a charge but did not finish it. They recoiled before the advancing avalanche."

Despite General Wickham's renewed efforts, the charge by the two Michigan regiments had drastically altered the situation on the right. A Virginian had to warn Wickham that the 7th Michigan was about to cut off the 3rd Virginia from Crooked Run. Wickham and his men about-faced and headed for safety across Crooked Run under the protection of their own guns.

As Paul related the incident, "The enemy broke, some dashed across the run, while others sought shelter under the artillery and skirmish line upon Round Top."

Historian Gregory Urwin calls the Crooked Run battle "one of the most brilliant actions George Custer ever directed."[10]

---

10. Urwin, *Custer Victorious*, 174.

The Confederates had been repulsed and suffered some four hundred casualties. While Anderson and his commanders on the field were pleased that they had fought the Union forces to a draw, Robert E. Lee was less than pleased with the loss of valuable veteran soldiers.

On the other hand, Sheridan was happy with the outcome. His cavalrymen had largely fought infantry troops at Crooked Run and come out ahead. As Patchan says, "The Battle of Crooked Run, Guard Hill or Second Front Royal proved to be a watershed occurrence in the Shenandoah Valley. Sheridan's Cavalry proved that they could stand toe-to-toe with the battle-hardened infantry of the Army of Northern Virginia."[11]

Sheridan also recognized that his army was in danger of being trapped in the Shenandoah Valley, unless it had reinforcements. Thus, he immediately began withdrawing his troops back to the vicinity of Harpers Ferry for the time being. Many more bloody battles loomed in the coming months before Sheridan could claim he had wrested control of the Shenandoah from the Confederacy.

Sadly, one young officer of Custer's staff would no longer be involved in the battlefield exploits of the Michigan Cavalry Brigade. Lt. Edward G. Granger had disappeared in the action that August 16. Months later, his friends and family would have to accept that he been killed in action. Two sources, Paul and Custer himself, recorded the final moments of the young aide from Detroit. Paul called Granger "one of the bravest of the brave," noting that he had ridden between the 1st and 7th as they charged. "The latter [7th] getting some rods in advance of the former, Lieut. Granger rode rapidly towards the First, and that was the last seen of him; he is missing, hope leads to the belief that he is alive and a prisoner. But fears are entertained that he has fallen—another victim."

On August 20 at Berryville, Virginia, Custer sat down to pen a letter of sorrow and condolences, all while expressing hope, to Granger's uncle Charles. The general immediately opened his letter by telling Walker: "Your nephew E. G. Granger serving on my staff has been missing since the engagement of the 16th near Front Royal, Va. I regret to convey to you and his many relatives this sad intelligence."

---

11. Patchan, "Battle of Crooked Run," 82.

Custer then outlined what he himself had observed of Granger's last actions: "He was with me until near the close of the fight when I ordered the 7th Michigan and a portion of the 1st Michigan Cavalry to charge the enemy with the sabre. Lieutenant Granger accompanied them in the charge. I saw him as the regiments charged over a hill on which the enemy was posted, he was riding at the head of the column encouraging the men forward to the charge. When last I saw him his horse was going full speed and he was brandishing his sabre over his head cheering the regiments on. The last words he was heard to speak were, 'come on boys, lets us give them fits.'" As Granger reportedly rode to the commander of the 1st Michigan, the young aide's final words were likely recorded by his friend Captain Buhl, who passed them on to the general.

Custer noted that he saw Granger late in the fighting as "the enemy were flying in utter confusion." He optimistically added that few shots were fired during this stage of the battle. "The above reasons induce me to think that there was but little chance for him to be wounded, much less killed."

He hoped the lieutenant had merely been captured because he was riding "a strange horse, one that has hitherto been unmanageable in battle, frequently running away with its rider." He believed that may have occurred with Granger. "While I would not lead you to indulge in false and unfounded hopes, I can assure you, for my part, that I entertain no other opinion than that your nephew is a prisoner, unhurt in the hands of the enemy, and that he became so by his horse running away with him; this is the universal belief here."

Custer is often criticized by writers for being careless with human life and thinking only of his own glory. That may be arguable, but clearly in this letter Custer was expressing genuine heartfelt concern for the fate of his aide and seeking to buoy the Granger family. "I sincerely regret even his temporary loss, as no officer of my command has been more faithful and attentive in the discharge of his duties than Lieutenant Granger. In addition to this, the personal relations existing between us from our being members of the same military family, are the most intimate and unreserved."

Mollie Granger in her wedding dress on her fiftieth anniversary. *Courtesy of Lisa Mower Gandelot.*

In closing his letter, Custer spoke personally to Mrs. Granger and Mollie: "Please convey to Mrs. Granger, to Miss Mollie and to all his relations, my heartfelt sympathy and assure his mother and sister that no effort will be spared by me to learn the exact condition and fate of the son and brother."

Paul, too, writes that the frantic horse Granger rode had "a history."

Sadly, by the next July, all hope had been lost for Granger's safe return. On July 2, 1865, the *Detroit Free Press* published its tribute to Granger: "The fate of this gallant young officer was so long wrapped in uncertainty and the conviction that his death is no longer doubtful has come upon his friends so gradually that no proper notice of him has ever appeared. The return of the regiment to which he belonged (the 5th Cavalry) seems a fitting occasion to speak of him."

The paper pointed out, "He was in various engagements and was very distinguished for his gallant courage, approaching to rashness and his faithful performance of every duty, and won the confidence and esteem of his illustrious commander."

For many months, the paper stated, "The most various and contradictory rumors were received; some of them giving particulars of his death and burial, others giving information of his capture." Reportedly, as late as December 24, 1864, Custer had kept open a position for Granger on his staff, should he return. However, in reality that September, Custer had been promoted to major general and appointed a divisional commander. Most of his Michigan Brigade staff remained with that unit.[12]

Finally, according to the *Free Press* article, on January 23, 1865, Lt. Col. Smith Hastings of the 5th Michigan wrote:

> No positive evidence has ever been received of Lieut. Granger's death. Yet from all information received we think that he is undoubtedly dead. Our reason for thinking him dead is that no person has ever heard from him either directly or indirectly, and that a mulatto man who is my servant and who resided near Front Royal at the time of the engagement tells of seeing a wounded rebel soldier who saw an officer of ours come riding into their line at the time of engagement at Front Royal, his horse apparently running away and was shot dead before he got through.
>
> As Lieutenant Granger's horse was known to have run away with him it is commonly believed that the officer referred to must have been the Lieutenant for the mulatto is a very truthful man and undoubtedly tells the truth of the story.

In its story, the newspaper concluded: "His name belongs to and ranks high in the list of Michigan heroes who have fallen fighting valiantly for the Union and the constitution as our fathers left it to us. His memory will be tenderly cherished by a large circle of attached friends and in the warmer circle of 'home' his place can never more be filled."

No more was heard of Lieutenant Granger, whose memory has receded into the history of the Civil War as one more of its 620,000

---

12. According to a letter Custer wrote to his wife on September 30, 1864, as commander of the 2nd Cavalry Division, he stated, "I had to leave my old brigade and staff, all but two aides." Merington, *Custer Story*, 119.

casualties.[13] His letters obviously were retained by either his mother or his sister. Given that most of them were written to Mollie, we can assume she safeguarded them for the rest of her life. On October 13, 1868, Mollie married Charles Henry Vernor in St. John's Church in Detroit.[14] The couple remained married until Mollie's death on December 12, 1922, in Detroit. Her husband and she were the parents of six children:

   —Edna L. Vernor, 1869–?[15]
   —Benjamin Granger Vernor, 1871–1961
   —Charles E. Vernor, 1875–1879
   —Ellen F. Vernor, 1876–1878
   —Winifred Vernor, 1878–1963
   —Frederick R. Vernor, 1883–1883

 On September 21, 1865, Mrs. Matilda Granger was granted a pension by the government for the loss of her son.[16] In a supporting affidavit dated June 14, 1865, her brother Edward Carey Walker stated that Matilda's son, Edward Granger, "faithfully devoted all his pay to the support of his mother." Charles I. Walker wrote similarly that day, noting that his sister was "dependent on said Edward for her main support, he being her only son + her other child being a daughter of nineteen years."

 He stated further that Mrs. Granger had moved from his house three years before to support herself and was working as a clerk in Edward Walker's law office. In addition, a day or two before Edward's

---

13. The figure of 620,000 casualties has generally been accepted for many decades. Some modern scholars have recently attempted to push the total up to as high as 750,000. See Guy Gugliotta, "New Estimate Raises Civil War Death Toll," *New York Times*, April 3, 2012; also, J. David Hacker, "A Census-Based Count of the Civil War Dead," *Civil War History* 57 (December 2011): 307–48.
14. This information is taken from the editor's family tree for Edward Gilbert Granger on Ancestry.com. Charles Vernor was born on September 18, 1839, in Albany, New York, and died on March 4, 1928, in Detroit. Both Mollie and Charles are buried in Elmwood Cemetery in Detroit.
15. While the death date for Edna is unknown, the 1940 U.S. census shows her still living in Detroit. Earlier census records showed her living with her parents, as she apparently never married. Her occupation was listed as a school teacher.
16. Matilda Granger Pension File, WC55924, National Archives and Records Administration, Washington, D.C.

death, Charles had received $100 from his nephew to be given to Mrs. Granger.

Edward Walker completed another affidavit the day before, on June 13, 1865. He related that the cause of Edward's death was "supposed to be wounds inflicted by the enemy. He was carried by his horse into the enemy's lines & his body was never recovered."

Mrs. Granger died on November 17, 1879, in Hillsdale, Michigan, but was buried in Detroit's Elmwood Cemetery. Her brother Charles Irish Walker, who had played such a large role in Edward's life, remained a prominent lawyer. He died February 10, 1895, in Flint, Michigan, and was buried in Detroit's Woodmere Cemetery.

Jerome Walker remembered his maternal first cousin Edward Granger in a traditional fashion, recording the following in the family Bible: "The only son of his mother and she a widow, was beloved by all. Brave to a fault, in a skirmish he was taken within the enemies lines by his horse and never more seen and his friends unsure. Horse had been captured from the rebels, and given him by General Custer, to whom he was aid."[17]

Besides Granger's direct family and Jerome, one more person deeply felt the lieutenant's loss in combat: the now-twelve-year-old Emma Walker, Jerome's sister. For the rest of her life, she would safeguard her letter that she had received from cousin Edward and the two photographs he had either sent home to her or had given her on one of his last visits home. The next March, the war caused further heartache for Emma and Jerome when their brother Hobart died in the sinking of the *Lyon*.

Sadly, Edward Granger never had an opportunity to marry or to father children. However, since two of Mollie's children, Winifred Vernor and Benjamin G. Vernor, had children, the family line continues today with numerous collateral descendants of Lt. Edward G. Granger.

---

17. John Ickes, great-grandson of Jerome Walker, email to the editor, March 16, 2015.

BIBLIOGRAPHY

Manuscript Sources

Amos Gould Papers. Clarke Historical Library, Central Michigan University, Mount Pleasant, Mich.

Edward G. Granger, Compiled Military Service Records. Record Group 94, Entry 519. National Archives and Records Administration, Washington, D.C.

Edward G. Granger, Journal. Michigan State University Archives and Historical Collections, East Lansing.

Governor Austin Blair Papers. Burton Historical Collection. Detroit Public Library.

Letter and Order Books, 5th Michigan Cavalry. National Archives and Records Administration, Washington, D.C.

Matilda Granger Pension File. WC55924. National Archives and Records Administration, Washington, D.C.

Muster Rolls, Returns and Regimental Papers, 5th Michigan Cavalry. National Archives and Records Administration, Washington, D.C.

Victor E. Comte Papers. Bentley Historical Library, University of Michigan, Ann Arbor.

W. H. Rockwell Letters. Waldo Library, Western Michigan University, Kalamazoo.

Federal and State Public Documents

1890 Veterans Schedules. Database at Ancestry.com. Original data from Special Schedules of the Eleventh Census, Enumerating Union Veterans and Widows of the Civil War, National Archives, Washington, D.C.

General Orders of the War Department, 1863 and 1864. U.S. Adjutant General's Office, Washington, D.C.

Michigan at Gettysburg, July 1st, 2nd and 3rd, 1863. Detroit: Winn & Hammond, 1889.

Michigan, Death Records, 1867–1950. Database at Ancestry.com. Original data from Michigan Department of Community Health, Division for Vital Records and Statistics, Lansing.

New York, Civil War Muster Roll Abstracts, 1861–1900. Database at Ancestry.com. Original data from Civil War Muster Roll Abstracts of New York State Volunteers, ca. 1861–1900, microfilm, 1185 rolls, New York State Archives, Albany.

Record of Service of Michigan Volunteers in the Civil War, 1861–1865. Vol. 31, *First Michigan Cavalry.* Kalamazoo, Mich.: Ihling Bros. & Everard, 1905.

———. Vol. 35, *Fifth Michigan Cavalry.* Kalamazoo, Mich.: Ihling Bros. & Everard, 1905.

———. Vol. 36, *Sixth Michigan Cavalry.* Kalamazoo, Mich.: Ihling Bros. & Everard, 1905.

———. Vol. 37, *Seventh Michigan Cavalry.* Kalamazoo, Mich.: Ihling Bros. & Everard, 1905.

Robertson, John, comp. *Michigan in the War.* Vols. 1–3. Lansing, Mich.: W. S. George, 1880.

United States, Civil War Draft Registrations Records, 1863–1865. Database at Ancestry.com. Original data from Consolidated Lists of Civil War Draft Registrations, 1863–1865, NM-65, entry 172, NAI 4213514, Records of the Provost Marshal General's Bureau (Civil War), Record Group 110, National Archives, Washington, D.C.

United States, Civil War Pension Index: General Index to Pension Files, 1861–1934. Database at Ancestry.com. Original data from National Archives and Records Administration, Washington, D.C.

United States, Civil War Soldier Records and Profiles, 1861–1865. Database at Ancestry.com. Original data from Historical Data Systems, Kingston, Mass., compiled 1997–2009.

United States, Registers of Deaths of Volunteers, 1861–1865. Database at Ancestry.com. Original data from Records of the Adjutant General's Office, 1780s–1917, Record Group 94, no. 656639, National Archives, Washington, D.C.

U.S. Civil War Soldiers, 1861–1865. Database at Ancestry.com. Original data from National Park Service, Civil War Soldiers and Sailors Database.

U.S. Federal Censuses for 1850, 1860, 1870, 1880, 1900, 1910, 1940. Database at Ancestry.com. Original data from National Archives and Records Administration, Washington, D.C. Images reproduced by FamilySearch.

U.S. National Cemetery Interment Control Forms, 1928–1962. Database at Ancestry.com. Original data from Records of the Office of the Quartermaster General, 1774–1985, Record Group 92, no. A1 2110-B, National Archives at College Park, Md.

The War of the Rebellion: A Compilation of the Official Records of the Union and Confederate Armies. 70 volumes in four series. Washington, D.C.: U.S. Government Printing Office, 1889–1904.

Books and Articles

Annual Report of the Superintendent of Public Instruction for the State of New York. Vol. 29. Albany, N.Y.: Weed, Parsons, 1883.

Bald, F. Clever. "Detroit's Little French Corporal." *Michigan History* 46 (1962).

Ball, Larry D. "Pioneer Lawman: Crawley P. Dake and Law Enforcement on the Southwestern Frontier." *Journal of Arizona History* 14, no. 3 (Autumn 1973).

Barnard, Sandy. *A Hoosier Quaker Goes to War.* Wake Forest, N.C.: AST Press, 2010.

———. *Shovels & Speculation: Archeology Hunts Custer.* Terre Haute, Ind.: AST Press, 1990.

Barnett, Louise. *Touched by Fire: The Life, Death, and Mythic Afterlife of George Armstrong Custer.* New York: Henry Holt, 1996.

Beal, William James. *History of the Michigan Agricultural College and Biographical Sketches of Trustees and Professors.* East Lansing, Mich.: Agricultural College, 1915. Reprint by Forgotten Books, 2012.

Beckendorf, John Peter. "The CDV Album of Major Robert C. Wallace, 5th Michigan Cavalry." *Military Images* (Export, Pa.) 26, no. 6 (May–June 2005).

———. "Finding Major Wallace of the 5th Michigan Cavalry." *Military Images* (Export, Pa.) 26, no. 5 (March–April 2005).

Bingham, S. D. *Early History of Michigan, with Biographies of State Officers, Members of Congress, Judges and Legislators.* Lansing, Mich.: Thorp & Godfrey, 1888.

Bixler, John W., ed. *Decisions of the Department of the Interior in Appeals Pension and Bounty-Land Claims.* Vol. 15. Washington, D.C.: Government Printing Office, 1905.

Block, Michael E. "The Battle of Cedar Mountain." *Blue & Gray Magazine* 32, no. 2 (2016).

Byrd, Joseph P., IV. *Confederate Sharpshooter: Major William E. Simmons.* Macon, Ga.: Mercer University Press, 2016.

Carlisle, Fred. *Wayne County Historical and Pioneer Society: Chronograph of Notable Events in the History of the Northwest Territory and Wayne County.* Detroit: O. S. Gulley, Bornman, 1890.

Carroll, John M., ed. *Custer in the Civil War: His Unfinished Memoirs.* San Rafael, Calif.: Presidio Press, 1977.

Clark, Charles F. *Annual Directory of the Inhabitants, Incorporated Companies, Business Firms, etc., in the City of Detroit for 1862–'63 Detroit.* Detroit: Charles F. Clark, 1862.

Cooper, Rev. David M. *Obituary Discourse on Occasion of the Death of Noah Henry Ferry, Major of the 5th Michigan Cavalry, Killed at Gettysburg, July 3, 1863.* New York: John F. Trow, Printer, 1863.

Davis, Daniel T., and Philip S. Greenwalt. *Hurricane from the Heavens: The Battle of Cold Harbor, May 26–June 5, 1864.* El Dorado Hills, Calif.: Savas Beatie, 2014.

Davis, Paul, ed. *I Rode with Custer: The Civil War Diary of Charles H. Safford, Brevet Major, 5th Michigan Cavalry.* Michigan: Ashton Z. Publishing, 2014.

Early History of Grand Rapids City, Kent County, Michigan. Grand Rapids, Mich.: Dillenback and Leavitt, 1870.

Egan, Timothy. *The Immortal Irishman: The Irish Revolutionary Who Became an American Hero*. New York: Houghton Mifflin Harcourt, 2016.
Eicher, John and David J. Eicher. *Civil War High Commands*. Stanford, Calif.: Stanford University Press, 2001.
Farmer, Silas. *History of Detroit and Wayne County and Early Michigan*. Vol. 2. Ann Arbor: University of Michigan Library, 1890.
Finny, David D., and Judith Stermer McIntosh. *Remembering Michigan's Civil War Soldiers*. Charleston, S.C.: Arcadia Publishing, March 2015.
Fisher, Ernest B., ed. *Grand Rapids and Kent County, Michigan: Historical Account of Their Progress from First Settlement to the Present Time*. Vol. 1. Chicago: Robert O. Law, 1918.
French, Albion H. "Old Gilmanton Matters." *Granite Monthly* 41, no. 8 (August 1909): 249–65.
Gibney, Abbott M. "Major Myron Hickey, Civil War Veteran is Mystery." *Lake Orion (Mich.) Review*, December 12, 1963.
Gottfried, Bradley M. *The Maps of The Wilderness: An Atlas of the Wilderness Campaign, including All Cavalry Operations, May 2–6, 1864*. El Dorado Hills, Calif.: Savas Beatie, 2016.
Gugliotta, Guy. "New Estimate Raises Civil War Death Toll." *New York Times*, April 3, 2012.
Hacker, J. David. "A Census-Based Count of the Civil War Dead." *Civil War History* 57 (December 2011): 307–48.
Haynes, Mark. "Chaplain's Corner." *Sons of Union Veterans of the Civil War: Picacho Peak Camp No. 1 Newsletter*, January 2008.
Hinsdale, Burke A., and Isaac N. Demmon. *History of the University of Michigan*. Ann Arbor: University of Michigan Press, 1906.
Historical Collections: Collections and Researches Made by the Michigan Pioneer and Historical Society. Vol. 35. Lansing, Mich.: Wynkoop, Hallenbeck, Crawford, 1907.
Historic Culpeper: Bicentennial Edition. 3rd ed. Culpeper, Va.: Culpeper Historical Society, 2002.
History of Oakland County, Michigan. Philadelphia: L. H. Everts, 1877.
History of Washtenaw County, Michigan. Vol. 2. Chicago: Chas. C. Chapman, 1881.
Ingall, David. "David Ingall's Speech for Civil War Monument Dedication." Monroenews.com, posted May 28, 2012.
———. "Lieutenant Frederick Nims." *River Raisin News & Dispatch* 3, no. 3 (July–September 2008). Newsletter of the Monroe County Historical Museum, Monroe, Mich.
Ingall, David, and Karin Risko. *Michigan Civil War Landmarks*. Charleston, S.C.: History Press, 2015.
Isham, Asa B. *Seventh Michigan Cavalry of Custer's Wolverine Brigade*. Huntington, W.Va.: Blue Acorn Press, 2000.

Johnson, William Page. "The Skirmish at Arellton and the Michigan Cavalry Brigade Hospital at Fairfax Court House." *Fare Facs Gazette* 11, no. 4 (Fall 2014).
Jones, R. Steven. *Right Hand of Command: Use and Disuse of Personal Staffs in the Civil War.* Mechanicsburg, Pa.: Stackpole Books, 2000. Kindle edition.
Jones, Virgil Carrington. *Ranger Mosby.* Chapel Hill: University of North Carolina Press, 1944.
Jopson, John H., ed. "Report of the Committee on Necrology." *Transactions of the American Surgical Association* 40 (1922).
Kidd, J. H. *A Cavalryman with Custer.* New York: Bantam Books, 1991.
———. *Personal Recollections of a Cavalryman.* Grand Rapids, Mich.: Black Letter Press, 1969. First published 1908.
Klement, Frank L., ed. "Edwin B. Bigelow: A Michigan Sergeant in the Civil War." *Michigan History* 38 (September 1954).
Kuhn, Madison. *Michigan State: The First Hundred Years 1855 to 1955.* Lansing: Michigan State University Press, 1955.
———. "Spartans in the Civil War." *Michigan State University Magazine,* March 1961.
Leckie, Shirley A. *Elizabeth Bacon Custer and the Making of a Myth.* Norman: University of Oklahoma Press, 1993.
Lee, William O., comp., *Personal and Historical Sketches and Facial History of and by Members of the Seventh Regiment Michigan Volunteer Cavalry 1862–1865.* Detroit: 7th Michigan Cavalry Association, 1902. Reprint by Forgotten Books, November 26, 2015.
LeMieux, Dave. "150 Years Ago, Muskegon Residents Filled Regimental Ranks after Attack on Fort Sumter." *Muskegon (Mich.) Chronicle* (online edition), April 12, 2011.
Longacre, Edward G. *Custer and His Wolverines: The Michigan Cavalry Brigade 1861–1865.* Conshohocken, Pa.: Combined Publishing, 1997.
———. *From Antietam to Fort Fisher: The Civil War Letters of Edward King Wightman, 1862–1865.* Cranbury, N.J.: Associated University Presses, 1985.
Maxwell, John Gary. *Gettysburg to Great Salt Lake: George R. Maxwell, Civil War Hero and Federal Marshal among the Mormons.* Norman, Okla.: Arthur H. Clark, 2010.
Merington, Marguerite, ed. *The Custer Story: The Life and Intimate Letters of General Custer and His Wife Elizabeth.* New York: Devin-Adair, 1950.
Mink, Eric. "'I Was in the Secret Service of the Army of the Potomac . . .'—Isaac Silver of Spotsylvania County." Pts. 1 and 2. October 7 and 8, 2010. *Mysteries & Conundrums, Exploring the Civil War–Era Landscape in the Fredericksburg & Spotsylvania Region* (historical blog). https://npsfrsp.wordpress.com/.
Monaghan, Jay. "Custer's 'Last Stand,'—Trevilian Station, 1864." In *The Custer Reader,* edited by Paul Andrew Hutton. Norman: University of Oklahoma Press, 2004.

Morris, Peter. *Baseball Fever: Early Baseball in Michigan.* Ann Arbor: University of Michigan Press, 2003.

Morris, Peter, William J. Ryczek, Jan Finkel, Leonard Levin, and Richard Malatzky, eds., *Base Ball Pioneers, 1850–1870.* Jefferson, N.C.: McFarland, 2012.

Nelson, Erik. "Historic Crossings of the Rappahannock and Rapidan Rivers That Played Critical Roles in Fredericksburg Area Battles." *Blue & Gray Magazine* 32, no. 3 (2016): 6–26, 46–65.

Neville, David. "Custer's Best Man: Brevet Lt. Col. Jacob Lyman Greene." *Military Images,* May–June 2004.

O'Neill, Robert. "Col. William Mann and the 7th Michigan Cavalry." *Gettysburg Magazine,* January 2013.

O'Neill, Robert F. *Chasing Jeb Stuart and John Mosby: The Union Cavalry in Northern Virginia from Second Manassas to Gettysburg.* Jefferson, N.C.: McFarland, 2012.

Ovies, Adolo. *Crossed Sabers, General George Armstrong Custer and the Shenandoah Valley Campaign.* Bloomington, Ind.: AuthorHouse, 2004.

Patchan, Scott C. "The Battle of Crooked Run: George Custer's Opening Act in the Shenandoah Valley." *North & South* 11, no. 2 (December 2008): 76–83.

Paul, E. A. "The Cavalry Engagement at Crooked Run." *New York Times,* August 25, 1864.

Portrait and Biographical Album of Hillsdale County, Mich. Chicago: Chapman Brothers, 1888.

Portrait and Biographical Record of Genesee, Lapeer and Tuscola Counties, Michigan. Chicago: Chapman Bros., 1892.

Reynolds, Arlene. *The Civil War Memories of Elizabeth Bacon Custer.* Austin: University of Texas Press, 1994.

Rhea, Gordon C. *The Battles for Spotsylvania Court House and the Road to Yellow Tavern, May 7–12, 1864.* Baton Rouge: Louisiana State University Press, 1997.

———. *Cold Harbor, Grant and Lee, May 26–June 3, 1864.* Baton Rouge: Louisiana State University Press, 2007 edition and 2014 reprint.

———. *To the North Anna River: Grant and Lee, May 13–25, 1864.* Baton Rouge: Louisiana State University Press, 2013 edition.

Rigdon, John C. *Historical Sketch and Roster of the Michigan 5th Cavalry Regiment.* Cartersville, Ga.: Eastern Digital Resources, 2015.

Ryan, Bill. "General Custer in the Corporate Archives." *New York Times,* April 14, 1996.

Scheel, Eugene M., and Culpeper Historical Society. *Culpeper: A Virginia County's History Through 1920.* Culpeper, Va.: Culpeper Historical Society, 1982.

The Semi-Centennial Celebration of the Organization of the University of Michigan, June 26–30, 1887. Ann Arbor: University of Michigan, 1888.

Stanford, Linda O., and C. Kurt Dewhurst. *MSU Campus, Buildings, Places, Spaces.* East Lansing: Michigan State University Press, 2002.

Starr, Stephen Z. *The Union Cavalry in the Civil War.* Vol. 2, *The War in the East From Gettysburg to Appomattox, 1863–1865.* Baton Rouge: Louisiana State University Press, 1981.
Stiles, T. J. *Custer's Trials: A Life on the Frontier of a New America.* New York: Alfred A. Knopf, 2015.
Taylor, Paul. *"Old Slow Town": Detroit during the Civil War.* Detroit: Wayne State University Press, 2000.
Tollo, R. P., and T. K. Lowe. "Geologic Map of the Robertson River Igneous Suite, Blue Ridge Province, Northern and Central Virginia." U.S. Geological Survey, no. 2229, 1994, http://pubs.er.usgs.gov/publication/mf2229.
Trout, Robert J., ed. *Memoirs of the Stuart Horse Artillery Battalion.* Vol. 2. Knoxville: University of Tennessee Press, 2010.
Ullery, Jacob G., comp. *Men of Vermont: An Illustrated Biographical History of Vermonters and Sons of Vermont.* Brattleboro, Vt.: Transcript Publishing, 1894.
Urwin, Gregory J. W. "Custer: The Civil War Years." In *The Custer Reader*, edited by Paul Andrew Hutton. Norman: University of Oklahoma Press, 2004.
———. *Custer Victorious: The Civil War Battles of General George Armstrong Custer.* Lincoln: University of Nebraska Press, 1990.
Utley, Robert M. *Cavalier in Buckskin, George Armstrong Custer and the Western Military Frontier.* Norman: University of Oklahoma Press, 1988.
Venter, Bruce M. *Kill Jeff Davis: The Union Raid on Richmond, 1864.* Norman: University of Oklahoma Press, 2016.
Wallace, Charles B. *Custer's Ohio Boyhood: A Brief Account of the Early Life of Major General George Armstrong Custer.* Cadiz, Ohio: Harrison County Historical Society, 1987.
Wallace, Robert C. *A Few Memories of a Long Life.* Edited by John M. Carroll. Fairfield, Wash.: Ye Galleon Press, 1988.
Warner, Ezra J. *Generals in Blue: Lives of the Union Commanders.* Baton Rouge: Louisiana State University Press, 1989.
———. *Generals in Gray: Lives of the Confederate Commanders.* Baton Rouge: Louisiana State University Press, 1959.
Wert, Jeffry D. *Custer: The Controversial Life of George Armstrong Custer.* New York: Simon & Schuster, 1996.
———. *Mosby's Rangers.* New York: Simon & Schuster, 1990.
Widder, Keith R. *Michigan Agricultural College: The Evolution of a Land-Grant Philosophy, 1855–1925.* East Lansing: Michigan State University Press, 2005.
Wittenberg, Eric. *Glory Enough for All: Sheridan's Second Raid and the Battle of Trevilian Station.* Washington, D.C.: Brassey's, 2000.
———, ed. *One of Custer's Wolverines: The Civil War Letters of Brevet Brigadier General James H. Kidd, 6th Michigan Cavalry.* Kent, Ohio: Kent State University Press, 2000.

———. *Under Custer's Command: The Civil War Journal of James Henry Avery*. Washington, D.C.: Brassey's, 2000.
Wurster, Nina Belle. "History of Chelsea." *Washtenaw Impressions* (Ann Arbor, Mich.) 10, no. 1 (February 1953).
Wylie, Paul R. *The Irish General: Thomas Francis Meagher*. Norman: University of Oklahoma Press, 2007.
Younkman, Tim. "Bay City Profile: Capt. James G. Birney IV Served under Gen. Custer in 7th Michigan Cavalry, Received Sword on Display at Bay County Historical Museum." *Bay City Times*, April 9, 2011.

Interviews and Other Correspondence

Adams, Jim. Multiple emails with Sandy Barnard, October 2016.
Beckendorf, John. Multiple emails with Sandy Barnard, 2015–2017.
Block, Michael. Email to Sandy Barnard, October 19, 2016.
Bushong, Julie. Interviews, in person and by phone, and multiple emails with Sandy Barnard, October–November 2016.
Carson, Patricia. Email to Sandy Barnard, March 20, 2016.
Corser, William F. Phone interview with Sandy Barnard, April 14, 2016.
Hall, Clark B. Multiple emails with Sandy Barnard, November–December 2016.
Ickes, John. Multiple emails with Sandy Barnard, March 2015.
O'Neill, Robert. Multiple emails and interview with Sandy Barnard, 2015–2016.
Roberts, Sarah. Multiple emails with Sandy Barnard, 2015–2016.
Wawrzyniec, Charmaine. Multiple emails with Sandy Barnard, January 2015.

INDEX

Page numbers in *italics* refer to illustrations.

Adams, Jarvis Martin, 36n16
Agricultural College of Michigan, 4, 7–18, 20–21
aide-de-camp (A.D.C.), 115, 117n, 118, 131, 150
alcohol, 159, 213–14; problems with, 5n, 53n, 62n36, 63, 102, 161, 179, 211n19
Aldie, Va., 5n, 53n, 72n58, 77, 78n65, 103; Battle of, 78n65
Alexandria, Va., 72n58, 125, 172
Alger, Russell A., 5n, 93, *94*, 102, 131, 177, 211–12, 228–31, 246, 255, 266
Allen, William H., 38
Alton, Illinois, 27n48
Ambulance Corps, 60, 63
Amissville, Va., 111, 113, 165n16
Anderson, Richard H., 262–63, 268
Andrews, George, 67n44
Anna Church, 245n86
Annapolis, Md., 22, 27n48
Antietam, Battle of, 150n74, 182, 186n50, 220n34

Arcola, Va., 77n62
Army of Northern Virginia, 53n, 56n, 97–98, 199n2, 209n16, 216n29, 231n57, 268
Army of the Cumberland, 191n56
Army of the James, 203, 215n, 232n59
Army of the Potomac, 3, 97–98, 102–3, 108, 148, 197–99, 209n16, 210, 223–24
Army of the Shenandoah, 199n, 261–62
Army of Virginia, 26n47, 56n
Arnold, John M., 38
Ash, Joseph P., 222
Ashby's Gap, 5n, 53n, 63, 65, 103n4
Atlanta Campaign, 31n1
Averell, William Woods, 167, 190, 262
Avery, James Henry, 29, 30n55, 44n5, 88n86, 245n86, 255
Axtell, Benjamin F., 227

Bailey's Cross Roads, 71n56
Baldwin, Lyman H., 37
Baltimore, Md., 260

283

INDEX

Barbour, James, 157n
Barnhart, Levant W., 266
Barrow, Caroline, 119n28
battlefields after battle, 56, 63, 108
Baylis, Richard, 117n, 143, 205, 213, 254
Bealeton (Station), Va., 136, 172
Beardsley, Dell, 36
Beaver Dam, Va., 199, 223–25, 256
Berea Baptist Church (Va.), 115n22
Bermuda Hundred Campaign, 215n
Berryville, Va., 268
Bethesda Church, Battle of, 205, 241n77
Beveridge, Robert, 37
Bibbins, Madison W., 89–90
Bigelow, Edwin B., 20, 81n
Birney, James G., IV, 21, 228
Bissell, Charles T., 144
Blair, Austin, 19n29, 22n39, 27, 45n11, 51n, 94n
Blue Ridge Mountains, 63, 103, 262
books and reading, 11–13, 18, 42, 116, 163, 166
Boonesville, Miss., 93n
Boonsboro, Md., 94n
Booth, John Wilkes, 176
Bottoms Bridge, 206, 232, 241, 245
Brainerd, Ann, 210
Brainerd, Miranda Aldis, 210
Brandy Station, Va., 95n94, 128n40, 134n, 139, 141, 160, 172–76; Battle of, 190n54, 198; combat at, 132–36
Brevoort, William M., 221, 224n33, 233n61, *234*, 244–45
Brewer, Melvin, 230n55, 243n82, 249, 265, 267
Brewster, Anna F., 91n91
Bristol, Jacob, 23, *25*, 44, 54–58, 69–72, 75, 78–81, 88, 106, 109–10, 139, 184, 207, 215, 256–57
Broad Run, Va., 138–40
Brodhead, Thornton, 26n47
Brown, Alexander, 80

Brown, James Ewell, 26n47
Brown, John, 229n53
Buchanan, Maggie, 68
Buckland Mills, Va., 48n16, 137–41; Battle of, 20n32, 168n21
Buckland Races, 138n
Buford, John, 103n4, 132–34, 140
Buhl, F. Augustus (Gus), 34n6, 105, 209, 221, 246, 267–69
Buhl, Walter, 34n6
Bull Run, First Battle of, 56n, 63. *See also* First Manassas, Battle of
Bull Run, Second Battle of, 63, 137, 186n50. *See also* Second Manassas, Battle of
Burnside, Ambrose, 167, 210, 211n18
Burnside Point, Ky., 191n57
Bush, Harvey, 12–15
Butler, Benjamin F., 215n, 232n59
Butler, Matthew C., 240–42

Calhoun, James, 158n3
Camp Banks (Banks Barracks), 24, 28–29
Campbell, John A., 48n16
Camp Copeland, Washington, D.C., 29–30, 39–41, 62n36, 65, 70n55
Cape Hatteras, N.C., 16n24
capture: of belongings, 153, 206, 254–56; of soldiers, 55, 72, 79–80, 94n108, 119n28, 153, 254, 267
careers prior to military, 16–19, 32
Carpenter, Otis W., 22
Carr, Alphonso W., 22
Carroll, William (Billy), 186–87, 195
Casey, Silas, 45
Caskey, Alexander Carey, 28n54, 31–32, 36n17, 146
Caskey, Caroline Walker, 31n1
Caskey, Edward G., 32
Caskey, Maria Louisa, 36n17, 175
Caskey, Samuel G., 32

INDEX

Cedar Creek, Battle of, 219n
Cedar Mountain, Va. *See under* headquarters of Custer
Cedarville, Va., 264; Battle of, 259n
celebrations, 121–23, 158–59
Cemetery Hill, 106
Cemetery Ridge, 99, 220n34
Centreville, Va., 53n, 54–55
Chambersburg, Pa., 98
Chancellorsville, Va., 178n40, 216, 221, 223n40; Battle of, 83n74, 151n75, 186n50, 190n54, 198, 216n28
Chancellorsville Campaign, 223n40
Chandler, William E., 176
Chantilly, Va., 77, 78n65, 83–84
chaplains, 116, 170
Charlottesville, Va., 178n39, 222
Chattanooga, Tenn., 20n32
Chesapeake Bay, 261
Chester, George, 164
Chesterfield Station (Va.), 215
Chester Gap, Va., 262
Cheyenne Crossing, S.Dak., 23n41
Chickahominy River, 229, 230n54, 232n59
Chickamauga, Battle of, 199n
Chickamauga Campaign, 31n1, 191n56
Chilesburg, Va., 223
Christiancy, Henry Clay, 150
Christiancy, Isaac P., 120n31, 150n73
Christiancy, James Isaac (Jim), 117n, 120, 144, 149–50, 158, 179, 182, 188–89, 195, 213–14, 233–35, 239
Christmas, 163, 170
church. *See* religious services
Civil War, beginning of, 21–25
Clark, Elbert J., 12
Clark, John E., 45, 131, 137–38
Clark, Lorenzo E., 38
Clemmer, David W., 251
Clemmer, Philena, 251n92
Cleveland, Grover, 216n29

Cleveland, Ohio, 124, 175
Clift, Mrs., 168, 175, 196, 214
clothing, 39, 52–53, 74, 87, 118, 163, 214, 254–55
Clover Hill. *See under* headquarters of Custer
Cold Harbor, Va., 232; Battle of, 186n50, 205, 221n38, 224n33, 234, 242n80, 243–44
Colerick, William, 117n, 118, 120, 124–26, 131, 133n, 136, 143–44, 148, 158–62, 165, 168–69, 174, 211
college. *See* Agricultural College of Michigan
combat, 97–110, 128–40, 149–53, 198–202, 215–32, 238–54, 259–69
Comte, Elize, 226
Comte, Victor E., 226–27
Cooke, Philip, 190n55
Cooper, Wickcliffe, 201
Cooperstown, N.Y., 210
Copeland, Joseph Tarr, 19n30, 26, 30n56, 35, 51n, 65n, 75, 77n61, 78n64, 97–98
Corser, Augustus Friend, 40, 61, 69, 126, 147
Corser, Marion Augustus, 40n
Corser, William F., 40n
Craig, James, 37, 38n34
Crater, Battle of the, 167n18, 211n18
Crooked Run, 126n, 131, 262–67; Battle of, 5, 24, 206, 258–59, 268
Cullen, James, 195n64
Culpeper (Court House), Va., 65, 121n33, *122*, 122n, *125*, 126–29, 132, 142, 155–57, 173, 192n58, 215–16; Battle of, 122n
Custer, Boston, 158n3
Custer, Elizabeth Bacon (Libbie), 119n28, 133n, 156–58, 165n16, 179–83, *183*, 186–89, 235n67, 240, 242n78, 254n97

Custer, Emmanuel, 158n3
Custer, George Armstrong, 5, 26n48, 99, *154*, *159*, *183*; and battling former roommate, 221n36; criticism of, 203, 269; on death of Granger, 260, 268–71; description of by Granger, 116–19; family of, 158n3; marriage of, 119, 156–58, 165, 179; statements by, 133n, 134n46, 138n49, 179n41, 242n78, 254n97, 271n12
Custer, Margaret, 158n3
Custer, Maria, 158n3
Custer, Nevin, 158n3
Custer, Thomas, 158n3

Dabney's Ford, 204, 238n71
Dahlgren, Ulric, 178n39
Dake, Crawley P., *46*, 47–50, 98, 104, 112, 160, 168, 177, 211
Dana, Amasa G., 254
Darling, Daniel H., 214
Davies, Henry Eugene, 132, 141, 148, 152
Davis, George, 35
Davisburg, Mich., 21
Davison, Eliza Brown, *159*, 165, 186, 188, 195–96
Dean, Joseph, 38
Deane, Charles W., 45n8, 231
deaths: accidental, 80–81, 81n; of family members, 191. *See also* Granger, Henry William: death of
Delano, Fredrick M., 176
Delano, Sarah E., 176
DeMill, Henrietta Marie Westbrook, 114n
DeMill, Peter Edward, 114n
Democratic Party, 6, 19, 63n37
Detroit, Mich., 4, 6, 16–18, 23–29
Detroit Free Press, 6n2, 7, 19, 27, 38n39, 47n14, 51n, 119n29, 120n31, 143n61, 270–71
Devin, Thomas C., 198, 201, 209, 218, 221, 230, 241n77, 242n80, 243n82, 262–67
Dewey, George, 190n55
diary. *See* journal
diphtheria, 87, 92
doctors, 34, 85, 92, 136
Dodge, Horace W., 23, *25*, 45, 48–50, 54, 72, 75, 78, 84, 110–11, 116n24, 160, 171, 177–79, 187, 240; erroneous death announcement of, 139, 146
Dodge, William H., 141n56
doughboys, 160
downtime, 85, 111, 115–16, 138–40, 148, 155, 162–66, 179, 195
Drake, George, 250
Dranesville, Va., 103
Drew, George A., 119, 153, 174, 182, 195, 213, 217, 235
Duggan, Andrew W., 245
Dunn, Miss, 145, 147, 161

Earle, Samuel, 79n
Early, Jubal A., 17n24, 34n6, 260–63
Earp, Virgil, 46n12
Earp, Wyatt, 46n12
East Cavalry Field, 99, 105n, 190n54, 216n29, 233n62
Easter, 72, 188, 191
Eastern Michigan University, 8
Edwards Ferry, 98, 103
Egan, William, 250, 253
Elder, Samuel S., *129*
Elizabethtown, Ky., 191n57
Elliott, Joel H., 201
Elmira, N.Y., 194
Ely's Ford (Va.), 178, 216
Emmitsburg, Md., 98, 108
Enon Church (Va.), 204–5, 239–42
entertainment, 111, 158–59, 163, 177, 182–87, 213–14
Ewell, Richard S., 157n
exercise, 92, 179

INDEX

Fairfax, John W., 78
Fairfax, Va., 72n58, 81, 85, 102–3, 113
Fairfax Court House, Va., 41, 45, 65–67, 71, 78n66, 81n
Fair Oaks, Va., Battle of, 13n22
Falling Waters, Battle of, 108
Falmouth, Va., 53n, 58, 61–65, 101, 113, 115n22, 116, 117n
Farmville, Va., 216n29
Ferry, Noah, 53n, 57–58, 59, 62n36, 89, 107, 112, 161
Ferry, William, 57n
fire and battle, 136, 224
First Manassas, Battle of, 55n28. *See also* Bull Run, First Battle of
Fisher's Hill, Va., 262; Battle of, 167n19
Five Forks, Va., Battle of, 85n79, 107n9
Fletcher, Ella, 7n3, 64n42
Flint, Mich., 273
Folsom, Frank, 38
Folsom, Simeon, 38n34
food, 54–58, 67–71, 80, 87, 117, 149, 152, 162–63, 187, 224
Foote, Charles Augustus, 13
Foote, Charles C. (father), 13n22
Forrest, Nathan Bedford, 217n30
Fort Laramie, 119n29, 171
Fort Leavenworth, Kans., 48n15
Fortress Monroe, Va., 17n24
Fort Scott, 30n56
Fort Stevens, 260
Fowlerville, Mich., 35
Franklin, Tenn., Battle of, 217n30
Frazer, Mrs., 86
Frazer, William A., 86n80
Frederick, Md., 98, 106–8, 260
Fredericksburg, Va., 40, 43, 58, 63–64, 115n22, 135, 178n40, 223; Battle of, 60, 64n39, 150n74, 167n18, 182, 198, 210
Frémont, John C., 63n37

French, William H., 150–51
Front Royal, Va., 5, 24, 34n6, 232n58, 254n96, 259, 262–64, 268, 271
furlough, 68–69, 82, 92, 165. *See also* leave of absence; sick leave

Gaines's Mill, Va., 230n54, 232
Gainesville, Va., 103, 138, 140, 147
Gale, Franklin, 226
Gale, Henry D., 168, 226
games, 85, 92, 163, 185–88, 213
Gardner, Ella, 141, 145, 172, 174, 181, 192–93, 195
Gardner, Olive Ann, 141n56
Gardner, Ransom, 141n56
Geigrich, George, 58
George, Elizabeth, 196n67
Germanna Ford, 149, 212
Gettysburg, Pa., 43; Battle of, 97–99, 104–8, 216n29, 220n34
Gettysburg Campaign, 42, 78n65, 96, 190n54
Gibbon, John, 186n50
Gibbs, Alfred, 201, 226
Goodell, Celia, 64
Gordon, James B., 231
Gordonsville, Va., 206, 245, 255
Gould, Ebenezer, 41, 51n, 52, 53n, 62n36, 64, 86, 94n, 183, 211–12
Gould, Mrs., 86
Grand Rapids, Mich., 6, 145, 168
Granger, Anna, 184n48
Granger, Austin, 58n32, 70, 112n15, 113n20, 198
Granger, Edward Gilbert, 2, 33, 260; in command, 84, 110; death of, 5, 24, 259–60, 267–73; and decision to join army, 19, 27, 35; and promotion to Custer's staff, 100–101, 117–20; and promotion to first lieutenant, 207; and promotion to second lieutenant, 22–24, 78, 81–83
Granger, George Warner, 70

Granger, Henry William, 112, 184, 191n57, 198, *204*, 227, 234; death of, 202–3, 215, 228, 237
Granger, Julia C., 70n54
Granger, Laura E. Thompson, 184
Granger, Lycurgus, 58–60, 63n37, 69–70, 105, 191n57
Granger, Matilda Walker, 4, 6, 18, 19n29, 27, 40–41, 50n19, 197, 259, 270–273
Granger, Mollie, 4, 6, 18, 35n11, 36, 39, *66*, 122n, 197, 207, *257*, 259, 270, 272–73
Granger, Rhoda Bostwick, 70n52, 112n15, 198
Granger, Sarah E., 113–14
Granger, Sylvester, 6, 58n32, 112n15
Granger, Thomas A., 58n32
Grant, Ulysses S., 48n16, 114, 167n18, 193, 198–99, 203–4, 208, 209n16, 215, 217n30, 261
Gray, Pharo, 213, 232
Gray, Wellington W., 75–77, 79, 88n86, 90, 102, 189
Great Sioux Campaign, 199n
Greeley, S. S. N., 170
Greene, Jacob Lyman, 117n, 119, 124, 145, 149, 153, *159*, 161, 179, 195, 205, 210, 213, 254, 266
Greenwood Hill (Va.), 122n
Gregg, David McMurtrie, 103n4, 105n, 140, 190, 198, 201, 205, 218, 220, 225, 239, 246
Grosse Isle, Mich., 121, 122n
Ground Squirrel Bridge, 225
Guard Hill, 262–66; Battle of, 268
Gum Spring Road, 77
Gunfight of the O.K. Corral, 46n12
guns, 27, 30n56, 80–81, 81n, 198, 238, 240–41
Guthrie, Mattie, 164, 174

Hagerstown, Md., 52, 108, 231
hairstyles, 53, 78, 147, 179
Hale, Elizabeth, 176
Hale, John P., 176
Hale, Lucy, 176
Hallock, Francis R., 37
Hallock, Horace, 37n21
Hamlin, Hannibal, 176
Hamlin, Sarah, 176
Hampton, Wade, 103n4, 204–5, 239n
Hancock, Winfield Scott, 220–21
Hanley, Timothy, 265–66
Hanover, Pa., 99, 104, 107
Hanovertown, Va., 205, 239n
Hansbrough Ridge, 155, 192n58
Harmon, Allen M., 80–81
Harpers Ferry, W.Va., 103, 260–62, 268
Harris, Georgie, 17
Harris, Samuel, 107
Harris, Sarah S., 107n10
Harrisburg, Pa., 175
Hart Island, N.Y., 17n24
Hartwood Church (Va.), 135
Hastings, Smith, *166*, 246, 271
Haw, John, 239n
Hawkhurst's Mills, Va., 79–80
Hawley, Carrie B., 36n17, 145, 161–62, 164, 171, 174, 177, 180, 195, 214, 237, 255
Haw's Shop, Va., 85n79, 204–5, 224n33, 239; Battle of, 95n94, 120n31, 205, 235nn67–68, 240
Hazel River, 121n33
headquarters of Custer: October 1863, Cedar Mountain, Va., 124, 126n, 140; winter 1863–64, Clover Hill, Stevensburg, Va., 142, *154*, 155–59, *159*
Heazlit, Lottie E., 233n62
Heazlit, Melissa D., 233n62
Heazlit, William M., 233, 245
Heintzelman, Samuel P., 83

INDEX

Henry, Patrick, 237
Herndon, Va., 88n85
Hickey, Myron, 20, 207
Hill, Ambrose Powell (A. P.), 151, 211
Hill, George W., 233, *234*
Hillsdale, Michigan, 273
Hinsdale, Edwin C., 37
Hobbs, John E., 89–90
Hobbs, Levant, 237
Hodge, Milton, 139
Holmes, Roswell H., 167, 196
homes in battle areas, 57, 62, 80, 98, 108, 137, 140, 152
Hooker, Joseph, 83, 98, 102, 114, 167n19
hospitals, 92, 106, 108, 233n67, 240
Howard, Alfred, 176
Howard, Ham, 176
Howrigan, Thomas M., 227–28
Hudson, Edon W., 37
Hudson, Jonathan, 116
Huff, John A., 203, 239n
humor, 120, 139, 163, 169, 172, 189, 193, 214
Humphrey, Annette, 119n28, 133n, 138
Humphreys, Andrew A., 150, 177
Hunt, George Wellington, 23, 35, 45–47, 50–54, 68, 72, 75
Hunter, David, 261
Hunter, Hammond, 35n8, 37, 143
huts, 60, 63, 166, 193; building of, 157–58, 165, 169–70

illness, 28, 87, 92, 136
Ingersoll, I. W., 34
Invalid Corps, 60n, 80n68, 194n63
Irish Brigade, 182–85
Isham, Asa B., 170n24
Ives, Albert, Jr., 38n31, 38n34

Jackson, Thomas "Stonewall," 60, 151n75

James City, Va., 130, 208; combat in, 128–31
James River, 86n81, 232n59, 261
Jomini, Antoine-Henri, 163
Jordan (servant), 186–88
journal, 4, 8, 11–18, 141
Judson, Robert F., 108, *109*, 111, 117n, 118, 120–21, 124, 131, 133n, 136, 142–43, 146, 163, 196

Kearny, Philip, 83n73
Keith, Mrs., 106
Keith, William, 91–92, *93*, 106, 147, 163
Keitt, Lawrence M., 244n83
Kellogg, Francis W., 145
Kelly's Ford, Va., 58n31, 135, 191n56, 216n29
Kershaw, Joseph, 262–63
Kidd, Eliza Ann, 59n32
Kidd, James, 225, 233n62
Kilpatrick, H. Judson, 23n42, 98, 108–10, 114, 122n, 128, 132–37, 138n, 140–43, 146, 160, 178n39, 183, 190, 209n16
Kilpatrick's Raid, 184n47, 185, 190
King, Rufus, Jr., *129*
Kirkpatrick, David, 158n3
Kirkpatrick, Lydia Ann, 158n3
Knoxville, Tenn., 167n20, 211n18

Lake Frederick, Va., 262
Lansing, Mich., 7–9
Lapham, Daniel, 265
leave of absence, 82, 108, 122, 158, 163, 169. *See also* furlough; sick leave
Lee, Edward M., 48
Lee, Fitzhugh, 53n, 140, 204–5, 216, 220, 232n58, 238, 242n80, 243n81, 244n83, 262–63
Lee, Robert E., 53n, 56n, 98, 103n4, 114, 142n59, 152, 166n, 199, 208–9, 215, 216n29, 260–62, 268

Leesburg, Va., 84n77, 104n, 261
Leggett, Percival S., 121
Lenn Park, 155
Lewis Ford, 26n47
Libby Prison, 79n, 86, 227n49
Lincoln, Abraham, 19n30, 24–27, 63n37, 176nn34–35, 261
Litchfield, Allyne C., 57n, 184
Little Big Horn, Battle of, 158n3, 199, 203, 219
Littlestown, Pa., 104, 107
Long Bridge, 71n56
Longstreet, James, 106, 107n9, 166, 167n20, 211n18, 218
Losee, Hepsebeth, 21n33
Louisa Court House, 206, 245
Loveland, William H., 172–74

MacDonald, Donald (Don), 35n11, 36, 68n48, 113, 140, 167, 171, 175, 180, 196, 214, 237, 255
Macon, Georgia, 217n30
Madison Court House, 208–9
Magoffin, William T., 212
mail, 42, 65, 141, 175, 212, 215–16, 235. *See also* postage stamps
Malvern Hill, Va., 215, 232; Battle of, 16n24, 226
Manassas, Va., 55n28
Manassas Gap, 51n
Mann, William D., 19n30, 26–27, 30n56, 47
marriage, 68, 147, 165–66, 210, 214. *See also* Custer, George Armstrong, marriage of
Martin, George H., 146
Massanutten Mountains, 262
Matadequin Creek, 241
Mattie (Cousin Mattie), 142, 145, 164, 174, 196, 256
Maxwell, George R., 85, 208, 233, 235, 239

McClellan, George B., 45n10, 51n, 94n
McGraw, Theodore A., 17, 34n5, 120n30
McKinley, William, 94n
Meade, George Gordon, 98, 102, 113–14, 142n59, 144, 149–53, 177, 190, 199, 209n16, 211n18, 218, 220n34, 221, 243n81, 244
Meadow Bridge, Battle of, 217, 229–31, 232n58, 234n
Meagher, Thomas Francis, 182
Merritt, Wesley, 137, 190, 201, 226, 230, 241n77, 242n80, 243nn81–82, 244–45, 261, 265
Michigan State Normal School, 8
Michigan State University, 8, 21
Middleburg, Va., 53n, 77n63, 78nn64–65, 103n4
Milford, Va., 233–34
Mine Run, Battle of, 148–53
Mine Run Campaign, 44n6
Missionary Ridge, Battle of, 199n
Mitchell, Margaret Julia (Maggie), 124
Mitchell, Robert Byington, 190
money, 52, 81–83, 87, 94, 169, 180, 207, 211, 255–57, 272–73; theft of, 153
Monocacy, Battle of, 260
Monroe, James, 78
Monroe, Mich., 119n28, 123, 143, 156
Monterey, Md., 85n79
Morton's Ford, 149, 153
Mosby, John Singleton, 3, 41, 53n, 62n36, 72, 73, 76, 78n65, 89, 93, 94n, 152
Mountain Run, 155
Mounted Riflemen, 27n50, 35
Munson, Benjamin G., 35, 191
Munson, Melvin C., 35, 191
music, 111, 128, 141, 159, 163, 218

Nash, Charles P. W., 170n24
Nashville, Tenn., Battle of, 31n1, 217n30

INDEX 291

Negus, Balina W., 195n64
Negus, Edward L., 194
New Baltimore, Va., 141
Newby's Crossroads, Va., 90n89, 246, 251n93
New Castle Ferry (Va.), 206, 224, 235, 241n76, 245
New Rumley, Ohio, 158n3
newspapers, 79n, 108, 136, 205, 240. See also *Detroit Free Press*
Nims, Frederick A., 72–73, 74, 104, 112–14, 147, 161, 168, 211–13, 222, 253
North Anna River, 203, 224
North Mountains, 262
Norvell, Dallas, 168
Norvell, Freeman, 30n56, 53n, 51, 62n36, 64, 168n22
numbers of losses, 26n47, 28, 183–84, 255, 268, 271–72, 272n13

Oak Hill mansion, 78
Oakley, Helen L., 193n
Old Church, Va., 107n10, 224n33, 245n86; Battle of, 205, 241, 242n79
Old Cold Harbor, Va., 205, 241n77, 242
Oliphant, David, 95, 237, 240
Osborn, Charles Y., 235, 240
Overland Campaign, 190n54, 198, 203, 216n29, 220n35, 240n75
Owen, Joshua T., 186

Paisley's Mills, 245n86
Paldi, Angelo, 266
Pamunkey River, 204, 206, 224, 238, 241n76, 245, 255
Parsley's Creek, 242n79
Parsley's Mill, 242
Parsons, P., 44n5
Pate, H. Clay, 229
Paul, E. A., 264–70
Peninsula Campaign, 83n33, 186n50, 190n54

Pennington, Alexander Cummings McWhorter, 129, 130–31, 137, 249–50, 253
Perkins, William Henry, 159
Perry, William, 81n
Petersburg, Va., 151, 211n18
Petersburg Campaign, 216n29
Philbrick, Henry, 36n14
photographs: exchanging of, 53, 64, 68, 82, 141, 145, 160–62, 171, 180, 189; making of, 70, 87, 160, 181, 193
Pickett, George E., 99, 107n8
Pickett's Charge, 106n, 220n34
Piedmont, Battle of, 84n77
Pierce, Robert, 165n16
Pierson, Warner H., 224
Pistorius, Frederick, 207
Pittsburgh, Pa., 27n48, 175
Pleasonton, Alfred, 65, 98, 99, 103–6, 121n33, 132–35, 152–53, 160, 177, 189–91, 209n16
poetry, 122n, 123
Pollay, E. M., 113, 169
Pontiac, Mich., 26, 35
Pony Mountain, 192
Poolesville, Md., 45, 98, 104
Pope, John, 26n47, 56n
Port Conway, Va., 120, 121n32
postage stamps, 42, 107, 113, 214, 255. *See also* mail
Potomac River, 71n56, 98, 103–4, 108, 260–62
Pratt, Sarah, 40n
Predmore, Sparling D., 187
Price, Richard Butler, 54
prison. *See* Libby Prison
prisoners, 78, 85, 90, 107–9, 122n, 153, 221, 223n40, 233n64, 238, 242, 251–55; rescue of, 199, 224
Pungs, William, 37n29
Purdy, Stephen P., 44, 47, 49, 171

Quinby, William E., 38
Quincy, Price, 34

Raccoon Ford, 149, 151–52
rain, 40, 54, 58, 63, 71, 80, 144–45, 148, 152, 193–94, 229, 237
Randol, Alanson M., *129*
Ransom, Dunbar R., 265–66
Rapidan River, 122n, 126, 128, 142n59, 144–45, 149n71, 151, 178n39, 208n12, 216
Rappahannock River, 53n, 58, 63, 121nn32–33, 128, 134, 136, 142n59, 145
Rappahannock Station, Va., 135
Read, H. B., *129*
Reed, Autie, 158n3
religious services, 13–14, 116, 131, 170
Reno, Marcus A., *219*
Republican Party, 19, 27, 63n37, 166n
review of division, 160, 177, 193
Reynolds, Ellen Jane, 90n90
Reynolds, Fred M., 90n90
Reynolds, John, 220n34
Reynolds, Polydore Milton, 90
Richards, George R., 228
Richardson, Israel B., 220n34
Richmond, Va., 178n39, 184n47, 198–99, 209n16, 223n40, 224, 229; Sheridan's raid on, 200–203, 215–217
Richmond Campaign, 234n
Riley, T., *129*
Rio Mills Bridge, 222n
Rivanna River, 222n
Robinson River, 208–9
romantic interests, 16, 80, 141n56, 171n26, 174, 214
Rose, David B., 202
Rosser, Thomas L., 221, 229n53
Round Top Hill, 262–67

Sabin, Alvin N., 90
Safford, Charles H., 20n31, 24n43, *29*, 30, 44n5, 51n, 71n56, 72n58, 98, 161, 242
Sailor's Creek, Battle of, 199
Saint's Rest Dormitory, 9, *10*
Salem Church, Va., 204, 238
Salisbury, N.C., 223n40
Sandisfield, Mass., 6
Saratoga, N.Y., 6
Savannah, Ga., 220n35
school. *See* Agricultural College of Michigan
Second Front Royal, Battle of, 268
Second Manassas, Battle of, 26n47, 55n, 56. *See also* Bull Run, Second Battle of
Sedgwick, John, 223
Selma, Alabama, 217n30
sermons. *See* religious services
servants, 159, 165, 186–88
Seven Pines, Battle of, 45n10
Shady Grove Church, Va., 206, 238
Sheldon, Mr., 70
Sheldon, Mrs., 61, 70, 189
Sheley, Alanson (father), 35n11, 38n38
Sheley, George Alanson, 35n11, 38, 160
Shenandoah Campaign of 1864, 216n29, 219n, 221n36
Shenandoah River, 262–66
Shenandoah Valley, 199n, 260–61, 268
Shepherdstown, Va., 34n6
Sheridan, Philip H., 20n33, 199–206, 209n16, 223n40, 224–25, 229n54, 232n59, 239, 241n77, 243n81, 244, 261–63, 268. *See also* Richmond, Va.: Sheridan's raid on
Sherman, William Tecumseh, 167n20, 199n, 217n30, 220n35
sick leave, 146, 189. *See also* furlough; leave of absence
Signal Hill, 192n58
Silver, Isaac, 223n40
Silver's farm (Va.), 223

INDEX

Simonds, Eli K., 44, 112
Simonds, Mrs., 86
Slaughter, John S., 126n, 128
slavery, 63n37, 229n53, 244n83
slaves, former, 13n, 165n16
Smith, J. Gregory, 210n17
Smithsonian Institute, 69
Snicker's Gap, 103n4
snow, 54, 73–74, 78n66
South Anna River, 225
Spotsylvania Court House, 222; Battle of, 186n50, 198, 222n, 223n40
SS *General Lyon*, 16n24, 17, 191, 273
St. Albans Raid, 210
St. Patrick's Day, 182–85
staff, Granger's description of, 118–20; structure of, 115n23
Stafford Court House, Va., 211
Stagg, Peter, 84–86, 103n5, 211, 244, 249, 253
Stahel, Julius, 84n77, 97–98, 103n6
Stanton, Stephen K., 35n9, 37
Stanton, William, 35n9, 37
Starkey, Henry, 47–48
Stedman, Elliott, 80
Stevensburg, Va., 40n, 149, 153–57, 166, 173, 189
Stevenson, John, 37
Stevenson, Walter, 37, 48, *49*
Stoneman, George, 190n55
Stony Mountain (or Stony Point), 155, 216
Stranahan, Farrand Stewart, 205, 210, 213
Strong, Miss, 17, 175
Stuart, J. E. B. (Jeb), 26n47, 71n56, 99, 103, *105*, 121n33, 137–40, 198–203, 220n35, 226, 229, 231n57, 239n
Sunday, combat on, 131
Sunday services. *See* religious services

Taylor, Lig, 164

tents, 58, 63, 69–71, 163–65, 169–70
theater, 88, 124
Thomas, William A., 12
Thompson, Carrie, 17
Todd's Tavern, Va., 198, 206, 216, 218, 221, 222n, 238
Toledo, Ohio, 175
Tom's Brook, Battle of, 219n
Torbert, Alfred T. A., 205, 209n16, 218, *219*, 239n, 241n77, 242n80, 243n82, 244n83, 254, 261
Totopotomoy Creek, 204–5, 224n33, 241n76, 242n79
training, 24, 27n50, 28–30, 39, 47n13, 48–49
trains: travel on, 29, 124–26, 173–75; and battle, 199, 224
Town, Charles H., 143–46, 174, 184, 192, 211
Trenton, Mich., 85n79
Trevilian Station, Va., 240n74, 246, 249; Battle of, 4, 22, 23n41, 143n61, 165n16, 206, 209n14, 212, 221n36, 230n55, 234n, 247–48, 252, 266
Trowbridge, Luther S., 52, 64, 112

University of Michigan, 6n3, 8, 42n4,
Upperville, Va., 84n77, 103n4
U.S. Horse Artillery, *129*

Vernor, Benjamin Granger, 66, 272–73
Vernor, Charles E., 66, 272
Vernor, Charles Henry, 272
Vernor, Edna L., *66*, 272
Vernor, Ellen F., 66, 272
Vernor, Frederick R., 66, 272
Vernor, Mollie Granger. *See* Granger, Mollie
Vernor, Winifred, 66, 272–73
veteran regiments, 30n56, 165
Vienna, Va., 83, 102

Wadsworth, Craig W., 251
Wadsworth, James S., 253
Walker (friend at headquarters), 213–14
Walker, Adaline (Ada), 17, 36, 64, 124, 175
Walker, Alexander, 230
Walker, Bryant, 19n29, 50n19, 192–93
Walker, Charles Irish, 6, 7, 18–19, 27, 32n4, 35n10, 41, 52, 63n37, 64n42, 78, 94, 117–18, 121, 143, 163, 207, 211, 255–56, 259–60, 268, 272–73
Walker, Edward Carey, 6n3, 7, 18–19, 22n39, 23n40, 27, 36–39, 50n19, 63n37, 78, 87, 142n58, 162, 174, 192n60, 237, 259, 272–73
Walker, Elmira, 17nn24–25, 36n16, *100*, 101n
Walker, Emma, 101, 113, 273
Walker, Ferdinand, 16, 17n24–25, 36n16, *100*, 101n, 210
Walker, Hobart M., 16, 175, 191n57, 273
Walker, Jerome, 16n24, 193n, 273
Walker, Jessie Rawson, 19n29, 50, 142, 192–93
Walker, Lucy Bryant, 19n29, 50, 87, 142n58, 192n60, 193
Walker, Lydia Gardner, 6n3
Walker, Mary Ann Hinsdale, 7n3, 64, 121
Walker, Polly, 67n44, 192
Walker, Samuel G., 60, 63, 105, 108, 172, 174, 180, 191n57, 215
Walker, Stephen, 6n3
Wallace, Lew, 260
Wallace, Robert C., 79, *81*, 86, *219*
Walter, Edward L., 42, 60, 63
Walter, Edwin, 42n4
Walter, Eugene E., 191
Walter, George Sheldon, 70n53
Walter, Hannah, 70n53
Walter, Sarah Walker, 42n4

Walton, Miss, 180, 192
Warner, C. K., *129*
Warren, Gouverneur K., 144, 149, 151, 177, 222
Warren, Robert Spies, 208, 209n14, 255
Warren, Samuel, 35n7
Warrenton (Junction), Va., 53n, 56, 63, 99, 103, 111–13, 116, 121, 136–38, 222n
Washington, D.C., 16n24, 26n47, 29, 39–41, 64–65, 70n55, 71n56, 83n74, 87, 124, 143, 175, 260–61
Washington, Va., 111n
Washita, Battle of the, 201
Watts, John W., 221n37
Welmore, C. W., 67
Western, Pauline Lucille, 88
Westminster, Md., 107
West Point, 118, 221
Whig Party, 19
White, Curran, 195n64
White, George Snow, 173
White House, Va., 235
White House Station, Va., 255
Whitwood, Deodatus B., 38
Wickham, Williams C., 231, 253, 263–67
Wilderness, Battle of the, 4, 19n29, 90n89, 172, 186n50, 198, 215, 222, 251n94
Williams, Joseph R. (college president), 13–14, 16n23
Williams, William C., 37
Wilmington, N.C., 17n24
Wilson, James H., 209n16, 217, 229
Winchester, Va., 48n15, 65n, 221n38, 262
Wofford, William T., 264–67
Wood, Malvina, 119n28
Woodruff, Carle, 251, 253
Wooster, Samuel R., 136
Wright, Horatio G., 260

writing, difficulties with, 11, 41, 62, 65, 82, 110, 112, 138, 141, 146, 148, 161, 170, 175, 180, 188, 197, 206–8, 256
Wyndham, Percy, 53n, 54, 61, 63

"Yankee Doodle," 218
Yazoo City, Miss., 191n57
Yellow Tavern, Va., Battle of, 112n15, 168n23, 191n57, 198, 203–4, 220n35, 223n40, 226–27, 229n53, 231, 232n58, 233n64, 234n, 239n
Young, Pierce M. B., 220, 253
Young's Island Ford, 98, 103n6

www.ingramcontent.com/pod-product-compliance
Lightning Source LLC
Chambersburg PA
CBHW021337230426
43666CB00006B/324